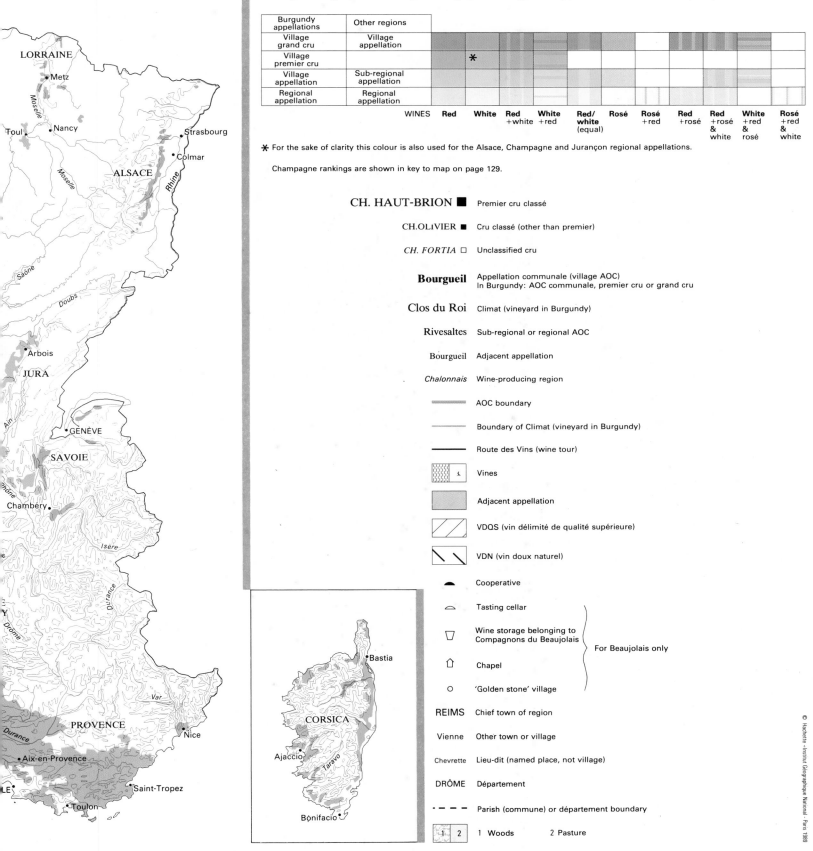

General key to maps in atlas

The colours indicate the type of wine (red, white or rosé) for AOC and VDQS wines.
Ranking – village (communal), sub-regional or regional appellation – is shown by depth of colour.

Burgundy appellations	Other regions												
Village grand cru	Village appellation												
Village premier cru				*									
Village appellation	Sub-regional appellation												
Regional appellation	Regional appellation												
	WINES	Red	White	Red +white	White +red	Red/ white (equal)	Rosé	Rosé +red	Red +rosé	Red +rosé & white	White +red & rosé	Rosé +red & white

✳ For the sake of clarity this colour is also used for the Alsace, Champagne and Jurançon regional appellations.

Champagne rankings are shown in key to map on page 129.

CH. HAUT-BRION ■	Premier cru classé
CH. OLIVIER ■	Cru classé (other than premier)
CH. FORTIA □	Unclassified cru
Bourgueil	Appellation communale (village AOC) In Burgundy: AOC communale, premier cru or grand cru
Clos du Roi	Climat (vineyard in Burgundy)
Rivesaltes	Sub-regional or regional AOC
Bourgueil	Adjacent appellation
Chalonnais	Wine-producing region
────	AOC boundary
────	Boundary of Climat (vineyard in Burgundy)
────	Route des Vins (wine tour)
	Vines
	Adjacent appellation
	VDQS (vin délimité de qualité supérieure)
	VDN (vin doux naturel)
◗	Cooperative
◠	Tasting cellar
▽	Wine storage belonging to Compagnons du Beaujolais
⬆	Chapel
○	'Golden stone' village
REIMS	Chief town of region
Vienne	Other town or village
Chevrette	Lieu-dit (named place, not village)
DRÔME	Département
– · – · –	Parish (commune) or département boundary
1 2	1 Woods 2 Pasture

(Tasting cellar / Wine storage / Chapel / 'Golden stone' village — For Beaujolais only)

THE
WINES
AND
VINEYARDS
OF
FRANCE

A

COMPLETE

ATLAS

AND

GUIDE

GENERAL EDITOR
PROFESSOR PASCAL RIBÉREAU-GAYON

FOREWORD BY
ROBERT PARKER

TRANSLATED FROM THE FRENCH BY ANNE ATKINSON
SPECIALIST ADVISER: SEBASTIAN PAYNE

WITH THE COLLABORATION
OF THE INSTITUT NATIONAL DES APPELLATIONS D'ORIGINE

VIKING

VIKING

Published by the Penguin Group

Penguin Books Ltd, 27 Wrights Lane, London W8 5TZ, England

Viking Penguin, a division of Penguin Books USA Inc,
375 Hudson Street, New York, New York 10014, USA

Penguin Books Australia Ltd, Ringwood, Victoria, Australia

Penguin Books Canada Ltd, 2801 John Street, Markham, Ontario, Canada L3R 1B4

Penguin Books (NZ) Ltd, 182–190 Wairau Road, Auckland 10, New Zealand

Penguin Books Ltd, Registered Offices: Harmondsworth, Middlesex, England

First published in France, under the title *Les Vins de France*, by Hachette 1989

This English translation first published by Viking 1990

10 9 8 7 6 5 4 3 2 1

Original text, treatment of maps and design copyright © Hachette, 1989
Base maps copyright © Institut Géographique National, 1989
This English translation copyright © Penguin Books Ltd, 1990

Filmset in Perpetua by KeyStar, St Ives, Cambridge

Printed in Italy by Canale Spa, Turin

A CIP catalogue record for this book is available from the British Library

Library of Congress Catalog Card Number: 89-40792

ISBN 0-670-81767-8

General editor: Professor Pascal Ribéreau-Gayon, Director of the Institut d'Œnologie, University of Bordeaux II

With the collaboration of the Institut National des Appellations d'Origine under the chairmanship of Jean Pinchon and with the following participating members: the Director, the Inspecteur Général, heads of divisional and regional sections, consultant technical engineers and technical assistants.

Other collaborators include:

Jean-Luc Barbier, General Secretary, Comité Interprofessionnel du Vin de Champagne

Jean-François Bazin

Pierre Bedot, President, Union Française des Œnologues; Vice-president, Union Internationale des Œnologues

Alain Berger, Technical Consultant, Ministère de l'Agriculture et de la Forêt

Jean Bisson, Director of viticultural research station at Cosne-Cours-sur-Loire, Institut National de la Recherche Agronomique

Jean-Michel Boursiquot, Ecole Nationale Supérieure Agronomique, Montpellier

Pierre Casamayor, Université Paul-Sabatier, Toulouse

Jean-Pierre Doazan, Director of Research, Institut National de la Recherche Agronomique

Jean-Pierre Jeancolas, Vice-President, Association Française de Recherche sur l'Histoire du Cinéma

Antoine Lebègue

Christine Montalbetti

Alain Razungles, Ecole Nationale Supérieure Agronomique, Montpellier

Hervé Renoult

Philippe Roudié, Professor of Geography, University of Bordeaux II

Gérard Seguin, Professor of Agronomy, Institut d'Œnologie, University of Bordeaux II

Pierre Torrès, Director, Station Vitivinicole du Roussillon

Editor
Adélaïde Barbey

Deputy Editors
François Monmarché
Catherine Montalbetti
Evelyne Grumberg

Art Direction
Bernard Père
Irène de Moucheron (assistant)
Nancy François (colour)
Gilles Tosello (design)

Picture Research
Explorer (Antoinette Charniot)

Production
Gérard Piassale
Maurice Malzieu

CONTENTS

MAPS

FOREWORD

HERE, I am happy to report, is a truly original, immensely useful book about wine that will prove of great value to anyone interested in the subject. My copy of *The Wines and Vineyards of France* will accompany me on all my travels in the future – it is that enlightening and helpful a book.

The Wines and Vineyards of France contains a wealth of information, presented in a concise, easy-to-read format. The chapters on the Origins of Wine and the Ecosystem of Great Wine offer a rare insight to the subject: the importance of wine in the culture of France, traced from its origins in antiquity, is fascinatingly explored, and the complex inter-relationship between man, weather, soil and the vine is succinctly yet brilliantly analysed.

When the atlas turns its attention to the specific viticultural regions of France, the excellent coverage of each area includes a wealth of interesting little-known facts. In the chapter on Burgundy, for example, one learns that in Jules Verne's *Journey Round the Moon* a bottle of Nuits (presumably a Nuits Saint-Georges) was drunk to celebrate 'the union of Earth and its satellite.' On 25 July 1971 this gustatory event was repeated when the Apollo XV space crew drank a bottle of Nuits Saint-Georges and baptized a lunar depression as the Saint-Georges Crater. Such nuggets of information sprinkled throughout the book add a quality of lightness without detracting from the comprehensiveness, conciseness and seriousness of the text.

Given the overwhelming coverage France's viticultural regions have received from wine writers in this century, one might have thought that any new book on the subject would be bound to read like a compilation of its predecessors. *The Wines and Vineyards of France* is highly original in text, style and presentation of information. History is adroitly blended with geography, and technical information is complemented by practical advice. The atlas shows a remarkable breadth of knowledge of contemporary conditions that influence every segment of the French wine industry.

France has long been the world's standard-bearer for wine quality. Not a single producer of wine from anywhere else in the world would offer his or her product without first measuring it against the yardstick established by French viticulture. This comprehensive book splendidly chronicles and describes the wines of France. It is to be applauded loudly by anyone with a fondness for that country's diverse and dynamic viticulture.

Robert Parker
December 1988

THE APPELLATION SYSTEM

IN the mind of the consumer, the names of wine and brandy suggest a connection between quality and a specific place. Bordeaux, Burgundy, Champagne and Cognac are all good examples of this implied connection, although most people do not realize what a precisely regulated system underpins these names. Since early in this century there have been attempts to codify the views of wine-growers and merchants, views based on generations of knowledge and experience of the best soils and the most suitable grapes, and of traditional methods of growing and making wine. All this experience, this special relationship between the land and the men who cultivate it, lies behind the production of wine.

The organization of the present-day wine industry is based on the *appellation d'origine*, which ensures that the wine actually comes from the place defined on the label. This concept developed slowly and tentatively and required much faith and persistence before it finally became reality. The pioneers in this field had a very difficult time, but succeeded in bequeathing a professional code of standards to their successors. This background of firm principles is vital to all decisions on maintaining and developing the French appellation system.

Serious over-production in the thirties led those concerned in high-quality wine-making to approach Senator Capus, then Minister of Agriculture, about setting up an organization to protect the national heritage of wine and brandy. This laid the foundations for the Institut National des Appellations d'Origine des Vins et Eaux de Vie (INAO), a body which for more than fifty years has been responsible for refining the concept of the *appellation d'origine contrôlée* (AOC), and ensuring that while old traditions are preserved, new technology and the commercial domain are not forgotten. In this way, there gradually came into being the unique system of regulations governing AOC wines and brandies.

The Comité National is the INAO's supreme court, the governing body of wine. At its head is the President, a ministerial appointment from among notable figures in the wine industry. The rest of the committee is made up of other members of the viticultural world: growers (30), *négociants* (20), well-known experts (16), and government officials (11). Baron Leroy, who succeeded Senator Capus as President of the INAO, summed up this unusual alliance of professions in the phrase: 'The INAO is a trinity uniting wine-growing, government, and the business world.'

The INAO governing body derives its strength from regional organizations. On the one hand, there are wine-growers' unions set up to protect their *appellations*, and which have to be consulted on any measure affecting production conditions in their districts. On the other hand, there are consultative bodies established in 1967 to avoid excessive centralization. These consist of twelve INAO regional committees: Alsace and Eastern France, Champagne,

South-west, Loire Valley, Burgundy, Languedoc-Roussillon, Rhône Valley, Provence-Corsica, *Vins Doux Naturels*, Cognac, Armagnac and *Eaux-de-Vie de Cidre*.

The complex AOC structure depends entirely on the professionals controlling it, from the beginnings on the land to the sale of the end-product. It is an autonomous system which regulates production but keeps a close eye on developments in technology and the business world.

The Comité National takes policy decisions which have to be confirmed by the government but which the government may not modify without previous consultation and agreement. These decisions are put into practice by the 150 INAO officials in Paris and twenty-three centres throughout the different wine regions.

In close collaboration with the wine unions and the government, the INAO has recognized 390 AOC wines, and 65 from the slightly

more lowly category of *Vin Délimité de Qualité Supérieure* (VDQS). It has laid down all the conditions for producing these wines: the specified area of production (those plots of land within a defined geographical zone which are recognized by INAO experts as most suitable for growing the AOC wine concerned), permitted grape varieties, specified yield, alcohol levels, cultivation methods, vinification, analysis and tasting procedures.

As well as making these decisions, the Comité National acts as consultant on all matters concerning wine-growing in the AOC areas: improvement of quality, product control, labelling, planting, technical procedures for changes or improvements in quality and productivity, threats to vineyards from compulsory purchase or urban expansion – all this and much more.

A SYSTEM OF PROTECTION

THE INAO's further mission is to protect the *appellations* both in France and abroad. All the rules applied at production level would be ineffective if very close checks were not enforced further afield. The INAO has instituted civil actions in a hundred or so cases uncovered by government departments dealing with tax and fraud. Indeed it is practically impossible for unscrupulous operators to get past the very fine mesh of controls at all levels, and permits are necessary for everything from grape varieties, pruning, fertilizers, volume of crops and stocks held and public *dégustations* (tastings), down to documents for selling and moving produce. Wine is clearly one of the most carefully supervised products in the entire agricultural industry.

A HERITAGE OF WINE *APPELLATIONS*

THE final duty of the INAO is a worldwide struggle to protect the *appellations d'origine* from every possible external threat. Unlike a brand name, which belongs to a single person or company and survives only as long as it is successful, the *appellation* is the joint, inalienable property of the whole community of people working the land to which it applies. As part of the French heritage, it should be protected from exploitation in any form. Unfortunately, some countries have hijacked some of the most famous AOC names and have applied them arbitrarily to certain products. Champagne has become an all-purpose name for sparkling wine, Chablis for dry and

Sauternes for sweet white wine, Burgundy for any red, and Cognac for all sorts of brandy.

Now that the world is becoming a more and more international place, and many more countries formerly producing anonymous bulk wines are coming round to the idea of *appellations*, it is essential to respect a code of conduct which is our only guarantee of commercial honesty.

THE INAO AND THE FUTURE

IN the fifty years of its existence, the INAO has drawn the wine map of France. As we come nearer to European Free Trade in 1992, the INAO still controls the wine market through the constraints it has imposed and will continue to impose, particularly in specifying AOC areas, yields, grape varieties and changes in planting. Since 1935, its essential brief has been altered only once, in 1984, when its powers were extended even further.

There is no doubt at all that the INAO has had exemplary success in setting up the *appellation* system. In thirty years the AOC share of French wine production has increased from 36 to 61 per cent, while in the same period the AOC area has increased by more than 75 per cent and production by 140 per cent. This expansion is a sign of great commercial energy, especially when we see that AOC wines are now being exported to more than 160 different countries, giving a net profit in 1986 of 17.8 billion francs (compared with 28 billion for the food and agriculture industry as a whole).

Remarkably, the principles laid down in 1935 have undergone no fundamental modification since then. Much has changed: wine-growing techniques, the consumer and the market are all different and the EEC has often upset all the rules. However, although it is now imitated in an increasing number of different countries, the INAO remains a unique body, as distinctive in its way as the French wine envied throughout the world as a living symbol of warmth, conviviality and enjoyment.

WINE:
Tradition
and Technique

Above, pot with impressed design from the Roman period (Sainte-Croix museum, Poitiers). Right, Bacchus, second to third century (Musée Gallo-Romain, Lyon).

THE LEGACY OF GREECE

WINE-GROWING in Gaul originates with the Phocaeans, who founded Massalia (the present-day Marseille) in about 600 BC and taught the people of the Mediterranean shore the art of pruning vines and producing wine; in exchange for metals and slaves they also sold drinks which the Gauls greatly appreciated.

It is not certain how vinification was accomplished at this time. On the other hand, we can guess how wine-growing came to be developed in Gaul. Originally importers of wines from Greece, the inhabitants of Massalia began to plant vineyards round their own city. Their product was sold throughout their zone of influence in large-bellied amphorae known as Marseillaises. Then all along the coast the local aristocracy began cultivating vines, particularly on the slopes close to the salt-marshes already under their control. It was probably around the third century BC that native production started to develop, as seems to be indicated by the appearance at this period of Catalan amphorae. For centuries this early form of vine-growing was to remain confined to the coastal area to the extent that the province of

Narbonne, pacified by the Roman conquest around 120 BC, became covered with vines and olive groves.

THE IMPACT OF ROME

INLAND Gauls were also lovers of this 'drink for gods and heroes'; Marseille exported its products northwards, by way of the Rhône corridor. Flourishing as early as the fifth century BC, Massalian trade was to find itself three centuries later in competition with Italian wines, whose importance was reinforced by the Roman occupation of southern France ('Provincia' and later Provence), then

of the whole of Gaul and Aquitaine. The Celtic tribes in turn imitated their colonizers. The coming of the Romans was the factor that determined the inception and development of vineyards. The Gauls became wine-growers; formerly wine had been limited to the ruling classes while the rest of the population drank ale made from barley, but now wine consumption began to spread more widely.

WINE AND ENJOYMENT

WITHOUT giving up their traditional drinks, the Gauls felt the

attraction of wine. Possibly they discovered in it a power to communicate both with the gods and with other men, like the German peoples who, according to Tacitus, viewed their 'warriors' feast' as a setting where business could be discussed or the inmost soul revealed. They certainly found gaiety in wine, judging by the inscriptions on drinking vessels. There was a whole range of toasts: congratulatory – 'Here's happiness' or 'Make the most of this', boastful – 'I'm the king of drinkers', amorous – 'I love you – love me too darling', and dialogues like 'Fill up and pour the wine' followed by the hostess's answer, 'Here's wine – I'm good to you!'.

NEW VINES AND NEW VINEYARDS

THE creation of vineyards in Gaul was made possible by a choice of grape varieties tolerant of the local climate, which was wetter and less hot than that of the Mediterranean regions. The Allobroges (natives of Dauphiné) 'invented' a species of cold-resistant vine soon known as *allobrogica*, which spread to the northeast, while the Bituriges, a Celtic tribe from south-east Aquitaine, adopted a damp-resistant variety, possibly from Albania, and known as *biturica*. New landscapes and new societies began to appear, as, for example, in the Bordeaux region where the poet Ausonius owned a villa. Gradually the wines of Gaul became known beyond its frontiers. Perhaps it was in order to supply the Roman legions in what is now Great Britain that the Bituriges became wine-growers and showed a vocation for this trade to be confirmed by centuries of Bordeaux history.

After the Mediterranean region and the valleys of the Rhône and Garonne, the vine reached Burgundy, the Loire valley and the Paris Basin. The fragmentary nature of archaeological finds and the brevity of available texts naturally prevent us making a

FRENCH WINE

precise estimate of the place occupied by the vine and by wine in the economic and social life of Roman Gaul. It has been pointed out that the vine is not once mentioned in Julius Caesar's *Gallic Wars*, in spite of his many battles in Gaul. But the reputation of this product of Gaul spread beyond the Alps, and soon came to rival wine production in Italy itself. It thus fell victim in 96 AD to an order by the Emperor Domitian that at least half the vines in the provinces of Gaul should be torn up. However, this early protectionist sanction had little effect, since in AD 276 the Emperor Probus allowed all Gauls to own vines and produce wine.

THE DISCOVERY OF THE CASK

THE amphorae used throughout the Mediterranean world to transport wine did not guarantee that it would keep well. The Gauls found a solution to this problem by adopting the wooden cask: this was more convenient and also ensured that there would be improvement with age, an advantage which wine-growers were to discover only centuries later.

WINE-GROWING BISHOPS

THE great Germanic invasions during the early medieval period caused the countryside to close in on itself, and vines were swept away in

the turmoil. At the end of these troubled times in the late classical period, it was the Church that rescued wine-growing in a land where the triumph of Christianity was now assured. The bishop, the most important person in his city, was also its most important wine producer. Vine cultivation was in fact one of his first duties. Wine was now charged with Christian symbolism and was linked with the celebration of the

Roman furrows at Saint-Emilion.

Mass. Like the bishop, chapters of canons soon also began to own vineyards close to towns. Throughout the countryside monasteries, which were centres of agriculture and religion as well as being inns for travellers, became interested in wine both for its connections with worship and as a product for consumption and trade. Monks showed consistent devotion to this plant of civilization. They extended its cultivation to the extreme edges of the Christian world, and were successful in regions such as Normandy and Flanders, producing wine in conditions that were climatically difficult but served as a model of technical achievement.

Left, crowned figure of Bacchus, Gallo-Roman period (Vichy museum).
Below, Gallo-Roman oil-lamp (museum at Lons-le-Saulnier, Jura).

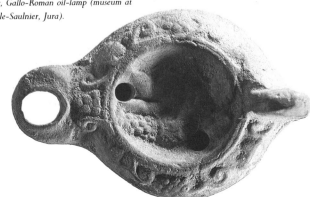

WHILE maintaining their vineyards, medieval abbeys also developed the custom of regularly doling out bread and wine to the men who worked for them. Perhaps certain peasants and rural craftsmen were thus encouraged to include a few vine-stocks among their crops in order to have their own wine to drink. In towns, on the other hand, wine consumption seems to have taken longer to develop.

WINE IN MEDIEVAL SOCIETY

MEDIEVAL society was also a feudal society and the secular powers could hardly allow bishops to keep a notable crop like wine to themselves. The aristocracy, with the great princes and the monarch in the forefront, therefore became wine-growers: the vine was perceived as both a sign of wealth and an adornment of the castle garden, and it allowed the proprietor to honour his guests or friends with a drink he had produced himself, or with the gift of a few barrels.

In Paris the king himself was setting an example. In 1035, Henri I possessed a considerable vineyard on the hill of Sainte Geneviève. Documents show that a royal vineyard existed, probably near the site of the present Faculty of Law in the rue Saint Jacques. The sovereign was copied by nobles and rich citizens; near towns almost everywhere, vineyards appeared in order to supply wine to the townspeople. The area around Paris thus became one of the most important centres of production, and sent a proportion of its wine out to Normandy, Picardy and the province of Artois.

This state of affairs was not limited to the Ile de France but spread to all parts of the country. Areas round towns all gradually acquired vineyards: near Bordeaux, the Graves region was planted with vines, while at Lyon they covered the steep hillside of Fourvière. As in Roman times, but on a different scale, wine production centred on key navigable routes, with the addition of a few important roads such as the one from Orléans to Paris, used by the ox-carts conveying wines from the Loire to Paris.

DEVELOPING MARKETS

RESERVED at first for the privileged, wine consumption in towns reached the working classes around the fourteenth century, in imitation of an aristocratic way of life. This encouraged the growth of a local wine trade and the appearance of bars and taverns. However, this 'democratic' development in wine drinking was not the only change in the market. The beginnings of specialization were visible with the evolution in taste favouring strong wines. The citizens of northern towns, who had formerly preferred light wines – 'no headache as long as you don't overindulge' – now inclined towards heavier wines, from Burgundy and the Loire valley in particular.

Rivers – the principal trade routes – became increasingly relevant to the wine trade during this period when consumption in towns was developing, a fact summed up by the saying that 'la vigne doit voir la rivière' ('the vine must be in sight of the river'). This was a reflection not so much of the climatic advantage of closeness to water and its cooling effects, as of the importance of the many ports from which wine could be despatched; and wine was now possibly the major commodity transported by river. All the shipping from the waterways upstream converged on Paris, especially from the river Yonne; boats could also go down the Loire as far as Orléans; Lyon was served by the Saône, and Bordeaux by the magnificent Garonne river system made up of the Lot, the Tarn, even the Ariège and the rivers in the Gers region of Gascony. In their turn, the vineyards of the Rhine and Moselle soon supplied a wine trade which, in the beginning at least, was mainly to benefit the natives of Friesland.

The most extraordinary event in large-scale commercial wine-growing in the Middle Ages was its shift towards the Atlantic seaboard, after the union of the Duchy of Aquitaine with the Kingdom of England. The wines of Poitou and Saintonge were the first

Above, The Winegrower's Temptation, church of Saint-Pierre-et-Saint-Paul, Andlau, Alsace.

Left, a detail from the Bayeux tapestry, eleventh century.

to benefit, because of the port of La Rochelle; but after this was captured by the French in 1224, Bordeaux took over and made the most of its monopoly of communications with England. The Bordeaux region and its hinterland became covered in vines to supply the London market with claret, still the English name for wine from Bordeaux. Each year from the Port de la Lune two wine flotillas would set off, at Martinmas and at Easter, their combined cargoes of from 100,000 to 800,000 hl representing the largest volume of trade known to the medieval world. The importance of this maritime route was so great that the custom grew up in England of calculating ship capacity in wine barrels or 'tuns' – hence the nautical 'tons' of the present day.

In 1453, the arrival of the French in Bordeaux for a time slowed down the Atlantic trade in wine from Gascony, but a second region trading in high-quality wine had now shown

map. It was the Dutch who brought into existence vineyards producing *eau de vie*: in order to sell certain Charentais wines from over-productive vine varieties such as *folle-blanche*, Dutch merchants distilled them and diluted them with water. This was the origin of *brandewijn* or 'burnt wine', from which came the English 'brandy' for spirits distilled from wine.

FROM *BRANDEWIJN* TO COGNAC

WITH its high cost and low volume, *eau de vie* had a great advantage: it was easily transported anywhere in the world, in particular to warehouses flourishing along tropical coasts. What is more, distillation could raise the price of mediocre white wines originating from vines that needed no special care or *terroir* (land) for their cultivation. In this way, white grapes would be introduced onto land which had been fairly marginal, as on some inland plateaux of the Bordeaux area or, more often, as in the districts of Armagnac, Aunis and Saintonge, onto land close to navigable rivers such as the Adour and the Charente. Cognac was quite rapidly to become the main centre for the production of these *eaux de vie*; with more refined techniques such as the adoption of lengthy ageing in oak casks and cultivation on the most chalky soil, these were to acquire an aristocratic reputation. Powerful merchants, often from outside France (from Flanders, and from England and Ireland as well) were to become securely entrenched in the small Charentais town of Cognac, which later gave its name to a product destined for extraordinary success.

During the eighteenth century the concept of quality was to be equally successful in other wine-growing regions, with the 'wine revolution' brought about largely by the changing taste of wealthy British consumers.

Bordeaux was gradually looking again in the direction of Great Britain, while at the same time seeking wider horizons for its sea trade. The

aristocratic members of the Bordeaux *Parlement* (governing council) were bringing out the *grands crus*, ancestors of nineteenth-century château wines. As early as 1670 Arnaud de Pontac, the first in a line of model wine-growers from Graves and the Médoc, thus had the idea of selling his Haut-Brion wine in fashionable London restaurants. Not content with exporting great quantities of red wine

(and Cognac) to lands round the North Sea and across the Atlantic, the port of Bordeaux also sent out its fine wines from *domaines* in the Médoc which were commanding constantly rising prices. The reputation of these *crus*, named after their proprietors, reached more and more distant lands, and by the end of the eighteenth century had travelled to the Russia of tsars and boyars and to Washington's United States.

The success of champagne was even more spectacular. For a long time the province of Champagne had

been producing reputable wines. But merchants and monasteries dealing in this wine had encountered a major drawback: it was impossible to check secondary fermentation and this was causing many bottles to break. History has credited Dom Pérignon, the administrator of the abbey of Haut-villers, with discovering how to control vinification in these temperamental wines. This resulted in the

Illuminated capital from the Abbey account book, Saint-Germain-des-Prés, 1530 (Archives nationales).

general use of corks, of metal wiring round the stopper and of pressure-resistant bottles, all essential adjuncts for this kind of sparkling wine, which was eventually to become the universal symbol of celebration. Vineyards with a genuine speciality were in this way stimulated by consumption outside the region and began to emerge from their anonymity.

---

what it could do. This was Burgundy. The move of the Papacy to Avignon had led the papal court from 1342 onwards to look for supplies in Burgundy and also to develop vine cultivation round the city of the Popes. The establishment of the Duchy of Burgundy in two main regions, especially the one that included the seaboard of Flanders stretching from Amiens to Dutch Friesland, gave a new impetus to these eastern vineyards. The Dukes of Burgundy were princes who lived in splendour. They promoted agriculture by opening up new markets, and sometimes intervened in vine production. In 1395, for instance, Philip the Bold substituted the *pinot* grape variety for *gamay*, that '*très desloyaut plant*' ('most treacherous plant'). The result was that by the end of the Middle Ages the wines of Beaune were of the very highest quality.

Up to the sixteenth century there were scarcely any basic changes in the world of wine, but this was not to be true of the seventeenth century. Now dominating the sea in place of the English, the Dutch were to have lasting influence on the French wine

THE LEGACY REINTERPRETED

AS the age of railways dawned, the geography of the wine industry in France looked extraordinarily complex. Vines were grown everywhere, except in a strip along the Channel coast and in a few wet mountain areas. They were more than ever a feature of peasant mixed farming, providing wine for everyday drinking. The choice of vine and methods of cultivation were completely unsystematic since every little group of growers was convinced that their traditionally handed-down practices were the best. Meanwhile other wine regions had been remarkably successful and were entering the export trade.

TRADITION AND SCIENCE

SINCE the end of the eighteenth century there had been a different attitude to wine-growing on the part of scientists, some of whom were attempting to determine what constituted good growing conditions. There were to be many distinguished researchers in this field during the first half of the nineteenth century, none more so of course than Chaptal. The son of a great landowner, he had a dual career under Napoleon I and Louis XVIII as a statesman and chemist, resulting in some important research on wine. The process known as 'chaptalization' (adding sugar to the grape juice to increase the alcoholic degree of the wine and make it more stable) was named after him. After Chaptal, many other scientists became interested in wine, simultaneously carrying out research and teaching wine-growers. Their interest could be attributed to the fact that wine-growing was regarded as the jewel of French agriculture and had advanced more than any other form of cultivation during the first third of the nineteenth century. The publication under the Second Empire (1852–70) of Dr Guyot's great investigation into wine-growing in France was to be the culmination of all this work.

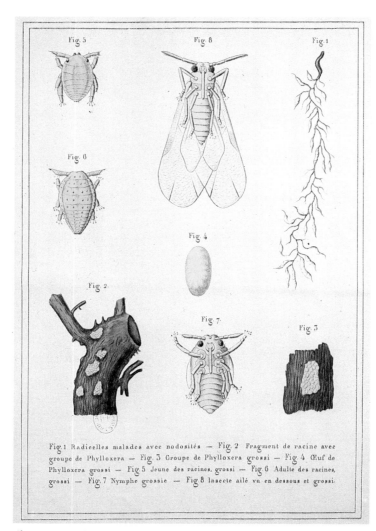

Above, an 1880 colour plate showing the life cycle of the phylloxera aphid. Infested vine roots are also illustrated (Bibliothèque nationale, Paris). Right, leaves affected by mildew, a disease caused by a parasitic fungus on the green parts of the vine.

Fig.1 Radicelles malades avec nodosités — Fig.2 Fragment de racine avec groupe de Phylloxera — Fig.3 Groupe de Phylloxera grossi — Fig.4 Œuf de Phylloxera grossi — Fig.5 Jeune des racines, grossi — Fig.6 Adulte des racines, grossi — Fig.7 Nymphe grossie — Fig.8 Insecte ailé vu en dessous et grossi.

WIDER MARKETS

ALTHOUGH scientific research contributed to the progress of French viticulture, the main factor in the remodelling of the wine map of France was the arrival of the railways. By bringing production areas closer to centres of consumption, the train precipitated the disappearance of many northern vineyards where mediocre wine was produced in difficult conditions. In the south, on the other hand, mass wine-growing became more and more common. During the Second Empire the area of vines in Languedoc increased by over two thirds and the rise in the price of vines brought considerable wealth to the region. This was noted in a report by the official (*sous-préfet*) with administrative responsibility for the Béziers area: 'The large amounts of capital now being invested in this region by the wine industry are producing an affluence which is having noticeable effects in all branches of commerce'.

The flourishing state of the major wine regions was also reinforced by Napoleon III's free trade policy. The trade agreements which he negotiated between 1860 and 1865 opened up a whole series of markets to good-quality wines: in Great Britain, and also in Belgium, the Netherlands, Scandinavia and Germany. This was an immense benefit to the French wine trade, whose production increased by more than 70 per cent in about twenty years. The great French wines (Bordeaux, Burgundy and Champagne) again found their way abroad, so that by 1875 around 6 per cent of the annual production was being exported.

THE PHYLLOXERA CRISIS

JUST as this unprecedented period of expansion seemed to be heralding a golden age for the wine industry, first oïdium and then phylloxera appeared. The first of these (between 1852 and 1855), although a near disaster which reduced the size of the grape harvests, was short-lived since the discovery of sulphur solution proved a very effective remedy.

This was not to be the case with phylloxera, a small insect from the United States. Phylloxera was spotted in the Rhône area in 1863, then in Bordeaux in 1869. From these two centres, the infection spread very slowly into Languedoc, the Charente districts and the heart of Aquitaine. Unlike oïdium, the disease developed very gradually, and the affected vines died off slowly. For this reason the unaffected regions, such as the Loire, at first benefited from this state of affairs and attracted financial speculation; and, similarly, there was a resurgence of northern vineyards thought to be safe from the disease. But by 1880 the evidence could not be denied: no region was going to escape.

In order to fight against what was regarded as a national catastrophe, the state promised large rewards to anyone finding a cure. Inventors throughout the country set to work and all sorts of schemes emerged, from the most simple-minded (cleaning the vine stems with an iron glove) to the most sophisticated. Some of these, such as treatment with carbon disulphide or potassium sulphocarbonate, were relatively effective but very expensive as each vine-stock had to be treated with a large, syringe-like copper injecting tube.

CURE BY WATER

IT was therefore decided to submerge the vines in winter during the three to nine weeks of the insect's reproductive cycle. This prevented the disease multiplying and was in fact a very effective system. The disadvantage was the need for ground that could be flooded. Wet land now had its compensations: vines were evacuated from the best *terroir*, the slopes and

Above, the new Quais de Bercy 1860–80 (wharfs on the Seine in Paris).
Below, dealing with vines suspected of phylloxera infestation (drawing by Claverie, 1878). The social and economic effects of vine disease justified intervention by scientists and government officials.

gravel terraces, and brought down to the plains and into river valleys, where plots changed hands at high prices. In many regions (Languedoc, Roussillon, Quercy, Périgord, the minor slopes of Burgundy) the best vine-growing soils lost their vines, sometimes for good. In the Charente districts this was a disaster: vine-growing was transferred to clay, while chalk soils were turned into meadow-land since it was impossible to replant quickly enough with root-stocks resistant to chlorosis, a particular problem on chalk. Whole areas of countryside turned to different types of agriculture. In the Côte d'Or there was a move towards soft fruit growing (raspberries and redcurrants); in Lorraine fruit trees were planted; the *grands crus* regions almost alone insisted on staying in high-quality wine-growing. In the end, the solution was to graft French vines, thus retaining quality, onto American root-stocks with natural resistance to the insect. Rebuilding the wine industry was then possible. But the phylloxera crisis was to leave scars, made all the worse by the effects on the industry at the end of the century of another disease – mildew. This spread from glasshouses in southern England and is a form of rot caused by a parasitic fungus which attacks the green parts of vines. It was mildew that was responsible for the crop failures between 1880 and 1980. E. David, from the Gironde, and the Bordeaux

scientists, U. Gayon and A. Millardet, succeeded in averting this danger by adopting the use of a copper sulphate solution, since known as *bouillie bordelaise*, or Bordeaux mixture.

In this curious manner, the railway, phylloxera and mildew were jointly responsible for the completely new appearance of the French wine industry at the end of the nineteenth century. The people of Languedoc were in the forefront of this fight to rebuild. With their vineyards now planted on low-lying plains, the world's most important mass-producers of wine were producing an everyday wine on deep soil. Such wine was drinkable only after it had been blended with wine from Algeria, where there was a large-scale migration of farmers encouraged to produce wine to correct the deficiencies of the French crop. These growers worked hard to produce strong-coloured, high-alcohol wines, which brought them a profit and, after transport across the Mediterranean from Oran or Algiers to Sète, would be invaluable for improving the wines of the Languedoc plain. Elsewhere, there remained a number of small vineyards producing wine suitable only for the peasant's own consumption, especially as these vineyards had often been replanted with American hybrids. On the whole, however, the focus of table wine production was now in the south.

THE TWENTIETH CENTURY – UNITY AND ORGANIZATION

THE post-phylloxera reconstruction of the wine industry had provided France with a new stock of high-yield vines. Over-production inevitably produced a slump in prices. In Languedoc, the price per hectolitre went down from 32.5 francs in 1880 to 6 francs in 1900. Producers were soon accusing the dealers of fraud, and blaming imports of Algerian wine and the blending procedures, as well as the legislation (favouring beet-growers in the north) that permitted sugaring the wine and therefore also the addition of water.

APPELLATIONS: THE BEGINNINGS

ONE of the first effects of the crisis was the emergence of cooperatives. Although the cooperative system had formerly seemed more difficult in the wine industry than in other sectors (no doubt because of the great diversity of wines), it now got under way in

such events that plans were formed for organizing the wine industry.

France to establish *appellations* as a protective measure for fine wines. The problems of over-production and of frontiers closed by the return of protectionism in 1892 had also hit areas producing *crus*, which were selling badly in spite of heavy investment. To safeguard themselves, producers were copying dealers and dressing up their wines with attractive names.

In the face of growing unsystematic and fraudulent practices everywhere, and under pressure from representatives of the quality wine regions, the government produced

d'origine of wines produced according to 'honest and consistent local practices'. Just before the First World War, the official existence of *appellations d'origine* was thus on the point of being recognized by the government.

Interrupted by the war, the process of establishing the boundaries of *appellations* started up again when peace returned, but it was not until 1927, with some vigorous action from Joseph Capus, born in Languedoc but settled in the Gironde, that the notion of quality in the product became as mandatory as its origin, and conditions

REBELLION IN THE SOUTH

ANGER intensified, and with it a feeling of rebelliousness towards northerners, whom public opinion was beginning to identify with the knights who in the past came south to subjugate Cathar heretics. The crisis turned into a massive peasant rising which endangered the Republic itself. In April 1907, the situation began to deteriorate badly and there were demonstrations involving larger and larger crowds. Prompted by a charismatic leader, a small wine-producer and bar-keeper called Marcellin Albert, the rioters rebelled and were backed up by a locally recruited infantry regiment (17th of the Line), which refused to take arms against the mutinous vine-growers.

The central authorities succeeded in discrediting Marcellin Albert and restoring calm, but this uprising nevertheless scarred the collective memory both of the vine-growers and of Languedoc as a whole. The lessons drawn from the crisis led the growers to form a powerful trade union: the Confédération générale des Vignerons du Midi. It was largely in order to avoid the repetition of

Above right, a postcard showing the leaflet for the Montpellier wine-growers' demonstration, June 1907.

ce que nous voulons

the Mediterranean south. In certain regions there was rapid progress. In the Var *département*, for instance, cooperatives controlled 30 per cent of production in 1915 and 50 per cent after the end of the First World War. In areas of fine wine, however, they were slow to make an impression, and it was only in the thirties that they became more common, when those in the trade found themselves facing the effects of the world economic crisis. Paradoxically, it was also the crisis in Languedoc that led

outline legislation for regulating the geography of *crus* from 1905 onwards. It was decided that the geographical boundaries of each authorized production zone should be set, and the demarcation of the zone for champagne was the first in the series. This pleased nobody, and in 1911 troops also had to intervene to restore order here. There followed a fresh study of the demarcation of *appellations d'origine*. On 6 May 1919, a bill established that civil tribunals would be able to acknowledge the right to an *appellation*

prescribing *terroir*, choice of vine, pruning methods, degree of alcohol and maximum yield were all laid down. The economic crisis of the thirties was responsible for lower prices, a situation which unfortunately coincided with the rich harvests of 1934 and 1935. On 30 July 1935, the system of *appellations d'origine contrôlée* (AOC) was established by a law setting out the main guidelines, which were to determine the fate of the French wine industry and which still apply today.

ENCOUNTERS WITH HISTORY

SHAKEN by internal crises and by social and economic changes, the world of wine was soon to undergo the pressure of historic events. After 1940, the Nazi occupation brought radical changes to the market in AOC wines. All exports to the United States, the United Kingdom and the British Empire were banned, whereas those to Continental Europe, especially Germany, were intensified, although this traffic often looked more like looting than trade. Since the Germans were enthusiasts for fine wine, especially sweet wines and

champagne, the Vichy government set up a system of taxes and tariffs for each *cru*, and published a lengthy decree fixing official prices.

Ten years later the wine industry was again struck by disaster, this time a natural one — the frosts of 1956. Similar in intensity to the great frosts of the eighteenth century, these started up at the end of February, after a very mild winter. The vines were caught just as they were starting into growth and were literally blasted by frost, at least in the southern half of the country where two thirds of them disappeared. In many cases, growers were obliged to replant. In some parts of the south, however, they preferred to give up planting in the plain and went up onto the hillsides, back to sites favoured in the eighteenth century. This move in the

direction of quality was a response to France's improved standard of living in the fifties and sixties. It was also reinforced by the establishment of the Common Market, which opened up the French market to imported Italian table wines.

THE NEW LOOK

THE social and economic aspects of the wine industry have since undergone major changes, with the rising value of land for vines now a threat to traditional small peasant owners, who cannot compete with influx of capital from business investors. The retreat from former colonies has added other problems: the fall in Algerian wine imports, the purchase of wine properties

by returning French colonials, the experience gained by Corsican growers on the Aléria plain — in the sixties all these helped to create a new image in the wine business.

The table wine sector, in recession throughout the world, has been influenced by the advent of the big companies. The present period has also

New wine technology: Top, automatic fermenting vats; above left, mechanised harvesting; above, on the Great Wall of China, in search of new markets.

been marked by demonstrations much in the news, in particular the riots of March 1976 at Montredon-Corbières, near Narbonne, which caused the death of a vine-grower and of a commander in the security police. For high-quality wines, however, development on the whole has been good and the market advantageous,

although expansion has also entailed some changes. The national press and public interest have tended to focus on the international groups that have bought their way into prestigious *appellations*, but the most striking phenomena have been the changes in the dealing sector. In Bordeaux especially, a good many traditional firms have disappeared or have been taken over by companies from outside the region; and in Champagne and Cognac, firms of *négociants* have managed to turn themselves into large-scale food and agriculture organizations. Certain firms have even made the most of wine's 'prestige' image and the hallmark of quality attached to France in order to extend their activities into the whole area of luxury products, as Moët-Hennessy has done with Dior. The commercial energy of these groups has found an outlet (and perhaps an image for themselves) in creating *domaines* and companies in countries that do not yet drink wine, as in eastern Asia. The outstanding project of this sort is the Rémy-Martin group's creation of the 'Dynasty' wine property in China.

After setbacks in the first half of the century, the wine industry is now making real progress in the realm of high-quality wine; progress which can be ascribed to the rise in standards of living in many parts of the developed world, and a steady and significant increase worldwide in the consumption of wine.

'*VINS, Café, Bar.*' This was the signboard you used to see on the little wooden shop-fronts which were once such a feature of working-class neighbourhoods.

THE EVERYDAY GLASS

THE small wine-merchant selling cheap wine in returnable bottles belongs to the world of the fifties, when a bottle stood on every French table and wine, in the popular mind, was associated mainly with manual workers.

Nowadays the local *cave* has become a curiosity, its gradual disappearance linked to the decrease in wine consumption in France. Around 1950 the average yearly consumption amounted to 120 l per person; thirty-five years later, the figure was 85 l, a drop of 35 per cent.

The downward curve in France is reflected in other traditional wine-drinking countries: in the fifteen years from 1970 to 1985 the annual consumption in Italy has gone down from 115 to 91 l per person; in Portugal, from 98 to 90 l; in Argentina, from 88 to 71 l; and in Spain, from 62 to 57 l.

PLEASURABLE DRINKING

THIS drop in consumption everywhere can be attributed in part to the decline of heavy manual labour because of mechanization and the move towards service industries, and in part to the development of non-alcoholic drinks such as colas. But it can also be attributed to a change in customer demands, as shown by the appearance in some places of elegant specialist wine shops where you can shop for a bottle of wine as you would for a book or a piece of antique furniture. People are drinking less, but

Percentages of different types of wine produced in France.

more discriminately, and customers for wine are showing the same tendencies as for other primary products where demand for higher quality reflects higher incomes and living standards.

The way money is spent on different categories of wine does not show up in the gross consumption figures. The consumption of table wine alone has gone down, while that of AOC wines has multiplied by three in thirty years. The average annual consumption per person of AOC wine was 4 l in 1950, and has gone up to 20 l in 1985.

The predominance in the past of basic table wine meant that people would toss back a glass of red at the bar at any time of day. Nowadays drinking is more infrequent: a good bottle is opened to go with a special meal. Wine now is not just an everyday drink, but a reason for conviviality, something to be discussed and savoured.

THE SEARCH FOR DIVERSIFICATION

THE wine industry has responded to those changing demands with an attempt to diversify production. This is partly a conscious tendency on the part of the AOC system to ensure that individual regions produce authentic wines based on specific grapes. *Vins de pays* also, though to a lesser degree, offer a range of wines of guaranteed origin. Consumers can choose as they like from a broad spectrum of wines — *vins de table* or AOC, wines with particular flavour characteristics or with a certain image or price.

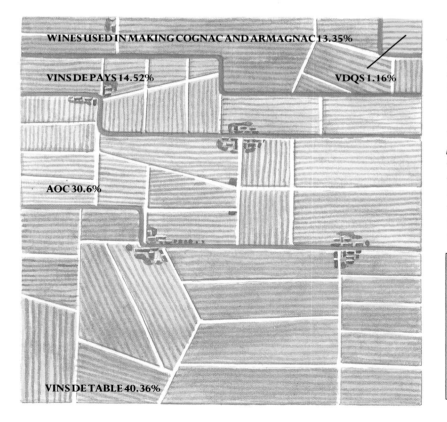

WINES USED IN MAKING COGNAC AND ARMAGNAC 13.35%

VINS DE PAYS 14.52%

VDQS 1.16%

AOC 30.6%

VINS DE TABLE 40.36%

French wine in the eighties: a reputation for quality both in France and abroad.

FLAVOURED WINE

THE specialist papers often feature headlines about flavoured wine (vins aromatisés). This is presented as new and revolutionary, although it may well have ancestors in Roussillon. The Coutume de Perpynia, *a book from the end of the twelfth century, mentions a 'nectar' which sounds like a wine flavoured with honey, herbs and spices. The recipe for this drink, said to 'drown the memory of earthly things', could perhaps have been bequeathed by the Greeks to the Catalans in classical times. Certainly the Greeks often blended all kinds of ingredients with wine to help preserve it. And, according to Pliny, in about 600 BC a certain Aristaeus used to make a mixture of wine and honey — 'two most excellent fruits of nature'.*

IID GOLD

RECEVEZ EN BORDEAUX.

LA COULEUR DU BON GOUT.

Vines in France cover one million hectares. Out of 69.4 million hl produced in 1987, including 10 million used to make cognac, 20.6 million hl are AOC wines (29.7 per cent of the whole), 0.9 million are VDQS (1.2 per cent), 10.1 million are *vins de pays* (14.5 per cent), and 27.8 million are basic table wines (40 per cent). So more than a third of the wines produced today in France have AOC labels. This has not always been true, and it is only in recent times that the wine industry has made a logical response to consumer trends by a notable increase in the volume of AOC wine.

If we go back to the early sixties (1962), we find vines occupying almost 1.3 million hectares (300,000 hectares more than today). However, the volume produced was comparable to that for 1986, but with a smaller proportion used for cognac (4.3 million hl), and for AOC wine (only 14.4 per cent). So, for the last two, there has been a significant growth in production.

New *appellations* have been created, but the growth is due essentially to increased production area and not to greater productivity. Exactly the reverse is true for the *vins de table* sector, where there is a decrease in area but a higher yield. There has also been a noticeable change in the ratio of white wine to red: twenty-five years ago, 62 per cent in volume of AOC wine was white; in 1987 the proportion is reversed, with 66 per cent of AOC wine now red or rosé.

A WORLDWIDE TOAST

AFTER Italy, France is the largest world producer of wine. But it is quality rather than volume which gives the wine industry its importance in the French economy: although covering only a modest 3.5 per cent of agricultural land, vines represent about 10 per cent in value of French agricultural resources. This divergence is even greater in regions such as Burgundy, where the figures are 1 per cent in land but 25 per cent in value. The wine sector is a notably high-value industry.

This high added value can be explained in part by the importance of the export market. Growers and shippers seem to have fulfilled their traditional ambition to 'make the whole world drink a toast in French wine', and the wines of Bordeaux, Burgundy and Champagne in particular are in the forefront of French exports. This is so much the case that, whenever some country has a political or economic disagreement with France, Champagne imports are often the first to be affected.

SALESMANSHIP

IN the agriculture and food sector, 60 per cent of the surplus in the French balance of trade comes from wine, a form of liquid gold in the view of some economists. This kind of performance on the foreign market can be explained in part by France's long wine tradition and her remarkable natural environment. But an additional factor is undoubtedly the technical achievement of all those involved in the wine industry in bringing their products up to the highest standard of quality. The move towards modernization was strikingly demonstrated with the advent in Bordeaux in the early eighties of the latest marketing techniques. Among other things, this has resulted in the logo of a glass with a bow-tie, a very successful trademark for the Bordeaux wine trade.

In addition to the use of such visual emblems, the whole wine industry has undergone a radical transformation in the course of one generation. This has taken place against a diminishing number of official crop declarations, which went down from 1.3 million in 1962 to 600,000 in 1986. However, there are still significant numbers of individual vineyards, often small in size, on an average 4.2 hectares of land. Production is consequently very fragmented and still much in the hands of the small-scale, individual grower. But this is surely what gives the French wine industry its special character and charm.

WHO DRINKS WHAT?

AT every social level, AOC wines are gradually replacing basic vins de table. *Where 100 is the index figure for French households as a whole, expenditure on high-quality wine is 55 for 'working-class' families and 180 for executives. On the other hand, basic wines run from 45 for the liberal professions up to 160 for agricultural workers. Another interesting trend in wine buying is the part now played by women: in the past women looked after everyday purchases, but the choice of special wine was a male prerogative. We have now reached a new stage when many talented women are taking up the profession of oenology.*

THE WORLD OF WINE

IN cartoons and comic writing France is commonly depicted as a land teeming with wine-growers in typical apron and beret. Yet, in an active population of over 21 million, only 420,000 are in fact engaged in wine-growing.

THE WINE COMMUNITY

MANY of these are only part-time growers who produce a little wine for family consumption. However, records list 236,000 producers making wine on a commercial scale. If we add the 3,000 firms of *négociants* (merchants), the 1,162 cooperatives and the 68,000 or so employees in these enterprises, there is a total of more than 300,000 people deriving their income directly from wine.

The wine community is fairly diverse, including both the top *négociant* with his established professional and social status and the workman who has to trundle some 120 casks per day. Between these is an infinitely varied list of landowners, large and small, of brokers and oenologists, administrators, cellar masters and vineyard managers.

WINE PRODUCTION

NOT everyone listed above actually produces wine. Some harvesting is controlled by brokerage firms, but this is fairly unusual, occurring only in a few regions such as Corsica and Champagne. Apart from this, most of the work of wine-making is in the hands of independent growers (about 125,000 of these, some of whom sell directly to the public) and of the cooperatives. The latter deal with crops from 51 per cent of the land under vines in France, and are thus responsible for 40.5 per cent of AOC wines and 63 per cent of *vins de table* (everyday wine) and *vins de pays* (regional wine).

The degree to which the cooperative system has established itself varies a great deal according to the region. In Languedoc-Roussillon as much as 73 per cent of production is in the hands of the 538 cooperatives, whereas in Burgundy only 26 per cent is controlled in this way.

WINE SALES

ALTHOUGH the cooperatives' main function is making wine, many of them are also involved in maturing, bottling and selling. In 1985 they processed some 500 million bottles.

Their sales rôle increased enormously during the thirty years after the Second World War, and the number of cooperatives grew by almost 15 per cent between the mid-fifties and the beginning of the seventies.

Except in Champagne, *négociants* play a comparatively small part in production although they are important at a later stage. Their name does not clearly define what they do and it is useful to make a distinction between the different sorts of *négociants*, known as *expéditeurs, embouteilleurs* and *éleveurs*. The first of these operate from the production area and are concerned with shipping wine, usually in bulk, to regions where it will be consumed; the second (often in the region of consumption) and the third (usually in the production area) keep permanent stocks of wine until it is ready for bottling or selling. The 800 *négociants–éleveurs* employ 18,000 people and have a business turnover of 30 thousand million francs. They are especially important on the foreign market as they are responsible for 88 per cent of exports.

Before the wine reaches the consumer there are further stages in which the restaurant industry and large stores such as supermarkets and hypermarkets play a surprisingly

Above, Paris export warehouse.
Below left, Beaujolais arriving in London.

important part. The latter are now the biggest distributors of AOC wines, selling 60 per cent of all such wines in France. In most cases they have managed to avoid poor storage, an often anticipated problem. According to a recent INAO survey, the majority of consumers consider that there is good wine available in supermarkets and hypermarkets.

This rise in large-scale distribution has been a striking feature of the last few years, at the same time as the development of direct selling by producers and cooperatives, now at

almost the same level as sales by small specialist concerns (18 per cent, compared with 20 per cent). The spread of direct selling from the producer has begun to give women a leading rôle, as they are usually in charge of sales to the public.

CONTROL OF THE SYSTEM

THE part played by government and professional bodies, with different effects on AOC wines and *vins de table*, contributes to the complex structure of the wine world. *Vins de*

pays are doing well, but the *vins de table* sector as a whole is declining, so measures are being taken by the French government and by the EEC to balance supply and demand. Increased grape yields are being discouraged by the provision of cheap distilling facilities, and growers are also being pressed to grub up vines so that potential production is more in line with present-day consumption.

Neither the state nor the EEC intervenes in the way the AOC is organized: its structure is left to the people who work in it. A virtue of the AOC organization is the fruitful interplay of different professional skills that it allows, encouraging deeper knowledge of both product and market, and improvements in quality,

sales management and product promotion. Decisions affecting the AOC sector are governed by a code of conduct much envied in other countries. Producers and *négociants* make collective decisions, forgoing personal interest for the sake of the AOC system as a whole. This is a system which owes far more to professional responsibility and service than to state control, and works again at a national level through the INAO.

The wine market, especially the price of wine, is affected by a variety of factors. One of these is the quality of the harvest, which obviously depends on weather conditions; there is also the question of availability, both of the present harvest and of previous stocks. Purchasing capacity of both *négociants* and distributors has an equally decisive effect. In certain years, too, speculation has had a damaging influence on sales.

Whether they work as independent producers, through cooperatives, or as *négociants*, all members of the wine community must accept changing demand and the new tendency to view

Left, a wine auction.
Below, Pommery: galleries named after towns importing the wine.

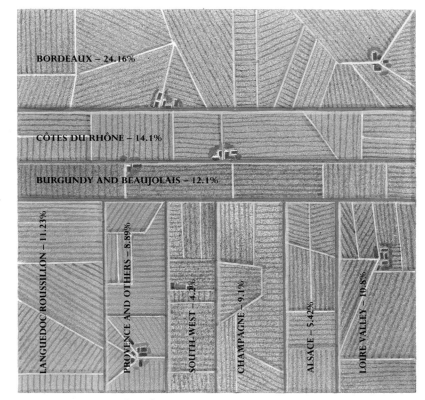

BORDEAUX – 24.16%

CÔTES DU RHÔNE – 14.1%

BURGUNDY AND BEAUJOLAIS – 12.1%

LANGUEDOC ROUSSILLON – 11.23%

PROVENCE AND OTHERS – 8.89%

SOUTH-WEST – 4.2%

CHAMPAGNE – 9.1%

ALSACE – 5.42%

LOIRE VALLEY – 10.8%

The main AOC production areas in France.

wine as an expression of social status. This trend could well result in the development of 'personalized' wines, grown in a particular locality or signed by a particular producer or *négociant*, or indeed marketed for a combination of the two.

MANCHESTER

FRENCH WINE ON THE WORLD MARKET

OVER 52 million hl of wine, the equivalent of more than 6 billion bottles, were put on the market in 1987. Nowadays French wine is oriented more and more towards the export market. France is second in the world after Italy for volume of wine exports, and first for value. In 1987, 13.2 million hl were exported and 38.2 million hl consumed in France. The 6.4 million hl of AOC wines (31 per cent of wine production) account for 48 per cent of wine export sales. French wine is becoming constantly more obtainable throughout the world, as the volume of AOC exports has been multiplied by four in the last twenty years. Champagne and Bordeaux are shipped to 160 different countries. The principal customers are Great Britain (18 per cent in value of sales), the United States (17 per cent), and the German Federal Republic (16 per cent).

soils, leached brown soils, leached acid soils, and even weathered podsols (very poor acid soils with accumulated layers of iron and organic matter sometimes compacted to form ironpan). To this list can also be added often heavily waterlogged

Left, vines grow best on slopes, as here at Bergerac.

Below, vines growing on limestone rock (Saint-Emilion).

IT was more than 2,500 years ago that Greek settlers began growing vines in France, but the present wine landscape has existed for hardly more than 200, or in some cases perhaps 500, years. So it has taken 2,000 years for French viticulture to develop the character it has today. The extraordinary slowness of this evolution, which still goes on, can be attributed to the problems encountered by generations of vine-growers seeking the perfect balance between grapes, soil, climate and cultivation.

In the beginning, the wine map seems not to have been planned with any precise concern for climatic or geological factors. Historians and geographers have shown that the important wine regions grew up close to navigable waterways, such as rivers and canals. It was trade, therefore, that shaped the map of French wine. But this should not be regarded as an accidental development made to work without reference to other considerations.

As early as the eighteenth century, growers were trying to determine which methods of cultivation, which grapes and vine-stocks were best suited to the weather, geology and soil conditions dictated by the demands of trade. If we exclude environmental influences, we overlook the fact that the wine map of France

today does not simply follow the outlines of the original map. Many former wine regions have since disappeared, the important Paris area for a start; only those fortunate enough to enjoy a favourable environment have managed to survive.

With quality wines, the *cru* can be regarded as the end-product of an ecosystem resulting from the interaction in a particular place of soil, subsoil, climate, plant (both grape variety and the stock on which it is grafted) and man.

NO OVER-SIMPLIFICATIONS

ARE all these elements of equal importance or is there one decisive factor determining the characteristics and quality of wine? The question has often been asked, especially since the growth in the eighteenth century of scientific interest in agricultural problems.

Attempts to establish a hierarchy of wine soon made it clear that vines do especially well on certain geological and soil formations, such as the chalk of the Champagne region or the gravel terraces of Bordeaux, whereas on others, such as heavy clay,

they grow with some reluctance. It also became apparent that the properties of soil and rock formations have a marked influence on the wine's colour, taste, aroma and later its whole bouquet.

However, it is dangerous to oversimplify the importance of geology: this is certainly a determining factor, but within limits. In France as elsewhere, wines, sometimes very famous ones, are produced on a vast range of different rock formations: on chalk, limestone, marl, molasse with varying limestone content, on alluvial sands and gravels which may be siliceous, and also on schist, granite and even clay. On the other hand, wines grown on a single rock formation may vary enormously in quality.

With such a diversity of parent-rock, it is not surprising that soils may vary, sometimes over quite a small area in one site. Over hardly more than 30 hectares in the best Montrachet zone, there are rendzinas (thin layers of pebbly soil over limestone subsoil) at Chevalier-Montrachet, brown calcareous soils at Montrachet and Bâtard-Montrachet, and in addition some brown soils at Bâtard-Montrachet. This is only a small sample of the sort of soils used for vine-growing. As well as soils containing high levels of limestone, a complete list would include brown

hydromorphic soils, the most famous examples of which can be found in some of the best Pomerol vineyards (Pétrus, Trotanoy, Latour à Pomerol and so on). These are geological aberrations, highly clayey formations theoretically unsuitable for high-quality vines. In fact they are very specific soils, with mineralogical properties lending themselves to special forms of water management.

THE COMPLEX REALITY

AS these examples show, the reality is very complex. However, even

INFLUENCES

without oversimplifying cause and effect, it does seem clear that soils are an important element in determining a wine's quality. They can have a negative influence, as when over-rich soils produce vigorous growth with grapes that do not ripen correctly, giving wines with a lack of balance. They can also have positive effects, especially in regions with a cool or temperate climate. Tasting shows up important differences in the way terrain can modify the properties of a wine. The Burgundian concept of the *climat*, meaning a small section within a larger vineyard, often with its own geological conditions, aspect and microclimate, demonstrates this particularly well: there may sometimes be fewer differences between two vines several hundred metres apart but within one *climat* than there are between practically neighbouring vines in two different *climats*. Montrachet is a very good example of this, with endless shades of difference between Montrachet itself and Chevalier-Montrachet, whose stonier soils result in a lighter, more delicate wine.

Topography too is important: the best plots are on fairly well defined slopes (ridges or hillsides), whereas cool damp plains and valley bottoms are unsuitable for growing high-quality wines. This is well illustrated by the hills of the Lower Vosges in Alsace, which provide excellent vine territory; by making the most of the sun's heat, the hillside situation allows the grapes to ripen correctly. Such sites often border on river valleys and it is easy to see why wine regions that grew up beside navigable rivers have never subsequently moved away from these hillsides.

In the great wine regions, wine quality does not seem to be linked to soil of very specific texture. It is clear that in fact there are considerable differences in clay content: this may be minute in certain soils, but above 50 per cent for some excellent growths in Burgundy and Bordeaux. Soil structure is much more important, however: by far the majority of

the best sites have soils of large pore structure where rapid drainage prevents waterlogged roots. This porousness allows the roots to penetrate several metres down into loose sand and gravel soils, or into fissured hard rock such as chalk or limestone. On the other hand, in some soils that lie on clay or dense limestone, roots may go down only half a metre or so. The depth of the roots and the way they penetrate the soil obviously have an effect on the vines' uptake of minerals and water. Greater depth

Good wine terrain is therefore based on an ecosystem with very complex interactions between its various components. There has to be a rigorous combination of circumstances, which occurs only in certain very precise areas; in France this may apply to some AOC wine regions run in line with the ecosystem of great wines.

Right, Cabernet vine-growing in gravel (Pauillac).

also helps to counterbalance the effect of climatic extremes. Studies in some of the best Bordeaux vineyards (in deep gravel areas, and also on dense limestone and on clay) have shown that a well-regulated water supply for the vines, linked with methods of rooting, can limit if not altogether suppress the damage caused by severe drought or excessive rainfall, especially during the time when grapes are ripening.

Above, a vineyard on chalk (Cramant in the Champagne region).

CLIMATE

GEOLOGY and soil structure are both important in the production of good wine, but only in conjunction with specific climatic conditions, so that together they create an environment suitable for high-quality vineyards.

EXTREME CONDITIONS

VINES can adapt to very varied climates. They manage to grow in cool northern countries with little sunshine; in a continental climate, provided root-stocks are not regularly destroyed by freezing winter temperatures; even sometimes in almost tropical regions. However, they do not flourish in extreme conditions: temperatures below −15°C can destroy all or part of the branches, roots and stocks, while excessively high

enough (without being excessive) to allow the synthesis of sugar in sufficient quantity for the natural production of something that deserves the name of wine.

In its turn, it is sunshine that determines the colour of wine. More light energy is needed for the synthesis of red colouring matter than for sugar production. This is why countries close to the northern limits of vine-growing produce almost solely white wines, as in Alsace and Chablis, sometimes even basing them on red grape varieties, as with Champagne: without adequate sunshine even red grapes do not have a strong colour.

Rainfall must not be too low, as it often is in Mediterranean regions; nor must it be too high, or quality may fall in some years, as in the temperate regions of the Atlantic seaboard or in the cooler climates of north-eastern France.

In hotter, sunnier regions where grapes ripen more easily and should therefore give better results, the same grape varieties give a 'soft' wine with a less developed bouquet, as if the fierce ripening process were burning off the essences that make for refinement in great wines. So the best wines are often produced at the northernmost fringes of an area where the best grape varieties are cultivated.

THE PERFECT CLIMATE

IN France, there are several hazardous periods in the wine-producer's year. It is rare for the vine-stocks to freeze in winter, but spring frosts may destroy young shoots. Heavy rain during the flowering and pollination period may cause *coulure* and *millerandage* (failure to pollinate and to set fruit), with subsequent loss of crops. Mild, rainy weather provides a favourable environment for fungus diseases such as mildew, oïdium and botrytis, which attack the vine's green parts or fruit. Hail, too, may cause local destruction of all or part of one crop and endanger those to come. Lastly, storms and heavy rain may damage vines and erode the soil through the torrents of water they create. This is especially true in Mediterranean regions where in the past the women used to carry back the soil washed down the hillside while the men repaired the walls protecting their plots.

Even if the vines are not affected by these hazards they will not necessarily give a good wine. It is not at all easy to determine just what are the ideal weather conditions for producing high-quality wine. However, there are clearly one or two basic premises. First, there must not be too much variation from year to year in the average annual temperature. Secondly, a determining factor for both quantity and quality in a vintage is rainfall. An adequate provision of water is necessary during the growth period of April to July inclusive. However, too much rainfall on

Frost danger in early spring. Heaters may be used to prevent bud damage.

THE GRAPE–WEATHER ALLIANCE

IT is a remarkable fact that high-quality wines are generally produced by grapes that only just ripen in the local climate: it is essential that grapes should ripen completely, but the ripening process must be slow and gradual.

temperatures may scorch leaves and grapes. The area favourable to vine cultivation lies between the latitudes of 50 and 35 degrees, extending in the northern hemisphere from the Ardennes to the northern fringes of Algeria, Morocco and Tunisia. Temperatures in this zone are high

Top, neutron gauge for measuring soil humidity.

Above, white grapes scorched by the sun.

relatively fertile soils would result in too vigorous growth and excess production of over-large grapes.

On the other hand, high temperatures, long hours of sunshine, and rainfall which is restricted but not inadequate during the period of ripening and harvest can often guarantee an excellent vintage. The year's weather conditions are what determine the quality of a vintage, even for the best *crus*. However, the latter can be very consistent in quality even when the weather is unfavourable, since other factors that contribute to their make-up (including the type and structure of soil, and the vine's root system) mitigate the effects of extreme weather and contribute to the healthy functioning of the vine. This all helps to explain how the *grands crus* manage to retain their superiority even in very poor years.

MESOCLIMATES AND MICROCLIMATES

WEATHER conditions on a general level are important, but what about weather on an intermediate level, within one plot or group of plots in a wine region? It is no accident that many French wine regions have an

Above, roots laid bare by heavy rain and landslips.

Below left, screened weather thermometer; right, analysing information at the Bordeaux-Mérignac weather station.

Left, water lying on badly draining soil.

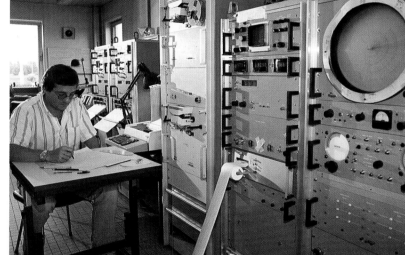

eastern aspect, as in Alsace and Burgundy. This lets the rising sun warm the soil gradually and gives some protection against rain from the west. It has also been shown that there is less daily temperature variation where there is convex relief, as on the brow of a hill, but on concave sites such as the foot of a hill or the bottom of a valley hours of sunshine are fewer and cold air is trapped, with the likelihood of night frosts in spring.

It would be dangerous to generalize from these few examples. However, it is certainly important when evaluating these intermediate climates to distinguish between hilly regions and others. In the former, altitude, slope and aspect all, to some degree, modify sunshine, temperature and rainfall rates and in this way have a direct influence on the quality and composition of harvests. In less hilly regions, variations in the intermediate climate

have a less decisive effect on crops.

There may be considerable differences in microclimate, however, at the level of a leaf, a bunch of grapes or even a single grape. The microclimate of warmth and light for different parts of the vine can be modified by procedures such as altering the layout and density of planting or the alignment of the rows, and by all the different methods of pruning, training, trimming or stripping the vines.

THE HUMAN CONTRIBUTION

MAN has had a decisive influence on the way the wine ecosystem works. The vineyards of France constitute an environment made almost entirely by man and remade a number of times in the course of the country's history. Man is therefore as much part of the wine ecosystem as soil, climate or grape. It is the interaction between these different factors that seems to determine the characteristics and quality of each site.

Above, planting vines.
Above right, pruning.

MATCHING SOIL AND GRAPES

A key to this ecosystem is the compatibility of grape and terrain. In general, no particular rock formations produce a monopoly of wine quality. However, for some unknown reason some grape varieties do seem to have a predilection for certain types of base-rock. The best Chardonnay wines are produced on marl terrain, and Viognier gives some remarkable white wines on granite at Condrieu and Château-Grillet. Gamay, which gives pleasant reds on the granite and schist of Beaujolais, produces fairly ordinary wines on marly limestone in Burgundy. In a particular regional climate, a choice between several grape varieties should take into account the type of soil and the microclimate of heat and water. In the Bordeaux area, for

instance, Cabernet Sauvignon grapes achieve their full ripeness and potential only on sandy gravel soils (Haut-Médoc and part of Graves) which are warm because of their lack of moisture. On more water-retentive cold silt or clay, these grapes ripen less easily and give herbaceous, less refined wines. On the other hand, Merlot Noir gives its best on the fine-textured soils of Saint-Emilion and the sometimes very clayey soils of Pomerol.

LIMITED INTERVENTION

MAN'S intervention is not restricted to the choice of grape and root-stock. It also affects the land. However, vines should not have to undergo constant interference, although it may sometimes be useful to remedy any deficiency, toxicity or chemical imbalance in the soil by appropriate fertilizers or improvers. If so, this should be done with restraint after thorough scientific analysis of the soil and subsoil. No attempt should be made to impose an optimum level of production. Research has confirmed growers' experiences by demonstrating in a number of regions that, above a certain threshold varying according to weather conditions that year, there is a negative

correlation between the volume of a crop and the quality. Closer study shows that a wine's quality seems to depend more on the weight of grapes produced by each vine-stock than on the total yield per hectare. This has brought about a return to very close planting (7,000 to 10,000 stocks per hectare of low, narrow vines), which for an equivalent output gives better quality wines than tall, spreading vines (less than 3,500 stocks per hectare). There is the additional finding that individual grapes, especially the red, have to be small in size so that the skin surface containing tannin and colouring matter is large in proportion to the volume of juice.

The chemical properties of the soil, the water supply and cultivation

procedures all have an effect on the yield–quality equation, but vine-stocks (see p. 17) are also important for the vigour they impart to the grafted vine. To produce good wine, it is essential to choose vine-stocks adapted to the soil, especially in resistance to chlorosis, and capable of drawing on its available water and fertility. Also, they must not make the grafted plant too vigorous, as limited production and early cessation of growth encourage the grapes to ripen properly.

Right, planting cuttings.

Below, soil composition may need improvement before vines are planted. Here sewage sludge has been added.

Below right, grafting a classic grape variety onto a phylloxera-resistant stock.

THE SPECIAL QUALITIES OF GREAT WINE

HUMAN intervention is important in establishing an ecosystem and essential when it comes to the harvest and to the vinification, treatment and storage of wine. Often in the past wines from very good vineyards used to develop excessive acidity and tannin which were not softened even

after a long time in the bottle. Modern improvements and greater knowledge of wine science have made poor vinification more unusual, without making all wines taste the same. For the *grands crus* at least, oenologists have aimed at quite the opposite, in an attempt to make the most of the specific, distinctive qualities in a wine;

and the very complex ecosystem of great wines itself helps to protect their individuality. The best sites are those where geographical situation, site, topography and soil properties (together with their effect on root systems) combine to allow the establishment of a *grand cru*, provided that climate and grape varieties are also suitable. For the most part, these are natural factors which man cannot readily modify, especially as we still understand too little about the differences between one vineyard and another or about the optimum

parameters for the proper functioning of the climate–soil–vine ecosystem. Research to date has hardly begun to account for all this, even if a start has been made in the best Bordeaux *crus* with the emphasis on a well-regulated supply of water to the vine in conjunction with study of the rooting system.

THE CHOICE OF GRAPE

CABERNET Sauvignon in Médoc, Ugni-Blanc in Cognac, Chardonnay in Burgundy, Chenin in the Loire Valley, not to mention Syrah, Sylvaner, Gewürztraminer and many others – these grape varieties are such an integral part of the French wine landscape that one might assume they had flourished since the beginning of time. Nowadays they are all officially classified and each *département* has its list of recommended varieties. Such regulations are even more strict for AOC areas, which may grow only those varieties listed.

These different grapes did not suddenly appear by magic. They have been brought into existence by generation after generation of hardworking growers. The thousands of

Above, training the vine into a 'lyre' shape.
Top, 'goblet' pruning.

varieties included in *Vitis vinifera*, the European vine, have been reduced by trial and error to a selection of about 250, of which only a hundred or so are economically worthwhile. The selection took into account the properties of each grape variety, and has become the basis of the present code of practice.

'THE GRAPE IS THE ESSENTIAL SPIRIT OF WINE'

EACH grape variety has its special character, derived from the way it adapts to its environment, the climate and the soil. What matters is to find a variety that has the right growth characteristics for a particular situation. The association of Cabernet Sauvignon and Merlot with the land round Bordeaux is well known: the growth cycle of these varieties enables them to resist spring frosts and allows the grapes to ripen during the generally mild and sunny local autumn.

Some varieties are exceptionally flexible in their ability to grow in all sorts of different soils and climates. Cabernet Sauvignon, for instance, flourishes in the moist, temperate climate of Bordeaux but, to judge by recent plantings in the Coteaux d'Aix, it also seems happy in the dry heat of Provence. Outside France, it seems equally content in California and the continental climate of Bulgaria and the USSR. This is nothing out of the ordinary: if we look at Merlot, Chenin, Pinot and Syrah, they are all just as adaptable.

The ability to produce a certain sort of wine in a specific place depends first and foremost on the biochemical constituents of the grapes: the study of what these constituents are and of their proportional importance has led to the establishment of a hierarchy of grape varieties. The so-called 'noble' varieties (Chardonnay, Pinot, Cabernet Sauvignon, etc.) are suitable for fine wines, while the others are consigned to producing everyday wines without much strong character. The constituents of these grapes, present also in the must, are numerous and complex. Four of them in particular have to be considered when choosing a grape variety:

Sugar: The level is not the same for all varieties as some produce more because of their leaves' greater capacity for photosynthesis.

Acidity: This is important in itself and also for the ratio of malic acid to tartaric acid, of great interest to the wine expert.

Phenolic compounds: These large organic compounds, predominantly in the skin of the grape, include anthocyanins, which contribute to the colour in black grapes, tannins, flavonoids and other components which determine the taste, flavour and texture of the wine.

Aromas: These are located in the grape skins and are very numerous. The difference in intensity between them is apparently what gives a variety its specific aroma and the wine its distinctive character.

In this way, the choice of grape variety determines the future quality of the wine. This has been well understood for many years, and it was Olivier de Serres in the early seventeenth century who insisted: 'The grape is the essential spirit of wine.' The golden rule is to find a grape variety where the yield is in quality rather than quantity.

REPLACING OLD VARIETIES

MOST grape varieties grown belong to the European species *Vitis vinifera* L., which has been cultivated for thousands of years and considerably transformed in the process of selection.

The nineteenth century was a period when much renewal of vines took place. In the second half of the century, various waves of diseases from the New World (oïdium, mildew, black-rot, phylloxera) threatened European vines with extinction. In spite of phylloxera, which was impossible to eradicate, vineyards were restored by grafting European varieties onto root-stocks derived from American species, chosen for resistance to phylloxera and for adaptability on different types of soil. Old *Vitis vinifera* varieties were thus conserved by grafting. Growers also learnt to protect them from fungal diseases by the use of chemicals.

On the basis of their success with grafts, some growers also tried

LTIVATION

Bordeaux or Burgundy, the selection of grape varieties has been perfected and it is unnecessary to seek out more; but this is not the case everywhere and, even for prestigious *appellations*, it is still possible to improve existing varieties. Also, economic conditions change, drinking tastes develop, methods of cultivation improve, competition increases and people are no longer willing to accept deficiencies which they put up with in the past.

Above, spraying by helicopter, a recently introduced technique (Champagne).

Left, spraying with sulphur (Burgundy).

Centre, the method of training vines in Entre-Deux-Mers.

to produce new graft varieties by hybridization, that is by crossing *Vitis vinifera* with hardy species such as *Vitis berlandieri* and *Vitis riparia*, in an attempt to combine grape quality with resistance to parasites. Hybrids were an obsession for about fifty years, and at their peak covered more than a third of the area under vines, though they could not be used for the production of *appellation contrôlée* wines. However, as none of them was really satisfactory in quality, they have been in decline since 1950.

This does not mean that the replacement of grape varieties has stopped altogether. In regions where there is a great tradition, as in

CLONAL SELECTION

THE propagation of vines has traditionally been carried out by the person responsible for cutting shoots to cultivate into new plants. This person chooses shoots from as many different healthy vines as possible, rather than propagating them all from one

individual particularly healthy-looking plant or clone. The selection is made by eye, avoiding any stocks which, whether for genetic or other incidental reasons such as the presence of viruses, show signs of weakness. This method, which is known as 'mass selection', has reduced virus disease and so led to an improvement in the quality of vine-stocks. It has also contributed to an increase in the average yield of grapes.

Clonal selection was initiated in the fifties and is based on scientific analysis of each original vine-stock. It represents 10 to 15 per cent of all selection today, compared with 0.5 per cent in 1980, and is very prominent in the Bordeaux, Champagne and Burgundy areas. By this method all plants propagated from the original vine-stock, whether by grafts or by cuttings, are its clones and behave identically to each other.

The characteristics of a great many vine-stocks of each grape variety are compared, especially for absence of decay, resistance to certain diseases, regular yield and aromatic intensity. These characteristics are analysed under strict experimental conditions, and special care is taken to eliminate bias due to fluctuations in mid-experiment and to the operator's subjectivity. After this only the clones with the highest ratings are kept; a small percentage of the original number. These are then propagated to produce sufficient vine-stocks for commercial purposes. It is very difficult to make morphological distinctions between different clones from the same grape variety, so very careful precautions have to be taken to safeguard the identity of each.

Selective cloning makes it possible to improve even the noble grape varieties. However, the improvement in aroma, colour or early ripening cannot exceed the level characteristic of each variety. The whole process is also very slow, as the effectiveness of clonal selection depends on extensive preliminary study and rigorous experimental methods, and a major drawback of the method is that, if the wrong clone is selected, the whole vineyard will suffer from the same weakness.

PESTS AND DISEASES

THE vine has a number of enemies. It is subject to attack from several viruses: the diseases of fan-leaf (court-noue) and leaf-roll (enroulement), various mosaic diseases causing mottling, and corky degeneration of the bark. All these are the result of a virus occupying the cells of the host plant and distorting its metabolism. Infection occurs when cuttings or grafts are being made and, since there is no readily available cure, preventive measures must always be taken. Vines are also vulnerable to fungal and parasitic infection. The most serious and widespread diseases, mildew, oïdium, phomopsis and black-rot, are caused by microscopic fungi. The different animal pests include various mites, leafhoppers and especially caterpillars, which eat the young grapes and set off grey-rot. The armoury of protective measures against all these pests has become much more substantial since the early days of chemical fungicides.

GRAPE VARIETIES

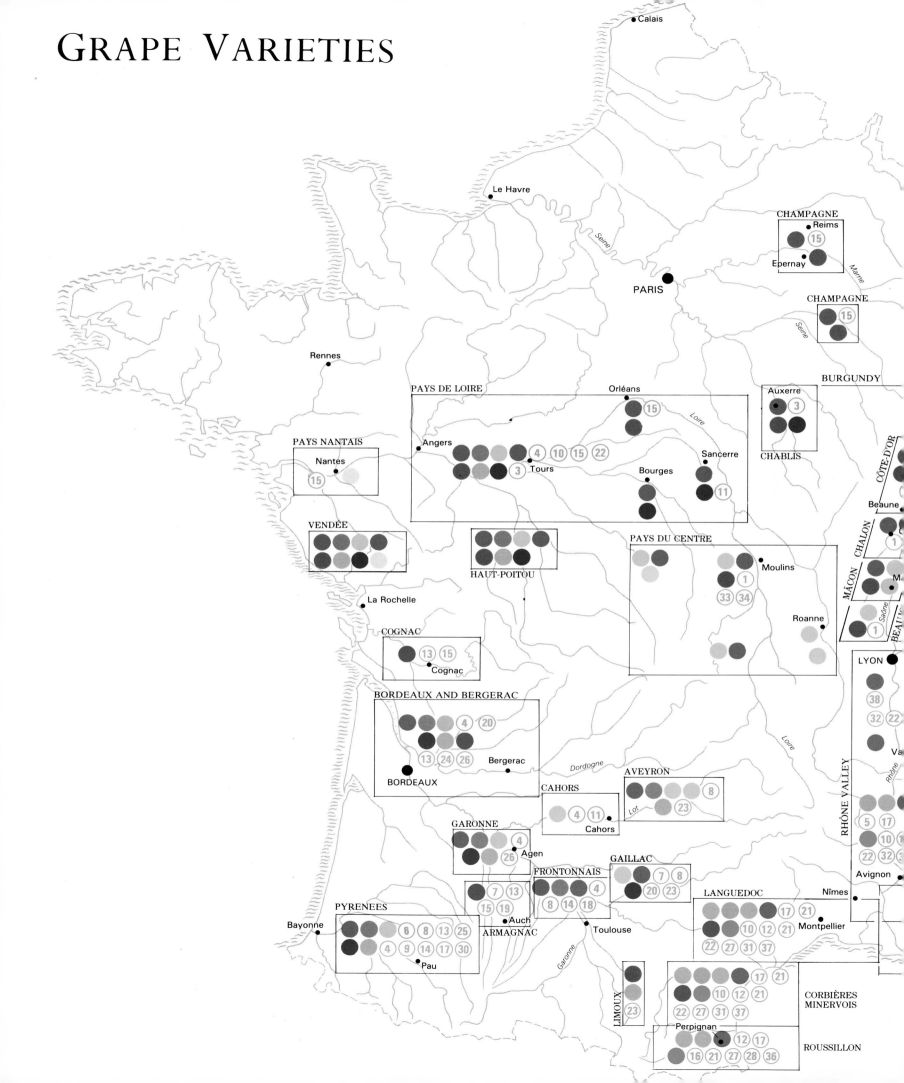

PRINCIPAL GRAPE VARIETIES FOR RED APPELLATIONS

Commonly grown varieties	Others		
● Cabernet-franc	① Braquet	⑩ Grolleau	⑲ Nielluccio
● Cabernet-sauvignon	② Calitor	⑪ Jurançon rouge	⑳ Petit verdot
● Carignan	③ César	⑫ LLadoner pelut	㉑ Picpoul noir
● Cinsault	④ Côt	⑬ Manseng noir	㉒ Pineau d'Aunis
● Gamay	⑤ Counoise	⑭ Mérille	㉓ Poulsard
● Grenache	⑥ Courbu noir	⑮ Meunier	㉔ Sciacarello
● Merlot	⑦ Duras	⑯ Mondeuse	㉕ Tannat
● Pinot noir	⑧ Fer servadou	⑰ Mourvèdre	㉖ Tibouren
● Syrah	⑨ Fuella nera	⑱ Négrette	㉗ Trousseau

PRINCIPAL GRAPE VARIETIES FOR WHITE APPELLATIONS
(AND FOR ROSÉ AND 'VINS GRIS')

Commonly grown varieties	Others		
● Chardonnay	① Aligoté	⑭ Courbu	㉗ Muscat à petits grains
● Chenin	② Altesse	⑮ Folle blanche	㉘ Muscat d'Alexandrie
● Gewurztraminer ✱	③ Arbois	⑯ Grenache gris ✱	㉙ Muscat ottonel
● Grenache blanc	④ Arrufiac	⑰ Gros manseng	㉚ Petit manseng
● Melon	⑤ Aubin	⑱ Jacquère	㉛ Picpoul
● Pinot blanc	⑥ Auxerrois	⑲ Jurançon blanc	㉜ Roussanne
● Pinot gris ✱	⑦ Baco 22a	⑳ Len de l'el	㉝ Sacy
● Riesling	⑧ Barbaroux ✱	㉑ Macabeu	㉞ Saint-pierre doré
● Sauvignon	⑨ Baroque	㉒ Marsanne	㉟ Savagnin
● Sémillon	⑩ Bourboulenc	㉓ Mauzac	㊱ Tourbat
● Sylvaner	⑪ Chasselas	㉔ Merlot blanc	㊲ Vermentino
● Ugni-blanc	⑫ Clairette	㉕ Molette	㊳ Viognier
	⑬ Colombard	㉖ Muscadelle	

✱ (rosé)   These lists are not exhaustive

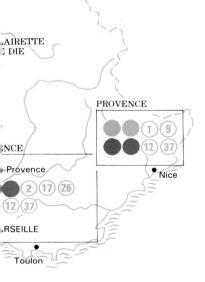

ONLY the grape varieties most representative of the different regions have been mentioned. The most widely planted varieties are shown by a coloured circle.

For the sake of clarity, the official name of each grape is being used, although there are a number of regional variations. For instance, several varieties may be known by the same name: the name Malvoisie may apply to the Bourboulenc grape in the Narbonne district, to Tourbat in Roussillon, or to Vermentino in Corsica..

Again, one variety may have different names in different regions. There are even more examples of this: in the Nantes area the Melon grape is called Muscadet; Côt may be known as Malbec or Auxerrois, depending on the district; Cabernet Franc may appear as Breton or Bouchet.

On the other hand, one variety has sometimes been confused with another in the past and may still be known by the wrong name.

These interchangeable names are closely linked to local customs and geography and can complicate the whole question of grape varieties. In France there is a relatively clear grasp of these problems. This is not always true at an international level, and in some countries there is still considerable confusion, even with the most commonly planted grapes.

THE SEASONS

'*POUDO-me dabant que pleure, foucho-me dabant que bourre, bino-me dabant que flouri, te farai béure de boun bí.*' ('Prune me before I weep, dig me before I bud, hoe me before I flower, and I'll give you good wine.') As this old proverb from Languedoc reminds us, the vine needs to be well tended before it can produce grapes for making good wine.

PRUNING

THE seasons of the wine calendar consist of an endless succession of chores, beginning in winter when the vines are still dormant. The grower has to bend double to prune the vines, his fingers numb with cold. The feast of Saint Vincent, the patron saint of vines (22 January), was the date traditionally fixed for the official start of this laborious task, although pruning is in fact carried out at intervals between December and March. Its

importance in the vine's annual cycle is considerable. It reduces the number of stems, fixes the number of buds to be retained and determines both the quality and volume of the future crop.

In spite of improved tools, and various pneumatic and electric secateurs in place of the old pruning knife, pruning is still lengthy and arduous. The secateurs have to cut into each plant four or five times so,

with an average of four to five thousand vine-stocks per hectare, the same action is repeated twenty to twenty-five thousand times over one hectare. Mechanized pruning by robot may be possible in the future but will run into the problem that growers have to treat each stock individually, each time making a guess about which shoots to remove from a particular position. Perhaps it is not surprising that they often feel sentimentally attached to the pruning operation, which is not just a decision about the future but a privileged moment of contact between man and plant. A real *vigneron* cannot help imagining that the vine is 'weeping' after pruning, when the rising sap forms beads of moisture round the cut.

Pruning is completed around 15 March, when vines start coming to life again. This is the time for ploughing the ground to destroy any intrusive weeds and to expose the base of the vines by moving soil towards the centre of the rows.

In many vineyards ploughing four or five times a year now tends to be replaced by the application of chemical weedkillers at the end of the winter.

In areas where vines are trained on supports, April is the time for fixing the shoots left after pruning, usually onto two or three lines of wire. There are a number of procedures to ensure that the vines continue to develop well. In May a second superficial

Merlot – in flower, turning colour and fully ripe.

ploughing is carried out so that weeds will not spread. At the beginning of May there is the first of a series of spraying operations against diseases and parasites. The Service de Protection des Végétaux (Plant Protection Service) advises what treatments to use.

For wire-trained vines June is the month for tying in, when the young growth is trained along wires. This is also the time for cutting back, an

operation which has to be repeated a number of times for vines grown low down. In Spring too there are various other procedures, such as thinning and disbudding, all intended to get rid of surplus growth. At the same time, the grower has to remember to spray against parasites whenever necessary. A mixture of lime and copper sulphate is still used against mildew, but is only one constituent of a chemical armoury now including some 36 active

ingredients and 300 brands. Most of these substances have a purely preventive function. There are two main types: products that affect only the surface of the plant and persist until rain washes them off, and products that are absorbed by the leaves, carried round by the sap and persist for about two weeks.

These treatments go on into early summer. In August work on the soil comes to an end once weed growth

Ploughing – an essential part of vineyard upkeep, but mechanized almost everywhere today.

slows down, but it is essential to continue watching over the vines, and protective measures may be necessary right into September if there is risk of disease.

VINE MANAGEMENT

THE vine-grower's calendar has inherited all the traditional popular wisdom passed on in sayings such as '*Le soleil de la Saint-Jean présage une année de vin*' ('Midsummer shine – a year of good wine'), and '*Quand il pleut à l'Assomption, le vin perd sa qualité*' ('Rain upon Assumption Day – for grapes and wine there'll be dismay'). Nowadays the calendar is also governed by scientific and technical ideas, and vine-growing is no longer a hit or miss affair. Indeed, it is now so strictly regulated that it can be called a 'vine management system'. This broadly covers all human intervention in vine-growing, including both work on the soil and protection against disease. In a narrower sense, it designates the organization of the basic structure of the vineyard: arrangement (density and spacing) of plantings; alignment of rows, according to topography and weather conditions; pruning methods; whether or not to train on wires or other supports; all the work on the vine itself. These systems can be reduced to two basic types, each involving a balance of various factors necessary for wine quality:

Vines grown untrained, pruned low on a short stock (*gobelet* pruning), sometimes planted in square formation with an average density of 4,500 stocks per hectare. This is the usual system in Mediterranean regions.

Vines trained on supports, a system necessary for producing adequate ripening in northern areas, pruned

Young vines tied in to stakes.

stock, in order to maintain an adequate yield per hectare. Because of slower ripening in the majority of cases, wines derived from these vines are inferior to those produced by the old system, so this type of vine is not used for high-quality production.

However, if foliage is trained into the so-called 'lyre' shape on a kind of double espalier, the leaves and grape clusters can enjoy an improved microclimate of heat and light. Recent research has shown that this encourages spreading vines grown at low

density to produce wine which is at least the equal of that from traditional vines. It is up to the growers in each wine region to judge the economic consequences of this and to determine the operating conditions best adapted to their particular environment.

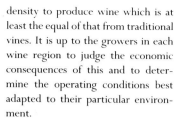

Pruning, here the Guyot method, determines the volume and quality of the crop.

Weedkillers simplify cultivation.

less severely and grown at a high density of 5,000 to 10,000 stocks per hectare. With a good many variants, this is the system met with in most non-Mediterranean wine regions.

From 1950 on, the need for lower production costs, with the increasing use of machines rather than men, led to the use of 'high-culture systems', typified by low-density planting (2,500 stocks per hectare) and by a taller trunk and spreading habit of growth. This in turn necessitates a larger number of shoots on each

DANGERS AND VIRTUES OF WEEDKILLERS

THE use of chemical weedkillers was cautiously introduced around 1955. Since then, it has completely transformed soil maintenance. A growing sector of the French wine industry has now gone over to 'non-cultivation' methods requiring no digging of the soil, a very cost-effective system compared with traditional methods of cultivation. As vines are extremely sensitive to most herbicides, there has to be very careful appraisal of the weeds to be eradicated, the type of soil and the level and distribution of rainfall. Non-cultivation methods have now been in use long enough to show that they have no harmful effects. As long as the rules are followed, there is no danger of residue in either the soil or the wine; nor does the productiveness or longevity of the vines seem to suffer. On the contrary, there is evidence of increased vigour, which can be put down to improved uptake of water and minerals when the vine roots are able to occupy more of the upper layer of soil.

FROM GRAPE TO WINE

Instead of cheerful bands of pickers, harvesting machines are now more commonly seen. These straddle the rows while their mechanical paddles flick the grapes onto a conveyor belt with plates that retract when they come up against a rootstock. The crop is blown clean of leaves and then tipped into hoppers for transport. This rough treatment is not conducive to quality, especially in white wines, and the most famous

'YOU burn a sulphur match in the barrel, you put in the juice, then you sit back and wait.' This was the advice given by an old wine-grower in the South-west to a son taking over the business. The son thought there might be better methods and managed to transform the wine without having to replace the vines. Winemaking may be an art but it is also a rigorous technique based on modern scientific knowledge and equipment.

RIPENESS IS ALL

AS every good wine-grower has known for centuries, to produce a wine that is good and true to type, first of all you have to have perfectly ripe grapes. The ripening process is linked initially to the weather conditions when growth starts at the beginning of spring, which may vary by more than twenty days according to the lateness of the season. Thereafter the grapes take about the same time to ripen each year.

The quality of the ripe grapes also depends on weather conditions from July to September; conditions that are preferably dry and hot. Great vintages generally occur in 'early' years, when

Top left, Corton-Charlemagne: traditional harvesting baskets.
Top right, filling the vat (Beaujolais).

the grapes can benefit most from long hours of summer sunshine.

HARVEST DATES

THE proclamation of the official harvest date is now an excuse for picturesque ceremony but is also a reminder that the choice of date has always been a very serious matter for the grower. For a long time it was based on the appearance of the grapes and their level of sweetness. Nowadays chemical analysis is more precise. In hot areas over-ripeness makes for soft, heavy wines, while in colder regions grapes have to be sufficiently ripe to avoid giving wines that are too green and harsh.

Harvest dates also depend on the

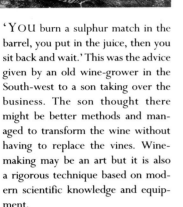

healthiness of the vines. Infected grapes may introduce unwelcome flavours and may also necessitate early picking to avoid losing the entire crop. Progress in the field of disease prevention has certainly helped to improve the quality of wine over the last twenty years.

Above, a mechanical harvester. Left, beaters which detach the grapes and the belt which conveys them to bins.

Picking used to be done by hand but is increasingly mechanized in many areas. The point of hand-picking is to gather whole grapes, rid of all extraneous matter such as earth, leaves and stems, and if necessary of rotten fruit. The crop then has to be taken quickly, uncrushed, to the vats.

vineyards, whose wines are particularly vulnerable to the impact of technology, continue to have reservations about these harvesting methods. However, there has been considerable improvement in the design and application of these machines. They also have much flexibility in use,

36

Yeasts are naturally present on the grapes and are brought into the fermenting rooms with the crop. If necessary, however, indigenous yeasts can be added to or even replaced altogether, and dried yeasts which are very easy to use are now readily available.

Alcoholic fermentation in certain cases is followed by a second, malolactic fermentation, a phenomenon only recently understood. It was only in the sixties that it was acknowledged as a factor in the improvement of red wine. For white wine its usefulness is less definite.

allowing producers to stop and start the harvest according to the ripeness of different grape varieties, healthiness of the vines or busy periods in the processing plant.

Differences in the composition of grapes and variations in weather sometimes make it necessary to rectify a crop: in years of poor ripening in particular, grapes have a low sugar level and the wine therefore has a low alcohol content. In very specific conditions chaptalization (the addition of sugar to the must) is legally permitted. During the last twenty years this procedure has become common in certain wine regions. However, the purpose of chaptalization is not to make wines with a higher level of alcohol but to achieve the level necessary for quality, whatever the weather conditions.

Large capacity vats used in cooperatives. These are equipped with various mechanical devices such as an automatic marc drainage system (Listrac).

They produce ethyl alcohol and the carbon dioxide responsible for the spectacular bubbling in the wine-vat. They also produce a number of side-products, such as glycerol and various acids, higher alcohols and esters, which contribute even in very low concentrations to the final flavour of the wine.

Alcoholic fermentation also gives off heat, which raises the temperature in the vats. Temperature control is essential and at times even refrigeration, in order not to exceed levels (20°C for white wines, 25 to 30°C for reds) detrimental to the quality of the wine.

Small lined steel vats used so that grapes of different origin can be vinified separately.

Surrounding conditions are not always propitious and fermentation may sometimes stop, leaving a residue of unconverted sugar which may be decomposed by bacteria, turning the wine vinegary. Greater expertise has contributed to the control of fermentation and hence to higher quality.

Yeasts (left) and lactic bacteria (right), the micro organisms which turn grapes into wine: they reproduce by budding and cell-division.

Malolactic fermentation is set off by certain bacteria which transform malic acid into lactic acid and carbon dioxide. This produces lowered acidity and more softness, as well as greater refinement and a more complex bouquet. At the same time, the wine becomes more stable and keeps better. However, it is undesirable for this second fermentation to take place once the wine is bottled, because of the difficulty of predicting or controlling it at that stage.

In spite of recent scientific work, controlling the timing of this second fermentation remains difficult. Attempts to start the process by injecting bacterial yeasts have been made for some time, but this procedure still involves problems to which it is hoped there may be a solution in the near future. At present, most growers deal with this difficulty by keeping the temperature of the must stable at about 20°C, or by introducing wine from another vat that has already started its malolactic fermentation.

When fermentation is over, wine has to be stabilized and various microbes are eliminated by clarification (racking, fining, filtering and centrifuging), by being subjected to heat (pasteurization), by the addition of an antiseptic such as sulphur dioxide, or by a combination of these procedures.

CONTROL OF FERMENTATION

GRAPES need only be crushed for spontaneous heating and effervescence to occur and the sweet taste to disappear, a phenomenon which has fascinated observers since classical times. This is the process of alcoholic fermentation which turns grapes into wine.

Wine yeasts are microscopic organisms which develop away from air and feed on the sugar in grapes.

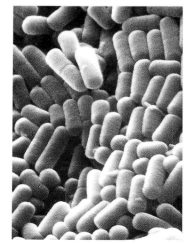

How Red Wine is Made

WINE-tasting vocabulary is so rich in words for appearance, smell and taste that it shows just how complex red wines are. Colour, and the tannins associated with it, are obtained by macerating the solid matter (skin, pips and if necessary even stalks) while the grape juice is fermenting. The length of this extraction process depends on the type of wine. The classic keeping wines need lengthy maceration using high-quality grapes, and this gives the depth of tannin

Harvested grapes at Gaillac.

essential for proper maturing, without too much astringency or bitterness. With less aristocratic grapes, it is better to macerate for a shorter time and concentrate on producing lighter, more delicate wines.

THE CLASSIC RED WINE METHOD

A certain number of specific procedures are involved in the making of red wine. Many of these are now mechanized, as with transporting the crop. As soon as the grapes are brought in from the vineyard, they are generally tipped into a machine that crushes and destalks them. The machine may vary in size and design according to type of grape and volume of production. Destalking has a number of advantages: the grapes need less space in the vats, and without the tannin from the stalks the wine may have a less harsh and astringent taste.

After the addition of a small amount of sulphur dioxide as protection against oxidation and bacterial contamination, the grapes proceed to the vat, where natural yeasts or an introduced cultured yeast will trigger fermentation. As soon as this begins, carbon dioxide churns up all the solid matter to the top of the vat to form a dense cap, called the *chapeau* or *marc*. Fermenting the sugar out completely generally takes five to eight days, and this process is helped along by the bubbling action necessary for the yeasts to grow.

For the fermentation to progress well, temperature has to be maintained at a level below 30°C so the yeasts are not killed. The most modern vats, made of stainless steel,

have built-in automatic temperature control. With older equipment the grower has to keep a constant eye on temperature changes and resort if necessary to hand-operated cooling methods to maintain the correct conditions.

While the wine is in the vat, there are various ways of influencing the maceration process, a period with crucial effects on the eventual constitution of the wine. To get the best results, a skilful wine-maker can exploit different elements: temperature;

the *remontage* or recycling through the *chapeau* of juice from the bottom of the vat; and length of vatting time, which has to be three to four days for table wines and usually three weeks and more for the great classic reds.

The juice is then drawn off the

pulp (*marc*) and this free-run wine is known as *vin de goutte*. The pulp is pressed to give *vin de presse*, which may later be blended as necessary with free-run wine.

Free-run and press wine are then put separately into vats to finish fermenting (the final alcoholic fermentation and the malolactic fermentation)

Above left, de-stalking grapes (Aloxe-Corton); above right, wine maturing in the chais at Château Pontet-Canet.

Below, the Joseph Drouhin cellars in Beaune.

to remove residual sugar and malic acid. These are really the final stages of vinification, during which the wine-making plant has to be kept between 18 and 20°C until the disappearance of all the sugar and malic acid. Very careful checks must be made during all this time.

THERMO-VINIFICATION AND CARBONIC MACERATION

THE classic vinification system just described is the most widespread method now practised in France, but not the only one. An alternative method extracts colour by heating the crushed grapes; the juice and pulp are then separated by pressing before fermentation. This is a technique known as thermo-vinification, which needs less vat-capacity and can be easily automated.

Carbonic maceration is related to traditional wine-making practice in Beaujolais. In this process, the grapes have to be brought whole to the vats without any preliminary crushing. Carbon dioxide is then pumped into the vats and fermentation inside the unbroken skins produces distinctive aromas. After a period of carbonic maceration lasting ten to twenty days the juice is run off, and free-run and press wine are blended and left to undergo classic alcoholic fermentation.

This technique is used for grapes with no special character and can give

Fermentation vats at the Château de Corcelles.

good results. Wines made by this method are supple, with a distinctive aroma which may overpower that of the grape variety. They are not intended for lengthy bottle ageing.

Shaping barrel staves.

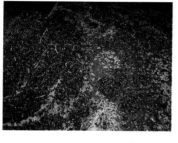

MATURATION

ONCE the vinification is over, the new wine, rough, turbid and fizzy, has to go through a process of maturation before being bottled. This stage varies in length according to the type of wine: for *primeur* wine it is not more than a few weeks or even a few days; classic keeping wines, on the other hand, will be matured for two years or more.

The first step in maturing is to clarify the wine, removing the cloudiness either by racking (drawing the wine off the sediment into a clean tank or barrel), or by filtering or centrifuging.

The new wine also has to have any excess carbon dioxide removed by racking. The amount of carbon dioxide left depends on the style of wine: it gives liveliness to young wines without much tannin, such as dry white wines, but makes red keeping wines too hard. Both the basic structure and the peculiar characteristics of each wine are refined during maturation. At the same time, oxidation plays an important part in softening tannins and stabilizing colour.

Below left, a vat of freshly picked grapes ready for fermentation to begin; right, cooling a stainless steel vat.

Bottom, two methods of keeping must circulating in the vat.

OAK BARRELS – THE ESSENTIAL LUXURY

CLASSIC red wines are traditionally matured in oak barrels. This is undeniably successful – a new wine

kept in a small wooden barrel will develop much sooner and more effectively than the same wine in a large-capacity vat – but wine stored too long in the barrel may deteriorate in flavour. Bad storage, especially in old, poorly maintained barrels, may result in thin flavour and diminished aroma.

The principal advantage of the oak barrel, especially one made of new wood, is that it contributes vanilla flavours, which blend perfectly with those from grapes. This is especially noticeable with the famous oak of the Forêt de Tronçais in the Allier *département*. However, to be effective, the wood has to be air-dried for three years before use: rapid kiln-drying does not impart such delicate aromas.

Storage in barrels has to be carried out properly. It is an expensive process, owing to both the cost of barrels and the manual labour involved. A certain amount of wine is lost by evaporation. It is also essential to gauge correctly just how much distinctive oakiness the wine should have, without the oak becoming overpowering. Nevertheless, in spite of its problems, this method of maturing is vital if classic red wines are to express their full potential.

ROSÉ WINE

ROSÉS fall between red and white wine but are never made from a mixture of the two. Such a mixture would in fact be illegal. There are different types of rosé and colour is an essential element in appraising them.

They are made in two possible ways. In the white wine method black grapes are pressed until just the right amount of colour is extracted, and the procedure is then as for white wine. In the 'partial maceration' method wine is obtained by saignée. *The vats are filled as for red wine and the early stages of fermentation cause the* marc *to rise. When enough colour has been extracted, after 12 to 24 hours, some of the juice is run off and fermented separately.*

MAKING WHITE WINE

THERE are many poems in which white wines have been compared to crystal, gold, sunshine or flowers. The diversity of these wines is what makes them so attractive and so delicious to drink. Each of them has to be harvested and produced in a special way.

STAGES IN MAKING DRY WHITE WINES

WHITE wine is most often produced by fermenting a pure grape juice. The grapes are pressed before fermentation in an attempt to avoid the diffusion of bitter, astringent elements from the solid matter into the wine, but the skins contribute aromatic depth, especially if high-

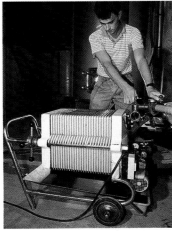

For brilliance of colour, white wines have to be filtered, using diatomaceous earth (top) or filter plates (above).

quality grapes are being used. So, to extract the aroma, the skins are sometimes macerated for a short time, but not long enough to acquire an unpleasant taste or smell. Juice extraction is carried out with the greatest care by puncturing, draining and pressing the grapes. Juice obtained from the final pressings is fermented separately, as it gives inferior wine. Throughout these operations, excessive exposure to oxygen has to be avoided as white must is very vulnerable to oxidation.

As well as the primary grape aromas giving different wines their special character, the aromas from fermentation (esters) are essential for quality in white wine. They are encouraged when yeast is working in clear juice at a relatively low temperature (not more than 20°C). Once extracted, the must is clarified by allowing the sediment to settle and then racking, and if necessary by using a centrifuge or filtering system. Throughout the fermentation process, the vat has to be cooled to keep the fermenting temperature below 20°C.

The majority of white wines are fermented in metal vats, although some prestigious wines are produced in oak casks, which should preferably be new. This system is particularly useful with small-capacity casks, as it allows contact between the yeast deposits and the wine, and helps to give

top-quality wines their distinctive character.

Vinification often ends when alcoholic fermentation finishes, as malolactic fermentation is not usually desirable. White wines can, in fact, stand a certain fresh acidity, and a second fermentation might affect the fruity flavours of the particular grape variety; but malolactic fermentation can give fatness and substance to fine wine matured in casks and intended for ageing. It can also stabilize the wine.

SWEET WINES

SWEET wine has to be made from grapes with a high sugar content. Part of this is turned into alcohol, but fermentation is artificially arrested by the addition of sulphur dioxide and the elimination of the yeasts.

Many sweet wines have a high level of alcohol (13 to 16°) and of sugar (50 to 100 g per l). Very ripe grapes are needed, infected with 'noble rot' (*Botrytis cinerea*), a mould responsible for other forms of rot. In certain environments, which are damp in the morning and sunny during the day, 'noble rot' can develop on a perfectly ripe grape without making the skin burst or spoiling it. The mould breaks down the skin of the grape, causing it to

shrivel and lose most of its moisture. The sweetness, glycerine and richness become more concentrated, and distinctive aromas start to appear. Since the mould develops gradually, the grapes have to be harvested in successive batches. For this kind of sweet wine a number of natural factors need to coincide and this occurs in only a

Left, checking wine in the cask (Entre-Deux-Mers).

Below, grapes affected by noble rot.

very few places. Some great vintages can be quite extraordinary and help to give these wines their reputation, but the disadvantages are labour-intensive production and small yield.

CHAMPAGNE

CHAMPAGNE occupies a special place in the spectrum of white wines. The balance and refinement of its flavours have contributed to its reputation, but the look of the wine and the way the bubbles fizz and sparkle in the glass have also helped to associate it with celebration. The prestige of Champagne has led to the development in other regions of wines produced on similar lines and grouped under the heading of *vins mousseux* (sparkling wines). In all cases, a second fermentation causes carbon dioxide to be released (which is what makes the bubbles). In the *méthode champenoise*, this second fermentation takes place in the bottle eventually bought by the consumer. When it occurs in the vat, before the wine is bottled, the process is known as the *cuve close* (sealed vat) method. With Champagne and Mousseux wines the pressure is around 6 atm, but ordinary *pétillant* wine (slightly sparkling) contains less carbon dioxide.

The base wine needs much care in preparation, if only because white wine is being made from black grapes. After the main alcoholic fermentation, malolactic fermentation is usually desirable for the sake of stability. Blending is essentially the result of tasting, according to the type of Champagne to be produced. The blending operation makes use of wines from different grapes and from different vineyards, and if necessary from older vintages.

When the blend has been stabilized, the *liqueur de tirage* is added,

Above, a wine-press in Champagne (Ecueil).

Below, clarifying must by centrifuge.

Left, the delicate blending process helps to give Champagne its character.

including sugar (25 g per l), yeasts and additives to boost fermentation. The wine is put in bottles with crown corks and stored on its side in the cellar. The second fermentation develops slowly, over several weeks or months, and at a low temperature (10 to 12°C). Then the wine has to mature for a year or more on its deposit of yeast, in order to make the most of the interchanges between wine and yeast.

To get rid of the yeast deposit, the bottles are fixed neck down in special frames called *pupitres*, where the deposit gradually moves down onto the cork. The makers are developing

methods of simplifying this operation with the use of mechanical frames called *giropalettes*, and with yeasts contained in an inert gel to make the sedimentation process easier.

Once collected on the cork, the deposit is removed by freezing the neck of the bottle and extracting the yeast in a lump of ice. The bottle is then filled up with the *liqueur d'expédition* based on wine with certain additives to aid conservation. Sugar can also be added to bring the sugar level into a range between 8 and 12 g per l for *brut*, or between 35 and 45 g per l for *demi-sec*. The bottle is then sealed with its final cork.

VINS DOUX NATURELS

THESE sweet fortified wines are produced mainly in Roussillon and can be white or red. They are based on grapes whose natural sugar level must be more than 252 g per l. In a process called mutage, alcohol is added to stop fermentation and leave some unconverted sugar (70 to 125 g per l) and a final alcohol level of 15 to 16°.

Some fairly light vins doux naturels are produced without maceration. These are not darkened by oxidation and are usually intended for early drinking, especially the Muscats. The red wines produced by maceration with the grapeskins are more rounded, with greater aromatic intensity. These are better for ageing, and to reach their full potential should be matured in casks for several years.

CARING FOR WINE

'THIS is a Gleiszeller I bought in myself – eight years back it must be. All the sediment must have settled by now so we should think about bottling it. A week from now I'll tell Schweyer the cooper and we'll start on it together. That Steinberg's been there eleven years. There was something wrong with it but that's gone now ... we'll have a look at that too. Ah! here's last year's Forstheimer which I've been fining with egg white. I'll have to taste it but I don't want to spoil my palate for today. Tomorrow or the day after will do.'

CONSTANT ATTENTION

IN this novel, set in Alsace, the hero's eight-year wait for wine to settle before bottling might make us smile today, with all our improved expertise, but his working methods at least indicate the depth of past interest in wine-making. They also show that

Tartar deposits in a vat. Because of the complex make-up of wine, natural deposits and cloudiness inevitably occur. Special treatment is necessary to prevent this process in the bottle.

human intervention does not come to an end when fermentation stops. Even when grape juice has turned into red or white wine, it still needs a great deal of care and attention before being bottled and offered for sale. Knowledgeable consumers are well

aware of this and are right to look for brilliance and clarity of appearance in the wine they buy.

Clarity may be achieved by keeping wine for some time in small-capacity containers, with regular racking to remove any particles that cause a deposit. With wines intended for early drinking, especially if they are kept in large-capacity vats, racking is not enough, and other processes such as using centrifuges or filters then become necessary.

Clarity alone is insufficient: the wine must be reliably stable. Wine is very complex in its make-up as, using the grapes, yeast and bacteria, the winemaker is manipulating living cells. Complicated chemical mechanisms mean that the different constituents may react with each other in such a way as to cause cloudiness and deposits in the wine.

In barrels or vats such mishaps do not matter, but they can be very serious if they take place in the bottle. The wine is not necessarily spoilt, but has to be taken out of the bottle, put back in the vat, reclarified and then bottled again, so it is obviously important for wine to be stabilized before bottling. Fortunately, it is possible nowadays to anticipate problems and apply preventive measures.

Alcohol and acidity have a stabilizing effect, but in certain conditions microorganisms may still develop and cause bacterial diseases which in some cases completely spoil the wine. These were first described by Louis

Top, wine in its first year of maturing: in the vast chai at Mouton-Rothschild.

Centre, fermenting must.

Below, fining with egg-whites.

Pasteur. Volatile acidity is linked to the level of bacterial growth and, for this reason, is limited by legislation. It is therefore essential to maintain scrupulous hygiene to stop bacterial growth, and to keep containers topped up so that no oxygen gets in. Sulphur dioxide is very effective as both a preservative and an antioxidant.

BOTTLING

AFTER careful attention through all these stages, the wine reaches the point where it has to be bottled. *Vins ordinaires* can make do with all sorts of packaging – 10 to 20 l cubitainers, waxed cardboard, even plastic – but fine wines must have glass bottles. There is a different bottle for every region, and the volume varies too, ranging from the Anjou *fillette*, a 35 cl half-bottle, to the famous 16 l Nebuchadnezzar. Usually the bottle contains between 72 and 80 cl, with the commonest, 75 cl, soon to be the standard size. This is traditionally the

---

FINING

FINING (collage) was first used in the eighteenth century and has the twofold effect of clarifying and stabilizing the wine. It consists of adding some form of protein, such as gelatine or egg white, which coagulates and gathers up suspended particles and other constituents likely to cloud the wine. Fining is essential for red wines, to remove colouring matter that might precipitate onto the inside of the bottle. With white wines, natural proteins are removed by fixing them with bentonite, a colloidal clay.

best size for ageing, as large-volume bottles such as magnums of 1.5 l or more slow the maturing process down, and half-bottles tend to speed it up.

At all events, the bottling process has to be carried out with enormous care and attention to cleanliness. Once properly clarified, the wine must not be contaminated during bottling, which often takes place at high speed.

The choice of material is very important for the bottle and even more so for the cork. For reasons of cost, metal and plastic seals are being developed for table wines, but for fine wines intended for ageing the preferred material is still cork. This carries the risk of leakages and of 'corked' wine, but with modern technology these are uncommon problems which in no way detract from the advantages of cork. Because of its elasticity, cork makes a reliable seal without needing brute strength to remove it, and it is also gas- and airtight. However, it does eventually deteriorate, so corks should preferably be replaced every 25 years.

SECRETS OF AGEING

A range of bottles: half-bottle, 75 cl, magnum, double-magnum, Jeroboam.

'AGEING' is a term applied specially to the gradual development of wine in the bottle, untouched by oxygen in the air. The cork is completely airtight and does not let the wine 'breathe'. Ageing ability is characteristic of fine wines, which undergo many complex changes in the bottle. Colour is most obviously affected, and this shows up very clearly in red wines. The colour starts as bright red in young wines, but in old wines takes on a more amber tone, rather like tile or brick – hence the terms 'brick-red' and '*tuilé*' ('tile-coloured') used by wine-tasters to describe the appearance of red wines after some years in the bottle. In very old wines, the red hue disappears altogether, leaving amber and brown as the dominant shades.

In the course of ageing, aromas develop and the characteristic bouquet of old wine appears. This is something which can be noted and enjoyed, but which remains rather puzzling: the chemical basis for these complex changes is still not clearly understood.

For wine to mature correctly, bottles must be stored in a suitable environment. First of all, they have to be laid horizontally so that the cork remains impermeable. For this, the cellar should have at least 50 per cent humidity. Although not altogether unsuitable, higher humidity levels (up to 100 per cent in some cases) may encourage weevils in the cork and damage labels and packaging.

The temperature also has to be controlled and kept at levels between 8 and 15°C. Below 8°C wine matures extremely slowly, and above 15°C it ages prematurely. More than heat, variation between summer and winter temperatures is especially harmful, as it causes successive expansion and contraction in wine. Light is another enemy, which is why tinted bottles are used and the cellars are kept in darkness.

Ageing wine is clearly a very demanding process, but organizing and running a cellar can be such a source of pleasure and satisfaction that it more than repays all the money and time spent on it.

Bottling procedures at Cellier des Sansons, a modern Beaujolais cooperative.

43

20TH-CENTURY VINTAGES – SUGGESTED RATINGS

	Bordeaux (Red)	Bordeaux (Sweet white)	Bordeaux (Dry white)	Burgundy (Red)	Burgundy (White)	Champagne	Loire	Rhône	Alsace
1900	19	19	17	13		17			
1901	11	14							
1902									
1903	14	7	11						
1904	15	17		16		19		18	
1905	14	12							
1906	16	16		19	18				
1907	12	10		15					
1908	13	16							
1909	10	7							
1910									
1911	14	14		19	19	20	19	19	
1912	10	11							
1913	7	7							
1914	13	15				18			
1915		16		16	15	15	12	15	
1916	15	15		13	11	12	11	10	
1917	14	16		11	11	13	12	9	
1918	16	12		13	12	12	11	14	
1919	15	10		18	18	15	18	15	15
1920	17	16		13	14	14	11	13	10
1921	16	20		16	20	20	20	13	20
1922	9	11		9	16	4	7	6	4
1923	12	13		16	18	17	18	18	14
1924	15	16		13	14	11	14	17	11
1925	6	11		6	5	3	4	8	6
1926	16	17		16	16	15	13	13	14
1927	7	14		7	5	5	3	4	
1928	19	17		18	20	20	17	17	17
1929	20	20		20	19	19	18	19	18

	Bordeaux (Red)	Bordeaux (Sweet white)	Bordeaux (Dry white)	Burgundy (Red)	Burgundy (White)	Champagne	Loire	Rhône	Alsace
1930							3	4	3
1931	2	2		2	3		3	5	3
1932				2	3	3	3	3	7
1933	11	9		16	18	16	17	17	15
1934	17	17		17	18	17	16	17	16
1935	7	12		13	16	10	15	5	14
1936	7	11		9	10	9	12	13	9
1937	16	20		18	18	18	16	17	17
1938	8	12		14	10	10	12	8	9
1939	11	16		9	9	9	10	8	3
1940	13	12		12	8	8	11	5	10
1941	12	10		9	12	10	7	5	5
1942	12	16		14	12	16	11	14	14
1943	15	17		17	16	17	13	17	16
1944	13	11	12	10	10		6	8	4
1945	20	20	18	20	18	20	19	18	20
1946	14	9	10	10	13	10	12	17	9
1947	18	20	18	18	18	18	20	18	17
1948	16	16	16	10	14	11	12		15
1949	19	20	18	20	18	17	16	17	19
1950	13	18	16	11	19	16	14	15	14
1951	8	6	6	7	6	7	7	8	8
1952	16	16	16	16	18	16	15	16	14
1953	19	17	16	18	17	17	18	14	18
1954	10			14	11	15	9	13	9
1955	16	19	18	15	18	19	16	15	17
1956	5						9	12	9
1957	10	15		14	15		13	16	13
1958	11	14		10	9		12	14	12
1959	19	20	18	19	17	17	19	15	20

OUT OF 20)

	Bordeaux (Red)	Bordeaux (Sweet white)	Bordeaux (Dry white)	Burgundy (Red)	Burgundy (White)	Cham-pagne	Loire	Rhône	Alsace
1960	11	10	10	10	7	14	9	12	12
1961	20	18	16	18	17	16	16	18	19
1962	16	16	16	17	19	17	15	16	14
1963					10				
1964	16	7	13	16	17	18	16	14	18
1965			12				8		
1966	17	15	16	18	18	17	15	16	12
1967	14	18	16	15	16		13	15	14
1968									
1969	10	13	12	19	18	16	15	16	16
1970	17	17	18	15	15	17	15	15	14
1971	16	17	19	18	20	16	17	15	18
1972	10		9	11	13		9	14	9
1973	13	12		12	16	16	16	13	16
1974	12	13		12	13	8	11	12	13
1975	18	17	18		11	18	15	10	15
1976	16	19	16	18	15	15	18	16	19
1977	12	9	14	11	12	9	11	11	12
1978	17	14	17	19	17	16	17	19	15
1979	16	16	16	15	16	15	14	16	16
1980	13	15	18	12	12	14	13	15	10
1981	17	16	17	14	15	15	15	14	17
1982	19	14	17	14	16	16	14	13	15
1983	17	15	16	15	16	13	12	16	20
1984	14	13	12	13	14	5	10	11	15
1985	18	15	15	17	17	17	16	16	19
1986	18	13	15	12	15	9	13	10	10
1987	13	11	16	12	11	10	13	8	13
1988									
1989									

THE FOUNDATIONS OF A GREAT VINTAGE

IT does not necessarily follow that the best wine is produced in the most apparently favourable climate. Excessive heat can make the grapes ripen too quickly, so they develop insufficient aroma and too much tannin. Elsewhere, in similar conditions, the predictability of the weather brings about such a uniform crop that vineyards lack individuality and every vintage tastes the same.

The most distinguished French wine comes from regions where weather conditions vary from year to year, influencing the growth cycle of the vine and the way the grapes ripen. At vintage time the composition of the grape may vary considerably, with distinctive characteristics apparent in each year's wine. No two vintages can ever be exactly the same. Weather affects both the start of the growth cycle, and hence the date when the crop ripens, and also the composition of the grape at the time of harvest. There is a popular saying that the weather in June, at flowering time, determines the size of the crop and August weather its quality. In fact, for a great vintage, at least in Bordeaux, Burgundy, Champagne or Alsace, you need fine sunny weather in September, and into October if harvesting is still going on. But in naturally hotter regions, such as the Rhône Valley and the Mediterranean basin, ripening may be held back by excessive dry heat.

Heat, light and humidity are the weather factors affecting the way the grape ripens. There have been many attempts to link grape and vintage quality with climatic conditions. Such connections clearly exist, but a precise formula cannot easily be derived from them as there are a number of interlinked climatic factors, with varying effects depending on the stage of the growth cycle.

As the grape ripens, a number of changes take place within it. The sour

taste of the juice diminishes with the increase in sugar, which will eventually become alcohol. The aromas become more intense and refined. At the same time, the skin of black grapes develops more tannin and stronger colour. This process of colour synthesis requires considerable energy and so is much affected by the weather, which in different years induces much greater variations in the compositions of the skin than in the juice of the grape. It is easy therefore to see why the concept of the vintage year is on the whole more clearly defined for red than for white wines, for which the skins are not an essential ingredient.

The year of vintage is again very important for the great sweet wines such as Sauternes and Barsac, as weather conditions in any particular year are crucial in determining the effects of noble rot on the grapes.

THE FUTURE

YOU would need a writer like Jules Verne to imagine what wine-growing will be like in the future, especially if it continues to develop at the speed of the last few decades. Contemporaries of H. G. Wells seeing a present-day tractor straddling rows of vines would think they were looking at some monster tripod from *The War of the Worlds*. However, we can deduce certain developments by basing our images of the future on present-day facts. In wine matters as in anything else, the future can to some extent be predicted from what we know about the present and even the immediate past.

In vitro cultivation techniques allow many new possibilities with the large-scale production of virus-free plants. Above, microplants growing in test-tubes; right, preparing plant material for test-tube culture.

BETTER RESISTANCE

ONE of the most interesting prospects for the future of the wine industry is the development of grape varieties with improved resistance to disease. European grapes are famous for the taste and fragrance of wines derived from them, but their susceptibility to various parasites requires constant treatment with fungicides and insecticides. Such chemicals are expensive and, even if their use can be limited by better forecasting, they may well cause harm to man and the environment.

It should be possible to find methods of treatment with fewer drawbacks and to take advantage, for instance, of the vine's inbuilt resistance. Recent studies have shown variations in susceptibility to parasites between different varieties of *Vitis vinifera*. These results deserve further investigation, even if they are not of immediate advantage. This approach fits in with the discovery of new chemical molecules that work against parasites by stimulating the plant's natural defence mechanisms. We shall have to make a great many very carefully matched crosses in order to select and reinforce the characteristic of reduced susceptibility present in different grape varieties. Another possibility would be to look for hidden resistance potential, using a system of reproducing plants *in vitro*.

In several countries research is in progress concerning genes for resistance in various American species. The results seem to be proving that, contrary to impressions based on previous unfortunate experiences with hybrids, resistance to parasites can be perfectly compatible with high-quality grapes and wine.

A future programme for protecting vines therefore ought to combine resistance to parasites with reduced use of fungicides. This programme is already being put into action with the development of new, so-called ornamental varieties, which are useful prototypes even if so far they are deliberately limited to amateurs growing grapes at home. Because of their high resistance to parasites, these varieties need only two or three multipurpose chemical treatments in the course of one growing season.

VINES *IN VITRO*

IN VITRO techniques, in a synthetic medium and aseptic laboratory conditions, do not lend themselves to vine cultivation. However, there may be interesting applications in the

46

future, and the technique is already used for propagating more than a hundred species for commercial purposes. It is now possible to propagate plants such as orchids, which will not grow from cuttings, and to produce plants of consistent high quality, such as virus-free strawberries and potatoes. There are no major problems with propagating vines, so *in vitro* techniques are not likely to revolutionize the present system. However, as a result of high reproduction rates, they may be able to improve the plant's natural potential. Also, it may be possible to grow cultures from different parts of the vine in well-controlled, germ-free conditions: these could have a number of different applications.

With few exceptions, *in vitro* propagation produces plants identical to the 'parent'. It is currently used in conjunction with heat treatment to produce plants free of virus infection. Miniature plants are used in this work, so it is possible at the same time to build up 'data banks' of grape varieties, taking the place of the old plant collections, which need space and are expensive to maintain.

These techniques also allow the study of several parasitic moulds which cannot be cultivated on their own in a synthetic medium as the host plant, in this case the vine, is their life-support system. The combined cultivation *in vitro* of each host–parasite pair (vine–mildew, vine–oïdium) allows varied stocks of each pathogen to be kept for long periods without further subculturing and possible adulteration. This is a remarkable tool for the study of the association of vine and moulds.

Finally, there are longer term prospects in genetic engineering: cell culture may make it possible to build into a grape variety a fragment of nucleic acid coded for a particular characteristic, and to do this without interfering with other inherited factors. On the other hand, *in vitro* techniques can also reveal possibilities not evident in the plant as a whole, but which may show up in specimens grown from tissue culture. Cells can be encouraged to multiply and produce, not copies of the original plant, but variants known as 'somaclones' (from so-called somatic embryogenesis derived from non-reproductive cells).

MEN OR MACHINES?

MECHANIZATION started off tentatively but is now increasing everywhere, for the very obvious reason that it is less expensive than manual labour. Armies of harvest-workers are already giving way to powerful picking machines; lasers could soon make straight planting lines; robots controlled by computers with electronic cameras could do the pruning; and there could be secateurs with rechargeable batteries fixed to operators' belts. Some people may be alarmed by this prospect, imagining vineyards where efficiency would come before quality and all the atmosphere and tradition of centuries-old practices would have disappeared.

Fortunately, both scientists and producers know where to stop, and are aware that, to be acceptable, mechanization must not endanger the quality of the harvest. Better machines allow improved performance of more and more complex operations. Some of these have been mechanized for a long time, as with pesticide spraying, which is now better measured and controlled, and consequently more economical. Elsewhere machines have taken over with good results, most dramatically in harvesting where mechanization has reached 80 per cent in certain vineyards. Refinements are still necessary where vines are trained in certain ways, such as the 'lyre' system, but even for cases like this there is now a prototype machine.

But there is still an essential rôle for the wine-grower. Machines may help in concrete ways, but men and women will always be there to choose how to run the vineyard and it is their character that the wine will always express.

OLD SAYINGS AND MODERN COMPUTERS

PREDICTING the harvest used to be a matter of consulting various old proverbs. Nowadays science provides several possible courses. According to a sample analysis from Alsace, it is possible to predict the approximate volume of the harvest only four or five weeks after the vines have flowered, by calculating the number of buds (which determines the number of bunches of grapes), the average number of flowers and the level of fruit-set (which affect the number of grapes per bunch) and the number of cells in each grape (which indicates the average weight of individual grapes). Research in Montpellier has focused on analysis of pollen levels in the atmosphere.

In fact, there is a close correlation between the number of pollen grains per cubic metre of air at the height of the pollination period and the eventual grape yield. Forecasts of almost 95 per cent accuracy are now available as soon as pollination is over.

Of course this sort of forecast cannot take into account every possible hazard in every possible plot of land, so hasty extrapolation can be risky. However, as well as its obvious economic importance in areas such as crop management and stock control, this kind of research is of considerable scientific interest for its detailed study of the elements affecting yield.

TOMORROW'S WINE

'WE'VE never needed a chemist here, Monsieur. Good bye.' It would be difficult to count the number of times this phrase must have been uttered in Burgundy, Bordeaux or Languedoc, in the days when growers were very mistrustful of men in white coats. That time is long past, and scientists and technicians now play an essential part in the wine-making process.

CHEMISTS AND CONSULTANTS

THE wine expert has undergone a radical change of image in the course of a few decades and is now brought in not so much to remedy problems as to advise. In the old days, a chemist would be called in to put matters right after the event and to advise on controlling levels of damage. The visit would be discreet, so as not to draw attention to the grower's mistakes or failures. It was in the sixties that attitudes to scientists changed and the chemist began to be accepted as an adviser. Improved knowledge of the wine-making process meant that it was possible to anticipate and prevent problems.

A technological revolution in wine-making has taken place and fine wines have attained a standard of excellence which has certainly contributed to the present worldwide interest in the subject of wine.

In 1955 a national diploma in oenology was established. Wine has become recognized as a serious subject for scientific work and is now a full university discipline, not just a sideline for specialists from other faculties, such as chemistry and pharmacy. By developing in this way, wine science has become more attractive to people in the industry, more and more of whom have themselves had some formal training in the subject. Better information and research are allowing the grape's maximum potential to be realized. By removing the risk of technical error, wine science today is making it possible for all the distinctive characteristics of different soils, vineyards or

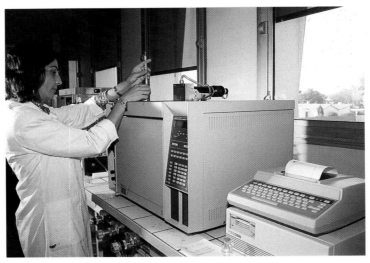

vintages to be reflected in the finished product.

INFORMED ACTION

WINE science has made, and is still making, considerable progress: more refined investigative techniques are in turn revealing possible new objectives. Oenology was originally based on chemistry and was a means of determining the composition of wine and of monitoring quality. The very complex chemistry of wine means that these procedures are still necessary. The number of constituents (several hundred, with some in very low concentrations) shows that the creation of an artificial wine is likely

to be just wishful thinking for some time to come.

Modern methods of chemical analysis have been especially effective in their application to wine, for instance the use of gas chromatography and mass spectroscopy to identify aromas, and of nuclear magnetic resonance to study the molecular structure of colouring matter and tannins.

Investigative methods such as these should make it possible to establish criteria for quality in grapes, a future objective for wine research; but it would be wrong to think that chemistry could take over completely from natural procedures.

There have been considerable developments affecting wine, first in the areas of microbiology and biochemistry, and now in biotechnology, molecular biology and genetic engineering. Research in these areas is extensive and promising. For instance, it may be possible to manufacture yeasts able to hydrolyse the natural

Wine is so complex in structure that modern scientific methods of analysis are invaluable. Above left, absorption spectrophotometry gives qualitative analysis of mineral elements, and left, gas chromatography analyses the constituents of aroma in wine.

Below, must analysis; measuring density.

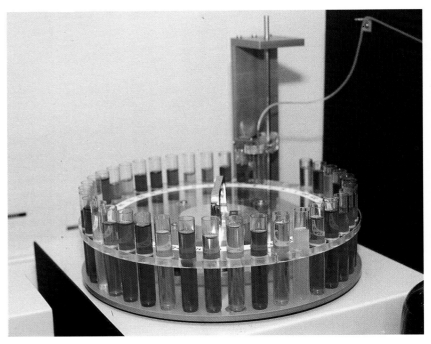

grape proteins that cause instability in white wines. The use of bentonite could then be avoided. Research is also in progress on cloning the gene for malolactic fermentation in bacteria, and then incorporating it in yeasts in order to produce simultaneous alcoholic and malolactic fermentation.

Industrial procedures are possible for better control of fermentation and for the provision of a standardized product in which the constituents of the grape are not of major importance. Despite such progress in biotechnology, there is no question of eliminating the natural element in great wines, although it is still important to understand their microbiology to achieve their full potential. The scientific study of fine wine has helped to develop knowledge and techniques in both chemistry and

Above, quality control by chemical analysis, a technique favoured for many years.

microbiology; more ordinary wine has benefited from these developments too.

MODERNIZATION

DURING the last few decades, the whole field of wine-making has been modernized extensively, and this will certainly continue. Improved mechanical methods make the work simpler and demand less labour. Illustrations in early twentieth-century wine books show that ten people were needed then for a job performed now by one person. Things will continue to change, but at the same time the traditional high standards must be maintained.

There is scope for improvements in wine-making apparatus, so that operations may be better controlled or even completely automated. Traditional wine-making vats in particular are gradually being replaced by fully automated systems. Control of temperature during fermentation is another advance. Appliances for heating and chilling are coupled with thermostats to maintain the right temperature for every phase of vinification.

Computers are beginning to be highly regarded as administrative tools. In the future they may also play a part in the wine-making process itself, especially in controlling fermentation; but their main rôle will probably be to open up new avenues for research. Multidimensional analysis of data produced by traditional chemical analysis means that there is a possible technique for classifying wines according to origin, year and grape variety.

NEW PRODUCTS

THE most revolutionary change is probably the development of non-alcoholic 'wines', or, since these do not conform to the legal definition of wine, beverages other than wine derived from grape juice. There have been experiments with these drinks from the mid-fifties, with some long-term success for sparkling grape juice.

Recently drinks have been introduced based on grape juice but with different fruit flavours. These so-called wine coolers were tried out in California in the mid-1970s, and are a refreshing mixture of white wine, fruit juice, lemon and soda water.

They have been on the market since 1981, with considerable success. It may also be possible to produce a low-calorie drink by microbiological processes other than alcoholic fermentation. By storing grape juice under refrigeration or as a concentrate, drinks like this could be manufactured throughout the year.

In the future, then, it is quite possible that vines may not be used simply for producing wine or table grapes. Jellies, preserves or grape 'beers' could be marketed; by-products of wine-making such as the lees, tartar and *marc* need not be wasted: the *marc*, for instance, could be used for animal feed or processed for use as a fertilizer.

These will probably be useful outlets when dealing with the changing patterns of wine-drinking in the world. Demand for fine wines is increasing, but everyday wines from some parts of France are distinctly less popular. Some areas may well cease to produce wine, but it is unlikely that these new and very different vine products could altogether take its place.

The techniques and equipment of wine-making will no doubt develop further, but human control and

decision-making will always be crucial. It is clear, for instance, that wine from traditional small-scale concerns is sometimes better than wine from big ultra-modern producers with all their sophisticated equipment. We are not talking about revolutions: progress in the science and technology of wine is a continuous process. Research deepens knowledge and shows how to make the most of the very complex natural characteristics of wine. This is why the taste of wine tomorrow probably will not be very different from its taste today; but surely that is just what everyone who loves wine would wish.

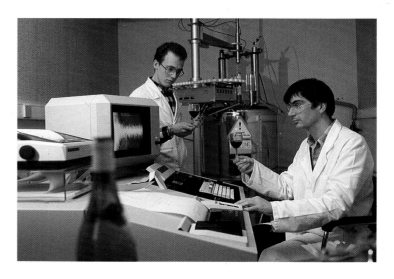

Above, wine experts use nuclear magnetic resonance to gauge the quantity and quality of sugar which the yeast has turned into alcohol.

IN ancient Rome the official wine-tasters would meet on 23 April in celebration of the festival of *Vinalia*. They had to follow established rituals for judging the new wine on this occasion: they were supposed to avoid certain strong-tasting foods, to spit out the wine and use a set form of words to comment on its colour, taste and smell. Wine was considered sacred in ancient times so they would end with a ceremony of deconsecration.

The ages of wine: below, white wines, and right, reds, at different stages of maturity.

WINE-TASTING: SCIENCE OR PLEASURE?

EVEN if wine-tasting no longer has religious connotations, it can still be approached in two ways: as a way of enhancing the pleasure of good wine, or as a scientific aid in wine production and consumer tests. Environmental conditions need to be such that they do not interfere with an objective opinion.

All the senses can come into play when tasting, in an analytical exercise that is both difficult and straightforward. Tasting does not demand exceptional aptitude, as is often imagined, but it does require a brief period of study, attention to detail and a memory sufficiently well trained to be able to make comparisons.

These are not enough on their own, however. Wine analysis cannot be limited to the taster's immediate likes or dislikes: it has to pinpoint and describe characteristics of appearance, taste and smell; their intensity; the way they interact; and the extent to which they conform to a type. This type may well be the opposite of the taster's own preferences, so an objective, disinterested approach is clearly essential.

This is not the only requirement: we are all much more sensitive than we think to the effects of our external surroundings. Pasteur was responsible for some significant findings on this topic. In order to find out the effect of heat sterilization on the taste of wine, he decided first to check the tasters themselves by giving them two samples of the same wine, letting them think one had been heated. The result was compelling: all of the tasters honestly thought that there was a clear difference between the samples.

A second problem may be the state of the taster's health or feelings. Even if the taster is not conscious of it, there are all sorts of circumstances that may affect his or her judgement: an annoying event, a touch of fever or indigestion, or even a minor cold can all disturb the acuteness of the senses. The main reason for having several people at a wine-tasting is to minimize the effects of variables that are unrelated to the wine itself.

Effective tasting requires the observance of three conditions: wines must be at the right temperature; one sample of wine should not bias your impression of the next; and you must give a clear and accurate analysis of your reaction.

Temperature is important as it may mask poor qualities or prevent good ones coming through. The recommended temperatures are 8 °C for sparkling and sweet wines, 12 °C for dry whites and rosés, 16 °C for young and 18 °C for older reds. It is essential too to taste a particular batch of wines in ascending order of

Wine-tasting consists of evaluating the colour (for shade, depth and clarity), then the smell, bouquet and taste.

strength of the principal common characteristic, whether this is richness in tannin or sugar, alcohol level or aromatic intensity.

If the *dégustation* is arranged for the most favourable time, usually as you are beginning to feel hungry in late morning; if detailed, fairly complicated tasting notes are made; and if all the other rules followed, there is a good chance of avoiding a subjective view of the wines tasted.

WINE

THE METHOD OF WINE-TASTING

THE technique of wine analysis is not something you can learn from books. Effective tasting comes with practice. The taster first has to acquire a certain amount of practical knowledge. Before a *dégustation* he or she has to avoid strongly flavoured food and drink, toothpaste and scented toilet-water. The glass, one third full, is held by the foot and the wine subjected first to a visual appraisal for clarity, intensity and range of colour, and, if it is a sparkling wine, for persistence of bubbles. The glass is then swirled so that the refraction can be seen at the edges of the wine.

As the glass is rotated, it is then the nose's turn to interpret the aromas, gauging their character, refinement, intensity and balance.

Finally, the wine is carefully swilled in the mouth, and a little air drawn in at the same time. While in contact with the palate, the wine sample is again rated for refinement, depth and balance. It is then spat out and the impression of the aftertaste and persistence or 'length' in the mouth summed up.

THE PLEASURE OF WINE

THE kind of wine analysis we have just described is what usually takes place at official and private tastings. On these occasions, it is essential to avoid influencing the taster's judgement. However, when wine is served to be enjoyed with a meal, every attempt should be made to enhance both food and drink with the appropriate surroundings.

Except for cocktails and apéritifs, wine is usually drunk with a meal. The setting for this is enormously important. No sensible person would

think of serving chilled rosé wine and *aïloli* (garlic mayonnaise with salt cod, boiled potatoes and other vegetables, served at all Provençal village festivals) with all the gala paraphernalia of silver, fine glass and china. It would be equally silly at a picnic to have Lobster Thermidor on paper plates and plastic beakers of Château d'Yquem.

'Le déjeuner sur l'herbe', Claude Monet, 1865–6 (Musée d'Orsay, Paris).

Below, a table set for a special occasion.

Lastly, wine and food should of course complement each other. This has caused plenty of hosts to agonize about entertaining supposedly knowledgeable guests. In fact, unsuitable

combinations are fairly obvious and not all that common. Experiments can turn out to be delightful, so it is a pity to be afraid of them. Some red wines will even go with oysters. Equally, we should not turn down the possibility of serving regional dishes with wine from the same area, especially as they often harmonize very well.

It is important not to be tied down by rigid theories, particularly at a time when so many new foods are coming our way; but we must certainly be aware of the few really hopeless partnerships, such as red wine with sardines in oil and other tinned fish, and also with chocolate; vinaigrette sauce with any delicate wine; fine red wine with blue cheese; or dry sparkling wine with a very sweet pudding.

Armed with this knowledge, we can use our imagination to enhance the delicious process of drinking wine.

WINE AND FOOD

'Les Cinq Sens' ('The Five Senses'), by the seventeenth-century painter Abraham Bosse (Musée des Beaux-Arts, Tours).

DARK spicy wine with winter stew, Sauternes and strawberries on a warm July evening, claret for a carefully planned dinner or Beaujolais with improvised suppers round the kitchen table – there are endless possible additions to the pleasurable catalogue of well-matched food and wine. Unexpected combinations can often be the most enjoyable so happily we need not suppose that there is only one 'correct' wine for every type of food. Fine wines clearly deserve a most carefully chosen meal. With others, it would be a pity to dismiss traditional partnerships, but nor should we be afraid of the occasional experiment, remembering that the aim is to find a wine to complement and enhance the flavours of a dish.

The game obviously has certain rules, the most important being to preserve a balance between wine and food in such areas as relative strength, sweetness or acidity. A delicate white wine will not survive the company of a robust peasant casserole, and a strong, dark Côtes du Rhône will overpower a creamy chicken dish. Equally, a bone-dry Muscadet will taste unpleasantly thin with a sweet pudding. A plate of sausages will not do justice to a magnificent Burgundy, and Sauternes cannot be enjoyed at its best with tinned fruit salad.

Some foods have exceptionally strong flavours which clash with almost any wine. A high proportion of tangy ingredients such as lemon or vinegar, highly spiced or peppery dishes like curry, and almost any chocolate dessert are very difficult to match with wine. Partnerships are not impossible but it is unfair to a very fine wine to set it against such demanding flavours. Other problem dishes are those containing eggs, which are best with a fairly acid or dry wine (Muscadet or a Sauvignon), and smoked or salty foods, which need something fairly assertive to stand up to them. The convention that only white wine should be drunk with fish is well founded, as red wine often acquires an unpleasant metallic taste. It has become fashionable to disregard this tradition, but on the whole orthodoxy is probably advisable except with some regional dishes of fish cooked in herbs and red wine.

The finest wines are often best with food which is simply cooked but of very high quality – a great red Bordeaux with roast lamb or poultry accompanied by exquisite but understated vegetables (no aggressively sharp tomatoes or fennel, for instance). Some experts even think such a wine is best drunk on its own. One could imagine drinking Yquem with a perfect ripe white peach, since each echoes the other's subtle combination of fragrance and acidity. Simpler wines are far less demanding and can be happily matched with all sorts of everyday food. Traditional local stews are customarily served with the same wine as that used for cooking.

The following list cannot possibly be exhaustive. It offers some traditional arranged marriages, and some which are less conventional. The vast range of French wines is a tremendous incitement to extend one's knowledge while enjoying the thoroughly civilized pleasure of wine with a meal.

FIRST COURSES

Artichokes *Tavel or Côtes du Ventoux rosé;* with hollandaise sauce, *Montagny or Mâcon blanc*

Asparagus *Full-bodied Chablis, Alsace Muscat or good southern rosé*

Caviare *Dry Champagne*

Confit d'oie (preserved goose), *Cahors red, Madiran or Corbières*

Egg dishes: with mayonnaise, *Loire Sauvignon such as Pouilly Fumé;* quiches, *dry white Bordeaux, Sauvignon or Alsace Pinot Gris;* soufflés (fish), *white Burgundy, Mâcon blanc;* (cheese), *young red Bordeaux or Côtes de Buzet*

Melon *Muscat de Beaumes de Venise;* with Parma ham, *Alsace Riesling*

Pasta *Red Minervois or Côtes du Rhône Villages*

Pâté de foie gras *Sauternes or Monbazillac are drunk with this in the Bordeaux region. An Alsace Pinot Gris would also go well*

Pizza *As for pasta, or a full-bodied rosé such as Tavel*

Quenelles de brochet (very lightly poached fish dumplings), *Chablis Premier Cru, Pouilly Fuissé*

Salad dishes (such as salade niçoise), *White Côtes du Rhône or Côtes du Luberon*

Smoked salmon *Pouilly Fumé or Sancerre*

Snails *Beaujolais-Villages, Fleurie*

Soups: *traditionally no wine with light soups;* bouillabaisse (Provençal fish soup), *Cassis or Bandol rosé when in the area, or a dry white wine such as Muscadet or Entre-Deux-Mers;* French onion soup, *generic Bourgogne rouge or Beaujolais*

Glass with enamel overlay, Joseph Brocard, 1877 (Musée national, Limoges).

Note: Vinaigrette sauce for salad dishes to be accompanied by wine should contain a high proportion of oil with either lemon juice or a very little wine vinegar. The same applies to mayonnaise.

FISH

Cod: cabillaud à la bordelaise (cooked with shallots/scallions and red wine), *young red Bordeaux, Fronsac or Côtes de Bourg*

Lobster *Meursault, good Chablis*

Mackerel *Muscadet, Sauvignon de Touraine, Sylvaner*

Mullet *White Côtes du Luberon or Corsican Patrimonio rosé*

Mussels *Muscadet or Gros Plant;* in a rich creamy sauce, *white Graves or Mâcon-Villages*

Oysters *Traditionally Chablis. Or Muscadet-de-Sèvres-et-Maine, dry white Bordeaux*

Salmon *When possible, the best white Burgundy – Le Montrachet, Meursault or Chablis Premier Cru*

Sardines (fresh) *Dry white Sauvignon (Loire Valley vin du pays), Bourgogne Aligoté or a Provençal rosé*

Scallops *Alsace Gewürztraminer, good white Burgundy or Chablis*

Sole *Chablis Grand Cru, good white Burgundy*

Trout *Alsace Riesling, white Crozes-Hermitage;* with almonds, *Pouilly-Fuissé, Montagny*

Note: Fish cooked in a cream sauce requires a correspondingly rich and fragrant wine, such as a fine white Burgundy.

MAIN COURSES

Beef: roast, *any fine red wine – Bordeaux, Burgundy, Hermitage;* casseroles, *robust reds such as Gigondas, Châteauneuf-du-Pape or Saint-Emilion;* Boeuf bourguignon (cooked with red Burgundy), *Beaune or other medium-priced Burgundy*

Cassoulet (rich peasant stew from SW France), *Cahors or Fitou*

Chicken, turkey: roast, *good neutral partners for most fine wines;* with cream sauces, *white Burgundy or intense, sweetish Loire white such as Savennières;* coq au vin, *traditionally a fine red Burgundy. Otherwise some reasonable equivalent of the wine used for cooking;* turkey with chestnuts, *Nuits-Saint-Georges*

Choucroute (milder version of sauerkraut, usually served with Strasbourg sausages), *Alsace Pinot Gris*

Duck *Pécharmant, Canon-Fronsac or a substantial white Burgundy*

Game birds *If possible a good Médoc or Pauillac for terrines, roast game and such dishes as wood-pigeon stew or woodcock. Older game needs a robust Châteauneuf-du-Pape, Gigondas or a Côtes du Rhône-Villages such as Vacqueyras*

Ham *Fruity Beaujolais (Côte de Brouilly) or Hautes Côtes de Beaune;* in a cream sauce, *white Burgundy, Alsace Pinot Gris Sauvignon-de-Saint-Bris*

Hare: jugged, *Pomerol or Saint-Emilion*

Kidneys *Substantial red Burgundy or Saint-Chinian*

Lamb: roast, *fine red Bordeaux, Bourgeuil;* Blanquette d'agneau à l'ancienne (lamb stewed in a sauce of onions and mushrooms with cream), *Médoc or Beaujolais-Villages;* Navarin printanier (casserole of young lamb with spring vegetables), *Médoc or Beaujolais-Villages*

Sixteenth-century wine glass (Louvre, Paris).

Liver: calves' liver (grilled or sautéed), *Beaujolais-Villages, red Crozes-Hermitage*

Rabbit: lapin aux herbes de Provence (sautéed rabbit with fresh herbs), *Côtes du Rhône-Villages or Bandol*

Steak *Almost any good red, depending on the sauce*

Sweetbreads: in brown sauce, *Chinon or Médoc;* in cream sauce, *white Graves or Rully*

Veal: roast or escalopes, *lightish red – Médoc or Savigny-lès-Beaune*

Venison *Saint-Joseph, Gigondas or Chateauneuf-du-Pape*

DESSERTS

CHAMPAGNE is sometimes served at this stage but should really be a demi-sec (or equivalent Crémant de Loire) to stand up to a sweet pudding. Otherwise, this is the time for Sauternes, Monbazillac and the *vins doux naturels* (Muscat wines from Beaumes de Venise, Rivesaltes and Frontignan). All are delicious with strawberries, raspberries, peaches and apricots (not citrus fruit) and with tarts or mousses made from these. Sauternes or Barsac taste delicious with custards or with crème brûlée. The problem of what to drink with chocolate desserts could be solved by serving liqueurs or brandy at this point. But a Banyuls or Muscat de Beaumes de Venise will probably withstand a not-too-intense chocolate mousse or gâteau, and even a red wine such as Pomerol has been suggested for soufflés or cakes made with bitter chocolate. If in doubt, serve champagne!

CHEESE

CHEESE and red wine are supposed to complement each other, but a strong or over-ripe cheese can dominate anything but very substantial wines. Camembert, Brie, Pont L'Evèque and other soft cheeses, if not pungently ripe, will partner claret and red Burgundy. Young Dutch cheeses, such as Gouda and Edam, are also suitable. Milder English cheeses are possible with claret, Chinon and Bourgueil; mature Cheddars need a substantial partner such as a Rhône Valley red. Blue cheeses often have such an intense flavour that they need a sweet wine to balance them: in France Roquefort is served with Sauternes. A late-harvested Alsace Gewürztraminer is sometimes suggested for the highly flavoured Münster cheese. Goat cheeses vary in taste according to maturity: when very fresh they can be eaten with Sancerre or almost any dry white wine; mature goat cheeses can be served with a sweeter white such as Maury (Roussillon), Sauternes or a strong red Côtes du Rhône. It is customary in France to serve the finest wine of the meal with the cheese course.

WINE

WINE is such an inherent part of the mythology and culture of France that inevitably it is also present everywhere in French art. In literature, music and the visual arts, wine appears in many contexts, both as a religious symbol and as a feature of everyday life.

Wine is depicted most directly in everyday scenes demonstrating the ways in which it is rooted in the lives of merchants and peasants. All the elements important in the making of wine can be represented: the harvest, the grapes themselves, the press and the casks, tasting and selling the wine.

THE GRAPE-HARVEST

HARVEST scenes are frequently featured in paintings of autumn, as part of the cycle of the seasons. The month of September in *Les très riches heures du duc de Berry*, the magnificent Book of Hours painted by the Limbourg brothers (1410–15) shows one such scene, with donkeys and ox-carts bearing grapes to the castle in the

THE WINE-MAKING PROCESS

background. There is even a certain consistency over the centuries in the way such scenes are represented. Similar pictures appear nowadays on wine labels: a spire pointing up behind a landscape of vines, or a château looking down over the vineyards that

Chartres cathedral, twelfth–thirteenth-century stained glass.

bear its name, with a half-open gate to give a sense of perspective. The figure of the grape-picker appears on a number of carved capitals, like those in the abbey of Mozac in Auvergne. There is no background landscape here, only a solitary vine, and emphasis

is all on the man and the three-dimensional moulding of the bunch of grapes. This is a subject that lends itself to sculpture as it is best represented in the round. Wine itself cannot easily be depicted in stone, but its colour is important in both paintings and stained glass. The grape-picker and his basket again provide the subject for scenes painted on china plates. In Dufy's watercolour, 'Vendanges' ('Grape-harvest'), the harvest

TIVE IMAGINATION

scene has become an exercise in the interplay of light and outline: the artist has concentrated on the oval shapes of hats and the checked pattern of shirts against the hillside.

Left hand page, 'August', from the Duchess of Burgundy's Book of Hours, c.1450 (Musée Condé, Chantilly).

Below, 'Les vendanges' ('Picking Grapes'), by Raoul Dufy, 1940 (Musée des Beaux-Arts, Nice).

Above, 'Wine Harvest', a sixteenth-century tapestry in the Musée de Cluny, Paris.

Below right, carving on a choir stall, in the Church of Saint-Nicholas, Rilly-la-Montagne.

THE ART OF WINE-MAKING

THE various stages of wine-making require a more technical approach. A painting by José Frappa depicts Dom Pérignon tasting grapes before the pressing. Pictures of the wine-press itself are frequent. The 'Vendanges' ('Grape-harvest') tapestry in the Musée de Cluny in Paris gives a traditional medieval presentation of events as if they were all happening simultaneously: against a flower-studded background we can see one person treading the grapes and, behind him, wine flowing from the press into a tub. A woman is filling her pitcher from the tub while a man empties his into a cask. The cask is a favourite subject for stained glass in wine-merchants' guild chapels, where everyday activities in the wine trade are often shown. At Chartres, for instance, a window in the side chapel of Saint-Jean-l'Hospitalier depicts the moment when an iron hoop is fixed round the cask, a subject repeated in Millet's painting 'Le tonnelier' ('The Cooper').

The final stage of selling the wine is often illustrated with scenes of wine-tasting, as in some of Daumier's prints, or with wine-merchants' shops lined up along the quayside as in Boudin's painting of the port of Bordeaux. The well-known wine firm, Nicolas, has a series of posters showing an imaginary deliveryman called Nectar, and also some leaflets by the artist Charles Martin with amusing portraits of people sampling wine.

In novels by such writers as Pagnol and Giono, vineyards are part of the background, simply a setting for the plot. Poets sometimes write about them, as Apollinaire does in *Les alcools* ('Spirits') (1913), bringing out touches of colour: '*Et les coteaux où les vignes rougissent là-bas*' ('Hills over there, with vines turning red'), or an impression of shape: '*Les vignobles aux ceps tordus*' ('vines with their twisted stems').

WINE AND THE DAILY MEAL

ACTIVITIES connected with wine-making are well represented in the visual arts. The everyday process of drinking it is illustrated in countless depictions of meals.

'Rafraîchissements' ('Refreshments'), by the eighteenth-century painter Chardin (Museum of Fine Arts, Springfield).

STILL LIFE

STILL-life paintings, on the other hand, focus on objects on a table or on meals with no human participants. Often they have a purely decorative function: paintings of a glass of wine can hang in a dining-room, like mirrors endlessly reflecting what is actually on the table. There is a painting by Vispré showing a bowl of peaches, a wine-glass and a biscuit, and similar subjects by the eighteenth-century artists Chardin, Desportes and Oudry. The precise wine may even be specified, as in a nineteenth-century painting called 'Nature morte aux huîtres et au chablis' ('Still Life with Chablis and Oysters') in the Saint-Brieuc museum (Britanny). In the eighteenth century there was a growing enthusiasm for still-life compositions of dessert on a table and for pictures of peasant meal-times and kitchen tables.

These can be an excuse for showing the play of light on wine or glass, often with added reflections from a window. Light has the same fascination for Don Balthasar, in Paul Claudel's play *Le soulier de satin* ('The Satin Slipper') (1929), where the following description is a still life in its own right: 'Peaches like globes of nectar ... delectably scented wine in a glittering decanter'. In the original French the emphatic use of '*étincelante*' ('glittering') is much better at conveying the impression of reflected light.

In the eighteenth century, still-life paintings are based on precise drawing. When we come to the Impressionists, this is no longer true: the object depicted often has no clear outline being made up of flecks of

'Still Life by a window', Pablo Picasso 1924 (Musée Picasso, Paris).

Left, 'Le dessert de gaufrettes' ('Dessert with wafer biscuits'), Lubin Baugin, seventeenth century (Louvre, Paris).

Below left, 'Nature morte à la bouteille' ('Still Life with Bottle'), Georges Braque 1910–11 (Musée d'Orsay, Paris).

light instead. So it is with the grapes, bottles and glasses which, with the repeated motif of an angled knife, form a small area of still life in Manet's 1865 'Déjeuner sur l'herbe' ('Luncheon on the Grass'). With Cubism, there is a return to precise outlines but this time they are reduced to abstract geometric shapes. Georges Braque, claiming that '*les sens déforment, mais l'esprit forme*' ('the senses distort, but the mind shapes'), turned the still life into an intellectual exercise. It was he who designed the 1955 label for Mouton-Rothschild, a half-filled wine-glass and a bunch of grapes. The Spanish-born Cubist Juan Gris also pointed out the relationship between geometry and what the artist sees: 'I turn a cylinder into a bottle'.

FEASTING AND DAILY FARE

AS well as being present on the table in all these still-life paintings, wine is a common factor at meal-times in every class of household. 'Le repas des paysans' ('Peasants' Meal'), by the seventeenth-century Le Nain brothers, uses a remarkably stylized still-life technique. The focus of the composition is a wine-glass against a dark indoor background and, in spite of the everyday presence of the peasants and the bread on the table, the balance of colour and mass and the predominant reds convey a heightened atmosphere. Outdoor paintings include such scenes of peasant merrymaking as Watteau's 'Noces de village' ('Village Wedding'), and others with a historical flavour like André Bauchant's 'Fête de la Libération en 1945' ('Liberation Celebrations, 1945'). This is a naïve painting showing people in local costume, a pair of musicians sitting on a barrel, bottles clustered on tables and in baskets, all in a mountain setting.

Peasant meals like these are set in dingy rooms or rustic landscapes, but elegant, finely detailed interiors are the rule for more affluent dinners. Troy's painting 'Le déjeuner d'huîtres',

('Lunching on Oysters') shows guests gazing at a popping cork with marble pillars and wall decorations behind them. The dozens of glasses in Ollivier's 'Souper chez le prince de Conti au temple' ('Supper with the Prince de Conti'), like the massed bottles and glasses in Hoffbauer's 'Banquet dans la grande salle de fêtes de l'Hôtel de Ville' ('Banquet in the Great Hall of the Hôtel de Ville'), are meant to indicate luxury. Peasant scenes tend to focus on wine, as they do on bread, as an essential symbol of food; in the grander scenes the profusion of bottles and glasses destroys this focus, and wine becomes a symbol of affluence.

Wine is shown in bars, inns and cafés, often linked with gambling and card-playing. It plays a basic part in the structure of Valentin de Boulogne's painting 'La diseuse de bonne aventure' ('The Fortune Teller'), and also in La Tour's 'Tricheur à l'as de trèfle' ('Card-sharper with Ace of Clubs'). In Manet's 'Bar at the

Folies-Bergère' rows of bottles are lined up in front of the mirror reflecting the whole room. There are endless references to Champagne in Offenbach's opera *La vie parisienne*, and Puccini's *Manon Lescaut* begins with a drinking scene in an Amiens inn. Renoir's painting 'Déjeuner des canotiers' ('The Boating Party at Lunch') suggests an atmosphere of overflowing abundance with its five wine bottles and grapes spilling from a basket of fruit. Wine appears in the drinking songs of the sixteenth-century composers, Clément Janequin, Orlando Lassus and Philippe de Monte, songs remarkable for their polyphonic innovation. In the twentieth century Poulenc brings

Far left, 'Le coin de table' ('Dinner Table'), Paul-Emile Chabas, 1904 (Musée des Beaux-Arts, Tourcoing).

Above, detail from 'Réunion dans un cabaret' ('Tavern Scene'), Valentin de Boulogne, seventeenth century (Louvre, Paris).

Right, 'Le joueurs de cartes' ('The Cardplayers'), Paul Cézanne, 1890–95 (Musée d'Orsay, Paris).

Left, detail from 'Le tricheur à l'as de trèfle' ('Card-sharper with Ace of Clubs'), Georges de la Tour, seventeenth century (Kimbell Art Museum, Fort Worth).

wine into his *Chansons gaillardes* ('Gallant Songs').

It is perhaps inevitable that far more red wine than white is depicted in these paintings. The colour red has great aesthetic importance, and is described in painting treatises as a colour that appears to come towards the viewer, whereas blues tend to recede. Writers too are susceptible to the attraction of red: Daudet's *Lettres de mon moulin* ('Letters from My Windmill'), set in nineteenth-century Provence, describes a meal accompanied by 'a

fine Châteauneuf-du-Pape, its rich colour showing up in the glass'.

In all these art forms, the pleasure involved in representing wine is related to the pleasure of actually drinking it, although at times it may, like bread, be a symbol of spiritual sustenance. Wine then takes on a richer, especially religious, significance.

Below, 'Scène galante', Nattier 1744 (Alte Pinakothek, Munich).

WINE: SYMBOL AND ALLEGORY

FOR the Christian religion, the first sacred meal was the Marriage at Cana, when water was miraculously turned to wine. Medieval historians saw the six wine-jars, often shown in paintings, as symbols of the 'six ages of Man' represented by Adam, Noah, Abraham, David, Jeconiah, John the Baptist, and finally Christ. The miracle was supposed to symbolize the transition from the Old Testament (water) to the New Testament (wine).

remind us of the liturgical and ritual function of wine. The wine at the Last Supper is a symbol of the blood of Christ and of Man's redemption. Images of Christ at the wine-press, like that in the church of Saint-Nicolas-de-Haguenau (Alsace), are an extension of this idea.

Literary allusions to the Last Supper often take the form of parody. In *Les diaboliques* ('The Satanists'), Barbey d'Aurévilly (1808–89) presents thirteen guests, including twelve women loved by Don Juan, at a table where there is Champagne in place of the red wine of the Last Supper. Similar blasphemous feasts are organized by Father Mesnilgrand in *A un dîner d'athées* ('At an Atheists' Dinner'): these take place on a Friday and the 'Satanic guests' are 'set ablaze with heady wine'. Wine at these sacrilegious events is clearly used with parodic intention.

THE VINE AS A MOTIF

THE metaphor of the vine is used to show the links between God, Christ and mankind: 'I am the true vine, and my Father is the husbandman…I am the vine, ye are the branches' (John 15: 1, 5). The same image occurs in the Old Testament when the miraculous, giant bunch of grapes is brought back from the Promised Land by the emissaries of Moses. Grapes like these, hung from a pole carried by two men, are a common motif in stained glass, as at Saint-Etienne-de-Mulhouse. They appear again in Poussin's 'Automne' ('Autumn'), and the two men from this painting seem to have inspired a similar pair in Derain's sketch for Nicolas brochures. Saint Augustine also referred to Jesus as the grapes

'La cene' ('Last Supper'), Philippe de Champaigne, seventeenth century (Louvre, Paris).

Below, detail from 'L'Automne' ('Autumn'), Nicolas Poussin, seventeenth century (Louvre).

THE LAST SUPPER

BREAD and wine, often placed at the centre of the table, are obligatory features in paintings of the Last Supper. In Philippe de Champaigne's 1648 replica of the Last Supper altarpiece at Port-Royal-des-Champs, near Paris, the slightly off-centre placing of the wine-cup is precisely what attracts the eye. The chalices on Henry Moore's labels for Mouton-Rothschild are meant to

from the Promised Land, and the miraculous bunch of grapes was seen in the Middle Ages as a metaphor for Christ on the cross.

THE CELEBRATION OF BACCHUS

THE religious aspects of wine are evident also in Greek mythology. The miracle of the wine at the Marriage at Cana has been compared to the annual transformation of water into wine at the temple of Dionysos on the island of Andros. Images of Christ at the wine-press echo those of Bacchus treading the grapes. They symbolize quite different things of course: the first is a metaphor for Christ's redeeming blood, the second for the wine, which can produce a state of ecstasy. But there are similarities of detail in the way they are presented in painting and sculpture.

The celebration of Bacchus, God of wine, is a frequent subject for music. The eleventh-century *Carmina Burana* contains invocations to Bacchus on the lines of the hymns to Iakkhos (the Greek name for Bacchus and another name for Dionysos) sung at the Eleusinian Mysteries. In the early eighteenth century, Rameau's opera *Platée* also included choruses in honour of Bacchus. 'Bacchic' scenes in French painting are not so much religious as a pretext for depicting sensual pleasure. 'L'enfance de Bacchus' ('The Childhood of Bacchus'), a painting often attributed to Poussin, shows the god drinking wine from a gold dish held by a faun, while a sleeping Bacchante and child are meant to remind us of Venus and Cupid. The analogy goes even further in Rilke's French poem 'Eros', in which the figures of Cupid and Bacchus are merged. Scenes like these explain the presence of wine in the amorous scenes painted by Nattier, for instance, or in Chagall's 'Double portrait au verre de vin' ('Lovers with a Glass of Wine'). Wine once symbolized Dionysos but has come to denote the ecstasy of love. Indeed, it has become more and more secular in its connotations.

Above, 'Loth et ses filles' ('Lot and his Daughters'), lid for wine cup, Pierre Reymond, 1544 (Musée de Cluny, Paris).

Right, detail from 'La Prudence amène la Paix et l'Abondance' ('Prudence bringing Peace and Plenty'), Simon Vouet, seventeenth century (Louvre, Paris).

Below, 'L'Apocalypse' ('Apocalypse'), tapestry, Nicolas Bataille, fourteenth century (Château, Angers).

THE ALLEGORY OF TASTE

THE still life, an attempt to imitate and compete with Nature, can also be an allegory for an inner world. The five senses can be suggested: smell by the presence of flowers, touch by dice or playing cards, hearing by musical instruments, sight by books or optical devices, and taste by wine. Linard's painting of 'Les cinq sens' ('The Five Senses') indicates taste by a wicker bottle and a half-filled glass. Baugin's 'Nature morte à l'échiquier' ('Still Life with Chessboard') also uses wine for taste, with pinks for smell, a lute for hearing, a chessboard for touch and a mirror for sight.

UNITY AND PEACE

WINE as an allegory for taste brings us almost back to wine in its everyday context as something enjoyable to drink; but wine can also be used to convey a more abstract idea, the idea of peace, for instance, and especially peace within society. In the late eighteenth century, a wine-merchant's signboard entitled 'Aux Trois Ordres Réunis' ('The Union of the Classes') depicts it as a unifying factor in society. A noblewoman is shown perched on a

swing pushed by a commoner; a bewigged man has his hand on the shoulder of a woman from the lower orders; a soldier raises his glass to a priest pouring wine. Wine safeguards peace between nations as well as peace within society. In Vouet's 'Allégorie de la paix' ('Allegory of Peace'), peace and plenty are symbolized by cupids holding grapes. The painting is in a long tradition which begins with Aristophanes' play *The Acharnians*, in which the hero Diceopolis attempts to bring the Peloponnesian War to an end with a pun on the word

spondai, meaning both 'peace' and 'libations of wine'. At the end of the play, the boastful warrior Lamachos is wounded by a vine stake, showing how wine can overcome war. In 1946, just after the Second World War, Jean Hugo's wine label for Mouton-Rothschild showed a dove of peace flying over vineyards, emphasizing once again the links between wine and peace.

Wine can both symbolize peace and bring it into existence. It can also stimulate the imagination. Indeed, it is often seen as a trigger for creativity.

WINE: INSPIRATION AND CREATIVITY

WINE is said to help the creative process, as Hoffmann's 'recipes' for composing music would seem to indicate: 'A conscientious musician should resort to Champagne when composing a comic opera. This will provide appropriate lightness and scintillation. Sacred music needs Jurançon or wine from the Rhine, which have an intoxicatingly bitter aftertaste, like serious thinking. Heroic music demands Burgundy, which has plenty of patriotic fire and passion.'

Wine may also inspire the painter. Matisse's 'Atelier rouge' ('Red Studio') underlines the links between wine and inspiration: the spreading red colour of the wine seems to suffuse the whole studio, the stage for artistic creation. Grapes are also used to illustrate the rules for painting light. The Académie des Beaux-Arts suggests that a painting should be lit like a bunch of grapes, with the light concentrated at the centre and darker edges. This is no magic formula but a serious rule for artists.

A PATH TO COMMUNICATION

THE links between wine and creativity are developed even more clearly in literature. The long quest of Rabelais's giant Pantagruel to find out if he ought to marry ends with a visit to the oracle of the *dive bouteille* (the sacred bottle) and with advice to drink. This advice perhaps extends to the writer, and the reader too, since Rabelais defines wine in the Prologue as the source of happiness and the best means of establishing fellow-feeling between his readers and himself.

In the *Paradis artificiels* ('Artificial Heavens'), Baudelaire makes wine say: '*notre intime réunion créera la poésie*' ('poetry will spring from this intimacy between us'), an idea repeated in the *Fleurs du mal* ('Flowers of Evil'), where the 'soul' of wine is made to say: '*pour que de notre amour naisse la poésie*' ('so that poetry can be born from our love').

Apollinaire's *Les alcools* takes this even further. In 'Poème lu au mariage d'André Salmon' ('Poem read at André Salmon's Wedding'), he suggests that artistic creation stems from links between wine and laughter:

Les verres tombèrent se brisèrent
Et nous apprîmes à rire.

('Glasses fell and broke and we learnt how to laugh'). There is a similar phrase in the last line of 'Nuit rhénane' ('Rhenish Nights'): '*Mon verre s'est brisé comme un éclat de rire*' ('My glass shattered like a shriek of laughter'). Apollinaire is referring to the laughter of creativity, generated by wine, which induces '*un lyrisme tout neuf*' ('a brand new lyricism'). In French the connection is reinforced by the possible pun on *verre* (glass) and *vers* (verse).

Above, 'The Shortest Way', Présence Panchounette, 1983 (Galerie de Paris).

TURNING THE WORLD INTO WINE

'VENDEMIAIRE' ('The Harvest Month'), the last poem in the collection, almost turns into an atlas of wine, giving the idea of poetic intoxication an even wider dimension. It begins with an invocation to all the cities of France, Europe and the world, the towns of western and northern France, of the whole South, the Rhône and Saône, the Moselle and the Rhine, to bring their wines to him. The poet can attain universal knowledge by swallowing the entire world in the form of wine, '*L'univers tout entier concentré dans ce vin*' ('The entire universe is concentrated in this wine').

Wine has often been seen as a key to truth, from the Latin proverb '*in vino veritas*' to Voltaire's '*ce n'est que dans le vin qu'on voit la vérité*' ('only in wine can truth be seen'). For many artists it has also opened the door to the world of the imagination. So it is a fascinating paradox that wine gives access both to truth and to artistic invention.

WINE AND THE CINEMA

SETTING THE SCENE

WINE – the bottle, the wine-glass, the gesture of drinking, the conviviality of drinkers – are so much a part of the French way of life that they are an inevitable feature in films all through the ninety years of the history of the cinema. With the comic actors of the early cinema or the edifying Pathé and Gaumont melodramas shown all over the world before 1914, it is not so much the wine itself that matters as the act of drinking and the companionable atmosphere suggested in the bar or round the family table. The essential images of conviviality – the bottle being opened, the glass raised, the toasts at receptions – rapidly became fixed as a modestly realistic screen convention unsurprising to the French but deliciously exotic and 'typically French' for an English-speaking audience.

Another film convention, especially in the twenties and thirties, was that of the champagne bottle on a tray carried by the inevitable butler in a striped waistcoat. Translated onto the screen, this was a basic and (for the producer) an inexpensive symbol of 'high life', the life of the rich, of society and its fringes, of the provincial living it up in town according to the image ingrained in the popular imagination. Like the opulent crimson velvet curtains in the cinema, Champagne catered to the dreams of Saturday night audiences.

A CENTRAL ROLE

ON the other hand, not many film-makers have brought out the true value and cultural significance of wine. In 1918, a few months before the end of the First World War, Louis Feuillade (from Languedoc) made the film *Vendémiaire* ('Harvest Month') for Gaumont. This is an allegorical story with a wine-harvest setting, where the wine which men laboriously extract from the earth is equated with the blood soaking the wartime trenches.

When we come to sound films, wine is seldom the main subject except in occasional brief sequences. Sometimes

Above, a scene from Flagrant désir, *directed by Claude Faraldo, 1986. Right,* Masques, *directed by Claude Chabrol, 1987. Below,* Vendémiaire ('Harvest Month'), *Louis Feuillade, 1918.*

these are more substantial, as in Claude Autant-Lara's 1946 film *Le diable au corps* (released as *The Devil in the Flesh*), based on the remarkable novel by Raymond Radiguet, published just before he died in 1923 at the age of twenty. The focus for an important scene in a grand Paris restaurant is a supposedly corked bottle of Pommard which the sixteen-year-old hero tries to send back, in a gesture to impress the young married woman with whom he is in love. This is an episode full of warmth and humour. However, in the

same restaurant a year later, the atmosphere darkens as the lovers confess the deception and we sense the cold reality of the love affair's approaching end.

There are a very few film directors who treat the topic of wine: Claude Sautet, Bertrand Tavernier, Claude Chabrol, Claude Faraldo. They all have the ability to discuss a great bottle (or to get their actors to do so) and to evoke the gestures connected with decanting wine against the light, while pouring it, inhaling its aroma,

savouring it in the mouth. A 1947 Château Margaux features at the beginning of Sautet's *Mado*: a little group of men is playing bridge when a case of wine arrives for their host, known to all as Papa. He opens it delicately, watches with anxiety while a friend opens a bottle and glasses are passed around – 'We should have let it rest.' In the 1987 film *Masques* directed by Chabrol (best known for sardonic

thrillers in the Hitchcock style) there is a shot where Burgundy is being carefully poured into a crystal decanter by Philippe Noiret's servant. Wine also appears where least expected: in *Providence* (made in 1977, with John Gielgud, Dirk Bogarde and Elaine Stritch) either the director Alain Resnais or his English scenario writer David Mercer has invented the leitmotiv of the bottle of Chablis, which is so crucial in stimulating the imagination of Clive Langham, the dying elderly novelist in the film.

WINE AND TOURISM

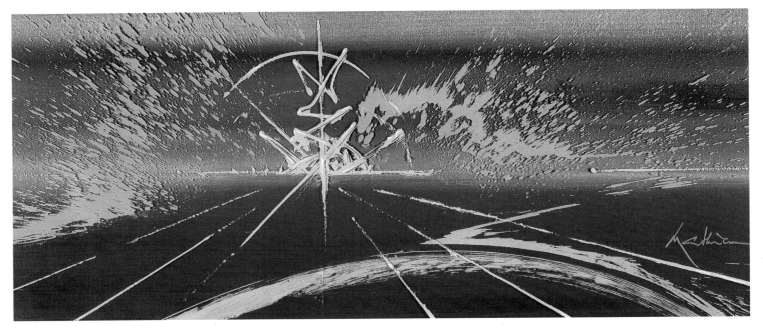

IT is a sign of the times that tourists nowadays 'do' Bordeaux châteaux, Burgundy vineyards or the *route des Vins* in Alsace just as they would the Loire Valley, the caves of the Dordogne or 'Paris by night'. Exploring wine regions and finding out about their produce has become yet another aspect of the tourist industry. This activity is not altogether new. Even before the Revolution, Bordeaux's reputation for wine led travellers to venture out of the city to the Graves estate of Haut-Brion. At a Pessac vineyard owned by Jesuits visitors were shown a vine planted by an archbishop of Bordeaux who later became Pope Clement V.

These early tourists took a fairly general interest in wine-growing procedures but a few of them did go further. Thomas Jefferson's enthusiasm for wine was such that, in 1787, he used a visit to take the waters at Aix-en-Provence as an excuse to go round a number of wine regions. He went in turn to Burgundy, Bordeaux, southern France and northern Italy, and the following year extended his explorations to the Rhine Valley and to Champagne, keeping regular travel diaries which are now invaluable documents for wine historians.

By the middle of the nineteenth century, constant demand by tourists for information about the great wine districts led to the publication in London in 1846 of the first edition of Charles Cocks's *Bordeaux, Its Wines and the Claret Country*, the precursor of the famous Cocks and Féret reference books on Bordeaux.

ROUTES DES VINS

ALTHOUGH tourist interest in wine goes back many years, it was a long time before the tourist and wine industries got together to satisfy this interest by setting up *route des Vins*. These 'wine trails' were marked out with pictorial signs which, like Mathieu's hoarding for the Rhône Valley, were sometimes the work of well-known artists. Itineraries were intended to combine places associated with wine (*chais*, wine-cellars and vineyards) and the more traditional tourist sites such as castles and churches.

In 1951 Alsace became the first region to acquire a *route des Vins*, which here followed a medieval track between Marlenheim and Thann. This was copied by other well-known *appellations* such as

Champagne, with three different routes, and by regions such as the Bergerac area and the Costières du Gard, which were better known in the past for their picturesque qualities than for their wine. Specially marked footpaths were also mapped out, again in Alsace, so that walkers could have a close view of grape varieties and methods of cultivation.

Vineyard owners have also started opening their cellars to visitors, and have sometimes set up miniature wine museums.

There are more ambitious wine collections in some city museums, at the Musée d'Aquitaine in Bordeaux, for instance, or the Musée du Vieux Biterrois in Béziers. A few museums are entirely devoted to wine: there is one in the historic setting of the fifteenth-century Hôtel des Ducs in Beaune, another at Epernay with a famous eighteenth-century wine-press, and an interesting Alsatian *cave* set up in the Colmar museum. It is not possible to list every museum, but Château Mouton-Rothschild deserves a special mention for its unique collection of works of art inspired by wine.

Visitors to vineyards are often concerned with the historical as well as the natural setting, and are clearly interested in buildings

A painting by Georges Mathieu, used as a hoarding along the Rhône Valley wine routes.

associated with the wine industry. For such visitors, wine châteaux become more than just names on a bottle. Often the châteaux are nineteenth-century buildings which are benefiting from fresh public interest in the period. Gothic and Classical 'imitations' are consequently now regarded as imaginative and characterful works of art in their own right.

Other visitors show a great deal of interest in the buildings where wine is made and stored. In Burgundy a special tour of old wine-presses is now possible, and the Médoc has an architectural guide devoted to buildings for fermenting and maturing wine (*cuviers* and *chais*).

Next to the *route des Vins*, the most striking trend is the development of guided wine tours and tasting courses. These can be enjoyed in groups, and are preferable to individual car tours for three reasons: places closed to visitors on their own are often open to accompanied groups; there is no need to drink and drive; a professional guide can give a much better introduction to the wine and background of a particular region. There are also more ambitious, highly organized wine tours taking in a number of *appellations*. Some of these even provide travel by limousine, helicopter and private jet.

Less sophisticated, but with rather closer focus on the wine, are the wine-tasting courses. Many such courses were launched in the fifties, when the Oenology Institute at Bordeaux University started allowing both experts and ordinary wine lovers to have access to its research findings. Wine courses now exist in most regions, notably at the Université du Vin housed in a magnificent castle at Suze-la-Rousse in the southern Rhône Valley. This attempts to provide rather more than the usual tasting courses, and regards itself as a centre for the dissemination of wine culture as a whole.

Right, vines growing beside the Etang de Diane, north-east of Cateraggio, Corsica.

Above, the spectacular hilltop village of Minerve.

PEACEFUL EXPLORATION

ALTHOUGH institutions such as these have contributed much to general knowledge about wine,

many people still prefer to make their own discoveries as they tour the wine regions. In Burgundy, if you leave the main *route des Vins* near Santenay, you can wander along hilly minor roads through villages full of the characteristic local *maisons vigneronnes* (wine-growers' houses). The delightful villages of Dezize-lès-Maranges and Sampigny-lès-Maranges, with its massive eighteenth-century wine-press, are typical examples. At Dracy-lès-Couches, the

sixteenth-century château has a simple and elegant wine store with a splendid collection of vats, some of which date from the seventeenth century. The Minervois region of Languedoc is not so well known but is full of beautifully austere Romanesque churches, such as Saint-Saturnin de Pouzols, the chapel of Saint-Etienne at Vaissière, southwest of Azille, and both church and castle at Puichéric. The wine-village of Rieux-Minervois, in the same region, has the interesting seven-sided church of Saint-Pierre-et-Saint-Paul, with its carved capitals.

Travellers venturing off the beaten track into the high Fenouillèdes region which separates Corbières and Roussillon will find enjoyable wine and wild countryside between Saint-Paul-de-Fenouillet and Montalba-le-Château. Here, in a remote and spectacular site, is one of the most important Roman monuments in Languedoc, the almost forgotten aqueduct of Ansignan. Touraine is noteworthy, at Bléré especially, for its curious *grottes* or *lubits*, vineyard shelters like precise miniature versions of the local houses and built of the same white tufa as the Loire châteaux.

In Corsica it takes some determination to leave the clear coastal waters, but it is very pleasant to seek out

vineyards growing wines which have been described as 'harsh, with traces of iodine, but subtle and fragrant nevertheless'. The new vineyards of Le Fiumorbo will perhaps compensate for the remoteness of the region. This is Corsica as one always imagines it: spectacularly situated bandit hideaways and hilltop villages such as Prunelli di Fiumorbo, with panoramic views over the whole eastern plain and on out to sea.

At the Provençal village of Villars-sur-Var, the home of the medieval Comtes du Beuil, every house has its own press and storage casks for the not very well-known local wine. This deserves to be tasted before you go on to see the remarkable statue of Saint John the Baptist by Mathieu d'Anvers, sculpted in 1524. This is in the local church, next to the romantic colonnades of the Allée des Grimaldi.

With the recent partnership between tourism and the wine industry, vineyards are now incorporated in the list of holiday destinations. Nevertheless, wine has not lost its primary virtue of bringing people together. Indeed, the whole of France is revealed as one travels round her vineyards, and exploration of these leads to knowledge of an entire civilization.

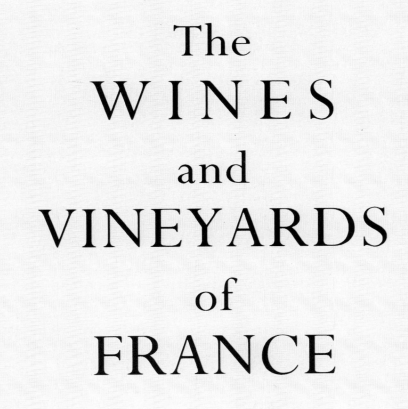

The
WINES
and
VINEYARDS
of
FRANCE

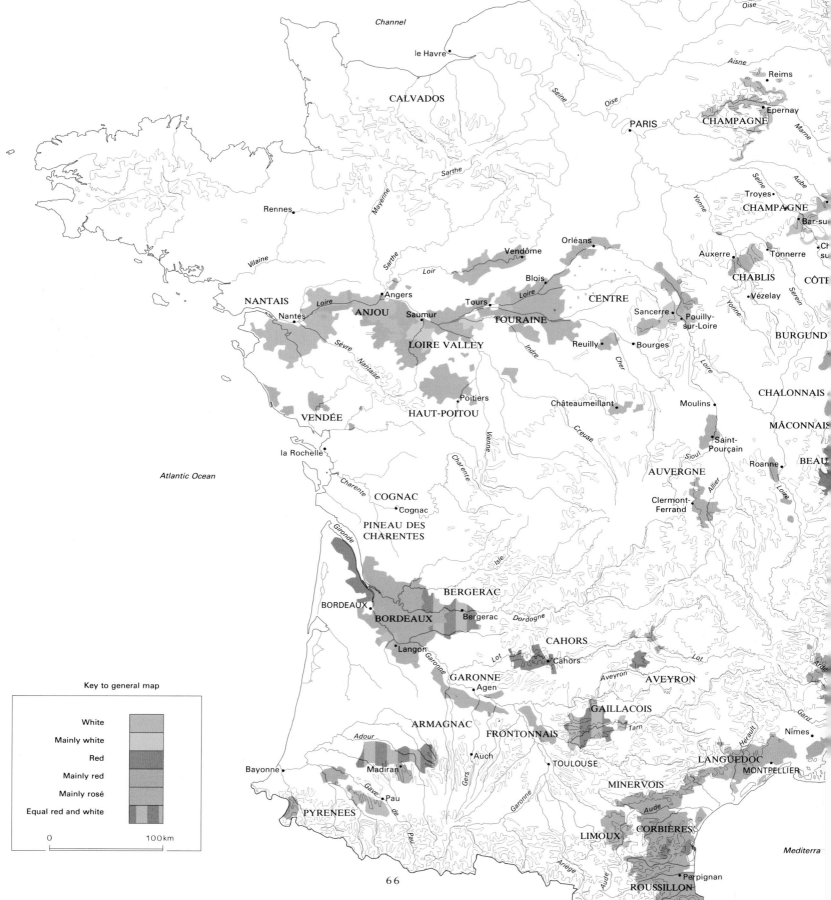

WINE IN FRANCE

Channel

le Havre•

Calais•

CALVADOS

•PARIS

CHAMPAGNE

•Reims
•Epernay

Oise

Aisne

Marne

Seine

Oise

Sarthe

Rennes•

Mayenne

Seine

Troyes•
CHAMPAGNE
•Bar-su

Yonne

Aube

Vilaine

Sarthe

Loir

Vendôme

Orléans•

Auxerre•
•Tonnerre
•Ch
su

CHABLIS
•Vézelay

CÔTE

NANTAIS

Loire

Blois•

Loire

CENTRE

Sancerre•
•Pouilly-
sur-Loire

Serein
Yonne

BURGUND

Nantes•
Angers•

ANJOU
Saumur•

Tours•

TOURAINE

Reuilly•

•Bourges

Loire

CHALONNAIS

Sèvre

LOIRE VALLEY

Indre

Cher

MÂCONNAIS

Nantaise

Poitiers•

Châteaumeillant•

Moulins•

Sioul

•Saint-
Pourçain
Roanne•

BEAU

VENDÉE

HAUT-POITOU

Vienne

Creuse

AUVERGNE

Allier

Loire

la Rochelle•

Atlantic Ocean

Charente

Charente

Clermont-
Ferrand•

COGNAC
•Cognac

PINEAU DES
CHARENTES

Isle

Gironde

BERGERAC

BORDEAUX•

BORDEAUX
•Bergerac

Dordogne

CAHORS

•Cahors

Lot

•Langon

Garonne

GARONNE
•Agen

Lot

Aveyron

AVEYRON

GAILLACOIS

Tarn

Gard

Key to general map

White

Mainly white

Red

Mainly red

Mainly rosé

Equal red and white

0   100km

ARMAGNAC

FRONTONNAIS

Adour

•Auch

Bayonne•

Madiran•

Gave

•Pau

Gers

Garonne

•TOULOUSE

MINERVOIS

Hérault

•Nîmes

LANGUEDOC
MONTPELLIER•

Aude

PYRENEES

Pau

LIMOUX

CORBIÈRES

Ariège

Aude

•Perpignan

ROUSSILLON

Mediterra

General key to maps in atlas

The colours indicate the type of wine (red, white or rosé) for AOC and VDQS wines.
Ranking – village (communal), sub-regional or regional appellation – is shown by depth of colour.

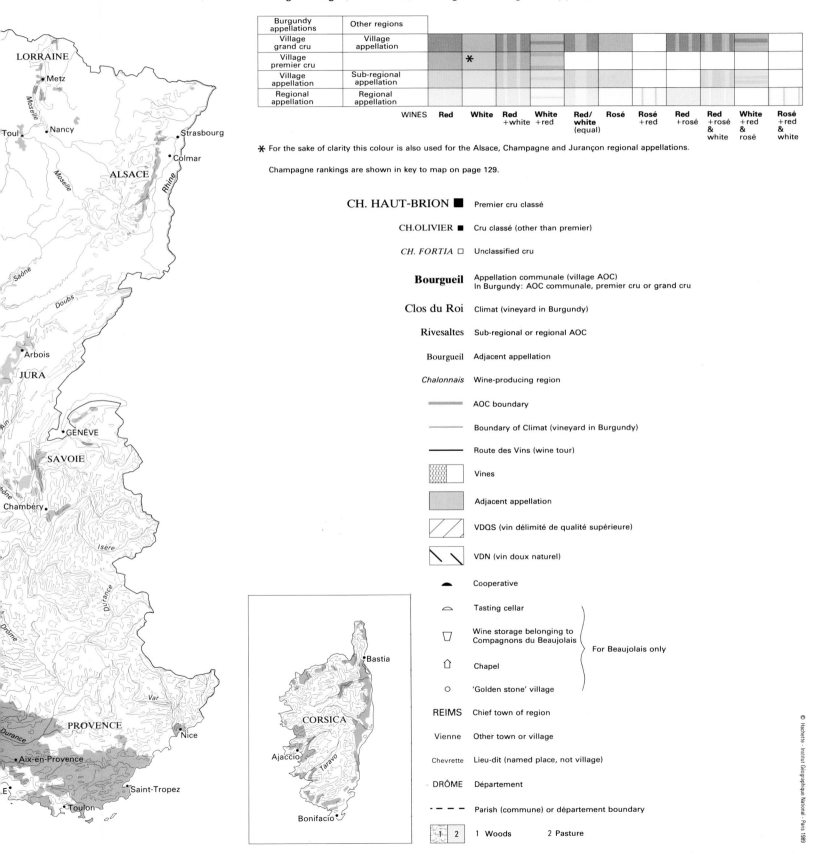

Burgundy appellations	Other regions											
Village grand cru	Village appellation											
Village premier cru				✱								
Village appellation	Sub-regional appellation											
Regional appellation	Regional appellation											
	WINES	**Red**	**White**	**Red +white**	**White +red**	**Red/ white (equal)**	**Rosé**	**Rosé +red**	**Red +rosé**	**Red +rosé & white**	**White +red & rosé**	**Rosé +red & white**

✱ For the sake of clarity this colour is also used for the Alsace, Champagne and Jurançon regional appellations.

Champagne rankings are shown in key to map on page 129.

CH. HAUT-BRION ■	Premier cru classé
CH. OLIVIER ■	Cru classé (other than premier)
CH. FORTIA □	Unclassified cru
Bourgueil	Appellation communale (village AOC) In Burgundy: AOC communale, premier cru or grand cru
Clos du Roi	Climat (vineyard in Burgundy)
Rivesaltes	Sub-regional or regional AOC
Bourgueil	Adjacent appellation
Chalonnais	Wine-producing region
	AOC boundary
	Boundary of Climat (vineyard in Burgundy)
	Route des Vins (wine tour)
	Vines
	Adjacent appellation
	VDQS (vin délimité de qualité supérieure)
	VDN (vin doux naturel)
◗	Cooperative
◠	Tasting cellar
▽	Wine storage belonging to Compagnons du Beaujolais
⬡	Chapel
○	'Golden stone' village
REIMS	Chief town of region
Vienne	Other town or village
Chevrette	Lieu-dit (named place, not village)
DRÔME	Département
– – –	Parish (commune) or département boundary
1 2	1 Woods 2 Pasture

For Beaujolais only

LORRAINE
Metz
Moselle
Nancy
Toul
Strasbourg
Colmar
ALSACE
Rhine
Moselle
Saône
Doubs
Arbois
JURA
GENÈVE
SAVOIE
Chambéry
Isère
Durance
Drôme
PROVENCE
Nice
Durance
Aix-en-Provence
Saint-Tropez
Toulon
Var

CORSICA
Bastia
Ajaccio
Tavaro
Bonifacio

© Hachette · Institut Géographique National · Paris 1989

ALSACE

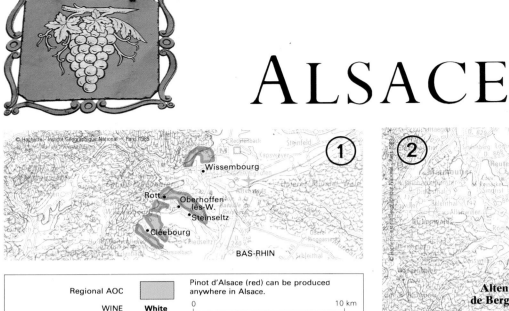

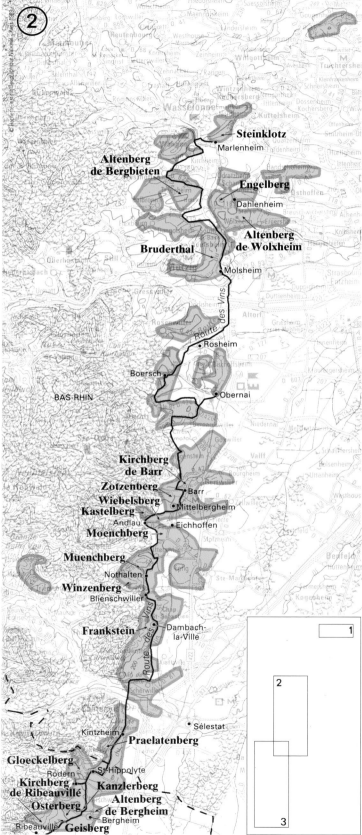

Regional AOC	Pinot d'Alsace (red) can be produced anywhere in Alsace.
WINE **White**	0 10 km

WHILE out for a walk one day, a child met a bear greedily eating berries that nobody had seen before. The bear was chased away and it soon became clear what these berries might be good for. According to legend, this was the origin of vines in Alsace. Celebrated for its rich folklore and colourful festivals, the Alsatian wine region stands out in relation to France as a whole for its northerly situation, its links with the Rhineland, its classification of wine according to grape variety (the type of soil, or *terroir*, is also important, of course) and, lastly, for its turbulent history.

A CHEQUERED PAST

ALSATIAN vineyards are established today on the slopes of the Lower Vosges, forming a link between mountain and plain, but they developed unevenly because of the chequered history of this much coveted province. Vine-growing first took shape under Roman influence, but it was only at the end of the great invasions, with the creation of the important episcopal and monastic estates, that it was able to prosper once more. The proximity of the Rhine, one of the principal communication routes in the Middle Ages, contributed early in this period to the rise in Alsatian wine exports both to countries at the mouth of the Rhine and, through trade with Hanseatic cities, as far as Scandinavia and England.

Wine production seems to have reached a peak in the sixteenth century. There were more than 180 wine-growing communes registered and vines spread widely over the Rhine plain. Wine-growing was in the hands of a great many different proprietors living in prosperous towns. These little towns with their Renaissance architecture grew up behind their ramparts in perfect sympathy with their natural surroundings and, by great good fortune, most of these architectural masterpieces survived a succession of wars. One of the bloodiest was the Thirty Years War (1618–48), which decimated the population and devastated the vines. When this conflict was over, Alsace was incorporated into France. Louis XIV then wisely encouraged new settlers from German Switzerland and from the Austrian Tyrol, regions then overpopulated but similar in culture to the local population. The situation both in the wine areas and in the province as a whole improved to the point that, in 1673, when Louis XIV saw Alsace for the first time from the top of the Saverne Pass, he was moved to exclaim, '*Ah quel beau jardin!*' ('Oh, what a beautiful garden').

Unfortunately, wine-growing was again to suffer, this time during the French Revolution. The great religious *domains* were demolished and the traditional trade outlets blocked, while the wines themselves tended to deteriorate.

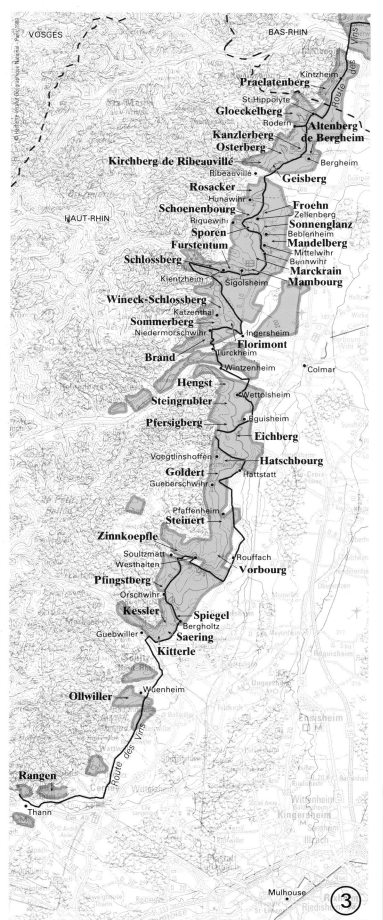

This situation was made worse by a law passed in 1822, intended to protect the internal market but causing reprisals against Alsatian wine exports: export sales fell from 70,000 hl in 1822 to 38,000 hl the following year. Later came competition from southern France, although Alsace was no longer exposed to this when annexed by the German Empire. At this stage, Alsatians saw their wine-growing take on a southern rather than a northern character and, until 1918, looked firmly in the direction of mass-produced wines sold locally and used to improve German wine. In 1893 the Alsace wine region covered 24,835 hectares, producing on average more than one million hectolitres every year.

The restoration of Alsace to France after the First World War confronted producers with an awkward choice. With great foresight, they chose the most difficult policy, which in the long run emerged as the best – to improve quality. For this reason, they had to replant with superior vine varieties and move from lowland sites up onto the hillsides.

HISTORICAL INSTABILITIES

MANY characteristic features of the wine industry in Alsace derive from the eventful history of the province. The frequent wars, in particular, explain the parcelling up of wine land into a great number of properties; for greater security, the inhabitants also gathered together in fortified villages. It was this concentration of housing that led to the division of inherited land through successive generations and finally to the extreme fragmentation seen today, with 8,163 owners declaring wine crops for only 12,600 hectares. The average plot-size

cultivated is around one tenth of a hectare and it is difficult, if not impossible, to reorganize or regroup these plots of land.

Wars and annexations have also had a distinct effect on the way wine-making is organized. From the beginning of this century, the German system has been in favour of establishing wine cooperatives. Because of destruction caused by fighting, from the Battle of Colmar until the Liberation of Alsace in 1918, the inhabitants of Bennwihr and Sigolsheim had to rebuild their villages completely. It was then that they decided to join together to form two new cooperatives.

These historical upheavals imposed frequent changes of direction in the way vineyards were exploited. The effect was to delay until the twenties the implementation of the policy to promote quality. Not all the historical effects were quite so negative. They also opened up to Alsace markets in the Rhineland, Benelux, Great Britain and Denmark, the Rhine being a major thoroughfare for the export trade. Finally, by helping cooperatives to develop, they were partly responsible for the present balance between merchant shippers, growers making and selling their own wine, and cooperatives.

Cask (Musée du Vin, Kientzheim).

ART IN THE WINE CELLAR

IN Alsace wine-growers have always been aware of belonging to an old civilization. In former times they felt a particular veneration for the tools of the trade; in their eyes these were not simple everyday objects, but a legacy from their ancestors. Among such objects, the wooden cask always had a special place and lent itself to carving, whether it was oval in shape or round like the 'Sainte Catherine' cask (dated 1715), the oldest still in service in an old Riquewihr cellar. Wealthy owners would have the front, or sometimes just the wooden fastening, carved with classical subjects such as Bacchus or sea-nymphs.

A Privileged Natural Setting

WITH their sunny terraces overhanging the Rhine Valley, the hills of the Lower Vosges are a perfect setting for vineyards and for the pleasantly civilized life these imply. The environment is exceptional, in its geology and soil structure as well as its general aspect.

COMPLEX CONDITIONS

AS in most of Alsace, these hills derive from the subsidence of the Rhine rift valley, a major tectonic movement which cut in two the former Vosges–Black Forest massif. The two north–south faults marked the boundaries of this trough and brought into play a vast network of primary and secondary faults forming a lattice of plateaux at different levels and with very varied geology.

On the Alsatian side, these faulted zones lie between the Vosges and Rhine faults (extending beyond the latter is the plain of Alsace, covered by an impressive mass of sedimentary deposits), and produced the hills that are now the principal planting area for vines. These vines also extend over the base of the mountains, that is, over the Hercynian platform, and

Le Brand vineyard at Turckheim.

over the alluvial cones in the Vosges valleys.

Vine-growing has thus been established on soil and subsoil of extreme complexity. However, it is possible to point out three main individual areas: the mountain scarp area, the hills of the Lower Vosges, and the alluvial plain.

The scarp, where vines are rarely grown above 400 m, consists of terrain of granitic or gneiss origin present from north to south in the vine-growing area. Here are sandy soils of high acidity, permeable and shallow (especially on sheer slopes), and often extremely steep, which has sometimes forced growers to construct terraces like those at

Guebwiller. In this category one can also include the schistous soils situated in the Andlau area, soils of volcanic origin as at Thann, and finally the widely represented sandstone soils. Owing to the fairly steep slopes, these soils are generally shallow, relatively young and highly acidic.

It is in the Lower Vosges that the typical Alsatian wine landscape can be found, with its beautiful large villages bright with geraniums and ringed by vine-covered hills. This is also an area where faults and erosion have uncovered very varied soil and where there are considerable changes of terrain over very short distances, particularly in the important fault areas of Saverne, Ribeauvillé, Wettolsheim-Guebwiller and Thann. The soils of the Lower Vosges hills are more or less calcareous or clayey, varying in depth according to situation and altitude (between 200 and 300 m). To these fairly weathered terrains of the Secondary era, limestone or rendzina over limestone in type, can be added conglomerates and interstratified marls, Tertiary fringe deposits which are present in the Rouffach region in particular. This whole area benefits from very favourable geology and soil structure, with soils that drain quickly while supplying the vine's natural requirements. In

the alluvial plain can be found a mixture of pebbles, sands and siliceous gravels, originating either from alluvial cones or from river terraces, at an altitude of between 170 and 220m. With a low proportion of clay, these immature soils are very permeable and tend to be acidic. In places they are covered by wind-blown deposits (superficial deposits of loess) that increase their fertility.

Seventeenth-century marriage chest (Boeckel cellars, Mittelbergheim).

SOUTHERN SUNSHINE

THE Rhine valley may be thought of as northern by the rest of the French, but to the Germans it looks like a land of gardens and sunlight, with almost southern characteristics. Each of these images contains an element of truth in a region whose

Soils of the Lower Vosges, providing perfect growing conditions for Alsace wines.

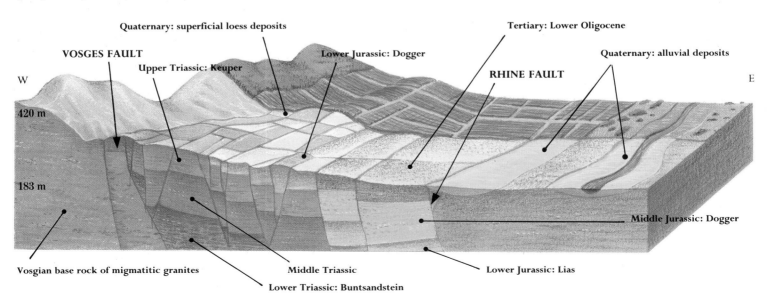

Quaternary: superficial loess deposits

Tertiary: Lower Oligocene

VOSGES FAULT

Lower Jurassic: Dogger

Upper Triassic: Keuper

RHINE FAULT

Quaternary: alluvial deposits

W

E

420 m

183 m

Middle Jurassic: Dogger

Vosgian base rock of migmatitic granites

Middle Triassic

Lower Jurassic: Lias

Lower Triassic: Buntsandstein

semi-continental climate possesses two very different aspects. In winter, under a blanket of snow, Alsace is certainly a northern land, but on a fine summer day one has only to walk down some quiet lane bathed in warmth and light to realize that to speak of the 'Mediterranean' sun is not out of place here.

Above left, the village of Niedermorschwir.
Above right, the Rangen vineyards at Thann.
Below, Saint Urban (Boeckel cellars, Mittelbergheim).

THE VOSGES BARRIER

THE source of this favoured micro-climate lies in the barrier formed by the Vosges, which restricts the effects of the Atlantic and allows the region to enjoy remarkably warm and sunny summers. At Colmar, for instance, the mean July temperature is above

20°C; and the sum of effective temperatures (that is, above 10°C) during the vine's growing period (1 April to 30 September) reaches 1253°C as opposed to 1129°C at Angers or 1175°C at Dijon.

Although summers are hot, winters are severe without reaching extremes that would prejudice wine-growing. Black frosts are fairly unusual: major damage has been recorded only in 1956 and 1985. The risk of spring frost does exist, but is kept in check by the broadening out of the Rhine Valley, and in reality affects only the outlets from valleys in the Vosges.

The Vosges barrier forms a shield against extremes of rainfall as well as of temperature: air masses from the Atlantic discharge moisture as they rise up against the western face and peaks of the range. On the Alsatian

side, the air warms up as it descends and precipitation becomes progressively less, reaching a minimum of 500 mm per year in the Colmar region. Over the vine-growing area as a whole, rainfall is between 500 and 650 mm per year, which ensures a natural check on water supply to the vines and optimizes the effects of sunshine. Favourable conditions in late autumn should also be mentioned, as these allow improved ripening and a late harvest. All this encourages the development of aroma in the wine and contributes to its individuality.

Good climatic conditions and favourable elements in both topography and soil structure have made these hillsides in the Lower Vosges a first-class *terroir* for wine. The people of Alsace have matched them to perfection with the grape varieties they have introduced.

TYPICAL GRAPE VARIETIES

Muscat d'Alsace.

WHEREAS with Champagne it is the brand-name that everyone looks for on the label, with Bordeaux the name of the château and with Burgundy the locality of vineyard, in the case of Alsace it is certainly the grape variety since this is always the name following the *appellation d'origine*. With Alsace, the usual tendency is to buy a Riesling or a Sylvaner, rather than the wine of a particular village or vineyard.

NAMING THE WINE

IN fact, this has not always been true. In the Middle Ages wines were essentially named after the commune where they originated and, until the phylloxera crisis, mixtures of vine varieties were cultivated. The grape expert Stolz pointed out in 1852 that, in the principal wine communes of the *département* of Haut-Rhin, mixed plantings were made of Riesling, Pinot Gris, Pinot Blanc and Chasselas, which, according to him, gave the best noble (*edel*) grapes in the region. Nevertheless, the vine variety already occupied a very important place in Alsatian viticulture. The situation on the Rhine river plain, a major route for trade and communications, favoured the planting of many different varieties in the course of the centuries. The diversity of soils and of microclimates allowed each one of these to find optimum conditions of growth.

However, solutions to the soil/grape/climate equation were sometimes affected by political choices, as,

for instance, when there was a directive to plant Trollinger, a now vanished variety, responsible in the last century for a large proportion of red wine production. The first consequence of phylloxera was the replacement of traditional old varieties by hybrids.

Riesling.

Fortunately, since it was necessary to use grafted vines, mixed planting was later gradually relinquished and replaced by the cultivation of single varieties. Each grape's typical properties, brought out by local climatic conditions, were naturally shown to advantage, and eventually it was decided to bring uniformity into wine-making and to produce and sell by the name of the grape variety.

BASIC GRAPE VARIETIES

THE usual practice is to classify Alsatian vines into two groups: one includes the basic varieties, the other the more noble grapes responsible for the most prestigious wines.

Chasselas, or Gutedel, had appeared in the Haut-Rhin by the end of the eighteenth century. It has become less common in the last few decades and now only represents about 2.5 per cent of the vines grown. Ripening early and adapting itself to a variety of sites, it gives fresh light wines, more neutral in taste than most of the grape varieties making up

Edelzwicker. In the Alsatian dialect this means 'noble blend', and is not a single variety but a blend including some Pinot Blanc or Sylvaner, with the addition, according to the year, of varying proportions of more aromatic varieties.

The Sylvaner grape originated in Austria and has been known in Alsace since the eighteenth century. It covers about 20 per cent of the vine area, principally in the Bas-Rhin region. It ripens late and prefers deep soils, sand and limestone, with fine particle structure. Together with Riesling it is

Pinot blanc.

the variety most regularly in production; its productivity is fairly high, on average 97 hl per hectare. It gives light wines, fairly lively and fruity, which sometimes turn out more robust on certain soils like those in the commune of Mittelbergheim.

Pinot Blanc and Auxerrois are two genetically distinct varieties, familiarly confused under the names of Pinot or Klevner owing to the similarity of the wine they produce. Whereas Pinot Blanc was present in the region from the sixteenth century, the Auxerrois grape, probably from Laquenexy in Lorraine, appeared rather later. These two are grown over an area that has gone up from 11 per cent of the whole in 1969 to 19 per cent today and owe their popularity to relatively early ripening. Wines of some breeding, they generally have good structure and a delicate bouquet.

THE GREAT NAMES

IT is the more prestigious grapes, rather than these basic varieties, that have given Alsatian wines their very definite character and reputation.

First Riesling, much cherished in Alsace, and probably the oldest local variety – early references to this can be found in an important botanical treatise, a herbal published by Bock in 1551. Today this grape covers some 21 per cent of the vine area; it is a late variety, very content on sandy clay or coarsely particled alluvial soils. With great consistency of output, it gives very distinctive, lively wines with a refined nose and considerable elegance.

The Muscat grape was also mentioned in the sixteenth century and is in fact a blend of two varieties:

Sylvaner.

Muscat d'Alsace, the older of the two, with small white grapes; and a more recent, early-ripening variety called Muscat Ottonel, possibly the result of crossing with Chasselas. The first of these gives relatively acid wines with intense aroma. The second is distinguished for its refined bouquet. The harmonious blending of the two varieties produces fresh, dry, very fragrant wines, which give a real impression of grapes in the mouth. However, Muscat now accounts for only 3 per cent of today's output as growers are concerned about inconsistent productivity.

Tokay, or Pinot Gris, is Hungarian according to legend, although in fact it is probably Burgundian in origin, and has been known in Alsace since the end of the seventeenth century. Since it accounts for only about 5 per cent of vine cultivation, it is still unusual, even if increasing. It has a special preference for the Tertiary soils (predominantly sand and clay) of the Cléebourg region in the north of the province, but is also happy on calcareous soil. Tokay wines are highly regarded because they are full-bodied, remarkably smooth and have excellent ageing ability.

Gewurztraminer is an aromatic form of the old Traminer grape, known from very early times. This selection with its very characteristic spicy bouquet ('spice' is the literal translation of *Gewürz*) appeared in Alsace towards the end of the nineteenth century and gradually replaced the old Traminer. It is constantly in production, occupying 20 per cent of the wine area despite some sensitivity to weather hazards and lowish productivity (55 hl per hectare). Early ripening, it prefers to grow on marly soil of good depth and medium limestone content. In spite of its pink-coloured grapes, it produces white wines with hints of gold, which turn out robust and

Haut-Kœnigsbourg.

which has survived in Heiligenstein and five neighbouring communes. It now occupies only a limited area and gives full, elegant wines.

Pinot Noir, which arrived very early on from Burgundy, is a prestigious red variety and ranked very high in medieval times. Over the centuries it had greatly diminished in importance, surviving only in a few places such as Ottrott, Rodern and Marlenheim, but during the last fifteen years it has been making a positive comeback and now accounts for 6.5 per cent of the area under vines. Fairly late and well adapted to sandy or calcareous soils, it is the only variety used for red and rosé wines. Although this variety was originally kept for producing fresh and fruity rosé wine, in the last few years producers have chosen to extend the fermentation period in order to produce more robust red wines.

Tokay pinot gris.

Gewürztraminer.

VIN D'ALSACE
GEWURZTRAMINER 70d
MISE A LA PROPRIÉTE PAR
J.-PH. & M BECKER, VITICULTEURS A ZELLENBERG 68340 - FRANCE

Pinot noir.

well structured, with a wonderfully intense bouquet. It is perfectly adapted to its environment on the slopes of the Lower Vosges and certainly fulfils its optimum potential in Alsace.

The Klevner grape from Heiligenstein is simply the old Traminer,

THE TOKAY LEGEND

TOKAY, or Pinot Gris, splendidly golden and substantial, is a wine of some panache so it is not surprising that there is a romantic story about its origins. In 1563 Baron Lazare de Schwendi, a General in the Austrian Imperial Army, is said to have bought the manor of Kientzheim near Colmar. Two years later he seized the city of Tokay in Hungary, discovered marvellous wines there and decided to bring back plants for propagation in his Alsatian vineyards. Since that time, the name of Tokay has always been used in the region, especially for Pinot Gris.

OVER some 180 km, the narrow ribbon of vineyards entitled to the Alsace *appellation* forms a barrier as well as a link between the plain bordering the Rhine and the *'ballons'* of the Vosges. These rounded hills are capped here and there with the ruins of medieval 'burgs' rich in history and legend. The forests, with their bright autumn colour at harvest-time, look down over vineyards perfectly integrated into the Alsation landscape.

Throughout the year, work is carried out on the vines in the same traditional manner as in the rest of the Rhine valley. They are planted out with a spacing all round of 1.5 m and each vine is pruned in the same way down to two long stems per plant, with each stem arched to encourage the first buds to sprout. It is specified that pruning should not leave more than twelve buds per square metre. Finally, the vine supports are very high, allowing growth up to 2 m from the ground – a system that encourages photosynthesis.

WISSEMBOURG

IN the north, there are already vines as we cross the frontier at Wissembourg, as if the Palatinate wine industry from Germany were overflowing into Alsace and reminding us of its links with the Rhineland. The entire output from the Wissembourg sector has been reorganized under the Cléebourg cooperative, famous for its Tokay and Auxerrois. This is delightful countryside, where the preservation of regional traditions is most important, but for tourists folklore is not allowed to overshadow a sense of local identity. Vines here are not predominant, but alternate with orchards, as they do in the little wine-growing area of Kienheim and Gimbrett, further south in the Kochersberg region, another very traditional area full of villages like those in old engravings.

Above, Riquewihr seen from Schoenenbourg.
Right, capital from the church at Marmoutier.

THE 'ROUTE DES VINS'

MARLENHEIM, with its famous roses, is where the *route des Vins* and uninterrupted vine-growing begin. This is where we find our first wine footpath (others are at Bergheim and Pfaffenheim); signposts point out varieties of Alsatian vines in their natural environment, which here is limestone and calcareous sandstone. The area of the former bishopric of Molsheim is part of the Saverne fracture zone. The usual north–south alignment of vines is replaced here by cultivation spreading from east to west, which perhaps explains the presence of mixed farming; direct selling to the public is also being developed.

After Wangen, where on the Sunday after 3 July wine flows from the fountain in front of the church, we come to Soultz-les-Bains with its salt-water spring, and then to Obernai and its breweries: these are all pleasant interludes on our journey but we must not go too far from the *route des Vins*. At Barr, where there is a festival every Sunday, we reach an area of genuine monoculture, particularly spectacular for the way the vines grow up to 2 m in height. Sylvaner represents a high percentage of the output. Selling is not all organized locally; it is from Barr onwards that we first come across firms of *négociants*. South of Barr, we should notice the picturesque small village of Mittelbergheim, with charming wine-growers' houses. This village has more than tourist interest: the Sylvaner here is planted on various very different soils and demonstrates the contribution of terrain to wine quality. Sylvaner may have less character on sedimentary soils at the foot of a slope, but it certainly displays plenty of freshness and roundness on the varied soils (overlaid with limestone) to the north-west of the village; this is even more evident in the Stein, south of Mittelbergheim, where good limestone slopes ensure exceptional ripening conditions. After this the fringes of the Lower Vosges thin out before the entrance to the Giessen valley at Sélestat.

Colmar, as at Turckheim, vines spread over much of the Fecht alluvial cone. South of Colmar, the wine road takes us to Rouffach and Westhalten, two villages where Alsace's climatic idiosyncrasies become apparent: on the tops of the dry limestone hills the unique flora (now protected) recalls that of the Mediterranean regions. Towards the south, where there is competition from very longstanding industry, we come to an elongated ribbon development of vineyards.

Halfway between the Vosges and the plain, the wine road forms a kind of backbone through the region but is not just a way of exploring vineyards and countryside. We may come across all sorts of traditional happenings, much loved by the people of Alsace, or study a living museum of the wine-maker's craft along what is one of the most interesting tourist routes in France.

RIBEAUVILLÉ, RIQUEWIHR AND COLMAR

DOMINATED by the imposing outline of Haut-Kœnigsbourg castle on a detached pinnacle of the Vosges, the foothill area broadens out again at Saint-Hippolyte. The vines look as if they enjoy this: Gewürztraminer increasingly makes an appearance on the marly soils, while Riesling is predominant on the granite slopes. Here also three delightful market towns are hidden: Ribeauvillé, where the Renaissance fountains and the houses of craftsmen and wine-growers show that the prosperity brought by wine is not a new situation; Riquewihr, a complete medieval town with no cars and no power lines; and Kaysersberg, the home-town of Dr Schweitzer. While enjoying the charm of these places, tourists should not forget their importance for the wine industry; towns like Ribeauvillé and Riquewihr contain some of the oldest wine businesses in the whole of

Alsace and there is a fairly high density of cooperatives in the Haut-Rhin wine region.

Kientzheim has its wine museum, but it is Colmar that most attracts our attention. The true wine capital of Alsace, it is also the home of the various wine trades and of the Bourse du Vin (in the Renaissance building known as the Maison des Têtes). At

Above, Kaysersberg and Schlossberg
Right, wine festival at Dambach.
Below, detail of porch lintel at Aloi.

WINE OF DEMANDING CHARACTER

WINE production in Alsace has many features distinguishing it from production in the rest of France. It is only in Alsace, for instance, that wines have to be bottled in the region, a situation envied by many other appellations. A second feature is the exclusive use of the famous long-necked bottle, 'la flûte du Rhin'. Dates for beginning the vendange have always been regulated by law. This also takes place later in Alsace than elsewhere, in order to make the most of autumn weather conditions which favour the slow ripening of the grapes and the harmonious development of aroma.

To preserve the aromatic potential, the harvested grapes are rapidly pressed in order to limit the phenomena of oxidation and maceration. Alcoholic fermentation is carried out at a sufficiently low temperature to restrict evaporation of the volatile aromas. Finally, it is essential to avoid initiating malolactic fermentation, which would spoil the wine's balance and prevent the development of its bouquet.

A REGION OF RICH DIVERSITY

Alsatian wine is no longer restricted to the regional *appellation*. Producers are now aware of the characteristic qualities of their wines and are trying to diversify. With the AOC Alsace *Grand Cru* they are returning to a regional and not simply varietal *appellation*. They are also restoring the old tradition of late-ripening grapes with the *vendanges tardives* and *sélection de grains nobles*. Crémant d'Alsace is a festive, sparkling wine now making an appearance.

THE *GRANDS CRUS*

THE main wine-growing area in Alsace consists of a strip between 1.5 and 3 km broad and stretching north and south over about 110 km as the crow flies. Variations in soil and micro-climate abound, giving the wine many different nuances of taste which

anywhere else would have been given legal classifications by the appearance of named *crus*. However, perhaps because of longstanding democratic tradition in the Rhineland, here in Alsace they date only from 1975, with the official definition of the *appellation* Alsace *Grand Cru*. In November 1983 this decision was carried through when boundaries were established for a first series of 25 *lieux-dits* (named localities), each consisting of from 6 to 80 hectares, with an average area of 35 hectares. However, the selection of *grands crus* is highly political and is an unreliable guide to quality. Some of the best sites were not delimited, while other mediocre ones were. When buying Alsatian wine, the best indication of quality is the name of the grower or the merchant.

An essential feature of the *appellation* Alsace *Grand Cru* is the individuality of each *terroir* under consideration, through its soil and

also its orientation and aspect. As a whole they are ideal for the production of the 'noble' vine varieties of Alsace (Riesling, Muscat, Pinot Gris and Gewurztraminer), which are alone entitled to the *appellation*. The output per hectare (70 hl) is much lower than that of the regional *appellation*, but allows the wines to develop their very characteristic properties (*typicité*), with additional nuances according to local conditions. A further feature is that these wines may only be made from grapes giving a minimum 10° of alcohol for the first two varieties and 11° for the others.

VENDANGES TARDIVES AND *SELECTION DE GRAINS NOBLES*

AUTUMN weather conditions, in

The seasons in Alsace; right, Hunawihr.

Alsace as in the Rhine Valley as a whole, have often favoured the development of *pourriture noble* (noble rot) and the concentration of the juice in each grape. For a long time now, this has enabled wine to be produced from very late harvests. However, the delicate and chancy nature of wine-making based on this kind of harvest, together with inevitably high prices, explains why in the last few decades only a few of the larger Alsatian houses have been interested in producing such wine. It might have had a limited future as a local curiosity if the regional pursuit of quality and a healthy sense of competition had not culminated in the recognition and defining (Decree of March 1984) of the terms *vendanges tardives* (late harvest) and *sélection de grains nobles*.

These terms may be applied to wines with the *appellation* Alsace as well as to the Alsace *Grand Cru*, but only on condition that their provenance is from 'noble' grapes (Riesling, Muscat, Pinot Gris and Gewürztraminer). The wine-makers have to adhere to the most rigorous methods since the legal minimum level of potential natural alcohol is higher for these wines, as for the Jura *vins de paille*, than for any other French AOC. For the *vendanges tardives* the minimum level is 12.9° for Riesling and Muscat and 14.3° for Pinot Gris and Gewürztraminer. For the *sélection de grains nobles* the minimum levels are 15.1° and 16.4°, respectively. The regulations are stringent and so too is the vigilance in seeing that they are carried out. When the grapes are harvested a systematic check is carried out by officials of INAO (Institut National des Appellations d'Origine) in order to provide a guarantee that the wines are authentic and have not been added to in any way. The wine may not be marketed without having undergone structural analyses eighteen months after the original harvest. The result of all this is wine with a remarkable concentration of flavour and very sustained aroma.

CELEBRATE WITH ALSACE!

THIS slogan, accompanied by a symbolic winking eye, has been used in a major advertising campaign to encourage the non-Alsatian French to drink Crémant, an uncomplicated sparkling wine. Its *appellation* area overlaps with the regional *appellation* and extends from north to south of the province. Crémant wines may be based on a number of different grapes: Pinot Blanc, Auxerrois, Pinot Gris, Pinot Noir, Chardonnay or Riesling. Unlike Alsace or Alsace *Grand Cru appellations,* Crémant wines are rarely designated by their grape variety. They are usually based on a blend of different grapes, in varying proportions according to the year, in order to ensure a consistent balance of acidity. The grapes have to be processed according to principles laid down in Champagne: for must of good quality, they have to be placed whole in the press and extraction levels must not exceed 100 litres of *appellation* wine for 150 kg of harvested grapes. The second fermentation has to take place in the bottle with a minimal *sur lie* (bottled directly from the cask) period of nine months.

In response to demand, a range of different Crémants has been introduced. Some are based on Riesling, with a highly characteristic nose; others, from Auxerrois or Pinot Blanc, are fuller and rounder with better ageing potential. By adapting itself to the market and sensibly pursuing quality, the Crémant *appellation* has achieved real commercial success with sales figures going from a few thousand hectolitres in 1975, up to more than 16,000 in 1982, and above 50,000 in 1988.

The wine of Alsace is still underrated. There are two major reasons for this: first, the adversities of history, which have delayed the introduction of quality standards; secondly, the complexity of the product itself, often regarded as a drawback. Nowadays consumers are in fact looking for individuality – a good thing for Alsace, since what was once a handicap is now a positive advantage.

Right, Ammerschwihr.
Below, drawing of Hunawihr by Hansi (1872–1951), an Alsatian writer and illustrator.

THE FEAST OF SAINT STEPHEN

ON *Saint Stephen's Day, the day after Christmas, the president of the Ammerschwihr Burghers' Society used to invite his fellow burghers to a magnificent meal – hence the name 'Confrérie Saint Etienne' for this cheerful fraternity, founded in the fourteenth century to control the quality of the wine produced in the parish. The society ceased to exist in 1848 but was revived a hundred years later, in 1947, with the encouragement of Joseph Dreyer, in an attempt to boost the wine trade in Alsace as a whole. Since 1972, its headquarters have been at Kientzheim, in the former home of the Barons de Schwendi, and the château has been turned into an important trade and publicity centre. Four official meetings are held at Kientzheim each year as well as a number of wine-tasting lectures. The society now has several thousand members who are unofficial ambassadors of Alsace and its wines to the world outside. It loyally follows the intentions of the original society and every year organizes a* concours des vins *where the best wines are awarded a seal of approval. Lastly, it owns the finest collection of Alsatian wines, today numbering more than 60,000 bottles, the oldest of which go as far back as 1834.*

BORDEAUX

BORDEAUX – THE CITY

IT is difficult to picture the Bordeaux waterfront without the rows of casks that appear in all the old engravings and which have helped to create the familiar image of the city. But there are no more wine barrels along the Port de la Lune and the great shipping firms have moved their storehouses from the Quai des Chartrons to more spacious surroundings on the outskirts. The great names that made this northern quarter of Bordeaux so famous have disappeared, and faceless companies and multinational food

...AND THE REGION

THE Gironde wine trade is in fact far more diverse and contradictory than it first appears. The Bordeaux AOC area is the largest in France, covering 86,000 hectares, and other Bordeaux wine statistics are equally impressive: the average annual yield is about 5 million hl (equivalent to 650 million bottles); some 20,000 growers declare their crops; there are 150 firms of brokers and 400 of *négociants* (merchants); altogether some 60,000 people, one in six of Gironde workers, are employed in the wine industry.

Finally, there are areas of molasse sandstone, *boulbènes* (stony silt/clay) and recent alluvial deposits. The latter are typical of soils alongside rivers and are known in the Gironde area as *palus* (from the Latin for 'marsh').

SIX GREAT FAMILIES OF WINE

THE variety of soils has encouraged the production of a broad range of wines. Without counting *vin mousseux*, there are six main official categories of wine: Bordeaux and Bordeaux Supérieur (red and rosé), yielding on average 2 million hl per year; the Côtes, 550,000 hl; Médoc and Graves, 750,000 hl; the Libourne region (Saint-Emilion, Pomerol, Fronsac), 550,000 hl; dry white wines, 900,000 hl; and, lastly, sweet white wines, 150,000 hl.

Despite these many variations, the Bordeaux region has a remarkably unified ecosystem. A temperate climate makes it possible to grow vines and to bring out the distinctive qualities of particular vineyards or years. Although the weather is often unpredictable, autumn can sometimes be rewardingly sunny, especially in great vintage years. Indeed, without such autumns, the wines of Bordeaux would be quite insignificant.

A WORLD FOCUS

'Le Port de Bordeaux' ('port of Bordeaux'), from a series of views of French ports by the eighteenth-century artist Yves le Gouaz.

organizations have taken their place.

It is sad perhaps that some local colour has vanished but, according to many Bordeaux people, the old picturesqueness has given way to a more realistic attitude on the part of the city, the region and the wine-growing community.

The Bordeaux wine trade involves many groups, and within each there are also vast differences of scale. There is very little in common between a *grand cru classé* proprietor in the Haut-Médoc and a small grower with a few hectares on the opposite side of the Gironde estuary at Bourg or Blaye. Accounts of the Gironde wine industry often fail to include the many small vineyards run by peasants, although such places are immensely valuable to the region, providing wine-lovers with good wine at low prices.

The variety of people and organiza-

tions is echoed in the diversity of the natural environment. First of all there are the distinctive local soils, beginning with the most famous, the gravels which have given their name to Graves and which are present throughout on the left bank of the Garonne and in the Libourne region (in Pomerol and part of Saint-Emilion). These provide ideal soil conditions for vines as they encourage deep root penetration and a well regulated intake of water. Limestone and clay/limestone soils on sites in Saint-Emilion, Sauternes and the Côtes also have specific characteristics.

WITH the help of various professional and commercial organizations, Bordeaux has become a world centre for the wine industry. Every two years, the Vinitech and Vinexpo exhibitions attract visitors from all over the world. There have been great developments in education and research, with the founding of an important Institute of Oenology at the University. With all the advances in information and technology, any site can be exploited to achieve its maximum potential. For red wines at least, Bordeaux is the undisputed leader.

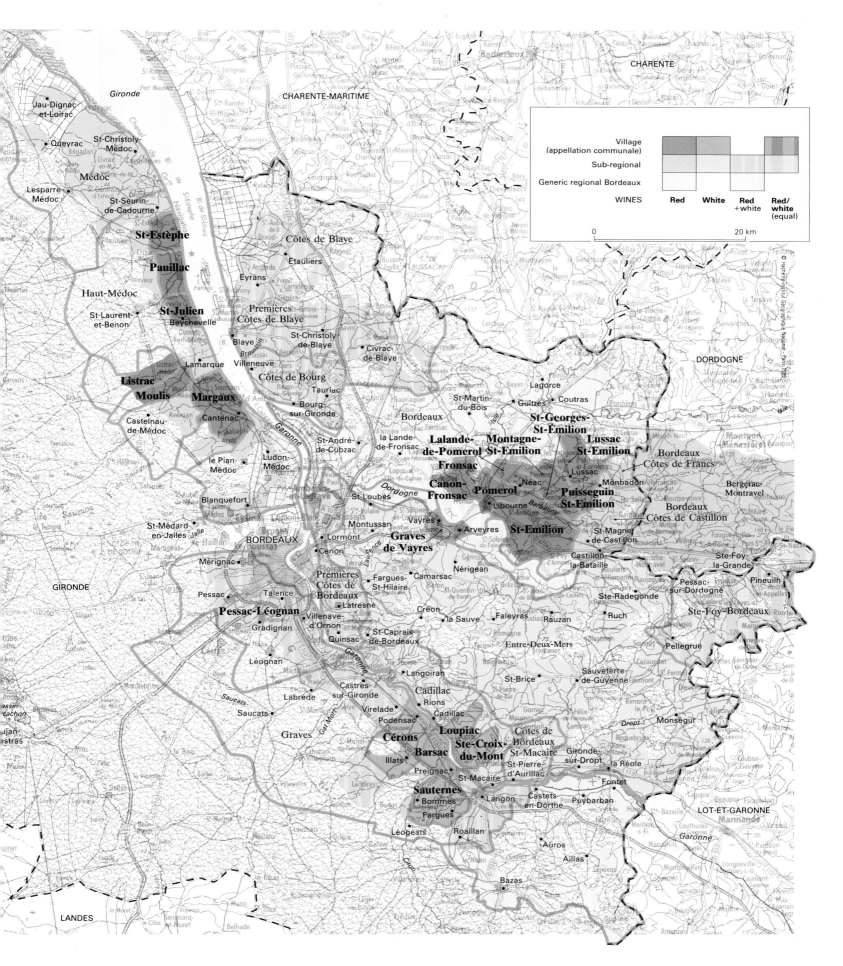

CHARENTE

CHARENTE-MARITIME

Gironde

Jau-Dignac-
et-Loirac

Queyrac

St-Christoly-
Médoc

Médoc

Lesparre-
Médoc

St-Seurin-
de-Cadourne

St-Estèphe

Côtes de Blaye

Etauliers

Pauillac

Eyrans

Haut-Médoc

St-Laurent-
et-Benon

St-Julien
Beychevelle

Premières
Côtes de Blaye

Blaye

St-Christoly-
de-Blaye

Lamarque

Villeneuve

DORDOGNE

Civrac-
de-Blaye

Listrac
Moulis

Margaux

Côtes de Bourg

Tauriac

Lagorce

Coutras

Castelnau-
de-Médoc

Cantenac

Bourg-
sur-Gironde

St-Martin-
du-Bois

Guîtres

Bordeaux

St-Georges-
St-Émilion

Bordeaux
Côtes de Francs

Ludon-
Médoc

le Pian-
Médoc

St-André-
de-Cubzac

la Lande-
de-Fronsac

Lalande-
de-Pomerol
Fronsac

Montagne-
St-Emilion

Lussac
St-Emilion

Lussac

Monbadon

Bergerac-
Montravel

St-Aubin-
de-Médoc

Blanquefort

St-Loubès

Canon-
Fronsac

Pomerol

Néac

Puisseguin
St-Emilion

Bordeaux
Côtes de Castillon

St-Médard-
en-Jalles

Montussan

Vayres

Libourne

St-Emilion

St-Magne-
de-Castillon

Graves
de Vayres

Arveyres

Castillon-
la-Bataille

Ste-Foy-
la-Grande

BORDEAUX

Lormont

Cenon

Nérigean

Mérignac

Pineuilh

GIRONDE

Pessac

Talence

Premières
Côtes de
Bordeaux

Fargues-
St-Hilaire

Camarsac

Ste-Radegonde

Pessac-
sur-Dordogne

Ste-Foy-Bordeaux

Pessac-Léognan

Latresne

Créon

la Sauve

Faleyras

Rauzan

Ruch

Pellegrue

Villenave-
d'Ornon

Gradignan

Quinsac

St-Caprais-
de-Bordeaux

Entre-Deux-Mers

Léognan

Romagne

Sauveterre-
de-Guyenne

Langoiran

St-Brice

St-Pierre-
de-Bat

Labrède

Castres-
sur-Gironde

Cadillac

Rions

Graves

Saucats

Virelade

Podensac

Cadillac

Côtes de
Bordeaux

Monségur

Cérons

Loupiac

St-Macaire

Barsac

Ste-Croix-
du-Mont

St-Pierre-
d'Aurillac

Gironde-
sur-Dropt

la Réole

Illats

Preignac

St-Macaire

Fontet

Sauternes

Bommes

Langon

Castets-
en-Dorthe

Puybarban

Fargues

LOT-ET-GARONNE

Léogeats

Roaillan

Marmande

Auros

Garonne

Bazas

Aillas

LANDES

Village (appellation communale)					
Sub-regional					
Generic regional Bordeaux					

WINES   Red   White   Red +white   Red/ white (equal)

0   20 km

THE LEGACY

ALTHOUGH the Bordeaux wine region owes a great deal to its natural situation, it has also been fortunate in its history. It is possible to date its origins almost to the day as, most unusually, these can be linked with a specific historical event. Historians all agree about this, though there is some disagreement about the date itself.

A FRUITFUL UNION

SOME think it should be 1152, the date of the marriage between the duchess Eleanor of Aquitaine and Henry Plantagenet, the future Henry II of England. This powerful union between England and Gascony was to be of crucial importance. Other historians claim that the real beginning was later, in 1224, when La Rochelle was captured by French royal troops. Until then, La Rochelle had been the essential port for shipping between England and Aquitaine, but this trade was now transferred to Bordeaux. With its rival out of action, the capital of Gascony became London's sole supplier for more than two centuries. Wine at that time was much sought after, as tea, coffee and chocolate, favourite drinks in today's Britain, had not yet come to Europe.

The Bordeaux region was then organized in accordance with the demands of the English market and vine-growing started to expand. It is rare in history to find such complete agreement between the interests of a king and those of his subjects, both peasantry and Bordeaux townspeople. Far from regarding themselves as under occupation, the people of Gascony had a very clear understanding of the advantages this Anglo–Gascon union could bring them. The whole countryside was planted with vines. Along the Garonne, the Dordogne and the Gironde, little river ports developed for transporting wine in sailing barges to Bordeaux and Libourne. Every year, at Easter and in the autumn, a great fleet of ships would take to sea and, after skirting the many dangers of the Breton peninsula, would cross the Channel on separate routes for the ports of London, Bristol and Hull. The volume of cargo was impressive: between 50 and 100 casks per year (450,000 to 900,000 hl). The trade between Bordeaux and England added up to the heaviest maritime traffic of the medieval period, the equivalent in its day of modern oil cargoes.

THE INFLUENCE OF DUTCH TASTE

TIES with Holland, although a less familiar story, have also made an important contribution to the development of the Gironde wine industry. In the seventeenth century the Dutch played a significant part, not simply as the largest buyers of wine from the South-west, but also because of all the technical and commercial reforms triggered by their demands. They bought wine at every level of quality, from the very finest down to the basic white wine used in distilling brandy. Bordeaux growers were thus encouraged to expand onto new sites and to initiate systematic ranking and classification for the region. Wines began to be described as Graves or Médoc, or as grown in Côtes or Palus districts. The custom gradually grew up of classifying first parishes, then individual estates, according to merit. In the eighteenth century, the English aristocracy was taking a great interest in fine wine and this in its turn encouraged Médoc and Sauternes

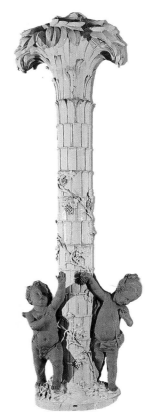

Stove decoration made by the Henry pottery in Rouen, 1780 (Musée des Arts Décoratifs, Bordeaux).

growers to age their wine in oak casks, and subsequently also in bottles for the Dutch market.

These beginnings were to culminate in the great wine region we know today. Its quality was to be officially acknowledged in 1855 with the 'Imperial' classification system, and in the twentieth century with the establishment of *appellations* and rankings.

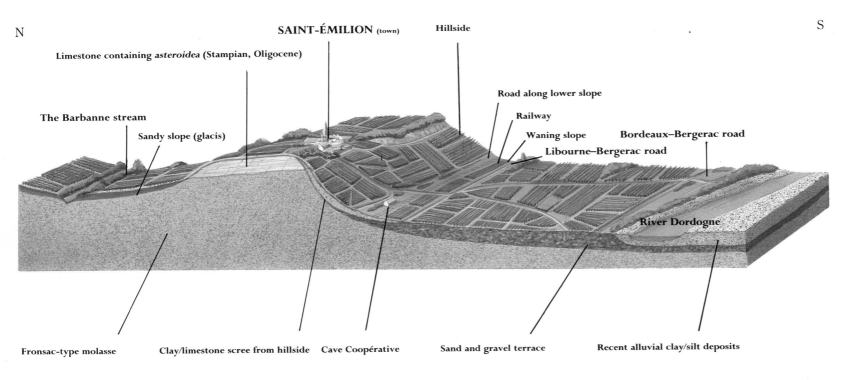

N   S

SAINT-ÉMILION (town)

Hillside

Limestone containing *asteroidea* (Stampian, Oligocene)

Road along lower slope

Railway

The Barbanne stream

Waning slope

Bordeaux–Bergerac road

Sandy slope (glacis)

Libourne–Bergerac road

River Dordogne

Fronsac-type molasse   Clay/limestone scree from hillside   Cave Coopérative   Sand and gravel terrace   Recent alluvial clay/silt deposits

BORDEAUX REGIONAL *APPELLATIONS*

THE area for the Bordeaux regional *appellations* (red, dry white, rosé, *clairet* and sparkling wine) and for Bordeaux Supérieur is not quite as extensive as the Gironde *département*, although often assumed to coincide with it. The damp valley bottoms and the sandy soils of the Landes pine forests are deliberately excluded from the *appellation*. These omissions are necessary so that wine quality can be guaranteed by reliable soils and sub-soils. In fact, everything is based on one simple principle: all Gironde sites suitable for growing vines are entitled to the Bordeaux *appellation*.

This apparent simplicity conceals extraordinary variety. The regional *appellations* cover more than 30,000 hectares and extend for 100 km, so it is obvious that Bordeaux is being produced on many different types of terrain. Certain regions, such as *palus* (recent alluvial deposits near rivers) and parts of the Libournais, may not be entitled to a specific *appellation*;

The Sauvignon grape: this and Sémillon are used for white Bordeaux.

Bordeaux and Bordeaux Supérieur may be produced in regions with an independent white wine *appellation*, such as Entre-Deux-Mers or Sauternes; on the other hand, some white wine is produced in regions with a red wine *appellation*, notably in the Médoc, where the yield is very small but of good quality and long-standing reputation. All Bordeaux vineyards, whether they are set comfortably in the plain or on steep limestone slopes and hilltops, have to follow rigorous rules covering yield and choice of grape. For red wines only six varieties, all classic, are permitted: Cabernet Sauvignon and Cabernet Franc, Carmenère (another local name for Cabernet Sauvignon), Merlot Noir, Malbec (also known as Côt), and Petit Verdot. Planting consists mainly of the two Cabernets and Merlot.

Cabernet-Sauvignon.

The production of regional Bordeaux amounts to more than 300 million bottles per year, and is divided into six *appellations*, all with considerable character.

The largest group, with 220,000 million bottles, includes Bordeaux and Bordeaux Supérieur. Bordeaux needs to be delicate and well balanced, fruity but not too robust, as it is meant for early drinking. Bordeaux Supérieur is not grown in special districts but is made from selected Bordeaux; it differs in its more powerful, full-bodied character and improved ageing capacity derived from high-quality grapes and very careful vinification.

Rosés and *clairets* are produced in smaller quantities (2 million bottles), and are pleasantly refreshing wines to be drunk within the year. *Clairets* are made by macerating red wine grapes for a short time and have a deeper colour than rosés.

With better wine-making techniques, dry white Bordeaux (85 million bottles) has been improving recently, and has a distinctively lively, fruity character. There is also a limited

Merlot.

production of a full sweet white Bordeaux Supérieur.

Finally, white and rosé sparkling wines (2.5 million bottles) are produced by the champagne method.

COUNTLESS CHÂTEAUX

THE famous '*mille châteaux*' ('thousand châteaux') title for the region derives from the innumerable estates of varying sizes scattered throughout the vast area of Bordeaux regional *appellations*. Some of these châteaux are genuinely large and impressive like the Château du Bouilh, a monumental though unfinished building in classical style. However, most of the others are no more than comfortable bourgeois homes or simple farmhouses, such as the typical low houses known locally as *échoppes*. These are on a modest human scale which makes them all the more attractive. Their owners, who often come from a long line of wine-growers, spend the summer working among the vines and the winter looking after their cellars. The reputation of these so-called *petits châteaux* ('little châteaux') is linked to the expansion of estate bottled wine, which has been made easier by advances in wine-making technology.

RICH HISTORY, PRESTIGIOUS WINE

A remarkable feature of these regions is the richness of both historical and natural heritage. One has only to think of the fortresses at both Bourg and Blaye, the prehistoric cave of Pair-non-Pair and the landscape of the Gironde Corniche. This heritage is highly valued by local people, who have made very successful use of history in promoting their wines to tourists, especially at the Clos de l'Echaugette, a prestige vineyard planted at the base of the Blaye citadel, and through the selection of Bourg as the site of the European Conference of Wine Regions.

GRAPE VARIETIES USED FOR RED BORDEAUX

BORDEAUX wines, particularly the reds, are not usually based on a single grape variety. The basic grape is Cabernet-Sauvignon or Cabernet-Franc, depending on the region. Traditionally this was supplemented by Merlot, whose low acidity softened the wine in years of poor ripening, and by the more acid Malbec and Petit Verdot for freshness in hot years. In fairly recent times, the trend towards softer wines and technical improvements in keeping wines with low acidity have caused Petit Verdot and Malbec to disappear and Merlot to be grown more widely. Merlot and Cabernet are complementary varieties. The former crops erratically, as a tendency to coulure damage sometimes prevents grapes from forming. It ripens easily, even in cold soils, but is susceptible to rot. Wines made from Merlot are robust without being too assertive, develop quickly and are soon ready to drink. Cabernet-Sauvignon needs the best soil if it is to ripen properly, but is not much affected by rot. High tannin content means that Cabernet wines require several years to develop their full potential.

MÉDOC

IN the Médoc the vines have been lined up in well-groomed rows, rather like soldiers on parade. There is even a rose bush to finish off each row with a touch of colour, like a flourish of braid on a uniform. In the background, trees cluster round châteaux in which sober classical architecture or even some fanciful hotchpotch of styles manages to suggest grandeur.

Countless similar details contribute to the image of the Médoc as a prestigious producer of wine. This image has been carried throughout the world on wine labels, in books and catalogues, newspaper articles and television programmes, and is now so familiar that it has become a cliché which no longer expresses the whole truth.

The picture may be glamorous, but the Médoc cannot be pinned down so easily. It should not be forgotten that the Médoc peninsula is a land of contrasts, where a few miles take you from *pignada* (pine forest) to marshes and polders on the banks of the Gironde. Within this very mixed landscape, vines occupy only a small strip some 5 to 12 km wide alongside the estuary.

CONTROVERSIAL GEOLOGY

THIS strip of vine-growing land is narrow, not because history or the local growers have happened to make it so, but because the only favourable sites run in a very constricted band from Blanquefort to Saint-Vivien on very distinctive terrain consisting of many gravel outcrops. These derive from the Pyrenees and, to a lesser extent, from the Massif Central, and were deposited by rivers which were precursors of the present Garonne and Dordogne.

Above, the windmill at Château La Tour Haut-Caussan.
Below right, a poster by Cappiello, 1905 (Arts Décoratifs library, Paris).

The gravel deposits are so extensive that some geologists have claimed that they must have been transported by the huge flows caused by torrential downpours or mass melting of glaciers. To put it simply, it used to be thought that there were two main periods when gravel was deposited in the Bordeaux region: first, during the Pliocene or Upper Tertiary period when violent torrential phenomena cut huge gullies in the Pyrenean mountainsides and caused rivers of debris (gravels, sands and green clays) to be swept towards the Bordeaux region; and, secondly, in the Günz glacial period of the Quaternary, when gravels were transported and deposited by the original Garonne and Dordogne rivers. In fact, as recent research has shown, the truth is perhaps more complicated. It now seems that the old 'catastrophe' scenario of vast sheets of material flowing down from the Pyrenees is all in the imagination, and that what really happened was a slow process of alluvial build-up which formed gravel into low hills, followed by inversion of relief. This process was caused by a succession of small rivers predating the Garonne and was continued throughout the Quaternary period, with results now apparent in the soils of the Gironde. The Gironde was

evidently the right length to encourage the best gravels to be deposited on the left bank, and they accumulated here because this was where tides and river current met.

THE IMPORTANCE OF GRAVEL SOILS

THE distinction between different types of gravel is important for the geologist and also for both the wine expert and amateur: all gravel types are excellent for wine-growing because they encourage good drainage and air circulation, and help to concentrate heat. However, the oldest gravel is less good than that from the Günz era, to use the classic Austrian chronology which is not altogether applicable in the Bordeaux region.

These more recent deposits are mainly close to the estuary, making it easy to understand the Médoc proverb: '*Les meilleures vignes regardent la rivière*' ('The best vines are in sight of the river').

The Médoc and Bordeaux regions are not unique in possessing these gravel soils. It could be said that the best gravel terraces in Europe are those between Saint-Gaudens and Pamiers, at the foot of the Pyrenees. However, there is a considerable difference between these terraces and those in the Médoc: the first have remained as intact layers covered

with silt, while in the Médoc they have been shaped into low-lying rounded hills. As is clear from various points throughout the peninsula such as La Lagune, Le Tertre, Loudenne and Grand-Poujeaux, this configuration is very suitable for vine-growing. Both topography and the balance this gives between soil and subsoil provide excellent conditions for drainage and water supply to the roots. This is certainly one key to the success of the Médoc, although not the only one. Other essential factors are climate, which is especially temperate because of the estuary and Atlantic Ocean nearby, and the choice of the Cabernet Sauvignon and Merlot grape varieties, which reach perfect ripeness in this particular environment.

The distinctive Médoc character is revealed in the typical ruby colour of the wine and the fruity bouquet with fragrant overtones of spice and vanilla.

MÉDOC AND HAUT-MÉDOC

APART from the classic villages, there are two sub-regional *appellations* for the area. 'Médoc' is the first of these and, although it can apply to the whole region, it is in fact used only by the villages north of Saint-Seurin de Cadourne. This district to the east of the small town of Lesparre is strongly affected by maritime weather conditions; it produces 175,000 hl of generally well-rounded, fragrant wines, the best of which are grown on isolated low gravel hills.

The Haut-Médoc *appellation* covers the area between Saint-Seurin and Blanquefort and has an output roughly equivalent to that of Médoc of around 155,000 hl per year. However, both soil and wine are superior to Médoc, as is evident from the five *crus classés* in the area. There are more gravelly hills here and a higher proportion of Cabernet Sauvignon is grown: these two factors give the remarkable refinement and powerful tannin, and hence the exceptional ageing potential which has made Médoc wine, and especially the village *appellations*, so famous.

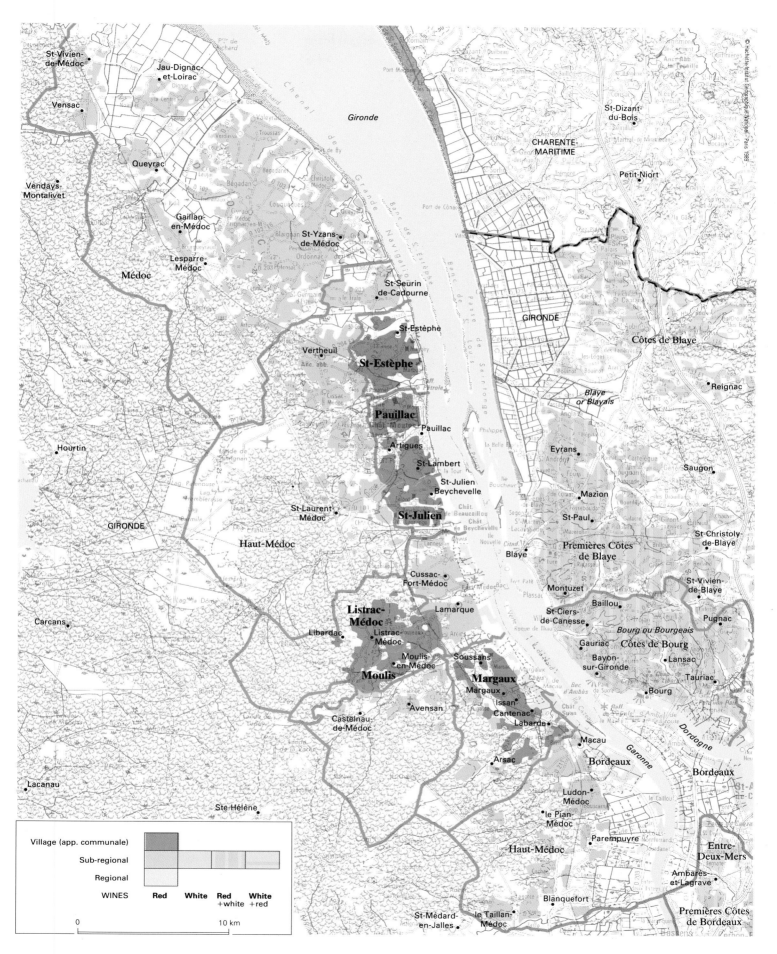

St-Vivien-
de-Médoc

Vensac

Vendays-
Montalivet

Queyrac

Gaillan-
en-Médoc

Lesparre-
Médoc

Médoc

Hourtin

St-Vivien-
de-Médoc

Jau-Dignac-
et-Loirac

Gironde

St-Dizant-
du-Bois

CHARENTE-
MARITIME

Petit-Niort

St-Yzans-
de-Médoc

St-Seurin-
de-Cadourne

St-Estèphe

Vertheuil

St-Estèphe

GIRONDE

Côtes de Blaye

Reignac

Blaye
or Blayais

Pauillac

Pauillac

Artigues

St-Lambert
la Tour

St-Julien
Beychevelle

St-Laurent-
Médoc

Chât.
Beaucaillou
Chât
de Beychevelle

St-Julien

Eyrans

Mazion

St-Paul

Saugon

St-Christoly-
de-Blaye

GIRONDE

Haut-Médoc

Blaye

Premières Côtes
de Blaye

Carcans

Cussac-
Fort-Médoc

Montuzet

Baillou

St-Vivien-
de-Blaye

Pugnac

Listrac-
Médoc

Libardac

Listrac-
Médoc

Lamarque

St-Ciers-
de-Canesse

Bourg ou Bourgeais

Gauriac

Côtes de Bourg

Lansac

Moulis-
en-Médoc

Soussans

Bayon-
sur-Gironde

Tauriac

Moulis

Margaux

Margaux

Bourg

Avensan

Issan

Cantenac

Labarde

Castelnau-
de-Médoc

Macau

Bordeaux

Garonne

Bordeaux

Arsac

Lacanau

Ludon-
Médoc

le Pian-
Médoc

Dordogne

Entre-
Deux-Mers

Ste-Hélène

Parempuyre

Haut-Médoc

Ambarès-
et-Lagrave

Blanquefort

St-Médard-
en-Jalles

le Taillan-
Médoc

Premières Côtes
de Bordeaux

Village (app. communale)			
Sub-regional			
Regional			

| WINES | **Red** | **White** | **Red + white** | **White + red** |

0   10 km

MARGAUX

AT first sight Margaux is rather disconcerting. With its cluster of nineteenth-century châteaux and group of comfortable houses and cottages, it tries hard to look like a town but cannot quite manage to do so. The whole village is threaded with vineyards and even the church stands on its own among them. Clearly, buildings take second place here to the vines, which dominate local life. Margaux itself is fairly small so the *appellation* area extends over the neighbouring villages of Cantenac, Soussans, Labarde and part of Arsac, and is consequently the largest of the Médoc village *appellations*. It also has the largest output of wine, between 30,000 and 60,000 hl, depending on the year.

The sheer volume may seem surprising and raises the question of how consistent in quality the wine could be. However, the *appellation* applies only to the best sites, not to all of them, and these sites include some of the finest gravel soils in the Bordeaux region. These gravels, together with layers of limestone, marl and sand, give Margaux its remarkably refined nose, balanced structure and excellent ageing potential. These qualities are present in all Margaux, and to a greater extent, of course, in the twenty-three *grands crus classés*.

The gravels take the form of a series of hillocks separated by streams and small valleys, and sometimes by peat bogs and marshland. The higher

Above, Château Margaux.
Left, Château Giscours.

land occasionally shows up in place names: at Arsac, for instance, the Château du Tertre (*tertre* means a mound) is the highest point in the village (24 m).

After crossing the Moulinat stream to the east, you come to a second series of small hills and the eighteenth-century Château d'Angludet, a country retreat in a delightfully romantic leafy setting.

FROM LABARDE TO SOUSSANS

A relatively low-lying area of woods and marshes then leads to Labarde, a small village which is unusual in that some 66 per cent of the wine is produced by three large growers, at Giscours, Dauzac and Siran. Labarde wines are grown on Günzian and Pyrenean gravel soils, and have all the aromatic intensity typical of Margaux. Giscours, the best known of the local châteaux, also has extensive fishing in a huge lake surrounded by wooded parkland. This was dug some years ago to give better natural drainage on the estate. The château and its dependencies, the staff cottages and all the

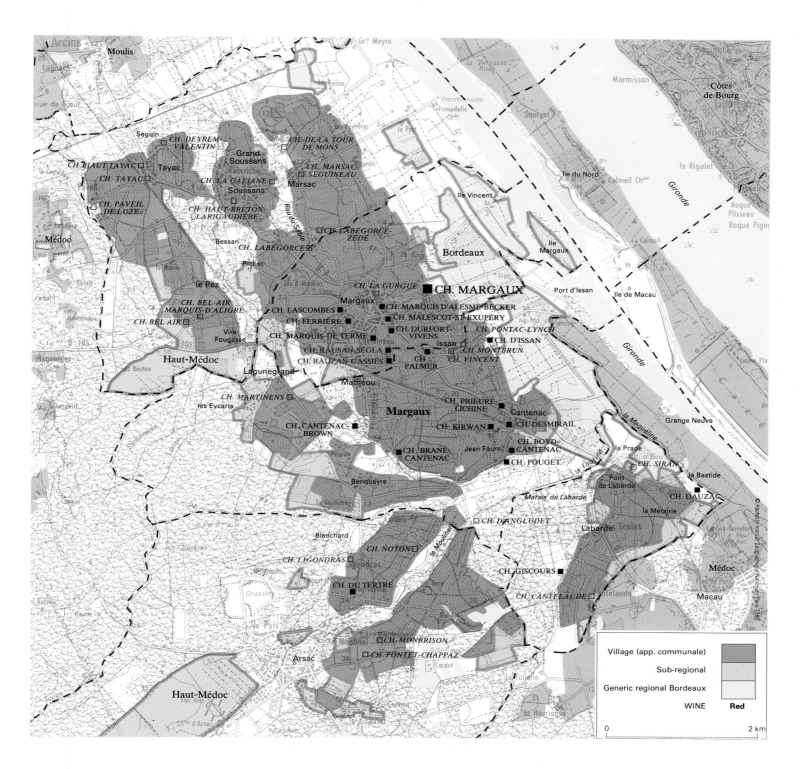

Village (app. communale)

Sub-regional

Generic regional Bordeaux

WINE   **Red**

0   2 km

buildings for making and storing wine show just how wealthy the Médoc wine industry was in the late nineteenth century.

Unlike Labarde, the village of Soussans, in the northern part of the Margaux district, is dominated by small growers. Plots are very fragmented, especially in the western part of the commune. There are one or two exceptions, but this is basically a village of peasant owners cultivating land that is less sloping and more low-lying than elsewhere in Margaux.

Soussans is a perfect example of a Médoc rural community. Dotted round the village, but separated by woods and vines, are no fewer than six hamlets: Le Pez, Bessan-Richet, Marsac (bigger than the main village), Grand Soussans, Bourriche and Tayac-Seguin. Each hamlet has its so-called château, usually a vast nineteenth-century affair which

almost amounts to a village in itself, with estate cottages and work buildings all clustered around the main house.

It is clear that Margaux has a fairly complex infrastructure. However small the business, three out of four growers mature and bottle their own wine. This shows just how intense the concern for quality is, not just in the best known vineyards, but throughout Margaux.

THE CENTRAL VILLAGES

CANTENAC and Margaux are the two villages that make up the core of the *appellation*. This extends over a series of small rises providing exceptionally good conditions for growing vines, as is evident from the large number of *crus classés* (eighteen of them).

The rising ground derives from remains of a Quaternary terrace formed by a long series of massive Garonne floods which washed down pebbles and gravels in a matrix of sand and silt, mainly from the Pyrenees but also from the Massif Central. These stones have been smoothed and polished over the years, to a degree that makes them dazzling in wet weather, although a geologist can still

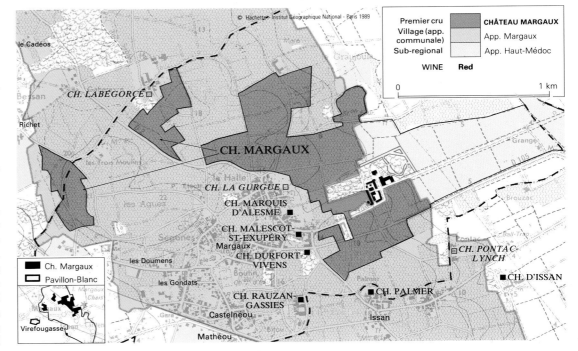

Left, Château Palmer: the building dates from 1856 but the vineyards have been well known since the early eighteenth century.

the left bank of the Garonne and the Gironde, distinctive characteristics are brought out on different sites, and soils are ranked according to quality.

CHÂTEAU MARGAUX, CHÂTEAU PALMER AND CHÂTEAU ISSAN

NOT surprisingly, the most favourable site is that of the Château Margaux vineyards, which run in a

pick out black lyddite, the deep marbled green of Pyrenean sandstone, white and bluish quartz from the Limousin region, and brown and black flints, probably from Périgord.

With very little clay or humus, these soils do not retain water and the roots of vines have to go down deep to find any. The best sites are on well-drained slopes or at the top of small hills where the water table is lowest and the vine root system

therefore needs to be very highly developed. Margaux vines are consequently remarkably drought-resistant, especially old vine-stocks whose roots often reach underground to a depth of several metres. Equally, water from heavy rain quickly sinks in without lingering in the upper levels of the soil where it could drown the vine roots. These are ideal conditions, requiring minimal use of fertilizers; and the larger the particle size of gravel,

the better the soil for producing fine wine. It is the combination of low water table and good soil permeability that gives vines a very deep layer of soil for growth and makes the Margaux *grand cru* sites so remarkable.

Apart from the marshes and the edges of the Landes, the whole of the Margaux and Cantenac district is suitable for producing wine of the highest quality. But, as everywhere on

prices. At Issan, for instance, there is the Château Vincent *cru bourgeois* surrounded by Palmer vineyards, and the

broken arc to the east and north of the village, between the château itself and the district of La Bégorce. Another look at place names throws light on the exceptional character of Château Margaux. There is a piece of land called Puch Sem Peyre, a Gascon name which means 'well with no stones', presumably because the vast number of pebbles meant that there was no need to put stones round the well. The pebbles here are smaller than further north at Saint-Julien and Pauillac, but the immense profusion makes up for their small size. This is not the only unusual feature of Château Margaux: it also has a limestone subsoil and a remarkable position on the eastern edge of the plateau.

South from Château Margaux there follow the two estates of Château Palmer and Château Issan, which are also remarkably well situated. The slight slope ensures excellent natural drainage and a good supply of rainwater to the vine roots. Issan was founded in medieval times and is one of the oldest estates in the region. For a long time it was called La Mothe de Cantenac, just as Château Margaux was once La Mothe Margaux. This is not all they have in common. Although the two châteaux are very different – Issan is a charming early seventeenth-century building while Margaux is imposingly neoclassical – they are both situated at points where vine slopes run down into low-lying countryside. This is because both are on the site of former medieval fortresses built to watch out for invaders sailing up the estuary.

A site similar to the two estates just described, although it faces the Labarde marshes rather than the estuary, is the southern edge of the Cantenac plateau where there are a number of well-known vineyards, including Pouget and Brane-Cantenac. The latter sits astride two excellent types of terrain: the plateau edge and the top of the ridge bearing the other Margaux *deuxièmes crus classés*, Rausan-Ségla, Rauzan-Gassies, Durfort-Vivens and Lascombes. This central sector of Margaux is not completely given up to *crus classés*, however.

Top, Château Issan.
Above, Château Rausan-Ségla.

There are a number of smaller estates among the aristocrats, and for winelovers these are a source of high-quality wine at very reasonable prices.

unclassed estate of Trois Chardons on the boundaries of Rausan-Ségla, Palmer and Brane. The existence of wines such as these is a great advantage, as it enables Margaux to offer a whole range extending beyond the *grands crus classés*.

MÉDOC DIAMONDS

ACCORDING to local tradition, the Comte d'Hargicourt is supposed to have appeared at the court of Louis XVI dressed in a coat with buttons glittering like precious stones. When the King expressed surprise at such wealth, the Count replied that he was wearing 'diamonds' from his estate. The same story is told at Latour about the Marquis de Ségur, so no doubt it is a fabrication, but d'Hargicourt's answer is not so improbable: quartz pebbles from the Médoc gravel were cut and polished and were used in those days for jewellery.

MOULIS runs in a surprisingly narrow ribbon to the west of the other villages and relatively far from the estuary. It is the least extensive of the Médoc *appellations*, covering only 350 hectares, but has much that a traveller would find both interesting and delightful.

SMALL BUT NOT SIMPLE

THIS small *appellation* has some puzzling features, although these can be readily explained. The countryside here is slightly more undulating, in a way that stands out from the rest of the region. The reason for this lies underground: tectonic movements beneath the Moulis territory have produced an anticline unusual in the Médoc subsoil. The underground

folding here has pushed up layers of limestone to form a dome, while elsewhere the layers have remained horizontal.

This configuration of the subsoil, also present in Listrac, is not especially obvious from the surface topography. Oddly enough, the anticlinal dome centred on Peyrelebade in Listrac has been worn by erosion into a basin-shaped depression.

MOULIS-EN-MÉDOC

Grape picking in Bordeaux.

VARIED SOILS...

BECAUSE of this accident of geology the *appellation* enjoys a wide range of soils. In the middle, next to the village of Moulis itself, are areas of clay/limestone. East of the village is a considerable stretch of fine ridges of Garonne gravels, including Grand-Poujeaux, Meaucaillou and Brillette. The two first have excellent drainage on well-defined slopes and have given rise to some well-known vineyards,

The soils of the central Médoc.

one being Château Chasse-Spleen, which is said to have earned this name because Byron claimed that its wine drove away spleen or melancholy.

Lastly, on the west side of the *appellation*, towards Bouqueyran, there is a small area spanning both the anticlinal slope and the ridge overlooking the basin formed by the inverted dome. These sites are also suitable for vines: the slope has Pyrenean gravel consisting of small pebbles like those of the Graves area; the ridge has a limestone crest over a layer of marl,

and provides a typical hill site, here indented by erosion which has created even better drainage conditions.

...AND VARIED WINES

VARIED growing conditions have led to the use of a number of different grape varieties. These are grown in the following proportions: Cabernet Sauvignon 50 to 70 per cent, Merlot 20 to 40 per cent, and Cabernet Franc 5 to 10 per cent, together occasionally with 5 per cent of Petit Verdot which is suitable in certain microclimates. Although there are only about thirty growers in the area, Moulis offers plenty of variety. Wines may vary from typical basic Médoc, like that produced on the flat gravel sites in the east, to something more full-bodied and rustic. All of them are intensely aromatic and age well.

— 10.5 km —

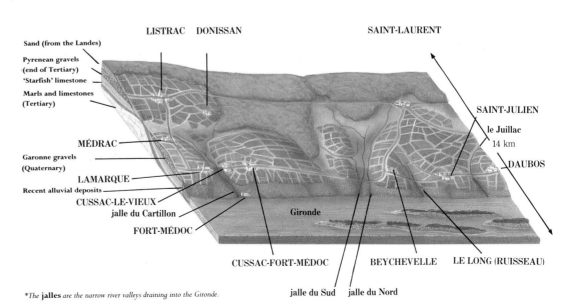

Sand (from the Landes)
Pyrenean gravels (end of Tertiary)
'Starfish' limestone
Marls and limestones (Tertiary)

LISTRAC   DONISSAN   SAINT-LAURENT

MÉDRAC

Garonne gravels (Quaternary)

LAMARQUE
Recent alluvial deposits
CUSSAC-LE-VIEUX
jalle du Cartillon
FORT-MÉDOC

Gironde

SAINT-JULIEN
le Juillac
14 km
DAUBOS

CUSSAC-FORT-MÉDOC   BEYCHEVELLE   LE LONG (RUISSEAU)

jalle du Sud   jalle du Nord

*The **jalles** are the narrow river valleys draining into the Gironde.*

A FRINGE OF VINEYARDS

THE name of Listrac means 'edge' or 'fringe', which gives some idea of the way the village lies between vineyards and woodland. The boundary edge of vine growing extends much further west than in other parts of the Médoc. A driver on the N215 through Listrac would see this very clearly. Before and after this section, the road passes through flat country-side with no vines, whereas between Bouqueyran and Listrac the hills are covered with them. It is clear too that the line of hills at this point lies much further west than the road.

The vineyards visible from the

main road cover the western side of the inverted Listrac dome. As at Moulis, this consists of a plateau of old gravel soils, bordered at Listrac itself by a strongly indented ridge. Here the suitable vine-growing sites are more extensive than at Moulis.

The same is true of the Peyrelebade plain, which is in the middle of the *appellation* area and the largest district within it. It coincides with the in-verted dome formation, on clay/

limestone soils over beds of lime-stone. This is a landscape that attracted and inspired the artist Odi-lon Redon, who wrote: 'I cannot tell you how much I was affected by leav-ing the old house at Peyrelebade, where all the most passionate, deeply felt and spontaneous elements of my work first came into being.'

Lastly, in the east and north, there are more ridges of Garonne gravel – here much less extensive than at Moulis. The best known is at Médrac, on a northerly extension of the Grand Poujeaux plateau.

Listrac covers an area of 550 hec-tares, more than Moulis to the south, and a larger number of growers are active here. More than 150 families, 99 of them vineyard owners, make a living from growing vines, but they

produce some consistent wine in spite of their number. Listrac has an instantly recognizable firmness and body with fine deep colour and plenty of tannin. They are 'chewy' wines, whose slightly closed character and harshness in youth need a few years to mellow.

The influence of the extensive cen-tral area of clay/limestone is one reason for the consistency of these wines and explains their tough, vigor-ous character. A second reason is the amount of Merlot grown – quite high proportions for the Médoc. Con-sistent quality has also been ensured by the local Cave Coopérative, which was founded to cope with the slump in the thirties, and has contributed to expansion by finding unusual outlets for their wine. One such outlet was the

Wagons-Lits company, which pro-vided a brilliant opportunity to take revenge on the local Médoc railways, which just touch on the eastern fringes of the district without coming as far as Listrac itself.

Today the reputation of Listrac has certainly spread beyond the French railways. New drive has come from the Château Clarke wine centre and from a younger generation of enterprising growers.

The Cave Coopérative had the idea of offering half-bottles to the Wagons-Lits service, and now in the Com-pany's handsome dark blue and gold carriages Listrac is served against all the panoply of fine linen, china and silver, and beside some of the very grandest wines.

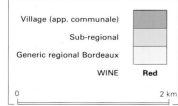

Village (app. communale)	
Sub-regional	
Generic regional Bordeaux	
WINE	Red

0   2 km

SAINT-JULIEN

IT is best to come to Saint-Julien by the *route des Vins*, travelling in the traditional direction from Bordeaux to Pauillac. Arriving in the region from this direction gives one of the best views in the whole of the Médoc. After passing through a strangely evocative landscape of marshy flatlands, the road climbs fairly steeply to reach the splendid estate of Beychevelle.

TWO IN ONE

THE château is a most imposing and elegant eighteenth-century building, which forms a magnificent introduction to Saint-Julien, one of the most aristocratic *appellations* in Bordeaux if not in France. It is also a reminder that the small Médoc village of Saint-Julien has a split personality, as shown in the commune's official double-barrelled name of Saint-Julien-Beychevelle, which is closer to the reality than plain Saint-Julien. In fact there are two villages of roughly the same size. Saint-Julien's church makes it look slightly more prominent, although both church and square stand modestly back from the main road. However, the *appellation* as a whole has a unified character which comes from homogeneous soils extending over a relatively small area, just over 700 hectares. The Beychevelle marshland cuts a slice some 4 km long through the district and separates Cussac from the gravelly plateau of Saint-Julien. The latter forms a tract 3.5 km long by about the same distance wide stretching alongside the Gironde, and consists of ridges indented by a series of small valleys. The soils are Garonne gravel (from the Günz Ice Age) on a gradual west to east slope, 22 m high where it borders on the wooded Landes, down to 16 m beside the marshland. This configuration provides good natural drainage, further emphasized by fairly

Above, Château Gruaud-Larose.
Below, Château Langoa.

Gateway into the walled vineyard of Léoville-Lascases.

steep convex slopes at the plateau edges.

All these conditions combine to produce good vine-growing terrain. The subsoil here is also very homogeneous, consisting of Ludian

THE WITCHES' SABBATH

BEYCHEVELLE is the Gascon version of baisse-voile (lower sail) and gets its name from the fact that ships had to strike sail when they reached a point level with the old fortress there. This incidentally gave the authorities the chance to levy a toll. The position of Beychevelle gave it strategic importance; it also had a rather sinister reputation, both in the Médoc and Aquitaine as a whole. It was in the Prat-Lauret, a broad meadow beside the castle, that witches and other demonic creatures were said to take part in Satanic orgies. A number of legends grew up around these supposed revels, including the story of Telet, a white horse which would fly in from further up the Gironde and carry away the Médoc witches.

limestone sediment (Saint-Estèphe limestone). The vine roots, especially those of the oldest stocks, can thus penetrate a very long way down in search of nourishment and water, right down to the upper level of the water table.

THE *GRANDS CRUS*

THESE soil qualities explain how the *grands crus classés* have come to be so important here, a fact visible in the landscape itself. Huge plantations of vines cover the countryside in a grid of regular lines stretching relentlessly up and down hills. It is obvious too that no peasants could have built these vast châteaux, some of which are of positively monumental size. This is clearly true of Château Beychevelle, a dignified single-storey building, long and low, with a pavilion at each end. This is rightly considered to be one of the finest country houses in Aquitaine. It was built in 1757 for the Duc d'Epernon, who was then Governor of the province of Guyenne and a Grand Admiral of France, and is a most successful example of a *chartreuse*, one of the elegant country retreats built by eminent Bordeaux citizens in the

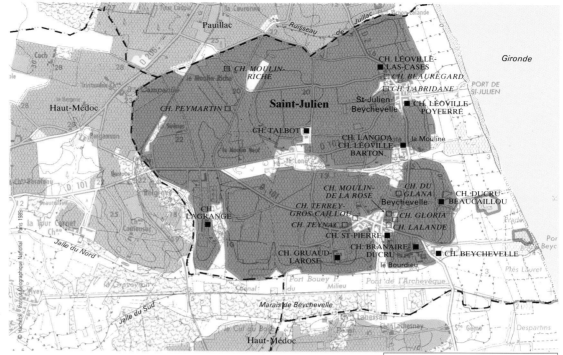

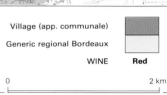

Village (app. communale)
Generic regional Bordeaux

WINE   **Red**

0   2 km

eighteenth century. Its terrace and formal French gardens, together with all the dependent buildings for wine-making, are all delightfully characteristic of the period. For all these reasons Beychevelle should certainly be visited, as well as for its importance in wine history and local legend (see inset).

Other châteaux should certainly be mentioned for their architecture, even if it does not quite come up to that of Beychevelle. However, it is the vineyards that really matter. On the southern edge of the region, above the marshes, are four *crus classés*: running from east to west, these are Branaire-Ducru, Gruaud-Larose,

Lagrange and Saint-Pierre. The lower, eastern edge, looking over *palus* pastureland, has three *grands crus*: Beychevelle, Ducru-Beaucaillou and Langoa. Finally, the northern edge is dominated by the three Léoville estates, including the walled vineyard of Lascases on a splendid isolated ridge just below the village of Saint-Julien.

At their best, all the Saint-Julien wines are a combination of Margaux refinement with Pauillac substance. This does not mean they have no character of their own. On the contrary, they are remarkable for their depth of colour, elegance and vigour. Their reputation and the emphasis on *crus classés* (75 per cent of the 5.5 million bottles produced each year) might encourage fears that Saint-Julien was inaccessibly expensive. Even though the *appellation* concentrates on *grands crus*, there are fortunately still a few pocket-sized vineyards on good gravel soils where peasant owners produce good wine at reasonable prices.

Château Beychevelle, an elegant eighteenth-century country house.

PAUILLAC

FROM the first sight of Pauillac it is clear that it is different from the other Médoc communes. Perhaps this is because, apart from the resorts along the Atlantic coast, it is the only town of any size in the peninsula which does not turn its back on the estuary.

LIFE ON THE RIVER

THE map shows this very clearly: the villages of Margaux, Saint-Julien, Saint-Estèphe, as well as Macau, Lamarque and Saint-Seurin de Cadourne among others, all seem to shun the banks of the Gironde. In Pauillac, on the other hand, rather than take refuge inland behind the natural barrier formed by marshland and *palus*, the inhabitants have chosen to cooperate with their river, a rather inadequate name for what amounts to an inland sea.

Activity is focused on the broad quays where stretches of grass give an oddly pastoral appearance. The little town lies halfway between Bordeaux and Pointe de Grave and its function as a port has always been important in its social and economic life. It started life as a port, and in its heyday carriage excursions to watch transatlantic ships steaming up the estuary were a favourite amusement for local land-owners and their families. There were many great social and sporting occasions such as the regattas when the river swarmed with splendid ocean racers.

CONDITIONS IN THE VINEYARDS

IN spite of the present-day marina, the fine river-front and the seafood cafés where you can eat tiny shrimps called *bichettes*, the importance of the harbour has declined with the ascendancy of wine. Pauillac has eighteen *crus classés*, including three *premiers* and two *deuxièmes crus*, and 150 growers declaring crops. It is not only the wine capital of the Médoc but a landmark for the entire wine world.

Like its neighbour Saint-Julien further south, the *appellation* area coincides with that of the commune and has unusually consistent soils throughout. The remarkably good terrain consists of a broad plain slop-ing gently down to the estuary from a high point in the west. The soils are based on very fine outcrops of gravel, transported, as elsewhere in the Médoc, by flooding from the rivers predating the Garonne. These rivers have built up a fine series of ridges overlying clays and Saint-Estèphe limestone. Gravels from different periods appear in varying forms and are identifiable by size, ranging from large pebbles down to finely particled shingle, and by depth of colour.

The successive phases of alluvial build-up followed by erosion have produced slopes that are convex at the top and concave lower down. This profile is also due to accumulations caused by soil creep: water-saturated clays and silts have gravitated to the bottom while larger pebbles have remained wedged higher up. Analysis has shown that finely particled soils are not very abundant here; certainly it is factors like this that have given the Pauillac slopes their unparalleled quality.

The gravel ridges are almost steep enough to count as hills and certainly make the landscape more attractive. In addition there is the narrow Gahet valley along which trains for the harbour used to run. Landforms such as these ensure very good soil drainage, emphasized, as at Saint-Julien, by the relatively high plateau edge facing both across the estuary and also northwards to Saint-Estèphe across the deeply embanked Breuil valley.

THE GREAT ESTATES

THE Pauillac wine region covers a thousand hectares and has a number of contrasting features. Small vineyards certainly exist and are apparent in the fragmented landholdings west of the line of villages between Dauprat and Bages, and again along the main road from Le Pouyalet to Anseillan. These scattered plots could lead in theory to very varied wine, especially with an annual production of 6 million bottles, but this fails to take into account the large Cave Coopérative which vinifies 5,000 hl, the high proportion of Cabernet Sauvignon

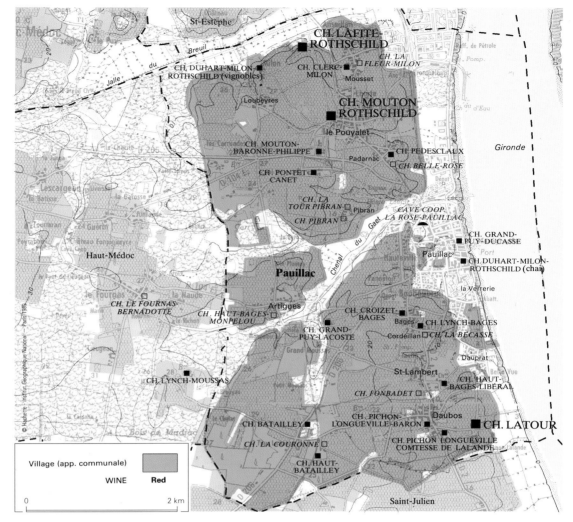

grown (on average 70 per cent for the *crus classés*), and the important rôle of the great estates. The latter are so predominant that small vineyards show up just as tiny pockets round some of the hamlets.

All this has the effect of reinforcing the special character of Pauillac wines. These are firm and robust, with powerful tannin and outstanding longevity, but they have refinement too and it is often these delicate nuances that distinguish individual vineyards.

Left hand page, top, Château Latour; below, Mouton-Rothschild.

Left, beauty and functionalism at Lafite-Rothschild: storage building designed by the contemporary architect Ricardo Bofill.

THE *PREMIERS CRUS*

AS a general rule, the vineyards with the finest reputations lie in the heart of an *appellation*. At Pauillac this is not the case: the prestigious châteaux are scattered all over the region, both north and south of the town. All the *premiers crus classés*, Lafite, Mouton and Latour, are situated round the edges, as are the two *deuxièmes crus*, Pichon-Longueville-Baron and Pichon-Longueville-Comtesse-de-Lalande. This situation has been brought about by the river Gahet, which flows through the middle of Pauillac territory into the estuary north of the town, and has created an enclosed valley forming a focus for erosion. The famous vineyards also have natural drainage in the *jalles*, the narrow river valleys that run alongside them, and in the Gironde itself.

One effect of this is that the best stretches of vineyard land, on the plateaux of Saint-Lambert and Le Pouyalet, share borders with Saint-Julien and Saint-Estèphe. This has led some experts to compare Latour and the two Pichon-Longuevilles with their southern neighbours, particularly the three Léovilles, while Lafite and Mouton are often thought to be similar to Saint-Estèphe, especially Cos d'Estournel. However interesting such comparisons may be, they do not really survive a serious tasting session.

In fact, the dominant feature of Pauillac is consistency of character, a character most perfectly expressed in the *grands crus*. Such consistency could almost certainly be attributed to the high proportion of homogeneous Garonne gravels on both northern and southern plateaux.

LE POUYALET, THE NORTHERN PLATEAU

THE highest point of the region is in the north, at Mouton, where the height of 30 m is rather unusual for the Médoc. Slopes are fairly steep, especially at Lafite, and are covered with medium and fine gravels over subsoils consisting of clayey sand,

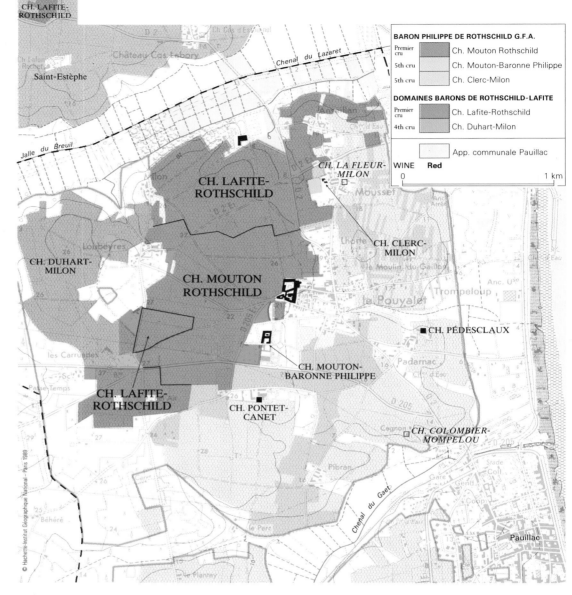

sandy gravel and limestone. It is almost certain that it is the harmonious balance of soil and rock that gives Lafite and Mouton their special character. Certainly it is slight gradations in the subsoil that make Mouton-Rothschild stand out from its southern neighbours, especially those south of the road between Pauillac and Hourtin.

The vineyards at Lafite-Rothschild have an exceptionally well drained situation. The château consists of some splendid buildings dating mainly from the eighteenth century, although without the classical severity of that period. In fact, it looks more like a charming Italian villa. The most impressive part is not the château itself, however, but the unique *chais* where wine is stored and matured. These buildings have now been complemented by magnificent

underground cellars designed by Ricardo Bofill.

In spite of a nineteenth-century château rather lacking in architectural interest, the overall impression of Mouton-Rothschild is attractive and

imposing. The buildings include a museum founded by Baron Philippe de Rothschild, who was noted for his interest in art. When he decided at the age of sixty to found a museum celebrating wine, he chose to have not

dominates the Saint-Lambert region. Its distinctive character also derives from the harmonious balance between the soil, large-pebbled gravel forming broad ridges, and the clay and marl subsoil. Its two neighbours, Pichon-Longueville-Baron and Pichon-Longueville-Comtesse-de-Lalande, are on especially favourable sites drained by the valley of the little river Juillac.

These natural advantages are an essential aspect of Pauillac's success, although they do not entirely explain it. It is notable also that growers here have often shown an interest in the latest technological advances: the barrel fumigation instigated by the Dutch in the eighteenth century, pottery soil drains in the nineteenth, the general use of malolactic fermentation, or, at the present time, the application of advanced computer techniques to the wine industry.

Left hand page, wine maturing in the chais *at Pontet-Canet.*

Left, Château Batailley.

Below, Château Pichon-Longueville-Comtesse-de-Lalande.

one more fashionable collection of bygones but original works of art inspired by wine. The former *chais,* partly underground, were chosen to display these works, which include some splendid pieces in precious metals and ivory, as well as tapestry and paintings. A major work in the museum is a betrothal cup in German silver, copied on Mouton Baron Philippe wine labels. For many years paintings have also been reproduced on Mouton-Rothschild bottles, and the label is always an original work designed each year by a different artist, including Braque, Chagall, Cocteau and Dali.

SAINT-LAMBERT, THE SOUTHERN PLATEAU

THE elegance of Lafite and Mouton is complemented further south by the powerful tannic quality of Latour, the château that undoubtedly

SAINT-ESTÈPHE

suggests a community more firmly rooted in peasant life than the luxurious nineteenth-century châteaux in the southern Médoc.

COS D'ESTOURNEL

THE low-lying countryside consists mainly of grassland and straight rows of fine trees. The soils here are too fertile for vine-growing, but higher up there are vineyards as far as the eye can see. The finest lie along the edge of the low hills, where convex slopes give better exposure to sunlight and excellent natural drainage.

All these favourable conditions are combined in the southernmost district of Saint-Estèphe, at Château Cos d'Estournel. This is famous for the architecture of the *chais* (see inset), and also for excellent soils consisting of Günz gravels.

Other districts in Saint-Estèphe have some fine gravel ridges. One of the best known of these is in the south

THE Church calendar makes no mention of Saint-Estèphe. There are only three parishes dedicated to him, all in the south-west, and the name is usually dismissed as a distorted version of Etienne or Stéphane. However, as a wine *appellation*, it is known all over the world.

A DIFFERENT ASPECT OF THE MÉDOC

AT first sight, the village does not particularly stand out from others in the Médoc. It stands on a plateau overlooking the Gironde and bordered by two streams, the Jalle du Breuil north of Pauillac, and the Estey d'Un south of Saint-Seurin de Cadourne. On the whole it is better to forget the map and the familiar wine route and wander down towards the estuary, where the atmosphere of the coastal marshlands anticipates the Pointe de Grave further up the Médoc peninsula. There are fishermen's huts with nets dangling in the water and hides for pigeon-shooting further inland. All of this

Top, Cos d'Estournel. Above, Château Montrose.

AN ORIENTAL FOLLY

LOUIS Gaspard d'Estournel, who was owner of the Cos estate in the early nineteenth century, had three great passions: horses, sea voyages and wine. He decided to build, not the customary château, but vast chais in a mixture of classical and oriental styles inspired by his travels in the Indian Ocean. The buildings that resulted from this were visited by the novelist Stendhal, who described them enthusiastically: 'This is a most elegant construction, brilliantly coloured in light yellow, and following no particular style; it is neither Greek nor Gothic, but looks very cheerfully in what I suppose to be the Chinese fashion.'

Village (app. communale)

WINE   **Red**

0   2 km

at Marbuzet, the site of a delightful château rather like the White House and of a quiet hamlet where the inhabitants once gathered to fetch their water from the pump. Along the three small hills that form the northern edge of the commune are the châteaux of Le Pez, Le Boscq and Calon-Ségur. Meyney and Montrose overlook the estuary in the east.

Even more conspicuously than further south in the Médoc, these gravels take the form of isolated hillocks surrounded by lower, more clayey terrain. An unusual feature is the presence, under the outer skin of pebbles, of either Saint-Estèphe limestone or *marne à huîtres* (marl containing fossil oysters) in place of the Stampian limestone, the usual sedimentary rock in the Bordeaux region, which has been eroded here. The vine roots are able to penetrate deep down through the different permeable layers in their search for water and nutrients.

The varied, rolling landscape of Saint-Estèphe includes more than a

thousand hectares of vines, with an annual yield of around 70,000 hl. More than a quarter of this comes from the big Cave Coopérative, while the five *crus classés* account for less than 20 per cent. It is clear from these statistics that *crus bourgeois* and small growers must play an important part in producing the varied wines of the region. It is rather more difficult to decide what constitutes a typical wine for Saint-Estèphe than it is for Margaux, Pauillac or Saint-Julien. However, possibly because of the clay subsoil, the local wines have certain elements in common: depth of colour, a certain acidity and exceptional tannic quality. They age extremely well, and after a few years develop great aromatic complexity with a mellow blend of tannins.

'Vendanges dans le Médoc' 'Medoc Wine Harvest', by the nineteenth-century painter Clément Boulanger (Musée des Beaux-Arts, Bordeaux).

PESSAC-LÉOGNAN

The arrival of the harvest at Haut-Brion.

THERE has been considerable indecision over the years about what to call the wines from the northern Graves region. This certainly does not mean that they lacked character, even before they acquired the present Pessac-Léognan *appellation*.

GEOLOGICAL ABERRATIONS

PESSAC-Léognan wines owe this special character to the rocks and soil of the region. They grow on the gravel terraces which are so magnificent a feature of the left bank of the Garonne and the Gironde estuary, but in this particular region the geology is slightly eccentric and has produced an area which is out of character in the Bordeaux landscape. Its unusualness is apparent as soon as one leaves the main routes, which do not penetrate much beyond the fringes of the *appellation* area. Walking through Léognan or Martillac one discovers a countryside with all sorts of ups and downs, and with valleys of an intense green.

This is not exactly hill country, but the land rises enough to seem surprising in such a low-lying region. This configuration was caused by rivers before the Garonne: the earliest of these seem to have branched to the east, leaving alluvial deposits added to by later streams. Subsequent weathering has created secondary gravel formations and these provide favourable sites for the many *crus classés* in the region. Poor soils and very

well-defined gravel ridges, such as those between Malartic-la-Gravière, Fieuzal and the village of Léognan, are exceptionally suitable for vine-growing.

The region also has very good exposure and drainage, with sharply sloping hillsides and an excellent water supply. This favourable natural environment is much more varied than in vineyards north and south of Pessac-Léognan, and white wines clearly do remarkably well on some of these sites.

The great Bordeaux landowners in the period before the Revolution were well aware of the land's possibilities and gradually added more and more of the best plots to their estates. This explains the present complicated pattern of land ownership, made even more awkward by the way some *grand cru* property is wedged into built-up areas of the city. Sometimes the

existence of a small stream or a tiny variation in slope or aspect is enough to transform the value of certain plots. This is very obvious if one visits Haut-Brion in autumn or late winter: even though differences in level are not very marked, vines clearly vary in their stage of development according to the height at which they are grown.

Pessac, Léognan and the ten villages nearby have made the most of their unusual terrain. During the last two decades the production area has expanded from less than 500 hectares to more than 900, with an annual yield of more than 5 million bottles.

PROBLEMS FOR THE FUTURE

ALTHOUGH the area is now at a transitional phase, growers here continue to produce wine in the traditional proportion of 80 per cent red and 20 per cent white. They have also persisted with wine of traditional character, and with their customary grape varieties: predominantly Cabernet Sauvignon with a little Merlot and Cabernet Franc for reds, and Sauvignon with some Sémillon for whites.

The very distinctive character of Pessac-Léognan wine means that it is sometimes even possible to guess the particular plot where certain red wines have been grown. Some of

these have an extraordinarily complex, almost smoky bouquet; others have a Médoc-like tannic quality and the smooth roundness of some Pomerol.

The dry white wines often mature very well when kept in wood, and

Château La Louvière.

develop crisp, delicate aromas of broom and lime-blossom.

Almost 75 per cent of the Pessac-Léognan output is exported, and is very well received abroad. It is unfortunate that such a reputable wine region, which owes its origins to the closeness of Bordeaux, should now be threatened by the expansion of that same city.

Urban development has encroached to such an amazing degree that world-famous châteaux such as Haut-Brion, La Mission Haut-Brion, Laville Haut-Brion and Pape Clément are now completely surrounded by houses, and streets run alongside vines. Perhaps this threat to their existence is the best guarantee for the future, as only focus on quality will prevent vineyards from being engulfed by the suburbs.

La Brède, the favourite home of the writer Montesquieu (1689–1755), who described it as '... Gothic indeed, but set off by a charming park which I have arranged to a plan I discovered in England ... Nature there appears as if rising unadorned from her bed attired only in her dressing-gown.'

BORDEAUX

Premières Côtes
de Bordeaux

CH. PICQUECAILLOU □

CH. LES CARMES
HAUT-BRION

CH. LA MISSION-
HAUT-BRION

CH. HAUT-BRION ■

CH. LATOUR-
HAUT-BRION

CH. LAVILLE-
HAUT-BRION

CH. PAPE-
CLÉMENT ■

Pessac

Talence

Bègles

Village (app. communale)

Generic regional Bordeaux

WINE   **Red**
        +white

0   2 km

CH. BARRET □

CH. DE
ROUILLAC

CH. POUMEY □

Villenave-d'Ornon

CH. PONTAC □

CH. BROWN □

Canéjean

CH. COUHINS ■

Cadaujac

CH. D'OLIVIER □

CH. HANNETOT □

CH. CARBONNIEUX ■

CH. BOUSCAUT ■

DOM. DE
GRAND-MAISON □

CH. COUCHEROY □

CH. LA LOUVIÈRE □

CH. SMITH-
HAUT-LAFITTE ■

CH. LARRIVET-
HAUT-BRION □

CH. HAUT-
BAILLY ■

Léognan

CH. GAZIN □   □ CH. HAUT-BERGEY

CH. MALLEPRAT □

CH. MALARTIC-
LAGRAVIÈRE ■

CH. DOMI □

DOMAINE
DE CHEVALIER ■

CH. DE FRANCE □

CH. LA TOUR
MARTILLAC ■   □ CH. LE FERRAND

CH. DE FIEUZAL ■

CH. HAUT-
GARDÈRE □

Martillac

CH. LAGARDE □

CH. LE SARTRE □

CH. LA SOLITUDE □

CH. HAUT-NOUCHET □

St-Médard-
d'Eyrans

FEW wines have had so much written about them as Sauternes and Barsac. There seems no end to the writers, journalists and historians who have produced some sort of thesis or theory to explain the origins of these certainly rather extraordinary wines.

THE SAUTERNES MYSTERY

SO far nobody has in fact succeeded in pinpointing the beginnings of present Sauternes, the sweet dessert wine made from grapes shrivelled to concentrated ripeness. Although Sauternes is a very ancient wine region, going back almost to the Romans, for a long time only *clairets* were produced, except in some medieval church *domaines* which developed a sweet white wine in the Mediterranean style. Since we lack convincing historical documentation, it is tempting to turn to oral tradition, which is abundant but probably unreliable.

According to the most plausible theory, the system of late harvesting for especially ripe grapes appeared in the seventeenth century. At this period there are already some

SAUTERNES AND BARSAC

documentary references and it is known that there was a market in Holland for sweet French wines. Sauternes, Barsac, Bommes and Preignac were the most prized of the sweet wines among the white Bordeaux exported to The Netherlands and northern Europe. In the eighteenth century their predominance increased and the local aristocracy, both old nobility and grand legal families, further ensured it by the introduction of batch picking and better vinification methods.

Sauternes' fame spread throughout the world, as shown by the following anecdote. On a visit to Bordeaux in 1787, Jefferson went to Yquem and ordered 250 bottles of the 1784 vintage. He tasted one of these when he returned to Washington and was so enthusiastic that he immediately ordered another thirty dozen.

THE 1855 CLASSIFICATION

THE rise of Sauternes and Barsac began before the Revolution and became even more marked in the first half of the nineteenth century. At this point history and oral tradition come together: the working methods that had formerly been confined to a few estates became more general and more systematic. Some owners also began to age the wine for long periods before bottling, in barrels made of oak or even acacia wood. The spread of oïdium in the mid nineteenth century led to increased cultivation of Sémillon, a variety that lends itself to the production of high-quality sweet wines.

The Sauternes region is famous for its fine houses as well as wine.
Below, Château Filhot, built in 1845.
Left, the seventeenth-century Château de Malle.

Sauternes by this stage was regarded as a wine for festive occasions and was drunk for celebration in all the royal courts of Europe. Prices began to soar and the Russian Grand Duke Constantine unhesitatingly paid the fabulous sum of 20,000 gold francs for a cask of the 1847 Yquem.

This triumphant situation was confirmed by the 1855 classification, in which Sauternes was the only white wine from the Gironde to be granted the same rank as red Médoc and Haut-Brion.

TWO ASTONISHING WINES

THE making of Sauternes and Barsac, wines with a high natural level of alcohol, has had a long history of trial and error. Yet even the patient method of batch picking, the meticulous selection of perfectly ripe grapes and long experience in wine-making would be nothing without the ideal natural environment.

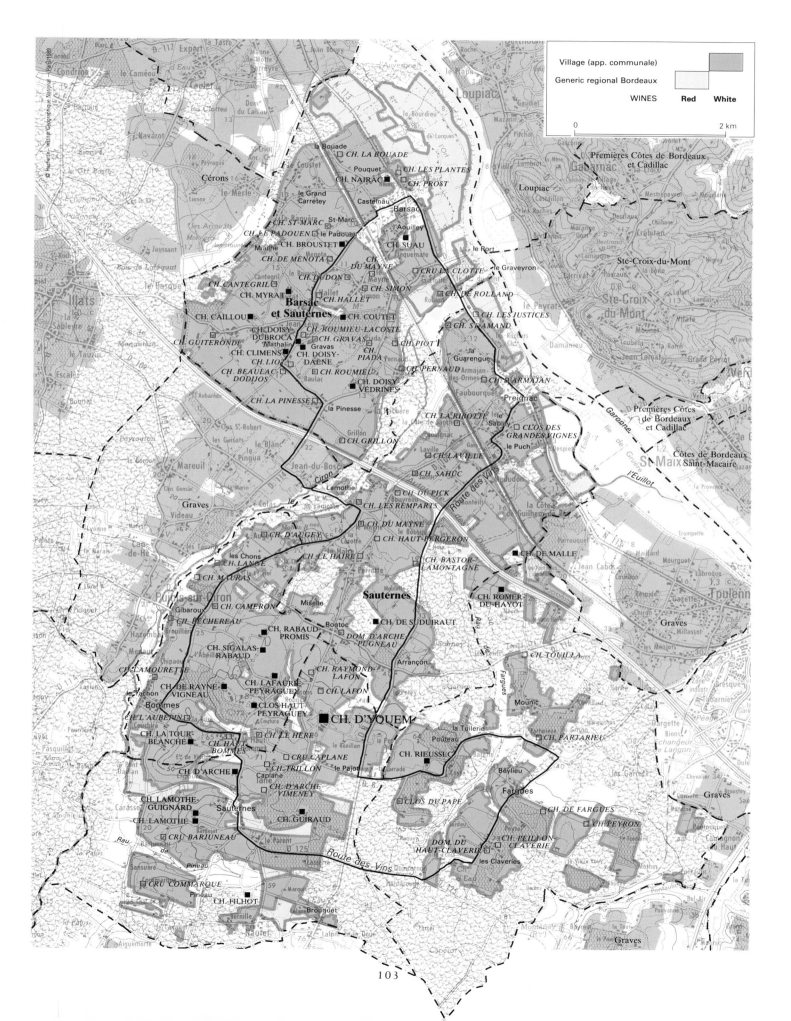

Village (app. communale)

Generic regional Bordeaux

WINES   Red   White

0   2 km

WEATHER FLUCTUATIONS AND SWEET *APPELLATIONS*

ANYONE visiting Sauternes in October might well be surprised by the local weather, the damp misty mornings and warm sunny afternoons. These daily fluctuations are crucial and are brought about by the particular environment at the confluence of the Garonne and the Ciron, a little river from the Landes. A map of the Gironde would certainly show how all the sweet wine *appellations* are centred on this confluence. It is not just chance that the river Ciron plays such a decisive part. Throughout its

CLIMATIC CONTRADICTIONS AND THE NOBLE ROT

THE Barsac and Sauternes region has an unusual advantage in possessing weather conditions which encourage, and indeed are essential for the development of 'noble rot'. This is spread by a minute fungus called *botrytis cinerea*, which is responsible for a number of chemical and biochemical changes in the grape, causing in particular an increase in sugar and a partial loss of water content. Normally this would result in rotten grapes covered with grey mould. In Sauternes, the process is quite different: the grapes shrivel and dry up, but the downy mould which develops on them has the deep brown colour of 'noble rot'. This effect is due to the splendidly contradictory

Top, Château Yquem.

Above, Château Coutet.
Right hand page, noble rot developing on Sauvignon grapes.
Right, Lafaurie-Peyraguey.

autumn weather, which generally manages to be both humid enough to encourage mould growth and warm enough to dry the grapes.

BOTRYTIS AND ITS PROBLEMS

BOTRYTIS *may be a blessing for the region but it presents problems too. It leads to noble rot only if certain conditions happen to coincide. In the first place, the fungus has to occur on perfectly ripe and healthy fruit. It works its way through the skin, which shrivels and turns brown, causing the berry as a whole to lose water. Concentrated sugar is produced but not concentrated acidity, and characteristic aromas appear. A serious problem is that* botrytis *does not occur everywhere at the same time, but spreads in stages over different bunches and even over different grapes within a bunch. This explains the necessity for picking in batches spread over a long period, and also the meticulous care in picking only grapes which have attained the ideal 'roasted' condition produced by noble rot.*

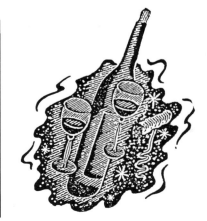

winding course beneath dense trees it is hardly ever in sunlight, so when its very cold waters join those of the much warmer Garonne, these special morning mists inevitably occur.

TWO GREAT
APPELLATIONS

AS well as enjoying this ideal weather, Sauternes has very favourable soils and subsoil, and these have allowed the development of two *appellations*.

Barsac vineyards also have the right to sell their wine under the Sauternes name. However, their individual character is visible in the landscape, which is less undulating, with

estates often surrounded by distinctive low walls. Barsac is situated on a depression where · erosion has laid bare layers of Stampian limestone. These have given rise in the centre of the district to a combination of limestone and red sandy soils which are excellent for growing fine white wines, as is clear from the many *crus classés* established there. Barsac wines are notable for their intense fragrance.

The Sauternes *appellation* covers a larger, more varied area, including the marvellous sites on the series of gravelly hills round Yquem. Although considerably higher (between 30 and 50 m at Rayne Vigneau in the west of the district, and more than 70 m towards Rieussec in the east) and more uneven, these stony hills are similar in formation to some in the Haut-Médoc, but often with veins containing more clay. This terrain is clearly ideal for sweet white wines. Both Sauternes and Barsac have a characteristically golden appearance, 'roasted' aromas, which evolve magnificently as the wine matures, and a

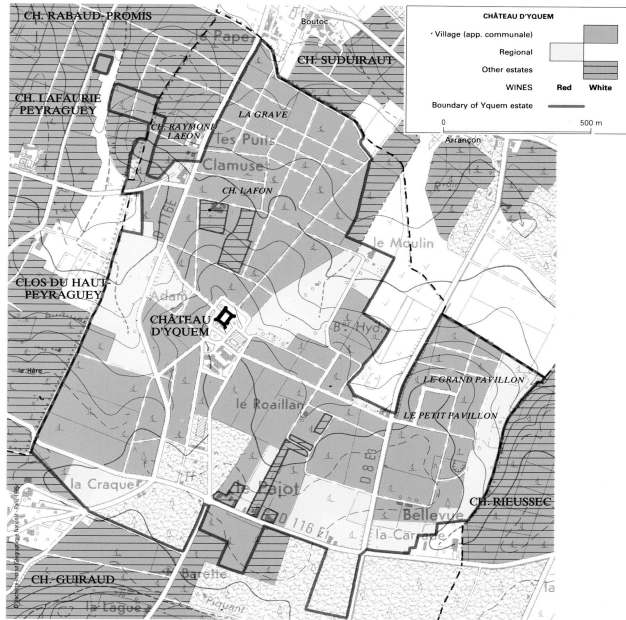

wonderful luscious smoothness.

Three grape varieties go into these wines: Sémillon (70 to 80 per cent), Sauvignon (20 to 30 per cent), and Muscadelle. Heavy investment is required for a very small output: yield per hectare is tiny, with a permitted maximum of only 25 hl. The special ripening process is a very chancy matter, depending on weather conditions. In spite of all this, the Sauternes region has remained very close in its basic structure to what it was in the last century, and in the Gironde this is a most unusual situation. In Barsac and Preignac there are still many estates of moderate size on 12 to 15 hectares, whereas elsewhere land is divided between great aristocratic

domaines like Yquem or minute family properties on one or two hectares, like those one can see at Bommes and Fargues.

Some very attractive estates can be found wedged in among the *grands crus classés*: Gravas (formerly Doisy-Gravas) in Barsac, and Lafon in

Sauternes, completely encircled by the vines of Yquem. When all the ups and downs of wine history are considered, such survivals seem amazing. One explanation is that most Sauternes growers, large or small, also have vineyards in Graves and woodland in the Landes nearby. By cushioning financial losses, this has certainly helped to preserve the character of the region.

ENTRE-DEUX-MERS

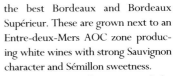

IN spite of its name, which means 'between two seas', the Entre-deux-Mers region has no sea coast at all. It consists of a stretch of Gironde territory lying between the Garonne and Dordogne rivers, and the name comes from the fact that both rivers are tidal for a long way upstream, as far as Sainte-Foy-la-Grande and La Réole.

This broad limestone plateau is often compared to the rolling Périgord region and has a surprisingly fragmented appearance for Bordeaux. The region is criss-crossed with valleys and little winding roads, which make the whole area look quite different from the endless flat vine prairies not far away. Vineyards are interspersed with woods and meadowland and there are many delightful secluded corners with contrasting water and greenery. The area's turbulent history, especially in the Middle Ages, can be guessed from the buildings – bastides (small medieval fortified towns) and Templar churches, fortified mills and houses.

The base rock of the plateau consists of Tertiary 'starfish' limestone (calcaire à astéries; limestone containing Asteroidea or starfish fossils). Where this has been quarried for building stone there are often immense underground galleries, some of which are now used for growing mushrooms. In many cases the rock surface has also decomposed or has surface layers of other rock, as in the Premières Côtes de Bordeaux area in the south on the steep plateau edge overlooking the Garonne.

The remoteness and fragmentation of the Entre-deux-Mers region has allowed it to retain its rural quality.

TEN APPELLATIONS

THE 23,000 hectares of vines between the Garonne and the Dordogne share not one but ten appellations, and a high proportion of the area is given up to Bordeaux and Bordeaux Supérieur. The Entre-deux-Mers appellation itself has the most distinctively local character and applies to a dry white wine zone stretching from the confluence of the Garonne and Dordogne in the west, to the département boundary of Lot-et-Garonne in the east. Nine communes centred on Targon are

Above, vines growing in the Camblanes region.

entitled to use the name Haut-Benauge in conjunction with the Entre-deux-Mers appellation.

The Entre-deux-Mers zone does not coincide exactly with the geographical region, as the AOC does not apply to districts with sub-regional appellations. Gravelly terrain in the villages of Vayres and Arveyres, for instance, has given rise to the minor appellation Graves de Vayres, covering 650 hectares for red wine and 350 for white. In the north-east, round Sainte-Foy-la-Grande, a wedge of land extending into the Dordogne département is entitled to the Sainte-Foy-Bordeaux AOC, although the red and white wine produced here is more often sold as Bordeaux or Bordeaux Supérieur.

Premières Côtes de Bordeaux is an appellation with a more concrete existence. The district runs for some 60 km between Entre-deux-Mers territory and the Garonne, devoting 3,600 hectares to red wine and 2,700 to white. Of the latter, only sweet wines are entitled to the AOC, while dry wines are covered by various regional Bordeaux appellations. Côtes de Bordeaux Saint-Macaire is a south-eastern extension of Premières Côtes de Bordeaux. Lastly, inserted among the Premières Côtes on the right bank of the river opposite Sauternes and Cérons, are the three sweet wine appellations of Sainte-Croix-du-Mont, Loupiac and Cadillac.

Below, Cazaugitat (Gascon term for a wild garden): self-sown tulips grow in the fields and vineyards.

THE WINE OF ENTRE-DEUX-MERS

THE very extensive Entre-deux-Mers appellation area lies in the middle of the region with the same name, with Bordeaux and Bordeaux Supérieur AOC zones as neighbours. The predominantly clay/limestone soils are suitable for all the local white varieties (Sémillon, Sauvignon and Muscadelle), for Merlot and, in certain conditions, for Cabernet. The district produces mainly red wines, including much of

the best Bordeaux and Bordeaux Supérieur. These are grown next to an Entre-deux-Mers AOC zone producing white wines with strong Sauvignon character and Sémillon sweetness.

The most significant part of the Entre-deux-Mers plateau (the Pellegrue, Sauveterre and Targon districts) has a clay capping which has resulted in the very distinctive soils known as boulbènes. These soils provide excellent conditions for white wine grapes, and give Sémillon in particular a delicate flowery perfume reminiscent of the local wild flowers. For good results, Sémillon needs to be combined with Sauvignon so that its sweetness can be balanced by a crisper, firmer fragrance.

Since local soils consist of clay and gravel it is possible to grow a number of grape varieties: reds include up to 55 per cent Merlot and 25 per cent Cabernet-Sauvignon, and whites some very fine Sauvignon. Red wines are powerful, with a strong colour; white wines are well balanced and smooth, dry whites are sold as basic Bordeaux and can be quite distinguished.

The Premières Côtes region, running along the southern edge of the Entre-deux-Mers plateau is worth a visit for its magnificent Château de Cadillac, a Gironde version of Fontainebleau, and the delightful little harbours and villages beside the Garonne.

The steep slopes overlooking the Garonne consist of limestone with outcrops of gravel which are very suitable for growing sweet white wines. As a local microclimate also encourages the spread of Botrytis, three appellations have established themselves here: Cadillac, Loupiac and Sainte-Croix-du-Mont.

CLASSIFICATION OF THE BORDEAUX CRUS

ONE of Bordeaux's most unusual features is the very strict classification of the various *crus* within the great *appellations*. This system was set up at different times, the earliest rankings being those for the Médoc (including Haut-Brion in the Graves region) and Sauternes. These were established in 1855 at the time of the Paris Exposition Universelle, where it was intended to exhibit all that was best in France, including wine from Bordeaux. In order to choose representative wines, the Bordeaux Chamber of Commerce asked brokers to provide a list of the most reputable estates. The yardstick for inclusion in the list was essentially the price of the wine, since it was thought to correspond to its quality. In spite of later criticism, the 1855 classification is still valid, with one modification in 1973 when Mouton-Rothschild was promoted from second to first growth. The finest estates of the Graves region (now known as Pessac-Léognan) were classified along the same lines in 1953, with a revision in 1959; they are all of equal rank. The first official classification for Saint-Emilion came in 1954 and was unusual for the clause specifying revised rankings every ten years. A revision took place in 1969 and again in 1986. There has never been an official classification of the best Pomerol estates.

Médoc: the classed growths (classified in 1855, revised in 1973)

Premiers crus
Château Lafite-Rothschild (Pauillac)
Château Latour (Pauillac)
Château Margaux (Margaux)
Château Mouton Rothschild (Pauillac)
Château Haut-Brion (Graves)

Deuxièmes crus
Château Brane-Cantenac (Margaux)
Château Cos d'Estournel (Saint-Estèphe)
Château Ducru-Beaucaillou (Saint-Julien)
Château Dufort-Vivens (Margaux)
Château Gruaud-Larose (Saint-Julien)
Château Lascombes (Margaux)
Château Léoville Las Cases (Saint-Julien)
Château Léoville-Poyferré (Saint-Julien)
Château Léoville-Barton (Saint-Julien)
Château Montrose (Saint-Estèphe)
Château Pichon Longueville Baron (Pauillac)
Château Pichon Longueville Comtesse de Lalande (Pauillac)
Château Raussan-Ségla (Margaux)
Château Rauzan-Gassies (Margaux)

Troisièmes crus
Château Boyd-Cantenac (Margaux)
Château Cantenac-Brown (Margaux)
Château Calon-Ségur (Saint-Estèphe)
Château Desmirail (Margaux)
Château Ferrière (Margaux)
Château Giscours (Margaux)
Château d'Issan (Margaux)
Château Kirwan (Margaux)
Château Lagrange (Saint-Julien)
Château La Lagune (Haut-Médoc)
Château Langoa (Saint-Julien)

Château Malescot-Saint-Exupéry (Margaux)
Château Marquis d'Alesme-Becker (Margaux)
Château Palmer (Margaux)

Quatrièmes crus
Château Beychevelle (Saint-Julien)
Château Branaire-Ducru (Saint-Julien)
Château Duhart-Milon-Rothschild (Pauillac)
Château Lafon-Rochet (Saint-Estèphe)
Château Marquis de Terme (Margaux)
Château Pouget (Margaux)
Château Prieuré-Lichine (Margaux)
Château Saint-Pierre (Saint-Julien)
Château Talbot (Saint-Julien)
Château La Tour-Carnet (Haut-Médoc)

Cinquièmes crus
Château Batailley (Pauillac)
Château Haut-Batailley (Pauillac)
Château Belgrave (Haut-Médoc)
Château Camensac (Haut-Médoc)
Château Cantemerle (Haut-Médoc)
Château Clerc-Milon (Pauillac)
Château Cos-Labory (Saint-Estèphe)
Château Croizet Bages (Pauillac)
Château Dauzac (Margaux)
Château Grand-Puy-Ducasse (Pauillac)
Château Grand-Puy-Lacoste (Pauillac)
Château Haut-Bages-Libéral (Pauillac)
Château Lynch-Bages (Pauillac)
Château Lynch-Moussas (Pauillac)
Château Mouton-Baronne Philippe (Pauillac)
Château Pédesclaux (Pauillac)
Château Pontet-Canet (Pauillac)
Château du Tertre (Margaux)

Sauternes: classed growths (1855)

Premier cru supérieur
Château d'Yquem

Premiers crus
Château Climens
Château Coutet
Château Guiraud
Château Lafaurie-Peyraguey
Clos Haut-Peyraguey
Château Rayne-Vigneau
Château Rabaud-Promis
Château Sigalas-Rabaud
Château Rieussec
Château Suduiraut
Château La Tour-Blanche

Seconds crus
Château d'Arche
Château Brousset
Château Nairac
Château Caillou
Château Doisy-Daëne
Château Doisy-Dubroca
Château Doisy-Védrines
Château Filhot
Château Lamothe (Despujols)
Château Lamothe (Guignard)
Château de Malle
Château Myrat
Château Romer
Château Romer-Du Hayot
Château Suau

Graves: classed growths

Château Bouscaut (red and white)
Château Carbonnieux (red and white)
Domaine de Chevalier (red and white)
Château Couhins (white)
Château Couhins-Lurton (white)
Château Fieuzal (red)
Château Haut-Bailly (red)
Château Haut-Brion (red)
Château Laville-Haut-Brion (white)

Château Malartic-Lagravière (red and white)
Château La Mission Haut-Brion (red)
Château Olivier (red and white)
Château Pape Clément (red)
Château Smith-Haut-Lafitte (red)
Château Latour-Haut-Brion (red)
Château La Tour-Martillac (red and white)

Saint-Emilion (*Grand cru* classification, decreed 1954, passed 1986)

Saint-Emilion, *premiers grands crus classés*

A Château Ausone
    Château Cheval Blanc

B Château Beauséjour (Duffau-Lagarosse)
    Château Belair
    Château Canon

Château Clos Fourtet
Château Figeac
Château La Gaffelière
Château Magdelaine
Château Pavie
Château Trottevieille

Saint-Emilion, *grands crus classés*

Château Balestard La Tonnelle
Château Beau-Séjour (Bécot)
Château Bellevue
Château Bergat
Château Berliquet
Château Cadet-Piola
Château Canon-La Gaffelière
Château Cap de Mourlin
Château Chauvin
Clos des Jacobins
Clos La Madeleine
Clos de l'Oratoire
Clos Saint-Martin
Château Corbin
Château Corbin-Michotte
Château Couvent des Jacobins
Château Croque-Michotte
Château Curé Bon La Madeleine
Château Dassault
Château Faurie de Souchard
Château Fonplegade
Château Fonroque
Château Franc-Mayne
Château Grand-Barrail-Lamarzelle-Figeac
Château Grand-Corbin
Château Grand-Corin-Despagne
Château Grand-Mayne
Château Grand-Pontet
Château Guadet-Saint-Julien
Château Haut-Corbin
Château Haut-Sarpe
Château La Clotte

Château La Clusière
Château La Dominique
Château L'Angelus
Château Laniote
Château Larcis-Ducasse
Château Lamarzelle
Château Larmande
Château Laroze
Château L'Arrosée
Château La Serre
Château La Tour du Pin-Figeac (Giraud-Belivier)
Château La Tour du Pin-Figeac (Moueix)
Château La Tour-Figeac
Château Le Châtelet
Château Le Prieuré
Château Matras
Château Mauvezin
Château Moulin du Cadet
Château Pavie-Decesse
Château Pavie-Macquin
Château Pavillon-Cadet
Château Petit-Faurie de Soutard
Château Ripeau
Château Sansonnet
Château Saint-Georges-Côte Pavie
Château Soutard
Château Tertre Daugay
Château Trimoulet
Château Troplong-Mondot
Château Villemaurine
Château Yon-Figeac

THE LIBOURNE REGION

ALTHOUGH Libourne has only 27,000 inhabitants, in drive and individuality it can be said to rival the great city of Bordeaux. This *bastide* town, founded in 1269 by Roger de Leyburn, has become one of the main wine centres of the Gironde, noted especially for the Saint-Emilion and Pomerol *appellations*. Wine in Bordeaux is only one industry among many, whereas in Libourne its rôle is central.

The importance of wine here is most obvious if one walks along the quays beside the Dordogne. The groups of *chais* at right angles to the river form a complete wine district within the town and would remind one of the Quai des Chartrons area in Bordeaux, if it were not for Libourne's very visible links with the local rural community.

A DORDOGNE RIVER PORT

ONCE again it is the existence of a river, this time the Dordogne, that explains why wine became such an important industry here. Libourne has a fortunate position at the confluence with the river Isle, and is the last port of any size before Bec d'Ambès at the mouth of the Dordogne. From here, past all the medieval castles, which still tower above the river, boats carry wine from Périgord and the northern Gironde would reach

Landscapes of the Libourne region. Top, vines growing on the banks of the Dordogne.

the Atlantic without having to go through Bordeaux, which for centuries had the right to give priority to its own regional wines. Libourne was able to develop independently and export its produce to Flanders and to Normandy and Britanny in northwest France. Its position between Paris and Bordeaux meant that it could retain its importance in the wine trade, even when sail declined and the shipping trade was focused on Bordeaux's Port de la Lune. Transport of wine to traditional external markets was later taken over by the railways.

SOILS

THE historical situation was only one factor in Libourne's success, the other being the existence of suitable wine-growing soils. The splendid hillside vineyards are situated on 'starfish' limestone, which appears as a largely continuous bench in the

Bordeaux region but has stood up to erosion only in the central area of the Libournais, at heights between 60 and 90 m. The limestone is overlaid by complex soils, sometimes in thick layers, but elsewhere much thinned and, in western areas, affected by human activity. At Castillon, surface soils and the underlying molasse, also of Tertiary formation, have not been stripped off the limestone base and

Village (app. communale)		
Sub-regional		
Generic regional Bordeaux		
WINES	Red	Red +white

0   4 km

THE MEN FROM CORRÈZE

AROUND 1830, more and more itinerant merchants from Meymac in Corrèze, a rather unproductive region in the Massif Central, began appearing in Libourne. There they would buy wine for resale in northern France, making the most of the fact that many fellow Coréziens had migrated to Paris at that time. They became a little too crafty and the ruse of printing 'négociant at Meymac, near Bordeaux' on wine labels goaded Libourne townspeople into taking legal proceedings.

Early in this century there was a second wave of merchants from Corrèze, a far more professional and scrupulous group. They settled in Libourne and began distributing the local wine even further afield, to Belgium, Holland and the Rhineland. As well as being remarkable wine salesmen and publicists, they established even stronger links with their adoptive region by acquiring their own vineyards in Pomerol and Saint-Emilion.

have formed steep scarps, very evident in the south of the region.

At heights below 40 m, elsewhere in the region, molasse is overlaid with Quaternary alluvium from the Dordogne and Isle rivers. Some of these deposits are coarse in structure, but they consist on the whole of sands where the water table is close to the surface for most of the year.

Winds have caused some of these sands to shift again more recently, driving them up onto the limestone table, especially on the northern side, where they have formed gradual slopes. Drainage here is very good.

The common denominator in Libourne geology is limestone. This gives the local wine its firm body and intense fruity bouquet. The region differs from the rest of Bordeaux in its weather, which is less maritime than on the left bank of the Garonne, with a tendency to drier summers and higher maximum day temperatures.

The wine community here has its own special character, influenced by the settlers from Corrèze, the emphasis on vine-growing to the exclusion of other farming, and the importance of the family wine business. Growers in Libourne itself and the countryside around have shown how perfectly they understand both terrain and grapes. Here the very fine Merlot, together with Cabernet Franc, flourishes on the local limestone, giving deep-coloured, intensely fragrant wine.

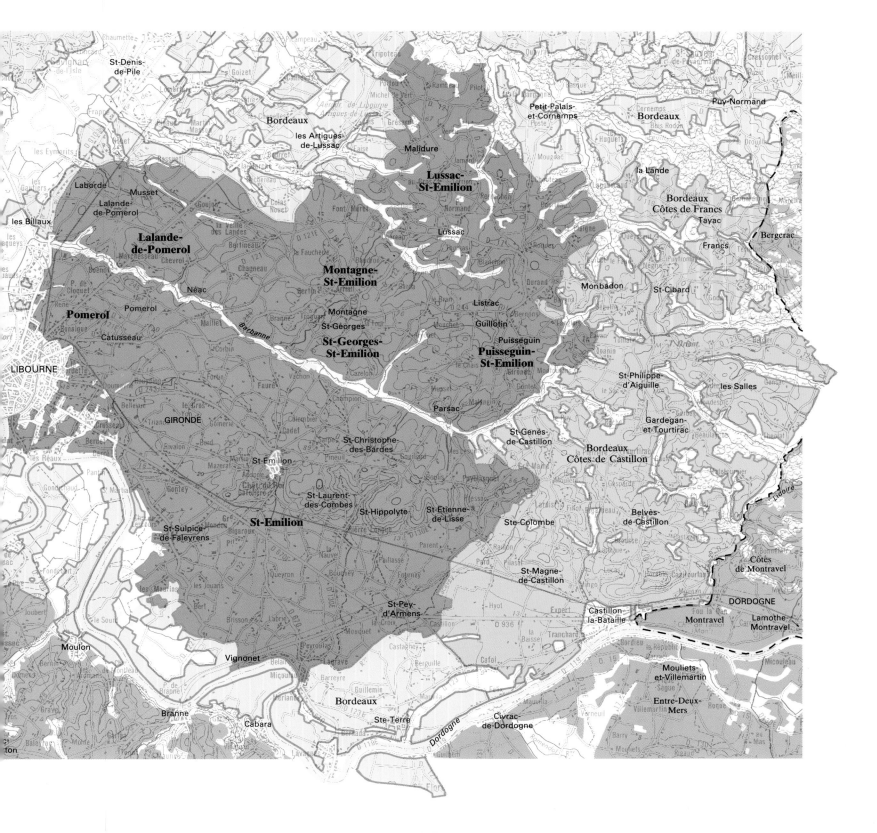

SAINT-EMILION

LIBOURNE, with its many *négociants*, is the commercial and administrative capital of the surrounding district, and dominates the wine industry of the north-eastern Gironde. It is strange that, despite this, there has been no Libourne *appellation* to spread the name of the town throughout the world. No doubt this misfortune is the result of being so close to Saint-Emilion.

A CAVE VILLAGE

IT is clear from one glance at that ancient hilltop city that its origins go back a very long way. The fortified *bastide* town of Libourne was built for strategic reasons fairly late in the Middle Ages, but Saint-Emilion dates from the end of the eighth century when the Breton monk Emilianus made himself a rock shelter in which to live as a hermit. Disciples

Column from the Roman Villa Ausonius at Château La Gaffelière.

subsequently dug out more caves, and these troglodyte dwellings eventually formed the nucleus of a village. At that time nobody could have imagined that this secluded spot would one day possess magnificent churches and fortifications, and that its wine would be world renowned.

Medieval grandeur is still visible in the well-preserved houses and ramparts of the old city. The visitor can wander through the narrow streets savouring the character of the place and acquiring at the same time some

understanding of its wine history. The present *appellation* in fact corresponds exactly to the area covered by the original charter and, as well as Saint-Emilion itself, covers seven further villages (Saint-Christophe-des-Bardes, Saint-Etienne-de-Lisse, Saint-Hippolyte, Saint-Laurent-des-Combes, Saint-Pey-d'Armens, Saint-Sulpice-de-Faleyrens and Vignonet) and part of Libourne. This gives an indication of the size of the *appellation* zone (5,200 hectares, which constitutes about 6 per cent of the Bordeaux vineyards) and of its diversity.

There are two *appellations* for Saint-Emilion and an unusual classification system. All wine produced in the AOC zone is entitled to be called Saint-Emilion, but only the best can use the name Saint-Emilion Grand Cru, which applies, not to specific sites, but to specially selected wines. Selection is based on annual tasting and is very rigorous.

AN UNUSUAL SYSTEM OF CLASSIFICATION

WITHIN the *grand cru appellation* are a number of classed growths, seventy-four in all, including sixty-three *grands crus classés* (the second rank of Saint-Emilion classed growths) and eleven *premiers grands crus classés* (the first rank of Saint-Emilion classed growths). The latter are subdivided further into two A and nine B growths. The Saint-Emilion system is relatively

recent, dating from only 1955. When Bordeaux was classified for the Paris Exhibition of 1855, Saint-Emilion was left out, as was the whole Libourne region. There were two reasons: classed wines were chosen by Bordeaux *courtiers* (wine-brokers) who had little to do with the northern Gironde, the province of the Libourne chamber of commerce; and Saint-Emilion also possessed very few large properties, even on gravel sites.

Although often thought to be a disadvantage, the delay in setting up an official classification system has in fact had some useful effects. The Saint-Emilion system, far from being just a repeat of what happened in Bordeaux

Left, members of the Jurade de Saint-Emilion on their way to proclaim the date of harvest. Below, wine maturing at Château-Ausone.

a century ago, has had the unusual foresight to insist on regular revisions, the last being in 1986.

MEDIEVAL SAINT-EMILION

VINEYARDS grew up here in early medieval times, independently of the town's development as a place of pilgrimage. At that stage Saint-Emilion had its own port at Pierrefitte, with later competition from the new bastide of Libourne, and wine made up a sizeable proportion of the Dordogne river trade. Saint-Emilion is one of the few wines from the south-west to be mentioned in thirteenth-century drinking songs and tales. A certain Geoffrey de Watersford refers in one of these to the white Saint-Emilion exported to England and credits it with power to give sweet sleep and no hangovers.

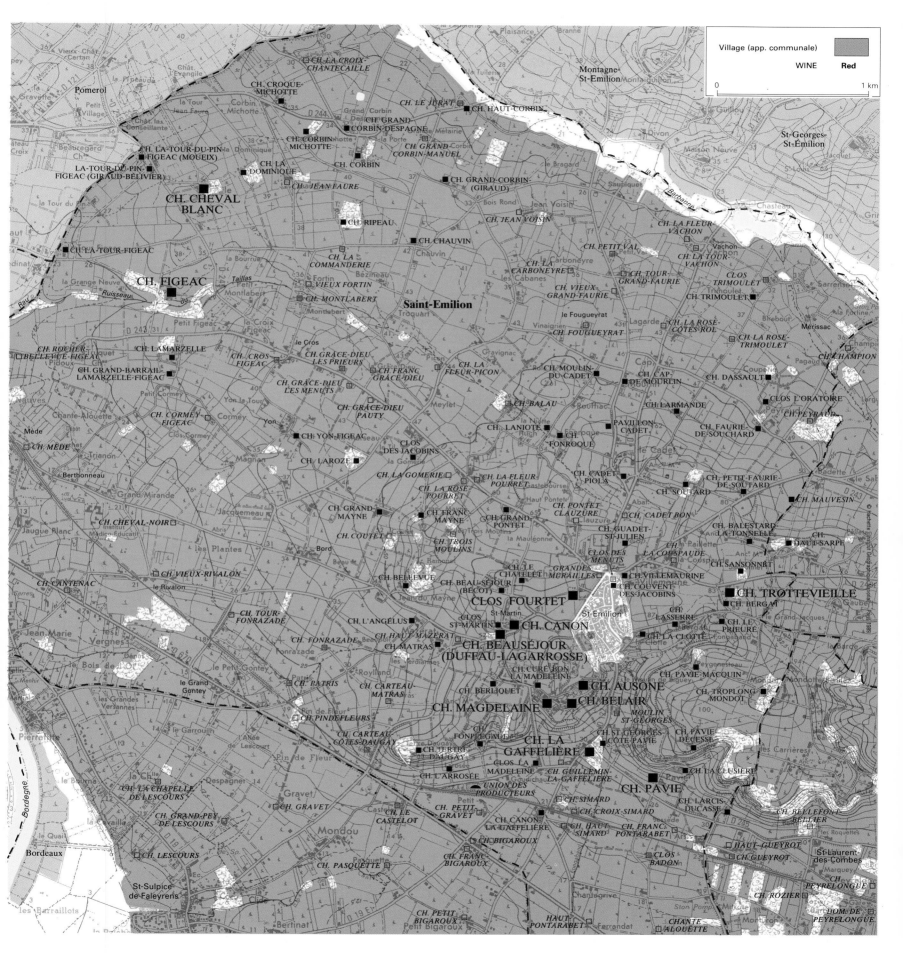

Village (app. communale)

WINE **Red**

0 ————————————————— 1 km

Montagne-
St-Emilion

St-Georges-
St-Émilion

Pomerol

CH. LA CROIX-
CHANTECAILLE

CH. CROQUE-
MICHOTTE

CH. LE JURAT

CH. HAUT-CORBIN

CH. GRAND
CORBIN-DESPAGNE

CH. CORBIN-
MICHOTTE

CH. GRAND-CORBIN
CORBIN-MANUEL

CH. LA-TOUR-DU-PIN-
FIGEAC (MOUEIX)

CH. LA
DOMINIQUE

CH. CORBIN

LA-TOUR-DU-PIN-
FIGEAC (GIRAUD-BÉLIVIER)

CH. JEAN FAURE

CH. GRAND-CORBIN
(GIRAUD)

CH. CHEVAL
BLANC

CH. RIPEAU

CH. JEAN VOISIN

CH. LA FLEUR-
VACHON

CH. CHAUVIN

CH. PETIT VAL

CH. LA TOUR-
VACHON

CH. LA-TOUR-FIGEAC

CH. LA
COMMANDERIE

CH. LA
CARBONEYRE

CH. TOUR-
GRAND-FAURIE

CLOS
TRIMOULET

CH. FIGEAC

VIEUX FORTIN

CH. VIEUX-
GRAND-FAURIE

CH. TRIMOULET

CH. MONTLABERT

Saint-Emilion

CH. FOUGUEYRAT

CH. LA ROSE-
CÔTES-ROL

CH. LA ROSE-
TRIMOULET

CH. ROCHER-
BELLEVUE-FIGEAC

CH. LAMARZELLE

CH. CROS-
FIGEAC

CH. GRÂCE-DIEU
LES PRIEURS

CH. LA
FLEUR-PICON

CH. MOULIN-
DU-CADET

CH. CHAMPION

CH. GRAND-BARRAIL
LAMARZELLE-FIGEAC

CH. FRANC
GRÂCE-DIEU

CH. CAP-
DE-MOURLIN

CH. DASSAULT

CH. GRÂCE-DIEU
LES MENUTS

CLOS L'ORATOIRE

CH. CORMEY-
FIGEAC

CH. GRÂCE-DIEU
PAUTY

CH. BALAU

CH. LARMANDE

CH. PEYRAUD

CH. MÈDE

CH. YON-FIGEAC

CH. LANIOTE

CH. ROC
FONROQUE

PAVILLON-
CADET

CH. FAURIE-
DE-SOUCHARD

CH. LAROZE

CLOS
DES JACOBINS

CH. PETIT-FAURIE-
DE-SOUTARD

CH. LA GOMERIE

CH. LA FLEUR-
POURRET

CH. CADET-
PIOLA

CH. SOUTARD

CH. CHEVAL-NOIR

CH. GRAND-
MAYNE

CH. LA ROSE-
POURRET

CH. GRAND-
PONTET

CH. PONTET-
CLAUZURE

CH. CADET BON

CH. MAUVESIN

CH. FRANC-
MAYNE

CH. GUADET-
ST-JULIEN

CH. BALESTARD-
LA-TONNELLE

CH. COUTET

CLOS DES
MENUTS

CH.
HAUT-SARPE

CH. VIEUX-RIVALON

CH. TROIS
MOULINS

LA COUSPAUDE

CH. SANSONNET

CH. CANTENAC

CH. BELLEVUE

CH. LE
CHÂTELET

GRANDES
MURAILLES

CH. VILLEMAURINE

CH. BEAU-SÉJOUR
(BÉCOT)

CH. COUVENT-
DES-JACOBINS

CH. TROTTEVIEILLE

CLOS FOURTET

CH. BERGAT

CH. TOUR-
FONRAZADE

CH. L'ANGÉLUS

CLOS
ST-MARTIN

CH.
LASSERRE

CH. LE
PRIEURE

CH. FONRAZADE

CH. HAUT-MAZERAT

CH. CANON

CH. LA CLOTTE

CH. MATRAS

CH. BEAUSÉJOUR
(DUFFAU-LAGARROSSE)

CH. LA CLOTTE

CH. PATRIS

CH. CURE-BON-
LA-MADELEINE

CH. PAVIE-MACQUIN

CH. CARTEAU-
MATRAS

CH. BERLIQUET

CH. AUSONE

CH. TROPLONG-
MONDOT

CH. MAGDELAINE

CH. BELAIR

MOULIN
ST-GEORGES

CH. PINDEFLEURS

CH. CARTEAU
CÔTES-DAUGAY

CH.
FONPLEGADE

CH. ST-GEORGES-
CÔTE-PAVIE

CH. PAVIE-
DÉCESSE

CH. LA CHAPELLE
DE LESCOURS

CH. TERTRE-
DAUGAY

CH. LA
GAFFELIÈRE

CLOS LA
MADELEINE

CH. L'ARROSÉE

CH. GUILLEMIN-
LA-GAFFELIÈRE

CH. LA CLUSIÈRE

UNION DES
PRODUCTEURS

CH. PAVIE

CH. GRAVET

CH. SIMARD

CH. LARCIS-
DUCASSE

CH. BELLEFONT-
BELLIER

CH. GRAND-PEY
DE LESCOURS

CH. LE
CASTELOT

CH. PETIT-
GRAVET

CH. CROIX-SIMARD

CH. CANON-
LA-GAFFELIÈRE

CH. HAUT-
SIMARD

CH. FRANC-
PONTARABET

CH. BIGAROUX

HAUT-GUEYROT

CH. LESCOURS

CH. PASQUETTE

CH. FRANC-
BIGAROUX

CLOS
BADON

CH. GUEYROT

St-Laurent-
des-Combes

St-Sulpice
de-Faleyrens

CH.
PEYRELONGUE

Bordeaux

CH. ROZIER

CH. PETIT
BIGAROUX

HAUT-
PONTARABET

CHANTE
ALOUETTE

DOM. DE
PEYRELONGUE

THE *CRUS*

THE sheer quantity of wine produced round the old town under the two Saint-Emilion *appellations* is surprising: an output of around 230,000 hl per year. The changing character of the environment ensures that this output is also very varied. Between the river Isle in the north and the Dordogne in the south, vines clearly dominate and shape the landscape, but at least they have not smoothed out all the pleasing irregularities of its hills and valleys.

The changing landscape is a delight in itself and evidence also of a varied geological background. Experts suggest anything from three to seven different geological types but, for the sake of simplicity, let us consider four main classes: the limestone plateau, the adjoining hillsides, gravel terraces on the Pomerol boundary, and the

plain. The latter runs all the way beside the Dordogne here and is made up of varied elements of occasional importance for vine-growing, especially a zone of gravels several metres deep in some places. Several different wines are grown here, distinctive in their character but all with pleasing suppleness and fruit.

Some of the vineyard sites on sands and in the plain are enviable enough,

Above, Château Canon.
Top, Château Cheval Blanc.

though they in no way equal the limestone plateau and hillsides. These cover 2,000 of the 5,200 hectares in the *appellation* and are, geographically and metaphorically, the true centre of Saint-Emilion.

The plateau overlooks the

Dordogne valley between Saint-Emilion and Castillon-la-Bataille and consists of a massive slab of Stampian limestone. Near Saint-Martin-de-Mazerat the rock has been laid bare but has broken down to form soils further east, towards Saint-Hippolyte and Saint-Etienne-de-Lisse. There is no doubt that the plateau area is exceptionally suitable for vines. This is demonstrated by the presence here of

Trottevieille, a *premier cru* yielding rich, fruity wine of great substance.

However, it is on the plateau edge in the south and south-west that the really great wines are concentrated. Every hillside there seems to harbour some famous name. Clos Fourtet in its enclosure of old walls is closest to the town. This one district contains eight out of the eleven *premiers crus*: Ausone, Beauséjour, Belair, Canon, Clos Fourtet, La Gaffelière, Magdelaine and Pavie. Each has its own special character, which varies with soil or aspect. There are many minute shades of difference between sites on the upper slopes, with thin limestone soils, and those on the mid-slopes where there is a combination of molasse and windblown sands. And there are always variations where a change of aspect creates a different microclimate. The most striking example of this is the hillside at Pavie. Holm oaks still grow here, and visitors once enjoyed excellent peaches in wine because of all the peach trees.

Everywhere in the district well-drained soil ensures high-quality crops. These plateau wines are extraordinarily lively and supple, and also possess the aromatic intensity and generous character that allow them to evolve over the years. All these qualities are present to the full in the wine of Ausone. One of the finest panoramic views in the whole region is of the château and vineyards there.

The final group of soils is on the boundary with Pomerol and consists

Château Figeac with an unusually high proportion of Cabernet Sauvignon.

LOCAL CHARACTER

AS with the wine itself, the local wine community has a fairly varied structure. The different kinds of house show this clearly. Outside the medieval city gate, we can see all this. What is evident most of all, however, is that Saint-Emilion is a region of small-scale properties, and that the 'château' owner is often a genuine workman getting his hands dirty in the vineyards. The average area of properties seldom exceeds 10 hectares. This fragmentation might be thought to diminish the consistency

Jurade, the administrative authority with roots in medieval times, and by the modern Syndicat Viticole and Union des Producteurs. The latter brings together 400 proprietors who cultivate more than 1,000 hectares overall, and is a splendid example of the vigour and energy to be found in Saint-Emilion.

Inside the unique monolithic church of Saint-Emilion, carved out of the limestone hillside between the eleventh and thirteenth centuries.

of gravels. Their suitability for Cabernet has encouraged cultivation of a high proportion of this variety on the edge of the Isle river terraces. Wine from this area is often regarded as halfway between Pomerol and hill-grown Saint-Emilion, and is notable for its structure and ageing potential. Two *premiers grands crus* indicate the quality of the area: Château Cheval-Blanc (Class A) growing mainly Cabernet Franc, and

prosperous eighteenth- and nineteenth-century mansions on the 5 to 15 hectares of vineyards belonging to the *crus classés*. Further west, near Libourne and Pomerol, we come to large manor-houses in their surrounding gardens. Everywhere else, especially on the edges of the region, there are innumerable long, low peasant houses.

The soft local limestone and neat appearance give a certain unity to

and distinctive character of the wine. In fact the special Saint-Emilion style comes from a number of different elements. The first is the widespread use of Merlot, which combines excellently with the local soils, especially limestone, to yield supple, long-keeping wines.

A second factor is the clear sense in everyone here of having a single interest at heart, an interest kept alive by traditional bodies such as the

AROUND SAINT-EMILION

TO the north and east of Saint-Emilion there are several AOC regions on soils of traditional character, halfway between the plateau limestone of Saint-Emilion and the Miocene sands of Périgord. Differences in situation, geology and local practices have led to these regions being divided into two groups, each with its special features: the Saint-Emilion 'satellites' and the Côtes (Côtes de Castillon and Côtes de Francs).

THE SATELLITES

EXTENDING northwards from the little river Barbanne are the villages of Montagne, Puisseguin and Lussac, now commonly known as the satellites of Saint-Emilion. Since two former villages have been incorporated into Montagne, the region is in fact shared by five *appellations*: Montagne, Lussac, Puisseguin, Saint-Georges and Parsac, all hyphenated with Saint-Emilion.

The château of Francs has buildings dating from the eleventh and sixteenth centuries.

The land here has not been entirely given up to vine-growing, as is the case south of the Barbanne. Vines in fact account for 3,100 hectares, half the total area, and yield an average of 200,000 hl per year. The countryside is a varied mixture of vineyards, meadows and woodland covering a jumble of fairly high hills and internal valleys, with occasional streams. All these ups and downs make for an attractive patchwork landscape, which also happens to be very suitable for vine-growing.

The region is divided between a number of small proprietors, both independent growers and Coopérative members, and some large châteaux. It is worth visiting a few of these, such as the Château des Tours with its Viollet-le-Duc restorations, and the elegantly eighteenth-century Saint-Georges. The wines are as varied as the countryside in which they grow, but have a similar agreeable and fairly forceful character. Further south in the region, there are vineyards that have soils and grape varieties like those of Saint-Emilion, and produce wines of comparable power and complexity.

CÔTES DE CASTILLON AND CÔTES DE FRANCS

CÔTES de Castillon is the *appellation* for an area east of Saint-Emilion. The small town of Castillon-la-Bataille, on the edge of Périgord, bears a historic name, since it was near here in July 1453 that the battle took place in which Talbot, the Earl of Shrewsbury, and his troops were defeated and the Hundred Years War between France and England was brought to an end.

The eighteenth-century Château Saint-Georges, at Saint-Georges-de-Montagne.

The Côtes de Castillon consist of very homogeneous land looking towards the Dordogne. There are two distinct types of terrain. Excellent sites on the plain 5 to 10 m above river level yield wine with considerable warmth and suppleness. Hillside and plateau sites give a more robust wine, which will mature well if yields are kept low.

Running north of this region are the Côtes de Francs, now producing much improved, powerful and generous wines.

THE WINE MUSEUM IN MONTAGNE

VINES are fascinating, not just for their ecology, but for the way of life they have inspired. Both aspects can be seen in a museum devoted to vine-growing and peasant life which was opened in the village of Montagne-Saint-Emilion in 1985. This contains an extensive and very interesting collection of documents and tools relating to life in the small peasant vineyard before the Second World War, and provides a splendid evocation of rural life and technical developments in wine-growing. The reconstructed buildings — houses, chais, *cooper's workshop, even a dove-cote — give a very clear sense of what it was like to live and work in this environment.*

FRONSAC

THE historic village of Fronsac lies on a massive wooded bluff towering some 70 m above meadows and marshland at the confluence of the Isle and the Dordogne. It is not necessary to climb right up to the castle to see that the site was bound to be of immense strategic importance.

HISTORY AND WINE

IN its commanding position above the roads from Bordeaux and the province of Périgord, the Fronsac bluff is a place steeped in history. According to his biographer Eginhard, Charlemagne built a fortress there in 769, although unfortunately nothing remains either of this or of the subsequent medieval castle. After becoming a place of refuge for Protestants in the sixteenth century, the huge edifice was razed to the ground and eventually replaced by the present rather characterless building.

Today Fronsac is better known for its wine than as a setting for great events. The village has a situation which is ideal for vine growing, in a landscape which is one of the most picturesque in the Bordeaux region.

Fronsac vineyards.

Fronsadais is a soft sandy clay rock interspersed with layers of sandstone. The formation has broken down most dramatically in the south-east, where it has been cut up into a series of steep bluffs with much weathered soils. Further to the north and west there are plateau areas on limestone, which has decomposed here to form reddish soils.

Fields and woodland add to the charm of the region. There is a vivid contrast between the sweeping molasse slopes under overhanging limestone ledges and the flat strips of watermeadow down by the river.

THE *APPELLATIONS*

THE apparently random ups and downs of this region are shared by two *appellations*. The Fronsac AOC extends over six communes and produces 5.4 million bottles per year. Canon-Fronsac applies to slopes in Fronsac and Saint-Michel-de-Fronsac, consisting of clay/limestone soils over a bench of 'starfish' limestone. It covers a more limited area and produces only 2 million bottles per year.

Grape varieties are restricted to four, as elsewhere in the Libourne region: the two Cabernet varieties, Malbec (or Cot), and Merlot. The latter tends to dominate and is ideally suited to the local soils. Fronsac wines, although neglected, and for a long time overshadowed by Saint-Emilion and Pomerol, have firm character, with both substance and refinement. Their strong colour led to their use in the past to remedy the appearance and body of other wines. They are generous wines, which can stand up to ageing. Canon-Fronsac has its own quite distinctive fruity intensity and delicately spicy flavour.

The visitor to Fronsac can enjoy other things besides wine. There are a number of beautiful Romanesque churches, and some elegant châteaux and manor-houses, including the imposing Château de la Rivière.

Left, the church of Saint-Aignan.

Below, the much restored sixteenth-century Château La Rivière. Its splendid cellars are hollowed out of the rock.

As well as the castle bluff, there is a complex group of hills and scarps, sometimes dissected into ridges. As in Libourne, this can be explained by the presence together of both Stampian 'starfish' limestone and Sannoisian (Oligocene) molasse. This very extensive tract of so-called *molasse du*

POMEROL AND LALANDE DE POMEROL

occurred during the catastrophic climatic changes of the Quaternary. The river completely wore away the limestone platform as it carved out a valley, a process that caused it to alter course towards the west. A million years ago, gigantic floods deposited sheets of pebbles, mainly quartz and flint, which in their turn were subject to weathering. Phases of extreme dry cold alternating with warmer periods scooped out hollows in the earlier alluvium and laid down fresh deposits of pebbles. All these changes culminated in the present system of interlocking gravel terraces and drift deposits of pebbles, often transported great distances from the Massif Central. As a final complication, there are wind deposits of sands which in places have formed a type of ferruginous sandstone, locally known as *crasse de fer* (iron dross).

NOW that Pomerol produces some of the most expensive wine in the world, the very name has potent connotations. In the past, however, its reputation was fairly obscure. This is one of many curious features of the district, like the fact that there is no focal village and no building of any note. The absence even of fragments of Romanesque or Gothic architecture is certainly remarkable, when such quantities of churches have survived elsewhere in the Libourne region.

PRESTIGE WITHOUT GRANDEUR

IN a district with such prestige it seems equally odd that there is no really grand château. Only the eighteenth-century elegance of Sales at the end of its long avenue, or the fine buildings of Beauregard and Vieux-Château-Certan are worth visiting for their architecture. Otherwise, there are only simple country houses no different from a thousand others in the Bordeaux region. Some hamlets, like the former barrel-making centre at Catusseau, look more like a suburban extension of Libourne, but perhaps a

prosaic appearance is inevitable in the predominantly flat Pomerol countryside.

One only has to look a little closer at this apparent dullness to discover terrain of remarkable interest. The surface limestone, which has elsewhere allowed the development of hillside vineyards, is replaced here by immense accumulations of gravel.

These have formed an extensive terrace upstream from Libourne, along the left bank of the Isle, and are interspersed with thin layers of clay which come almost to the surface at the highest point in Pomerol.

If one surveys this peaceful countryside from the river, it is almost impossible today to imagine the immense scale of the activity that

Top, Sales, the château.
Above, fermenting vats at Château Gazin.

THE VILLAGE OF POMEROL

ROCK and soil conditions in Pomerol are ideal for growing vines

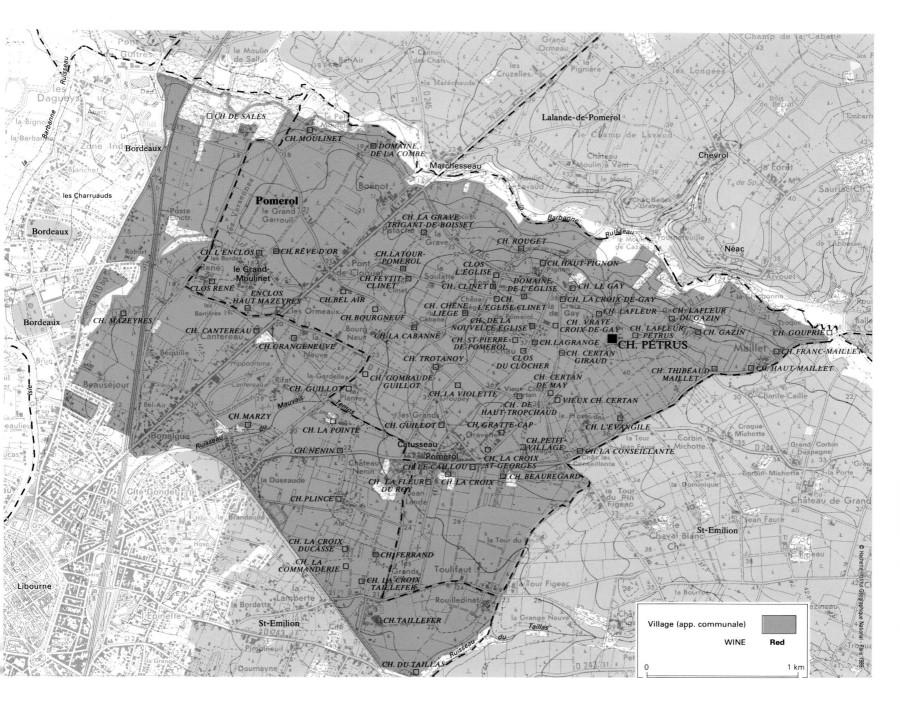

but not for much else. This probably explains why people in the district have acquired a fairly independent attitude to the world.

Before the Revolution, the extreme dryness of the sand and gravel soils discouraged effective agricultural development, especially as the land was divided between a number of owners, often leading figures in Libourne, who let plots out to small tenant farmers.

Heavy investment was necessary before the potential of this region could be properly exploited. With the absence of aristocratic owners and general fragmentation of the land, it was a long time before Pomerol wines emerged from their state of honourable anonymity. Brokers and travellers in the late eighteenth and early nineteenth centuries do not include Pomerol in their various lists and classifications, and it was only from 1850 onwards that it began to gain a reputation. This was helped too when the old system of cultivation between the rows of vines was abandoned, and improved agricultural techniques were developed.

DISTINCTION WITHOUT CLASSIFICATION

TODAY the success of Pomerol is clear, and confirmed by the price and reputation of its great wines. The star of the region is Château Petrus, but other great vineyards run close, such as l'Evangile, Trotanoy, Lafleur, Vieux-Château-Certan, La Conseillante, Petit Village, Certan de Mays, Lafleur Pétrus and many others. All

Carving of the Maltese cross at the Château de la Commanderie.

have belonged for generations to families that have been unashamed of their peasant roots.

The Lalande plateau is divided from Pomerol by the river Barbanne and has excellent soils in the southern half, with very good drainage in summer. The wines, which are similar in style to those of Pomerol though with rather less breeding, have notable power together with intense colour and fragrance. They are regarded as being of a very fine quality.

these rank on a level with the *crus classés* of Saint-Emilion and the Médoc. In fact, there has never been an official classification, which might perhaps have threatened the traditional cohesiveness of this community.

The distinction of Pomerol wines is very clear: their power and aromatic intensity go with remarkable smoothness and ageing potential. It is tempting to regard them as a cross between Saint-Emilion and Médoc. This is not altogether wrong but does not do justice to their distinctive character, especially their ability to mature to such perfection: after about five years they acquire the extraordinary subtlety and richness that are the products of ageing. Certainly this is one of the reasons why Pomerol has been accorded its reputation as one of the finest wines available.

Top, Vieux-Château-Certan.

Above, wine maturing at Château Pétrus.

Below, Château Siaurac.

LALANDE DE POMEROL

THIS *appellation* is slightly larger in both area (890 hectares instead of 735) and output (6 instead of 5 million bottles), but is otherwise similar to Pomerol further south. As in Pomerol, the 'châteaux' are traditional unpretentious houses which

CHÂTEAU PÉTRUS

CHÂTEAU Pétrus (the name's derivation is mysterious) is both characteristic of Pomerol and utterly distinctive. Its tiny 11-hectare vineyard is typical of the district, as is the unpretentious building with its turquoise-painted windows, like a doll's house in size. Nothing in its past seems to foreshadow its present illustrious rank.

Beneath the everyday surface the château's exceptional features are evident: the land itself, much of it consisting of very clayey soils, and the long series of remarkable owners: the Arnauds, Mme Loubat and Monsieur Christian Moueix. They have been consistent in using old vine-stocks, even after the great frosts of 1956, and in harvesting at speed and at the best possible moment. Their methods have included limited destemming, lengthy fermentation and ageing for two to two and a half years in new wood. The success of Petrus clearly owes nothing to chance.

CÔTES DE BOURG AND CÔTES DE BLAYE

THE old ports of Bourg and Blaye lie on the left bank of the Gironde at the edge of the Charente region. The altitude here is relatively high, about 100 m, and the district forms a link between the wooded country round Saintes and the silty edges of the estuary.

A LOCAL BRANDY

THESE two districts are on a prolongation of the Libourne lime-stone platform and stand out from the rest of the Gironde region. Inland one sees similarities with the Charente valley, especially as the people there also have more northern origins. They were known as *Gabailhs* or *Gavaches* to the Gascons and for a long time used to make Cognac like their neighbours in the Charente. There are still a few small businesses that use a two-stage distillation process to manufacture *Fine de Bordeaux*, a brandy *appellation* set up in 1974.

This inland plateau is almost entirely covered with sands, and vines are still grown here for dry white wine sold as Blaye, but essentially this is country far more suitable for crops such as cereal and asparagus, as well as some stock farming.

THE WINE REGION

THE present AOC zone has grown up mainly on the edge of the plateau. This terminates as a steep hillside overlooking the Gironde and is tunnelled through by caves and galleries where stone was quarried for local towns and villages. Immediately inland from the plateau face are the deep valleys of the attractive countryside known locally as Little Switzerland. The land here is entirely given up to vines and is shared by two *appellations*, Côtes de Bourg and Côtes de Blaye.

For many years these wines were little known and were used mainly to

Above, Côtes de Bourg vineyards overlooking the Gironde estuary. Below, the castle at Blaye.

improve blends in other regions. They have begun to have a clearer identity now that bolder commercial methods are being used, with emphasis on improved maturing, estate bottling and direct sales.

Production in both districts is concentrated on red wines: Premières Côtes de Blaye yields an average 130,000 hl per year of red wines and 11,000 of white; at Bourg the figures are 157,000 hl of red and 3,000 of white.

Although the two *appellations* are neighbours, they have slightly different characteristics. The whites from Blaye tend to be fresh and light, while those from Bourg are more fragrant, with a more defined local character. The reds of both districts have plenty of fruit and colour, but Bourg wines have more body and tannin and Blaye greater refinement.

RICH HISTORY, PRESTIGIOUS WINE

A remarkable feature of these regions is the richness of both historical and natural heritage. One has only to think of the fortresses at both Bourg and Blaye, the prehistoric cave of Pair-non-Pair and the landscape of the Gironde Corniche. This heritage is highly valued by local people, who have made very successful use of history in promoting their wines to tourists, especially at the Clos de l'Echaugette, a prestige vineyard planted at the base of the Blaye citadel, and through the selection of Bourg as the site of the European Conference of Wine Regions.

CHAMPAGNE

CHAMPAGNE is so much a symbol of celebration that it is difficult to think of one without the other. In spite of this festive image, it comes from an austere and sober part of the world. The Champagne region lies over the sloping side of a spur protruding from the Ile de France, 120 km east of Paris. Vineyards stretch for 200 km between upland forests and endless lowlands, in a narrow band whose colours change with the seasons. Towards Lorraine, the land is a vast granary. Towards Paris, it is more undulating and there is a changing landscape of woods, pools and meadows.

There is nothing obviously remarkable about the land. Vines grow on chalk, deposited here by a sea that receded 100 million years ago. The very shallow layer of sand or clay does not provide enough nourishment and the soils constantly need enriching. Roots have to find their way deep into the chalk, which may be 100 or even 200 m thick and acts as a storage heater for the vines.

This is a land for passing through, the land of the great medieval fairs, of wars and invasions. But vines seem to flourish in tough conditions; one can suddenly come across a tranquil vineyard, as charming as the statue of the smiling angel in Reims Cathedral, and surrounded by gently rolling hills. The landscape is the colour of sackcloth in winter and the freshest of green in summer. At the beginning of spring, this harsh expanse of greyish-white earth, studded with little posts, comes to life as the blossom reappears on the vines.

Fossil vine-leaves from 60 million years ago have been found near Sézanne, and the Romans were well aware that vines can flourish in a challenging climate. Since the fourth century AD they have been spreading

Above, a sixteenth-century tapestry depicting the life of Saint Rémi (Saint-Rémi Museum of Archaeology, Reims). Top left, young man drinking, detail from a painting by Quentin de la Tour, eighteenth century (Musée Lécuyer, Saint Quentin).

Below, map of the Aube wine region.

in fits and starts through the former province of Champagne, which was joined to France in 1361. Only in Germany are vines successful so far north and in so harsh an environment. The average annual temperature here is 10.4°C. Grapes do not ripen at temperatures lower than 9.6°C.

THE STRUGGLE FOR SUCCESS

VINES in Champagne certainly suffer from cold. During the winters of 1985 and 1986 the temperature went down to −25°C and, in spite of their remarkable resistance to cold, hundreds of hectares of vines were destroyed. Such catastrophes mean waiting a number of years before another harvest is possible. The 1981 spring frosts were a threat to buds and setting fruit, and on some nights heaters had to be put beside each vine. The more unusual autumn frosts, such as those of 1972, can cause irrevocable damage.

There are only about 1,550 hours of sunshine each year, but the annual rainfall is high (670 mm). If there is

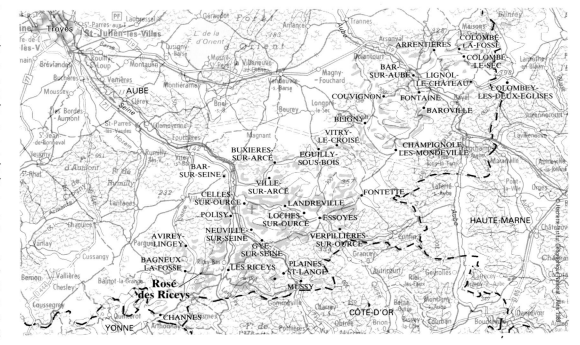

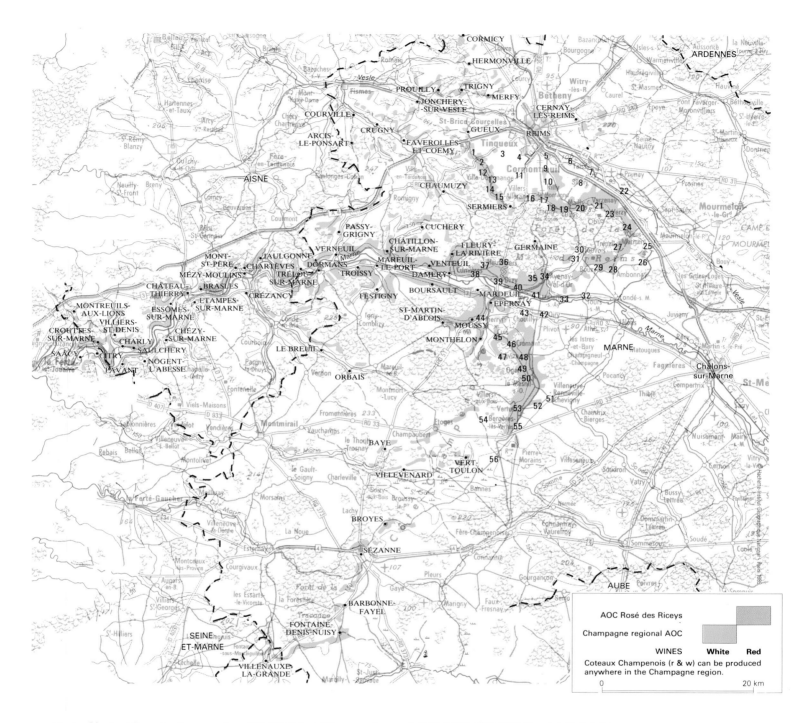

AOC Rosé des Riceys

Champagne regional AOC

WINES   **White**   **Red**

Coteaux Champenois (r & w) can be produced anywhere in the Champagne region.

0   20 km

persistent cold rain at flowering time, there can be a low rate of pollination and setting of fruit and consequently small crops, as in 1980. August thunderstorms can sometimes ravage an entire village.

In spite of great progress in combating vine diseases and parasites, nature continues to be the wine-grower's most persistent enemy: one harvest in five is reduced by hail, one in seven by freezing winter temperatures and one in three by spring frosts. This explains the enormous discrepancies in the harvests: less

than 600,000 hl in 1978, more than 2,200,000 hl in 1983.

The Champagne vineyards are shared by three *départements*. The Marne has the largest share, with 20,530 hectares, including the historic nucleus formed by the Montagne de Reims, the Marne valley and the Côte des Blancs. Vines are also grown west of Reims in the valleys of the river Ardre and the Vesle, further south between Epernay and Sézanne, and in the east near Vitry-le-François. The Aube *département* has 5,700 hectares where vine-growing has

1 PARGNY-LÈS-REIMS   2 JOUY-LÈS-REIMS   3 LES MESNEUX 4 BEZANNES   5 CORMONTREUIL   6 TAISSY   7 **SILLERY** 8 **PUISIEULX**   9 TROIS-PUITS   10 MONTBRÉ   11 VILLERS-AUX-NŒUDS 12 VILLEDOMMANGE 13 SACY 14 ECUEIL 15 CHAMERY 16 VILLERS-ALLERAND 17 RILLY-LA-MONTAGNE 18 CHIGNY-LES-ROSES 19 LUDES 20 **MAILLY-CHAMPAGNE** 21 **VERZENAY** 22 **BEAUMONT-SUR-VESLE**   23 **VERZY**   24 VILLERS-MARMERY 25 BILLY-LE- GRAND 26 VAUDEMANGES 27 TRÉPAIL 28 **AMBON-NAY** 29 **BOUZY** 30 **LOUVOIS** 31 TAUXIÈRES 32 **TOURS-SUR-MARNE** 33 BISSEUIL   34 AVENAY   35 MUTIGNY   36 CHAMPILLON 37 HAUTVILLERS 38 CUMIÈRES 39 DIZY 40 **AY** 41 MAREUIL-SUR-AY 42 **OIRY** 43 **CHOUILLY** 44 PIERRY 45 CUIS 46 **CRAMANT** 47 GRAUVES   48 **AVIZE**   49 **OGER**   50 LE MESNIL-SUR-OGER 51 VILLENEUVE-RENEVILLE   52 VOIPREUX   53 VERTUS 54 ETRECHY 55 BERGÈRES-LÈS-VERTUS 56 COLIGNY

developed round the towns of Bar-sur-Seine and Bar-sur-Aube and near Troyes. Round Château-Thierry, in the Aisne *département*, there are 2,400 hectares of vines. And finally, there are 40 hectares in the Haute-Marne and 30 in the Seine-et-Marne *départements*.

Still wine continues to be made in Champagne, although production nowadays amounts to only a modest one million bottles per year. Bouzy, the most famous, has a charming violet-scented bouquet, whereas the

Above, a wine press at Moët et Chandon.
Below right, adding the liqueur de tirage *for Bollinger champagne, one of the few still made in wood.*

historic Rosé de Riceys is a wine of real character.

Between 1930 and 1950 vines covered only 11,000 hectares. Recent planting has brought this area up to 28,600 hectares today, a total which will certainly rise to 30,000 hectares by the year 2000.

The wine-growers have shown immense persistence in facing all these difficulties and in caring for the vines. Champagne owes its soul to this precarious environment. The wine of celebration starts life in toil and drudgery.

EVERY year an army of 100,000 workers picks the grapes for Champagne by hand. No harvesting machines are allowed here as the bunches of grapes have to be put uncrushed into the wine-press. Since the white wine is made out of mainly black grapes, the pressing operation is extremely delicate and the colouring matter in the skins must not be allowed to darken the juice. Great numbers of special presses are installed in all the wine villages so that the grapes do not have to be moved any distance and perhaps spoilt in the process. Everything has to be done at speed: damaged and rotten grapes removed, and the must extracted. Only a proportion of the juice derived from pressing is entitled to the Champagne *appellation*.

One method of quality control, still practised today, began at the end of the seventeenth century. The *cuvée* or first pressing of juice is kept separate from later pressings (the so-called first and second *taille*). After pressing, the must undergoes an initial alcoholic fermentation caused by the action of yeasts. These transform the grape sugars into alcohol and other components (esters and higher alcohols), which help to give a wine its taste and smell. In November or December malolactic fermentation begins, transforming the malic acid from the grapes into lactic acid. The wine thereby becomes biologically stable and diminished acidity gives it much more suppleness.

Krug: choosing wine for blending.

THE PERFECT BLEND

BEFORE the wine is bottled it has to be blended. In the past this was done at the grape stage, but blending now consists of marrying wines from particular years, plots or grape varieties to give a basic wine. Each grape variety has its own characteristics. Chardonnay gives wine with a greenish-gold tinge, refined and long on the palate, rather assertively crisp when young but more expansive once it has acquired its sparkle. Pinot Noir vinified as a white wine (not red as in Burgundy) gives a pale gold wine with a sustained but unaggressive nose, full-bodied and generous – a wine for keeping. Meunier is slightly pink and lacks the backbone of Pinot Noir, but has a fruity, well-rounded flavour. Apart from these three grape varieties, 302 different vineyards and a half-dozen vintages help to make up the vast spectrum of possibilities for any blender attempting to compose his particular Champagne. Each component influences the finished product. Any one wine in isolation might lack grace and expressiveness but the *chef de cave*, like the conductor

of an orchestra, blends them into a subtle and harmonious whole. Every producer is very secretive about the ingredients and proportions of the blend. All this helps to explain why every Champagne is unique in character and why sixty or seventy different wines can be blended before the vital spark appears. The charm of Champagne derives from the sustained skill of the blender, who is rather like a medieval stained-glass maker with his personal version of blue or green.

FERMENTATION IN THE BOTTLE

ONCE bottled, the Champagne undergoes more fermentation, on the same principle as the first but with a fundamental difference: instead of escaping, the carbon dioxide now stays in the bottle and sets off the *prise de mousse*, the development of the bubbles in the wine. It is said that the *prise de mousse* enhances the bouquet of the Champagne, bringing out its true quality and giving it a vivacity and liveliness possessed by no other wine. This process takes place when the wine is bottled and the *liqueur de tirage* is added, consisting of selected yeasts and

CHAMPAGNE STYLES

ACCORDING to sugar content Champagne is defined as:

- extra-brut *(0–6 g of sugar per l)*
- brut *(less than 15 g per l)*
- extra-dry *(12–20 g per l)*
- sec *(17–35 g per l)*
- demi-sec *(33–55 g per l)*

The term blanc de blancs *(white wine made from white grapes) refers to Champagne made exclusively from Chardonnay grapes. As 63 per cent of the area is planted with black grape varieties (Pinot Noir and Meunier), Champagne is usually based on a blend of black and white grapes. If based on black grapes only, it can be called* blanc de noirs. *There is no red Champagne. Pink champagne, which has been in fashion for a number of years, is produced by an old technique of partially macerating grapes before pressing, with or without their stems. The must is run off and separated from the marc once the pink colour has been achieved. It can also be produced by blending 15 to 20 per cent of red wine, usually from the best areas of the Montagne de Reims, with white wine based on black or white grapes from different Champagne vineyards. This is in fact the only wine region in France entitled to make rosé from a blend of red and white wines.*

Above, Laurent-Perrier remueur: *turning the bottles to shift the deposit.*
*Below, deposit trapped in ice before extraction (*dégorgement).

cane sugar dissolved in Champagne.

The Champagne spends a long time in its bottle while the yeasts of this last fermentation are working. These yeasts take what is needed for their temporary survival, are then destroyed by the action of their own enzymes, and gradually give back substances which enrich the wine. The exchanges taking place between wine and yeasts allow maximum development of those qualities that will affect the drinker's sense of smell and taste. To achieve this, Champagne is not sold until it has spent an average of three years in the bottle, or much more if it is a vintage wine.

Before the bottles are taken out of the cellar in a special rack and sold, *remuage* has to take place, a process which involves standing the bottles neck-downwards in a special rack and tapping and turning them each day to shift the deposit from the sides of the bottle down onto the cap. In the next stage, known as *dégorgement*, the necks of the bottles are frozen and the corks, with the frozen sediment attached, are removed. Although this whole process is increasingly mechanized, in the past it was carried out entirely by hand and a good craftsman could deal with more than 35,000 bottles in a day. Before the bottle gets its final cork, the *liqueur de dosage* is added, consisting of a solution of cane sugar in Champagne.

DOM PÉRIGNON

BEFORE sparkling wine was invented, the Champagne region was the first to make white wine out of black grapes and to blend wines with complementary characteristics from different vineyards. Dom Pérignon, the cellarer of the Benedictine abbey of Hautvillers, is supposed to have discovered the secret of Champagne in about 1695. However, there is still some mystery about the precise origins of this revolution in wine-making. It was probably a gradual, cooperative process, in which Dom Pérignon played some part. Whether the story of his invention is legend or historical fact is uncertain. What is certain is that sparkling wine first appeared in the late seventeenth century in the Epernay region and that monasteries had an important hand in it. It was only in the eighteenth century that the wine achieved fame, and in the nineteenth century its present aristocratic reputation.

CHAMPAGNE HOUSES

CHAMPAGNE
MUMM de **CRAMANT**
Blanc de Blancs
Brut

G.H. MUMM & CIE

REIMS

750 ml   PRODUCT OF FRANCE   N M - 257 - 001   PRODUIT DE FRANCE   12 % vol.

IN the middle of the last century, a letter arrived in Paris from Russia bearing just these words on the envelope: 'To the greatest poet in France.' It was delivered to Victor Hugo, who in turn courteously sent it on to Lamartine. When it was finally opened it turned out to be from Prince Zirov to Monsieur Moët, director of one of the most distinguished Champagne Houses.

These firms are always known as 'houses', perhaps because of their deep local and family roots. It is they who, with help from both art and science, have brought about the universal recognition of Champagne. The product was excellent but the marketing skill of the Champagne Houses has also been extraordinary, and Champagne has inspired one of

Marie-Antoinette receiving Florent Heidsieck (Piper-Heidsieck collection).

THE CHAMPAGNE CAVES

THE chalky subsoil of the region is ideal for vine-growing and for encouraging both prise de mousse and slow maturing of the wine. Champagne gradually develops its qualities in a labyrinth of galleries tunnelled at depths of 10 to 50 m in the chalk, at a constant temperature of 8 to 12°C, and well away from any light or noise. Hundreds of millions of bottles spend their time peacefully maturing down here.

If one could put them all end to end these galleries beneath Reims and Epernay would reach for 300 km. Some négociants have access to 50 or 60 km of caves and need electric cars to move about in them. In Reims there are galleries in the chalk-pits used in Gallo-Roman times as quarries for building the town; some of these chalk-pits are even classified as historical monuments. Others were dug out by hand after the end of the seventeenth century.

---

the most remarkable public relations campaigns of all time.

Burgundy has been known and appreciated since medieval times. Champagne has been in existence for barely two centuries but has certainly been making up for lost time. In 1760 a few thousand bottles were sold; in 1860 a few million; nowadays the figure can be more than 200 million in a good year.

CHAMPAGNE – AN AMBASSADOR FOR FRANCE

ONCE the production of good-quality wine could be controlled in the nineteenth century, some very determined *négociants* from Reims and Epernay set off to conquer the world. They turned up everywhere from

The cellars of the Deutz firm.

Russia to the United States, managing along the way to get themselves shipwrecked and put in prison, to lose their belongings and to fall in love, and all the time obsessed with converting all five continents to their wine. The Champagne Houses were founded in the eighteenth and nineteenth centuries and a hundred years ago were already exporting three quarters of the 30 million bottles produced each year, mainly to England, the United States, Belgium, Germany and Russia. Few people in France were then privileged to drink Champagne, as in 1900 a bottle cost the equivalent of one man's weekly wages.

The promotion of Champagne was held back for half a century by such problems as war, the Russian Revolution and American Prohibition laws, but after 1950 there was another marketing drive. The total of 50 million bottles sold in 1960 became 100 million in 1970, 150 million in 1976 and 218 million in 1987. Expansion of the area under vines and technical improvements in production and vinification help to explain this growth, as does the increased buying power of the French: in 1988 a bottle of Champagne is worth the equivalent of two man-hours. With 136 million bottles, France is now the principal market for Champagne.

However, thirst for Champagne is universal. It is a brilliant ambassador for France, with exports amounting to 40 per cent of production. Eight

out of ten bottles exported are drunk in only eleven countries: Great Britain and the United States first, with more than 15 million bottles each, then the German Federal Republic, Switzerland, Italy, Belgium, Australia, The Netherlands, Canada, Spain and Japan.

New plantings in the early eighties will make it possible to produce 230 to 260 million bottles each year. Wines now maturing would fill more than 700 million bottles, which if

The Laurent-Perrier vineyards.

placed end to end would almost reach from the earth to the moon.

Although covering only 2.9 per cent of the area under vines in France (5.7 per cent if only the AOC wines are counted), Champagne represents 25 per cent of the business sector in wines and spirits, one third of exports of French AOC wines, and 0.6 per cent of all exports. The government's profit on this is almost incalculable!

GRAND HOUSES, GREAT FAMILIES

IN dim cellars so vast that electric trains are provided, or surrounded by mellow panelling in *fin de siècle* drawing-rooms, among stockbrokers at the Bourse or workers at harvest-time, the great Champagne families

manipulants (growers who both harvest and process their own grapes) each sell on average just under 12,000 bottles per year. A few dozen cooperatives also sell their own named Champagne. Together these account for 47 per cent of sales in France, but only 7 per cent of exports.

Left, scene carved into the chalk in Pommery's underground cellars.

Far left, the statue of Dom Pérignon at Moët & Chandon.

Below, La Marquetterie (the château belonging to Taittinger).

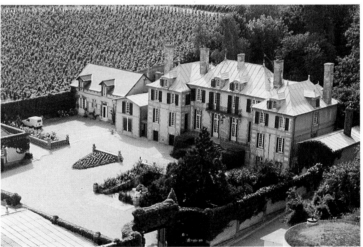

are still much in evidence. Their Houses are sometimes bought and sold but they are proud of their ancestors with their determined expressions and prosperous paunches, and stand by the precept that you have to live up to a great name.

Women take pride of place in the annals of many Champagne Houses. Veuve Clicquot was a woman of absolute dedication: between 1806 and 1860 her business turnover expanded by 2,000 per cent. But there were other remarkable women in Champagne, such as Louise Pommery, Mathilde Laurent-Perrier and Elisabeth Bollinger. If a widow did not found the House, then a monk probably did, as with Ruinart, the first House to be founded in 1729 by the family of Dom Thierry Ruinart. Other founders include settlers from Germany, as with the Houses of Krug, Heidsieck, Mumm and Roederer; or simply local men such as Henriot, Pol Roger and Lanson.

The *négociants'* houses have also taken over a number of firms with differing interests, a process which has done no harm to the reputation of Champagne and has even produced some dynamic partnerships. Taittinger, for instance, has become one of the foremost hotel groups in France, owning several of the most exclusive properties, such as the Hôtel de Gillon in Paris, built in 1758. Moët et Chandon joined with Cognac Hennessy in 1971 and has been following a programme of diversification. In 1987 the Moët-Hennessy and Louis Vuitton groups combined to form the first international group of prestige products, with a turnover of 13 thousand million francs. In Champagne the new grouping (Moët et Chandon, Mercier, Ruinart, Veuve Clicquot-Ponsardin, Canard-Duchêne, Henriot) represents 30 per cent of *négoce* sales and 20 per cent of total sales. It also has connections with Cognac (Hennessy, Hine),

Calvados (Père Magloire), sparkling wines (in California, Australia and Argentina), port (Rozès), luggage and luxury leather goods (Louis Vuitton), high fashion, the handling and distribution of alcoholic drinks, horticulture, and genetic engineering.

Most of the 15,000 growers who work 87 per cent of the area under vines in Champagne pass on all or part of their crops to about a hundred *négociants*. Since 1950, however, more of them have been making and selling their own wine. These *récoltants/*

Below, portrait of the widow Clicquot (Veuve Clicquot) by Léon Cogniet.

TIME FOR CELEBRATION

EVERY second throughout the world there are seven Champagne bottles being uncorked – not a bad gift to mankind! In France, Champagne fizzed all through the Regency period in the early eighteenth century, and in its maturity it has become the essential symbol for gracious living.

Champagne is a wine that inspires and enhances. The Marquise de Pompadour thought it the only wine to leave a woman's beauty unimpaired by drinking. Baths of Champagne became popular in the days of the Revolution and among the dancers and actresses of the Belle Epoque. Sarah Bernhardt was offered a Champagne-bath, and Marilyn Monroe used 250 bottles to fill her bath one night.

Frisky, spontaneous, light-hearted, good company at every possible party or ceremony – Champagne fits the life of film-stars and actresses, the froth of feathers and sequins. It can occupy the whole stage and play every part there is. And the sparkle makes the whole company feel witty.

Above, Greta Garbo in a scene from Goulding's film Love *(1927–8).*

Above left, from a 1900 advertisement for Moët & Chandon.

A TOAST TO HAPPINESS, LOVE AND PEACE

BUT Champagne is also a great wine with soul and character – elegant, complex, harmonious. Real happiness and rejoicing are a much more congenial background for it than hymns and official speeches. Christenings, lovers' meetings, the intimate pleasures of life – they all seem even more luminous in the company of Champagne.

Like no other wine, Champagne is charged with images, feelings and memories. A bottle of Champagne is broken over the stern for luck when a boat is launched, and drunk inside an aeroplane on its maiden flight. There is always Champagne to celebrate a Grand Prix victory or smooth over a theatrical flop. Wagner drank it for consolation after his opera, *Tannhäuser*, and Hemingway always had a bottle if breakfasting alone. But it should really be a convivial wine – a 'civilizing' wine, according to Talleyrand. His fellow diplomat, Metternich, claimed that the most successful treaties were inspired by Champagne rather than guns, so perhaps a peaceful world should be grateful to it.

ART AND INSPIRATION

THERE is Champagne in Verdi's *La Traviata*, in Richard Strauss's *Arabella*, in Lehar's *The Merry Widow*, of course, in Johann Strauss's *Die Fledermaus*, and the American musical *Gigi*. And of course it has a starring rôle in any number of films by King Vidor, Jean Delannoy, Billy Wilder, Andrej Wajda, Jacques Demy, Joseph Losey, John Ford, René Clair, George Cukor, David Lean...Where would the cinema be with no Champagne?

Champagne appears in posters by Cappiello and Mucha, in Manet's 'Bar at the Folies-Bergères', and even in Lurçat's tapestry, 'Le chant du monde' ('Song of the World'). It also appears in Watteau's painting of 'L'amour au Théâtre Français' ('Love at the Théâtre Français').

The poet La Fontaine, who was born not far from Reims, would certainly have written a fable about Champagne, if only it had existed in the seventeenth century. Voltaire did write about it: 'The cool frothy sparkle of this wine is a brilliant reflection of the French themselves.' So too did Stendhal in the novel *Lucien*

HOW TO DRINK CHAMPAGNE

OPENING a bottle of Champagne is easier than you think. With the cork held firmly in one hand, hold the bottle in the other at an angle of 45° and turn it so the carbon dioxide escapes slowly. If the cork refuses to budge, there are special pliers for the job. An elegant wine demands behaviour to match, so no pops and explosions. As for spraying it around – that's up to you.

It is better to 'sabler le Champagne' – enjoy it without swallowing a whole glassful at once. The ideal temperature for it is between 6 and 9°C, and ice-buckets containing a mixture of ice and water are preferable to the fridge. The expression 'Champagne frappé' comes from the bits of ice clinking against the bottle (*frapper* means to knock).

Over the years, Champagne glasses have gradually evolved into their present tulip shape, elongated to show off the bubbles, wide enough to make the most of the bouquet but not so wide that you lose it. The glass has a long slender foot so that it can be held without warming up the wine. And obviously it has to be crystal.

Debrett or *Who's Who*, since this is a wine drunk by all the best people and in every royal palace. It would be easier to try to count present-day monarchs and princes who have never drunk any, if such people in fact exist.

As an AOC wine, Champagne is part of the heritage of the Champagne region, of France and of the whole world. The name and the wine have both been imitated and plagiarized internationally. Worthy but straightforward *mousseux* are passed off as Champagne; fizzy lemonade, cider, bubble-baths and cigarettes have all

Above, eighteenth-century drinking glasses. Right, 'Le déjeuner d'huîtres' ('Oyster Dinner') by Jean-François De Troy (Musée Condé, Chantilly).

Far right, a staff with a carving of St Vincent, patron saint of wine (Ay).

Leuwen. 'Scintillating with Champagne, supper was coming to an end.'

Balzac, Zola, Maupassant, Shaw, Paul Fort, Apollinaire, Colette, Hemingway...good literature and poetry does not exist without Champagne. In *Don Juan* Byron writes rapturously of 'Champagne with foaming whirls, / As white as Cleopatra's melted pearls', and compares the 'evaporation of a joyous day' with 'the last, glass of Champagne without / The foam which made its virgin bumper gay'.

Any background suits it: Regency suppers or dinners at Maxim's, eighteenth-century wigs and lace or the top-hats and monocles of nineteenth-century Russia. You can drink it wearing a dinner-jacket, but just as well in denims. According to the poet Vigny: '*Dans la mousse d'Ay luit l'éclair d'un, bonheur*' ('Happiness gleams in this foaming wine').

A list of all the famous lovers of Champagne would be as long as

been called after it. The method of making Champagne has been widely followed, leading to the production of various lightly sparkling wines such as *crémants*, but there is still only one Champagne – the wine made in the Champagne region itself. Despite vicissitudes, Champagne producers are making an honourable attempt to win respect for the name and character of their wine. Their constant battle is the inevitable result of unprecedented success.

IN THE CHAMPAGNE REGION

DRIVING rapidly through Champagne you might in fact see very few vineyards. They tend not to be concentrated along main roads but inconspicuously tucked away in unexpected corners. You have to take your time and venture down twisting minor roads before you come across low, gently sloping hillsides across which lie the long narrow ribbons of vines. There are woods of oak or fir-trees on practically all the hilltops and slow, winding rivers in the valleys. Woods and water prevent extremes of temperature and provide the vines with coolness in summer and warmth in winter. Most vineyards face east or south-east, but in fact the situations vary, some facing south near Epernay and some even north near Reims. All these positions are the result of long experience by growers constantly searching out the best sites.

VILLEDOMMANGE

THIS is not a region of isolated houses, châteaux and estates, but of villages clustering on hilltops and in clefts in the landscape. Everywhere there are reminders of the First World War, especially the Battle of the Marne. The Montagne de Reims curves in an enormous horseshoe between Reims and Epernay and is edged with a string of large and affluent wine villages cultivating Pinot Noir. At Villedommange a Gallo-Roman mound with a twelfth-century chapel to Saint Lié gives a remarkable view over vineyards and the whole of the plain of Reims, and at Verzenay there is another view-point from the old windmill. Leading on to the Marne valley are the wine-growing areas of Ambonnay, which celebrates Saint Vincent's Day on 22 January, and Bouzy, with a wine festival in June.

Just before Château-Thierry the river runs between vineyards and, nearer Epernay, flows at the foot of some splendid châteaux (Dormans, Boursault, Mareuil-sur-Ay) and fine churches (Mézy-Moulins, Oeuilly, Vauciennes). At Châtillon-sur-Marne there is an imposing statue in honour of Pope Urban II who advocated the first Crusade of 1095. Dom Pérignon lived as a Benedictine monk at the abbey of Hautvillers, founded in 650, and his tomb can still be seen in the church of this typically flowery village. From here, as from Champillon and Mutigny, there are more superb views across the valley. It is claimed that Pope Leo X, the Emperor Charles V, Henry VIII of England, and François I and Henry IV of France all owned vines and presses in the old village of Ay with its late Gothic church and narrow streets. This is a region of Pinot Noir, but other parts of the Marne valley concentrate on growing Meunier.

CHARDONNAY

HOWEVER, it is Chardonnay that dominates the Côte des Blancs, a wooded cliff looking down over vine-covered slopes and the many twists and turns of the road. The villages are often clustered round churches of Romanesque origin, as at Cuis, Chouilly, Cramant, Avize, Oger and Le Mesnil-sur-Oger. At Vertus, where the fourteenth-century poet Eustache Deschamps was born, Pinot Noir is grown again. A little further on, smothered with vines, is the enigmatic Mont-Aimé which in its time has been a camp for Gauls and then Romans, a powerful fortress, the place where local Cathars were burned at the stake in 1259, and the site of one of the grandest military parades of all time, when Czar Alexander I was celebrating the Allied defeat of Napoleon.

Further south there are vines round the little towns of Bar-sur-Aube and Bar-sur-Seine, both with a rich heritage but still active today. At Essoyes the Maison de la Vigne has exhibitions devoted to local wine-growing traditions and also to the

Vines growing on limestone at Ay.

The Verzenay windmill, on the slopes of the Montagne de Reims.

painter Renoir, who lived here. Les Riceys is a village with three churches, the largest area of vines in Champagne (more than 600 hectares), and the only place entitled to all three local *appellations* (Champagne, Coteaux Champenois, Rosé des Riceys). Colombey-les-Deux-Eglises, at the edge of this region, is famous for its historical connections,

as it was here that General de Gaulle lived and was buried.

ROYAL REIMS

REIMS is the city where once the kings of France were crowned and is now the principal regional university and business centre. Its magnificent thirteenth-century Gothic cathedral contains a modern stained glass window showing the crafts associated with Champagne. The Saint-Rémi Basilica, the Palais de Tau and the Saint-Denis museum are all well worth a visit. The Champagne Houses are all in the Champ-de-Mars district and the old chalk quarries of the Butte Nicaise. Further on, the town of Epernay lies amongst vineyards, its life apparently devoted to the production of Champagne. Along its massive Avenue de Champagne are the Musée du Vin de Champagne and a succession of Champagne Houses.

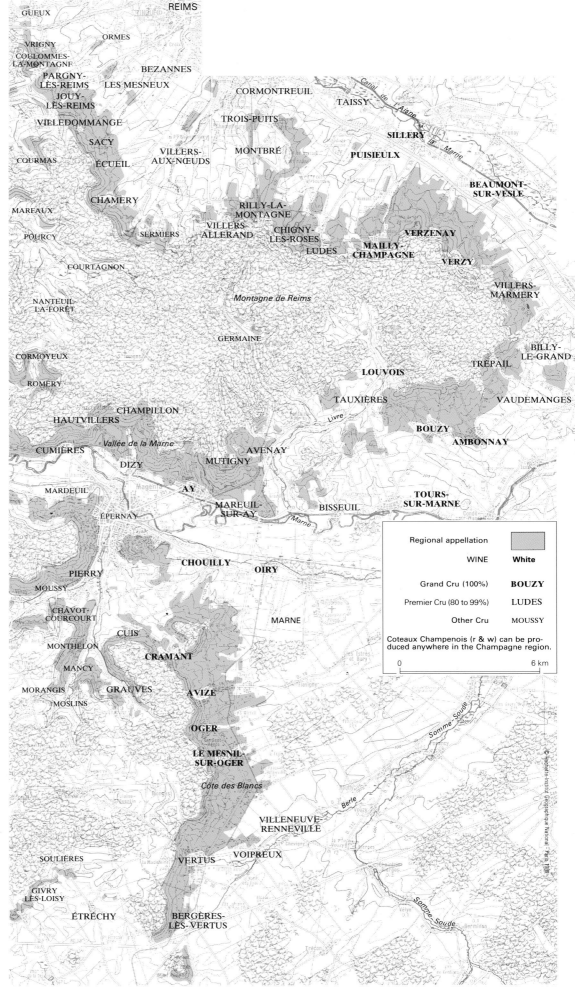

Regional appellation	
WINE	**White**
Grand Cru (100%)	**BOUZY**
Premier Cru (80 to 99%)	LUDES
Other Cru	MOUSSY

Coteaux Champenois (r & w) can be produced anywhere in the Champagne region.

0   6 km

BURGUNDY

'LE *Bourguignon tape un peu fort ce tan-tôt!*' ('The old man of Burgundy is beating down a bit!'): with the afternoon sun high over the vines, this is what the workers would say as they put down their baskets. Certainly the sun seems to have a special relationship with Burgundy if one thinks of the bright summer light on the rooftops of the Hôtel-Dieu in Beaune, the blazing autumn colour of the vines, even the reputation for opulence inherited from the time of the great dukes.

The history of Burgundy has twice overlapped with that of Europe: at the time when Cluny and the Cistercian movement were dominant in the tenth and eleventh centuries and again during the period of the Valois Dukes in the fourteenth and fifteenth centuries. It is wine, however, that has ensured it the longest period of historical dominance. The present Burgundy wine region covers the *départements* of Yonne, Côte d'Or, Saône-et-Loire and Rhône, according to the 1935 definition still valid today. It scarcely differs from the royal statute of 1416, which recognized as Burgundy the wine from all vineyards between the bridge at Sens and the Mâcon region. In 1935 Beaujolais (in the Rhône *département* and the La-Chapelle-de-Guinchay district of Saône-et-Loire) had not achieved its present status. Today we can still use the term 'Grande Bourgogne' or 'Greater Burgundy' when referring to Burgundy and Beaujolais together.

GRANDE BOURGOGNE

SO-called Grande Bourgogne extends over an area of 40,000 hectares, scarcely more than 10 per cent of the entire French AOC wine area. Its average output is 2.3 million hl per year, or 300 million bottles. Regional *appellations* represent 66 per cent of the crop, village *appellations* 33 per cent and the *crus* only 1 per cent, so Burgundy adds only one drop of fine wine to the immense sea produced by vines as a whole. Her success is due to the development of choice grape varieties ideally suited to local soils, to the commanding influence of the *crus*, and to 1,500 years of human effort.

Detail from 'Les Vendanges' ('Wine Harvest'), by the eighteenth-century painter Jean-Baptiste Lallemand (Musée des Beaux-Arts, Dijon).

There are more than 10,000 wine-producing enterprises in Burgundy. The average area is 4 hectares, a figure especially typical of family-run *domaines*. There are forty-four cooperatives, mostly in the south of the region, and these account for a quarter of the annual output. Seventy-five per cent of local wine is marketed through 165 shipping concerns (*négociants/éleveurs*) and the rest is sold directly by growers. These amounts vary of course according to the harvest. More than half is exported (the United States and Switzerland are the best customers, together with Germany, Benelux, The Netherlands and the United Kingdom).

One might well be confused by Burgundy's countless different *appellations*. The image of a finely stitched tapestry would apply very well to the intricacy of these *climats* (a Burgundian expression summing up one or more named vineyards in terms of soil, subsoil, aspect and microclimate), of the 'honest and consistent' local practices, and of the system of small-scale ownership allowing individuals to continue to own their own vines. When the AOC system was set up, other wine regions chose to use a brand-name, the name of the estate or the grape variety as their distinctive *appellation*. For Burgundy the *cru* or individual vineyard was the natural choice. In wine country it is easy to understand why history and geography are so closely linked.

The landscape here is one of great diversity, especially as the furthest regional boundaries are 300 km away from each other. In the Côte d'Or the vines look as if they have been carefully trimmed and combed, but this is far from being their natural appearance. Until the phylloxera crisis in the late nineteenth century, vines were planted '*en foule*', in completely random fashion. It was the use of horses and later of tractors that made it necessary for the grower to line up the plants and train them along wires.

A FAMILY OF FOUR

GREATER Burgundy can be subdivided into four regions: the Auxerre, Chablis, Tonnerre and Vézelay wine districts in the Yonne *département*; the Côte, Hautes Côtes and Côte d'Or (with the revived Châtillon district); the wine districts of the Côte Chalonnaise, Couches and the Mâconnais in the Saône-et-Loire *département*; Beaujolais, mainly in the Rhône *département*.

There are elements in all these scattered regions which add up to a 'family likeness'; only Beaujolais has a clearly different character.

The Yonne wine district, now in the process of expanding, covers a little more than 3,000 hectares. The area of the Côte d'Or is about 7,500 hectares and cannot easily be enlarged. There is the possibility of some limited expansion among the regional *appellations*, in the Hautes Côtes, and to a lesser degree in the Châtillon district. In the 10,000 hectares in Saône-et-Loire some expansion is taking place in the Mâconnais. The remaining 20,000 hectares are in Beaujolais.

The vineyards that used to produce wine for local consumption have almost disappeared, except for a small nucleus near Beaune and Chalon-sur-Saône. In pre-phylloxera days the area

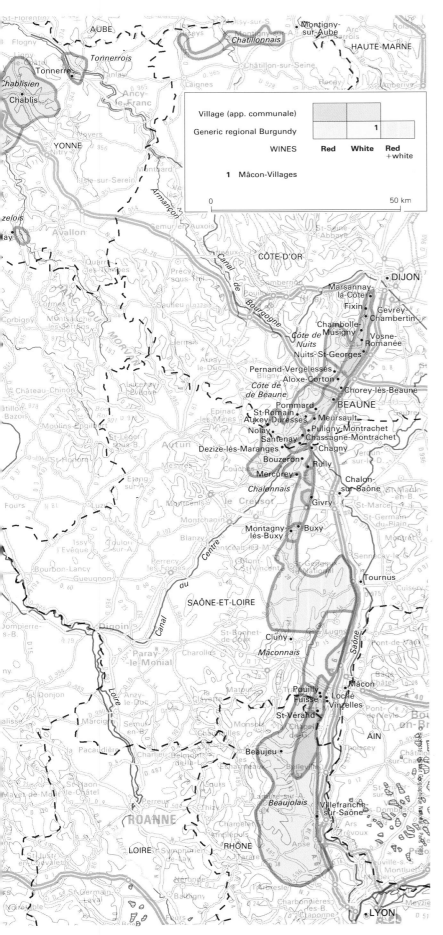

of vines here was four times greater. These everyday wines are no longer produced and wine-growing now continues only on the best *terroirs*.

THE IMPORTANCE OF *COTEAUX*

BECAUSE the wine-growing area is so extensive, there are some variations in the basically semi-continental, northern climate. Mediterranean influences are perceptible as far as the Côte de Beaune, while north of Dijon weather patterns are modified by the presence of the Burgundy Sill which forms the Seine/Saône watershed, and by effects of altitude and hilly country. As everywhere, annual weather variations have a marked effect on production, which consisted of 1.4 million hl in 1981 and 2.6 million hl in 1982.

This is an area where slopes (*coteaux*) are of prime importance for wine-growing. East or south aspects are preferable, but in good local conditions vines may be grown on hillsides facing slightly north-east or north-west. The vines grow at altitudes of about 150 m in the Serein and Yonne valleys, and at 400 m or higher in the Hautes Côtes de Beaune and in the Saône-et-Loire *département*. There are some winding minor rivers near the vine-growing area, providing a useful focus of warmth. The parent-rock very strongly affects the character of the wine produced: in Burgundy this is limestone, in Beaujolais granite or schist.

GRAPE VARIETIES

THERE are three grape varieties that make the most of the land's potential. In almost all the limestone regions Pinot Noir is grown and gives wines of well-defined style if not of strong colour. Their remarkable refinement shows itself after a few years of keeping. Chardonnay is perfectly suited to limestone soils and on marly terrains in particular will produce fantastic dry white wines. Gamay Noir is happy on granite sands or schist and gives delectable easy-

drinking Primeur wines, which can be drunk from mid-November onwards. Beaujolais-Villages and Crus can of course be kept and will

Above, Chardonnay. Below, Pinot noir.

then mysteriously develop a bouquet quite like that of a Burgundy.

Three other grape varieties are cultivated: Aligoté for light and lively white wines (Yonne Côte d'Or and Saône-et-Loire); and in the Yonne *département* Sacy for crisp and dry, possibly sparkling whites, and César for robust and tannic reds. Also in the Yonne, the Melon (for white wine) is dying out and Tressot (red) is extinct.

ONE LARGE CHESSBOARD

WINE-growing on the hillsides of Burgundy presents a very fragmented picture, rather like a bumpy chessboard made up of very uneven and sometimes very small plots of land. Ancient vineyard walls show that vines must have been grown here for centuries. How they came here is not certain, but they were known to exist in Gallo-Roman times. At the height of the medieval period they were grown in abundance and the foundation of the Clos de Vougeot can be dated to the early twelfth century.

ANCESTRY

PEOPLE in Burgundy have taken little notice of changes made at the time of the Revolution. Even local notaries still calculate area and volume in *ouvrées* and *pièces*. The *ouvrée* (4 to 28 m²), which is equivalent to the area dug (with a *fessou* or mattock) by one man in one day, is still the unit of area for wine-growers in the Côte d'Or. The *journal* is equivalent to 4 *ouvrées*. The *pièce* (228 l) and the *feuillette* (114 l) are the units of volume on

which prices are based but the volume can vary anywhere between Chablis and Villefranche-sur-Saône.

Vinification is governed by age-old procedures; grapes are picked then put in vats or pressed. Wooden poles (*piges*) are used to push down the cap of grapeskins (*chapeau*) which forms on the juice during fermentation. After this the wine is run off and allowed to mature. These are very 'natural' processes; science may improve quality but is not the answer to everything.

The grower carries out all this work, from making the graft to selling the produce. However, the *négociant/éleveur* also has a long tradition dating from the eighteenth century of maturing, blending and marketing wine,

making the wine of Burgundy well known throughout the world.

Crus and blends are classified according to criteria which have been in use since the middle of the nineteenth century. Variations are limited since each *cuvée* consists of a single grape variety.

There are increasingly stringent conditions defining the hierarchy of wines from regional AOC to that of the *grands crus*. There are also two levels, each with variations, in the regional classification. These levels occur because of the way sites are defined. Bourgogne Aligoté, Bourgogne Grand Ordinaire, with its uncertain future, and Bourgogne Passe-Tout-Grains, made from blending at least a third of Pinot Noir with Gamay Noir, make up the largest production area.

In addition, a Bourgogne *appellation* can be given for wine based on Pinot Noir for reds and on Chardonnay for whites. To the basic Bourgogne *appellation* can be added a district name (Hautes Côtes de Nuits or Hautes Côtes de Beaune), or, more rarely, that of a village (Irancy, Saint Bris). Bouzeron is another special case as it can be associated with Bourgogne Aligoté, a basic level *appellation*.

In the village *appellations*, the best *climats* are classed as *premiers crus*: these have to conform to a specified degree of alcohol and to a more stringent demarcation of the vineyards producing them. The name of the *climat* may appear on the label, next to that of the *appellation*.

CHABLIS AND THE YONNE REGION

THE Chablis wine region runs along the valley of the river Serein for about 20 km. Overlooking its gently rolling hills and valleys for most of the way is a long chalk cliff topped with clumps of trees. The little town of Chablis, known as the Golden Gate of Burgundy, is entirely devoted to wine and still contains the fine twelfth century cellar of Petit-Pontigny. This was built by monks from the nearby Cistercian abbey, the site of the vineyard of Clos la Vieille Plante.

Chablis has the principal vineyards in the Yonne region, where waterways facilitated an important wine trade with Paris and the north of France. The phylloxera epidemic at the end of the nineteenth century destroyed 40,000 hectares of vines in this *département* and only the sites most suited to wine-growing were able to continue and develop. The area of wine-growing in Chablis has more than doubled in the last fifteen years and has now reached over 2,500 hectares.

Chablis has successfully maintained its high reputation, to the point where the name is exploited as practically the generic term for white wine. However, only here is the real thing produced. For many years spring frost was a constant threat to the vines. Vines are now sprayed with water to protect them from this, as buds coated with ice are more resistant to intense cold and chilling wind. This is why there are now stretches of water throughout the countryside, and even swans can sometimes be seen there.

The AOC for Chablis was defined in 1938 and has certain distinguishing characteristics. It is regarded as a 'communal' *appellation* although the conditions specified for producing it are similar to those for regional

appellations. The *appellation* forms a homogeneous unit within Burgundy itself; the Chablis name is applied to the whole output and within this a Burgundy-type ranking system of *crus* and *grands crus* has been set up. As well as defining the area of production, the 1938 Decree includes a rather unusual geological specification (Kimmeridgian). Such precision may seem insignificant but was to have a considerable effect on the region. For growers here, Kimmeridgian applies to the marl facies which suits Chardonnay so well: layers sometimes almost 80 m deep, of marl interspersed with small benches of limestone, which help to create the gentle rolling hills of Chablis.

Much expert study has finally produced the 1978 Decree modifying the specification for this AOC and redefining the *appellation* areas, except those of the *grands crus*. The Kimmeridgian specification is being replaced by a group of criteria applying to high-quality wine, which cover soil, subsoil, relief, aspect and suitability for cultivation. Sometimes the boundaries have been extended westward as at Maligny, La Chapelle-Vaupelteigne and Beine; in other places such as Préhy and Viviers, extensive areas have gone back to farming.

CHABLIS
GRAND CRU

THE Chablis *Grand Cru* area consists of about 100 hectares, almost entirely under vines. This sloping terrain on the right bank of the river Serein faces mainly west-south-west, sometimes east-south-east, and even north-west, depending on the alignment of the valleys. Except for a minute portion of the lower slopes

Above, eighteenth-century wine-merchant's signboard (Wine Museum, Beaune).

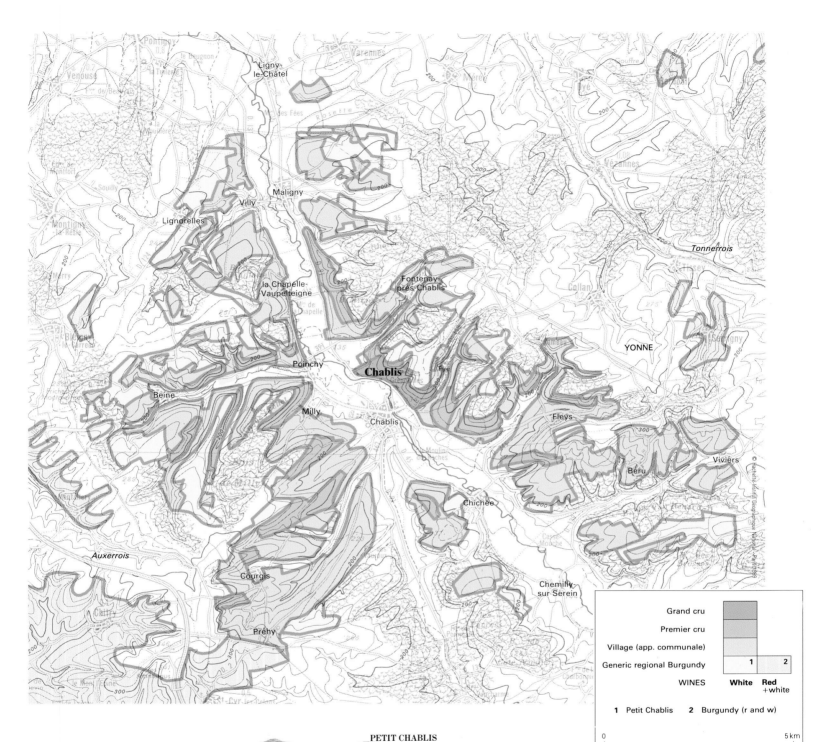

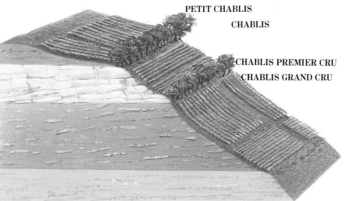

Sands, clays and marls
(Barremian stage of Lower Cretaceous)

Portlandian limestones

Clayey limestones and marls
containing Exogyra virgula
(Middle and Upper Kimmeridgian)

Sublithographic limestones
of the Lower Kimmeridgian
(Sequanian)

240 m

130 m

PETIT CHABLIS

CHABLIS

CHABLIS PREMIER CRU

CHABLIS GRAND CRU

Chablis: the three types of soil.

of Les Clos and Blanchot, the soils consist of grey rendzina over Kimmeridgian marls.

The soils on the upper parts of the slope are coarser in texture and are enriched by small pebbles of limestone from the spur-shaped Portlandian cliff, which shelters the vines from north winds. Further down, there is white clayey marl, which is actively chalky and sometimes harmful to growth. Too strong a solution of carbonates in the soil inhibits the transfer of iron necessary for the formation of chlorophyll. When this happens, chlorosis occurs and the plant turns yellow and is unable to process minerals from the soil: normal development ceases and the plant is unable to manufacture sugars. In areas where soils cause chlorosis, Chardonnay is often grafted onto a stock able to withstand excess chalk.

The ground here slopes steeply and the heavy, sticky soil is full of small fossil oysters (*Exegyra virgula*). The river Serein is close enough to influence conditions suitable for producing fine wine.

generally rather firm wines. Les Preuses wines are often considered the softest. Vaudésir and Valmur are close together but variations in soil and aspect bring out different qualities in their wine: both have good structure and ageing potential, but Vaudésir is sometimes livelier and Valmur more charming. Chablis *Grand Cru* is a translucent green when young but later turns pale gold, with a bouquet of exquisite elegance.

Right-hand page, Saint Vincent (Confrérie des Trois Ceps, Saint-Bris-le-Vineux) Below, a rounded hilltop at Chablis.

limestone becomes more noticeable: sheer slopes with shallow soil on which vines are sometimes grown. The 'cliff' forming the plateau edge is never more than a few metres high and is rarely included in the zone of Chablis *Premier Cru*, which generally comes from the marl slopes. The soils are all similar, but varying aspects produce some very different wines.

After the delimitations were revised, seventy-nine of these *lieux-dits* were classified either completely or in part as *premiers crus*. Growers have also regrouped themselves under the names of seventeen *climats* (Fourchaume, Montée de Tonnerre, Mont de Milieu and so on).

climat name of Fourchaume. These are wines of remarkable refinement with scents of meadow flowers and new mown hay.

East of the *grands crus*, beside the road leading to Fyé, is the group of vineyards entitled to use the name Montée de Tonnerre: Les Chapelots, which is on a steep south slope, Montée de Tonnerre, Pied d'Aloup just above it and Côte de Bréchain. The wines are very refined, with a firm backbone and slight harshness, enabling them to age well.

On the south side of the Mont de Milieu, on the hill which once marked the boundary between the provinces of Burgundy and Champagne, there now grow some of the most firm and robust of the *premiers crus*. After the village of Fleys we come to the corn-growing plateaux round Tonnerre and have to go still further south, down to the villages of Béru and Viviers, to find hillsides of vines. Here only Vaucoupins in the commune of Chichée counts as a *premier cru*.

An immense number of *lieux-dits* with enchanting names are classified as *premiers crus*; on the left bank of the Serein are Butteaux, Montmains, Malinots, Roncières and Epinottes. Nearer Chablis there is Les Lys, then Côte de Léchet in the village of Milly, and, finally, Les Troesmes with its good southern aspect. Vau Vigneau, Vau de Vey and Vaux Ragons all give drier-tasting wines.

Chablis *Grand Cru* is situated entirely on Chablis village land. Each of the seven *grands crus* has its own distinctive character: Grenouilles is in the middle, on steep, fairly consistent land at the foot of the slope, giving pleasingly ample and generous wines. Les Clos has the largest area and the most uniform situation, on a regular south-west facing slope, and gives firm wine which will keep on improving. Blanchot, on a steep eastern slope, produces light, refined wines. Bougros, or Bouguerots, in the extreme west, is near the river and more subject to frost; the very steeply sloping land here is difficult to work but very rewarding for its rich,

CHABLIS *PREMIER CRU*

IN this region the sedimentary layers slope slightly towards the Paris Basin. Over the same altitude, the Kimmeridgian marl therefore appears as a plateau in the east (at Viviers, Béru and Poilly-sur-Serein) and in the south (at Chemilly-sur-Serein, Chichée and Préhy), while forming most of the slopes in the heartland of the *appellation*. Further down the valley of the Serin, the low cliff made of hard Portlandian

The *premiers crus* on the right bank, with their better exposed sites, have justifiably acquired a higher reputation. The slopes on each side of the *grands crus* can boast a succession of famous names. In the west, L'Homme Mort in the village of Maligny, La Fourchaume in La Chapelle-Vaupelteigne and Poinchy, and Vaupulent in Poinchy, are all part of a consistent gentle slope facing south-west. The south-east-facing Côte de Fontenay and Vaulorent, with its varying aspects, are on either side of the valley enclosing the village of Fontenay-près-Chablis, and complete the list of vineyards entitled to sell under the

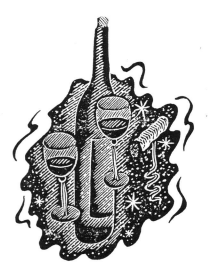

Chablis and Petit Chablis

PLATEAU land unsuitable for cultivation is covered in woodland. When easy development of slightly sloping ground is possible, on a sufficiently thick layer of good arable clay, there may be plantings of vines on the edges of the *grand cru* and *premier cru* areas. Sites with a maximum number of suitable factors have been classed as AOC Chablis, and produce 70,000 hl from about 1,400 hectares spread over twenty villages. Sites producing adequate wine are included in the Petit Chablis *appellation* (140 hectares giving 6,000 hl).

Chablis is grown on marl slopes (at Viviers and Béru), on the edge of the Portlandian limestone plateau (Fontenay, Maligny and Beine) or on Tertiary clay plateaux (Lignorelles). The wines are of different types, though with some characteristics in common. The first is firm and solid, with some ageing potential; the other two are more immediately tasty and should be drunk at once.

The choice of Chardonnay in the Chablis region is quite recent and probably goes back only to the post-phylloxera period. Since 1970 there has been a spectacular expansion of vine-growing in this area. As well as more effective means of protection, there has been greater specialization and a move from mixed farming to vines. At the same time, with a guaranteed supply, business enterprises have been able to create more stable markets. An additional advantage has been the fashion for white wines, especially in America.

The wine is always light and dry with a remarkably rich bouquet and ageing ability. There are predominant scents of mushroom and truffle, together with iodine and a green sappy flavour. Vinification techniques have made some progress. The 136 l chestnut wood *feuillettes* have been replaced by stainless steel vats which allow a greater volume of more consistent wine to be made. Certain enterprises, as in the neighbouring Côte d'Or and Saône-et-Loire, raise the wine in new Burgundian *pièces* (large casks). This is a new development for Chablis and gives the wine the refinement of oak.

Between the Yonne and the Armançon

Auxerre

IT is possible to go from one end to the other of the Yonne *département* without seeing a single vine. The main roads are up on the plateaux and pass only immense fields of corn. Nearer Auxerre, the capital of Lower Burgundy, the hills in spring are covered with cherry blossom and these orchards are sometimes interspersed with vines.

Between Auxerre and Nitry the Paris – Lyon motorway runs along the rocky ridge separating the much lusher river basins of the Serein and Yonne and crosses the outer ring of the Upper Jurassic. In the west is land whose soils and aspects resemble those of Chablis, and hence there are also old wine villages such as Chitry and Saint-Bris-le-Vineux. Further north, land less suitable for vines produces little wine except for the VDQS Sauvignon de Saint-Bris made from the only Sauvignon grown in Burgundy, a variety once called Epicier. The use of this grape indicates that this is a transition zone between

St Vincent

Burgundy and the Loire Valley. This is a fragrant white wine made in Burgundian fashion and less sharp than Sancerre. It has quite a reputation although the output is only about 3,000 hl.

Further south, towards the valley of the Cure, the red wine tradition in

Irancy extends to the villages of Cravant (Côte de Palotte), which stands at the confluence of the Cure and the Yonne rivers, and Vincelottes. The name Irancy may go with a Bourgogne *appellation*. A very old local grape variety known as César or Romain is sometimes used and the tannin from this means that the wine matures well.

On the right bank of the Yonne, vines are grown on marl slopes and on the plateau edge of hard limestone, where some excellent burgundy is made from Chardonnay and Pinot Noir. Aligoté gives some pleasant wines. Sacy used to be grown for making sparkling wines but is now being replaced by more refined grape varieties. This region was in fact one of the earliest producing the slightly sparkling Crémant de Bourgogne and now has a cooperative to improve the wine and ensure its survival. At Bailly there are 3 hectares of amazing underground galleries from which the stone for Auxerre cathedral, a fine example of gothic architecture, and the Panthéon in Paris was quarried. These are used by the growers making sparkling wine and can hold more than 10 million bottles.

On the other side of the river Yonne similar wines are produced in the villages of Jussy and Coulanges-la-Vineuse, where a superb eighteenth-century wine-press still exists. Auxerre was a major wine producer in the eighteenth and nineteenth centuries but now has only one vineyard, the Clos de la Chaînette. Vine-growing was abandoned after the phylloxera epidemic which devastated the area in 1878 and urban development has taken over.

There is classified wine territory in fourteen other local villages, but only in scattered vineyards without much reputation.

Tonnerre

TEN villages near Tonnerre, an attractive little town built on terraces and surrounded by vineyards, are also entitled to Burgundy regional *appellations*, but this small wine district just

west of Chablis now consists of only 50 hectares situated mainly in Epineuil. The wines of Tonnerre and the Tonnerre region, on the river Armançon, used to have a considerable reputation as the best in the Yonne. These were white wines of strength and refinement which were often thought comparable to the best Chablis and Meursault. 'Pineau' Noir and Blanc were grown at Tonnerre, and Morillon Blanc gave white wines at Epineuil and Dannemoine. Good-quality red wine was based on 'Pineau'. There were also some sparkling wines, based on the same grapes.

Joigny

NORTH of Auxerre, the Armançon and the Serein flow into the Yonne near Joigny, the gateway to Burgundy, and these rivers apparently brought along some good wine-growing techniques, as in the eighteenth century Joigny wines had a reputable 'bourgeois' name. The local chalky tufa is ideal for Cabernet Franc (Touraine) and produces the Côte Saint Jacques *vin gris*, the last remnant of this Burgundy wine region.

Vézelay

OVERLOOKING the valley of the Cure, the marvellous hill on which the pilgrimage town of Vézelay has grown up is gradually being clothed in vines. Slopes at Saint-Père-sous-Vézelay, Asquins, Tharoiseau and Vézelay itself have been replanted with vines during the last ten years or so. Pinot Noir and Chardonnay are growing on sites identical to those in the rest of Burgundy in their gradient, aspect and soils overlying hard limestone or Liassic marly limestone. These favourable conditions have made it possible to include this small production area with Burgundy vineyards. However, there are limited possibilities for expansion here and ripening the grapes is sometimes difficult.

CÔTE DE NUITS AND HAUTES CÔTES DE NUITS

THE Côte de Nuits is little more than a corrugation in the landscape, a modest fault scarp between two monotonously flat regions – the Burgundy plateaux on one side and the Saône valley plain on the other. To the east it faces out towards the distant Jura. Vines are grown along a narrow, sloping strip of land running first south as far as Nuits-Saint-Georges, then south-east, which is rarely more than 1 k wide. The altitude is between 230 and 260 m in the south, and between 270 and 300 m nearer Dijon.

However, this is the Champs-Elysées of Burgundy, a road along which the name of every village or *climat* is familiar throughout the world. The Côte de Nuits is a masterpiece of human determination to conquer the environment. At times the vines have to compete with clumps of trees, as at Gevrey-Chambertin, or with barren patches of stunted oaks and junipers such as those at Vosne-Romanée. Fields and woodland soon take over on the plain.

From village to village, the dry Alpine-type valleys make deep gashes in the side of the escarpment and lead up to the Hautes Côtes on their plateau between the lower vineyards of the Côte de Nuits and the valley of the river Ouche. The Hautes Côtes have a sombre, lonely atmosphere which brightens up further south but is still very unlike that of the bustling, congested territory below.

The most noticeable feature is the stone: stone walls enclosing vineyards as in the Clos Saint-Jacques at Gevrey-Chambertin; the piles of pebbles dug out of the soil over the centuries and now occupied by dozing grass-snakes; the stone roof-slates on churches, cottages and washhouses such as those at Fixin; or the impressive marble-like quarry face near Comblanchien. The villages are very distinctive in character and the splendid houses (*maisons de vignerons*) are hidden by high walls since there is a local saying that '*on ne fait pas le vin sur la place publique*' ('you don't make wine in the market place'). Vines grow well on stony terrain, consisting here of marl and Bathonian limestone. People are living and vines are growing in

valleys formed during the Quaternary Ice Age. If you walk through these vines, you often come across fossil shells left by prehistoric seas.

The Côte de Nuits has consistent soil and weather, it is planted with a single grape variety, the Pinot Noir, and it is the site of almost all the great red Burgundy *crus*. So the region is all of a piece, although geographically it is made up of four distinct areas.

Between Dijon and Marsannay-la-Côte there were once considerable areas of vines, now replaced by urban development. The vines remaining at Les Montreculs are evidence of the

Vines on the hillside at Vosne-Romanée, with woodland above.

once vigorous Dijon wine industry, which produced white wine comparable to Meursault. At Chenôve the Clos du Roy and a vat room that belonged to the Dukes of Burgundy survive. After Marsannay, vines take over completely. The regional *appellations* are predominant as far as the Combe de Lavaux at Gevrey-Chambertin. Between here and the Combe de la Serrée at Nuits-Saint-Georges there are no fewer than twenty-two *grands crus*. Then, as far as the Combe de Magny, vines grow in high stony country. The Côte de Nuits finally stops at the little road just before Buisson: the noticeboard by the Clos de Langres really should be moved a few hundred metres to the south.

There are differences in these four areas, but the style of wine is similar. This is apparent as you reach La Corvée sur Ladoix, where you find real Côte de Nuits wine: clean, bright, robust, with strong aromas of soft fruit and needing time to mature. This style of wine is general, with subtle local variations resulting from the soil, the vintage or the individual maker's touch.

In the hinterland west of the Côte, some slopes on the undulating plateau lend themselves to wine-growing. Depending on the type of soil, here less uniform, the best exposed hillsides can use the Burgundy regional *appellation* with the addition of Hautes Côtes de Nuits as the place of origin. Aligoté tends to be grown on less favoured sites and produces a crisp and lively dry white wine, very pleasant to drink young (Villers-la-Faye, Magny-lès-Villers, Marey-lès-Fussey). At Villars-Fontaine, Meuilley and

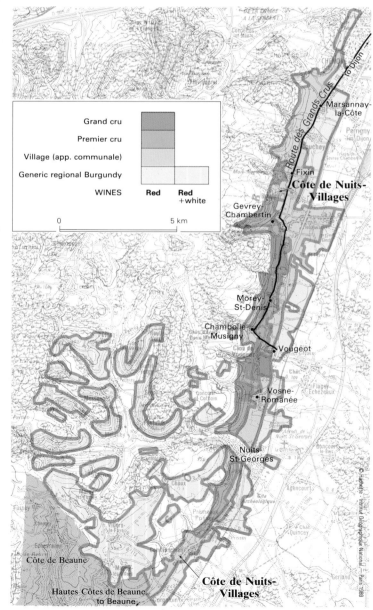

WINES	Red	Red + white
Grand cru		
Premier cru		
Village (app. communale)		
Generic regional Burgundy		

0   5 km

Echevronne some excellent Burgundy is produced from Pinot Noir and especially Chardonnay. Les Vergy (from Reulle, Curtil and L'Etang) evokes the name of a great medieval family in Burgundy.

There is harsher weather in the Hautes Côtes than on the Côte itself. Wine-growing extends no further north than Chambolle-Musigny and is restricted to the triangle formed by Chambolle, Bévy and Magny-lès-Villers. The Côte de Nuits vines bud, flower and ripen a few days later than those of the Côte de Beaune, and the Hautes Côtes are later still. They are on higher ground here and the vines are grown higher up the hillsides.

CÔTE DE NUITS-VILLAGES

THE reputation of the *crus*, of Chambertin or Clos de Vougeot, has been established for centuries. Village *appellations* go back only to the last century or the beginning of this, in their present form. *Appellations* received protective legislation only in 1919 and again in 1935. Each village on the Côte de Nuits has its own *appellation* although, like Vougeot, some are very small in area. Others with a limited area of production chose to call themselves Vins Fins de la Côte de Nuits. This later became Côte de Nuits-Villages and is an *appellation* restricted to five villages. In the north it applies to Fixin, which may also use its own name, and to Brochon for the area not classified as AOC Gevrey-Chambertin; in the south it applies to part of Prissey and to Comblanchien and Corgoloin. The *appellation* is governed by similar production conditions to the village *appellations* and produces some very good-quality red wine (6,400 hl).

MARSANNAY AND FIXIN

MARSANNAY

EVEN before the phylloxera epidemic, Pinot Noir was being replaced by Gamay on the slopes of Marsannay-la-Côte. With the large urban area of Dijon nearby, a rapid turnover of everyday wine was easily ensured. Conditions locally were not

suitable for a village-type *appellation* and growers applied unsuccessfully for inclusion in the Côte de Nuits-Villages. More recently there has been replanting with Pinot Noir and Chardonnay and a 1987 decree has defined conditions of production for AOC Marsannay: red and white wines are produced above the road through the *grands crus*, on a defined area of land in Chenôve, Marsanny-la-Cote and Couchey. Since 1965 Marsannay has been acquiring a reputation, almost unique in Burgundy, for some elegant and distinctive rosé wines. Appellation Bourgogne wines could already use the AOC Bourgogne followed by Marsannay, and the rosés, in acknowledgement of their individuality, are now also entitled to the village *appellation* but applicable to a much larger production area. They are grown on slopes with a consistent aspect and soil composed of thick scree deposits.

FIXIN

THE slopes at Fixin are dominated by the Clos de la Perrière, which once belonged to the monks of Cîteaux

South of the Combe d'Orveau.

and has buildings dating back to the eleventh century. This *climat* (vineyard site) extends into the village of Brochon and has a well-founded reputation. Between 1741 and 1843 it belonged to the Marquis de Montmort and could sell its red wines at the same rates as Chambertin.

Fixin produces 1,150 hl of powerful tannic wine which keeps well. The finest *climats* are Les Arvelets, Les Hervelets and Le Chapitre, along with La Perrière and the Clos Napoléon.

This once belonged to Noisot, a veteran of the Napoleonic wars and so passionate an admirer of the Emperor

Fixin.

that he commissioned a monument called 'Le Réveil de Napoléon' from the Dijon sculptor François Rude. This can still be seen in the Parc Noisot at Fixin.

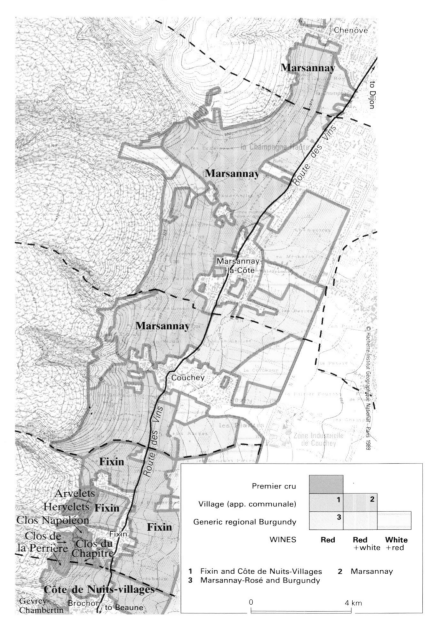

GEVREY-CHAMBERTIN

The château at Gevrey-Chambertin.

THE old village of Gevrey-Chambertin lies at the foot of the Combe de Lavaux, a cool, deep gorge sloping down from the Hautes Côtes and forming a crossing point in the Côte de Nuits. It is said that the cement facing on the church is pink because of all the wine used in making it. The château was built by an Abbot of Cluny to store his wine crop and is practically a cellar with fortifications. Even the chapterhouse is a Romanesque wine-store. Along narrow streets in the hub of the village of Gevrey, behind high walls covered with ivy and wistaria, there are old houses, *cuveries* (where fermenting takes place) and storage buildings, all in some way connected with wine. On the *Route des Grands Crus* is the handsome Hôtel Jobert de Chambertin, named after the man who launched Chambertin in the eighteenth century. Lower down the valley, beyond the main road and the Baraques quarter, is 'Nouveau' Gevrey, which has been expanding in the last twenty years and is no longer mainly concerned with wine. The village has 2,500 inhabitants, with eighty families connected with wine-growing.

A SPECTRUM OF *APPELLATIONS*

THE Côte itself starts at Dijon, but the landscape broadens out at Gevrey-Chambertin. Every corner of the region is used for vines, which grow in dense rows all the way up the stony hillsides on soil coloured red by iron salts.

The whole spectrum of Burgundy *appellations* can be found at Gevrey-Chambertin. First there are the *grands crus*, with Chambertin and the seven accompanying *crus*. Gevrey-Chambertin is the largest village *appellation* with more than 300 hectares,

50 hectares of which extend into the southern part of the village of Brochon. The main road (RN 74) forms a boundary between the fine wines and the ordinary ones. However, the village *appellation* extends a long way eastwards over the main road. Gevrey-Chambertin is in fact situated in the middle of the Côte-de-Nuits anticline, on outcrops formed in different eras and producing different soil types. Vines can be grown a long way into the plain because of the broad alluvial deposits fanning out from the Combe de Lavaux.

All these natural factors have an effect on the wines. The *grands crus* and *premiers crus* are grown on the slopes, while wines of the Gevrey-Chambertin *appellation*, which are more often grown at the foot of the hills, have characteristics which vary according to the consistency of the soil.

On the slope north of the Combe de Lavaux you can see outcrops of marl layers from the middle Jurassic (marl containing *Ostrea acuminata* oyster fossils). These layers are overlaid with scree or with deposits of red silt brought down from the plateau, as at the *premier cru* vineyards of Les Etournelles, Clos des Varoilles, and the upper areas of Lavaux, Clos Saint-Jacques and Les Cazetiers. The wines from here acquire a fully rounded character, with elegance and refinement from the gravel layers and ageing ability from the clay-rich marl nearby.

The monks of Cluny Abbey were once the biggest vine-owners in Gevrey-Chambertin and the *premier cru* of Combe les Moines was named after them. Other famous vineyards are Les Champeaux and Les Evocelles in Brochon, though the latter is not a *premier cru*. These are all east facing but, from the southern part of Les Cazetiers onwards, the exposure is more to the south-east. Clos Saint-Jacques behind its superb stone walls has some remarkably high-quality wines, which are frequently compared to the neighbouring *grands crus*. Just below, at the top of the village, is the equally historic Clos du Chapitre, contemporary with Clos de Vougeot;

this was ceded by the monks of Bèze Abbey to the Chapter of Langres Cathedral, in whose domain Dijon was at that time.

THE EPITOME OF GREAT BURGUNDY

FURTHER south, the hillside narrows but provides the site for all the *grands crus*. Along with Romanée-Conti and Clos de Vougeot, Chambertin is historically the earliest red wine in Burgundy. Chambertin includes Clos de Bèze (28 hectares in all, producing 650 hl) and these two count as a single *appellation*. The vines stretch along the best section of the slope with woods above and the *Route des Grands Crus* below. All the factors for producing splendidly rounded wines are united here: a limestone foundation very close to the surface, shallow soil and a gentle slope facing east so that it gets all the sun from dawn onwards. Substance, colour, bouquet, refinement, strength – Chambertin has them all. The wine-writer G. Roupnel used to say: 'This one wine contains the qualities of all Great Burgundy.'

The other *grands crus* (2,000 hl from 73 hectares) are on neighbouring sites to the north and south. Mazis-Chambertin and Latricières-Chambertin are comparable to Chambertin in every respect. Ruchottes-Chambertin is a separate case: this small area of very shallow, more pebbly soil, almost down to the rock base, generally produces elegant and subtle wines. Chapelle-Chambertin and Griotte-Chambertin,

Vineyards at Gevrey-Chambertin.

NAPOLEON'S WINE

NAPOLEON was loyal all his life to the Chambertin recommended by his doctors. The wine was supplied to him in bottles made at Sèvres and marked with a crowned letter N. It was five or six years old and the emperor drank it watered down, never more than half a bottle at a meal. A carriage known as 'La Grande Cave' ('the great cellar') would accompany Napoleon on his campaigns and on the field of battle he would sometimes send a glass of his own wine to a wounded soldier.

CLAUDE JOBERT DE CHAMBERTIN

IN Burgundy one cannot call oneself after a grand cru. There may be people called Romanée-Conti or Corton-Grancey but in these cases it is the family that has given its name to the wine: the reverse process goes against all tradition. Claude Jobert (1701–68) was one man who challenged this. Employed as a farmer by the canons of Langres cathedral, he managed to acquire a sizeable area of Chambertin and Clos de Bèze. He sold his wine to German royal courts, made his fortune and called himself Jobert de Chambertin. However, he had no descendants and the name died out in the next generation.

with its scent of cherries, have the advantage of an intermediate climate in a dip east of the *Route des Grands Crus*. But Charmes-Chambertin and Mazoyères-Chambertin are less well-placed: the curving aspect means that wines from higher up are better than those from the lower section beside the main road. Since 1945, Mazoyères has also been entitled to use the name Charmes-Chambertin.

The *premiers crus* (2,500 hl from 85 hectares) include some magnificent neighbours of the Chambertin family, such as Fonteny, Les Corbeaux and Les Combettes, which lies between Latricières and Clos de la Roche.

In the Gevrey-Chambertin AOC

Les Goulots (a premier cru *vineyard at Gevrey-Chambertin).*

production area (10,000 hl from 350 hectares), the foot of the slope, between the *premiers crus* and the RN 74, gives robust, tannin-rich wines which age well, while the wines from east of the road, on the more gravelly soils of the alluvial outflow from the Combe de Lavaux, have a fragrance and refinement from early youth. A blend of the two is best for a really rounded wine, but this is not always necessary, and the wine from Crais is good enough on its own.

In 1963 producers sensibly removed some sites not up to the village *appellation* standard by revising the *appellation* area in the plain. This revision has recently been implemented and a study at the University of Burgundy under Professor N. Leneuf has confirmed that these new boundaries are appropriate.

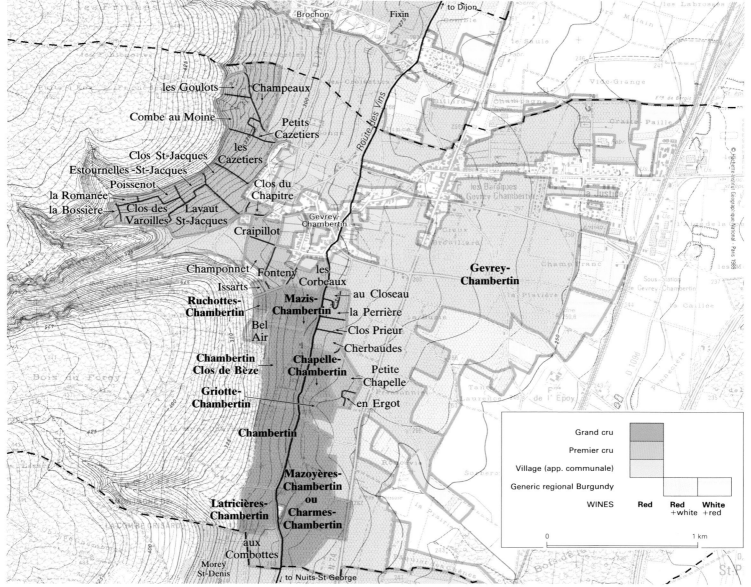

MOREY-SAINT-DENIS

Grand cru
Premier cru
Village (app. communale)
Generic regional Burgundy
WINES **Red** **Red** **White**
       +white **+red**

0   1 km

ONCE past Les Latricières and into the territory of Morey-Saint-Denis, the vineyards suddenly climb a hundred or so metres higher up the hillside, where small transverse faults have exposed good vine-growing soil near the Combe Grisard. There is a miniature château here which has the Monts-Luisants vines almost as its private garden. Such places were known locally as '*maisons de quatre heures*' ('four o'clock houses') as the owners used to hold lavish tea-parties at four o'clock or spend whole Sundays there in the fresh air.

Since the vineyards formerly belonged to abbeys such as Cîteaux, La Bussière and Saint-Germain des Prés in Paris, the workers cleared and planted land for themselves higher up the hill. These large plots enclosed by modern walls are not an attractive addition to the present-day countryside. The Combe-Grisard lies between Gevrey and Morey. The Mansouse stream has its source here but does not affect vineyard soils. The other valley, directly above the village, does influence the terrain, by causing variations in the usual topography of the hillside and by shaping the land in the plain east of the main road where the village *appellation* vines grow.

Morey is a small village with a vine area of about 275 hectares, 150 of which are used for the village *appellation* and for *premiers* and *grands crus*, and the rest for regional *appellation* wines. Production consists essentially of red wines, although the regional *appellation* may also apply to white. Monts-Luisants have a solid reputation for their *premiers crus*. The family of *grands crus*, which already included Clos de la Roche, Clos Saint-Denis and part of Bonnes-Mares, was extended to cover Clos des Lambrays in 1981. It is possible to visit the *domaine*

park and admire its fine trees and ornamental rockeries and grottoes, all very much in the taste of the bourgeois families who stayed here.

Clos de la Roche borders on Gevrey-Chambertin to the north, and is the first and largest of the *grands crus*, covering more than 16 hectares and producing 450 hl annually. The *appellation* includes eight different holdings and takes its name from one with an area of a little over 4.50 hectares. Like Clos de Bèze in Gevrey, it is not enclosed by walls. (The word '*clos*' normally applies to a walled garden or vineyard.) In 1969 it acquired almost a whole hectare of land with the addition of a plot from Les Genavrières and a small section of Les Chaffots.

Clos Saint-Denis also has no walls enclosing it. It takes its name from the Collegiate Church of Saint-Denis in Vergy (Hautes-Côtes). In 1927 the vineyard name was added to the village name of Morey to form Morey-Saint-Denis. This *climat* produces 170 hl from 6.6 hectares on the central part of the slope between the village and Clos de la Roche. Less well

known than Clos de la Roche, the wines from Clos Saint-Denis are full-bodied, substantial and long-lasting. The southern part of the vineyard receives more of the midday sun and produces warmer-flavoured wines.

The opposite bank of the valley with its north-north-east aspect has a quite different atmosphere. The vines here at Clos des Lambrays are grown higher up the hillside and need their sheltering walls. Wines from here are lively and age well. One hundred and sixty hl are produced on 8.8 hectares.

The southern part of Morey-Saint-Denis ends with Clos de Tart and a small section of Bonnes Mares. Clos de Tart produces 200 hl from 7.5 hectares and, like Les Lambrays, is virtually autonomous. The *grand cru* has a long-established reputation and vines were cultivated here in medieval times by Bernardine nuns from the Abbey of Tart, a village in the Tilles plain east of the Côte. The vineyard walls date from the late nineteenth century and there are interesting cellars on two levels. Clos de Tart wines are elegant and fruity and they mature well without any loss of refinement.

Besides these *grands crus* there are about ten *premiers crus*, including Les Charmes, the upper part of Clos des Ormes, Les Millandes, Les Ruchots and Les Sorbés, all giving wines of considerable class.

Morey-Saint-Denis may not have such a long established reputation as its neighbours but is otherwise entirely comparable. Before the AOC system was organized, the wines were often sold as Gevrey or Chambolle, but they have recently been promoted in their own right, notably at the Festival of Dionysos held every spring.

Solid and substantial Morey-Saint-Denis wines are produced at the top and bottom of the hillside, above and below the *crus*. They tend to be lighter when grown on the gravel outflow from the valley.

CHAMBOLLE-MUSIGNY

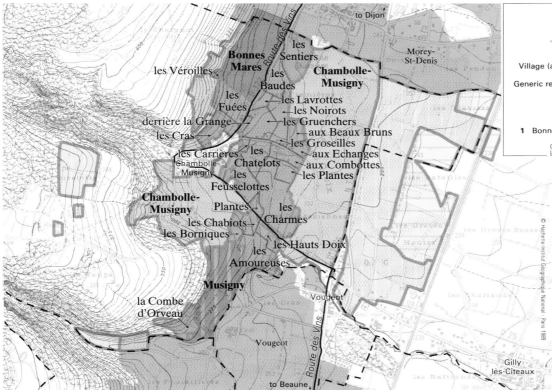

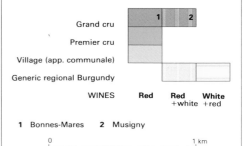

	Red	Red +white	White +red
Grand cru			1 2
Premier cru			
Village (app. communale)			
Generic regional Burgundy			

WINES

1 Bonnes-Mares 2 Musigny

0   1 km

GEVREY is a fair-sized market town and Morey a small village, but Chambolle-Musigny is a hamlet compressed along each side of one street along the valley. There are one or two rows of houses and then you are out among the vines again. Chambolle has acquired a magnificent reputation among the *grands crus*. It was formerly known as Gilly, but its name was changed to Chambolle-Musigny in 1882.

This village is entirely dedicated to wine, which is produced on very shallow soil and is famous for its elegance. Almost without exception, the base-rock is very close to the surface and on the hillside there is solid limestone only a few centimetres down. The *grands crus* and *premiers crus* are grown in the central area. The alluvial deposits fanning out from the valley have a substratum of blocks and limestone pebbles (oolitic limestone) which are also close to the surface and ensure good drainage, even if the topography appears at first glance to be less favourable.

The Combotte ravine has merged just above the village with the Combe

Ambin, bringing down from the plateau Quaternary material, which lies over a homogeneous layer of Bathonian limestone. The valley divides Chambolle-Musigny into two: a northern part which extends from Morey-Saint-Denis, and a southern part where the aspects, soil and gradient are all slightly different.

BONNES-MARES AND MUSIGNY

BONNES-Mares, which stretches up to the south wall of Clos de Tart, covers 15 hectares (1.5 in Morey and the rest in Chambolle) and produces 410 hl. This one *grand cru* seems to possess all the Côte de Nuits qualities. Its wines (red only) are grown on an almost ideal site and are powerful and fleshy yet balanced and refined. Only the small quarry area along the *Route des Grands Crus* gives wine with different characteristics, but the amount of wine produced here is insignificant.

The village's other *grand cru* comes from the hill between the Chambolle-

Musigny valley and that of Orveau. Musigny is the most refined and aristocratic wine of the entire Côte. Only 270 hl are produced on 10.7 hectares in three *lieux-dits*: Les Musigny, Les Petits Musigny and Combe d'Orveau. There are some differences in soil and aspect, which reveal themselves in different batches of wine. Les Musigny has a steeper gradient and red alluvial soils with a high proportion of pebbly debris from the Quaternary Ice Age. These light poor soils produce a small yield, but the wines are of great elegance.

However, in Les Petits Musigny there is no red silt or pebble debris. The soils here are a little deeper and

produce wines with more tannin, from vines with roots almost in the rock. One oddity in the sea of Côte de Nuits is a tiny island of Chardonnay giving 10 hl of white AOC Musigny.

THE FAMOUS AMOUREUSES

THERE is a small group of *premiers crus* on about 20 hectares with similar soils and aspect. These are: Les Plantes and the lower section of Les Charmes, Les Hauts Doix and Les Amoureuses, which give rich and elegant wines. Les Amoureuses has both refinement and remarkable persistence and, partly because of its delightful name, is now as famous as a *grand cru*. Other high-quality wines close to the Musigny are Les Chabiots and Les Borniques.

Close to Bonnes-Mares are Les Fuées, Les Gruenchers, Les Cras, Les Lavrottes, Les Baudes, Les Feusselottes, Les Chatelots and Les Combottes, all giving very well-structured wines. Out of 200 hectares of fine wine, there are more than 80 hectares of *grands* and *premiers crus,* which give this village its splendid reputation.

Vines at Chambolle-Musigny.

VOUGEOT

CLOS de Vougeot and its château make a majestic picture in the heart of the Côte de Nuits landscape. Vougeot itself is a tiny commune of only 88 hectares, of which 69 are under vines, including 51 for the *grand cru* alone.

This is a genuine *clos*, the largest walled vineyard in Burgundy, with one wall going right around it. It is a pity that the main road now runs on the corniche above and that the wall is not better maintained. All the same, you cannot help being impressed by this great vineyard and by the château, a rare example in Burgundy of a country house built among the vines and not at all pretentious or overpowering. Here everything is secondary to wine and nowhere are the links between history and topography more visible.

produce excellent wine. There used to be a number of individually named plots within the Clos, such as Musigny, Plante-l'Abbé, Chioures and others, but these have been absorbed under the general name.

Clos de Vougeot had a very high reputation for Burgundy as far back as the seventeenth century, as a result of the wide influence in the Christian world of the Abbey of Cîteaux and the real quality of the wine. The vineyard was sold as public property at the time of the Revolution and passed through various hands before being bought by J. Ouvrard. He and his heirs had sole ownership until 1889, when it was first split up. Today the Clos consists of ninety plots

divided among eighty owners. Some reorganization has taken place so that there are in fact sixty working units, producing about 1,500 hl. Some owners have even built gates in front of their own part of the vineyard, rather like private chapels in a cathedral.

The single *appellation* of Clos de Vougeot applies to the whole vineyard. Perhaps another course could or should have been followed, especially as the lower portion of the Clos corresponds only to the village *appellation* in plots alongside. At the same time it seems right to pay tribute to a name of such significance throughout Burgundy.

The Clos de Vougeot red wine is full of body and strength – a wine to

Pitcher (Perrin-de-Puycousin Museum of Burgundian Life, Dijon).

lay down. It has hints of violet, truffle and wild mint, with remarkable length in the mouth. You have to live up to a wine like this: it will never welcome you with open arms.

The wine is as much a historical monument as the château, which has a thirteenth-century Romanesque cellar, built at ground level with a sloping roof to maintain the constant temperature suitable for wine storage.

A HISTORIC SITE

CLOS de Vougeot was established in about 1110 by the Abbey of Cîteaux and continued to be run by the Cistercian community until the French Revolution in 1789. By choosing this site, the monks hoped to control the little river Vouge too, which rises at Vougeot and provided the Abbey water supply. They also collected building stone for the Abbey from the hillside here.

The vineyard was an immensely ambitious project based on centuries of piecing together plots of land. It is the lowest of the *grands crus*, at the foot of the slope just where the land flattens out. On each side of it are Musigny and Echezeaux on their sunny hillsides, while above Clos de Vougeot the vegetation is almost as sparse as in Arizona.

It is usual to distinguish three different areas of the Clos: the gently sloping gravelly upper section, with a thin covering of soil over the limestone base; the middle section on a very slight slope, with brown clay over limestone debris; and the lower section of deep brown soil over a layer of marl. These soil types ought to produce three types of wine whose quality rises with the level of the Clos. This traditional belief is not always confirmed by tasting, although the plots in the middle area generally

The walled vineyard at Clos de Vougeot.

The *cuverie* is also a model of appropriate architecture, a cloister-like later construction with a huge antique wine-press in each corner. The château is a Burgundian Renaissance building commissioned by an Abbot of Cîteaux around 1550 and restored first by L. Bocquet in 1900 and later by the Confrérie des Chevaliers du Tastevin.

CLOS BLANC

CLOS Blanc, on the other side of the north wall, is a Côte de Nuits oddity. Chardonnay has survived here although abandoned in the rest of Clos de Vougeot where, in the early nineteenth century, it was still blended with Noirien (Pinot Noir) to give some finesse. It had been gradually replaced first by Beurot, which gave finesse without loss of colour,

and then altogether by Pinot Noir. The area now has the administrative name of La Vigne Blanche but the *cru* is still Clos Blanc. Clos de la Perrière has a site in the former stone quarry of Les Petits Vougeots where red wines, as in the rest of the *crus*, are classed as *premiers crus*.

A few plots around the village and in the lower part of Les Petits Vougeots are entitled to the Vougeot village *appellation*. This is restricted to less than 5 hectares and such a small area is really only a curiosity.

A twelfth-century wine-press at the château of Clos de Vougeot.

LES CHEVALIERS DU TASTEVIN

THIS Confrérie was founded in 1934 and is the oldest such wine organization. Since 1945 it has occupied the château of Clos de Vougeot, where 500 guests are convened to chapter-meetings twenty times a year. Throughout the world there are 10,000 members who have all sworn 'blameless devotion to wine' before being granted the purple and gold sash with the wine-taster's essential **tâtevin** (wine-tasting cup): 'In the name of Noah father of wine, in the name of Bacchus god of wine, in the name of Saint Vincent patron saint of wine-growers, we dub you Knight of the Tastevin.'

Tastevins *(for tasting wine) from the collection at the château of Clos de Vougeot.*

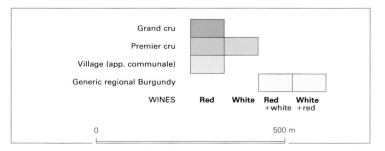

VOSNE-ROMANÉE

The church of Saint Martin at Vosne-Romanée. Right, seasoning casks.

BETWEEN Vosne-Romanée and Nuits-Saint-Georges the Côte starts to look rather bare on top. One cannot help thinking of Stendhal's comment that: 'If it were not for the admirable wine I should think nothing in the world could be uglier than our famous Côte d'Or'. Vines stop halfway up the hillside where the soil turns into plain rock. Yet this is where Romanée-Conti comes from.

It is customary to say that there is no common *appellation* in Vosne-Romanée. This is quite true. It is not just a village but a treasure-house of such marvels as Romanée, Romanée-Conti, Romanée Saint-Vivant, Richebourg, La Tâche, Echezeaux, Grands-Echezeaux… There is a surfeit of riches.

If you take the road to the right of the church you come directly to Romanée-Conti behind a cross erected in 1804, a patch of vines apparently unconscious of its glorious reputation. Flagey-Echezeaux is in the plain and adjoins Vosne-Romanée. The *grand cru* of Grands Echezeaux has a very consistent situation on little more than 9 hectares, producing 250 hl. Its closeness to Clos de Vougeot encourages comparisons with wine from the higher section of the Clos and with Bonnes Mares. Its qualities of strength, breeding and longevity certainly have something to do with growing in mid-slope, on a gentle gradient.

Echezeaux covers a much larger area, 40 hectares with an output of 1,000 hl. There are eleven different holdings, all or part of which are included in the production area.

Eighty producers make wine for this *appellation*, and most of their production is absorbed by the best *premiers crus* in the Côte. Here, too, the siting of the vines brings out differences in the wine. The Combe d'Orveau alone, one of the few valleys to be partly planted with vines, has a plot called En Orveau in a site quite unusual for a *grand cru* and altogether different from others in this *cru*.

Continuing south, we go through the excellent *premiers crus* of Les Suchots and return to the heights with Romanée Saint-Vivant, Richebourg, La Romanée, Romanée-Conti, and finally La Tâche. Three of these have single owners: La Tâche and Romanée-Conti belong to the Domaine de la Romanée-Conti, and La Romanée to Canon J. Liger-Belair. LaTâche now produces 170 hl from 6 hectares; it covered a smaller area earlier this century, before Les Gaudichots was included. Richebourg extends over 8 hectares producing 230 hl.

LA ROMANÉE, ROMANÉE-CONTI AND ROMANÉE SAINT-VIVANT

OTHER villages have holdings in Romanée (Gevrey-Chambertin, including a section classed as *premier cru*, and Chassagne-Montrachet). These holdings are always on the hillside. The vineyards of Vosne-Romanée were much coveted in the Middle Ages. In the twelfth century, the monks of Saint-Vivant owned a plot in Romanée and gradually added others, including those which were gifts from Alix de Vergy, the Duchess of Burgundy. It seems likely that the Abbey of Saint-Vivant owned what are today the three *grands crus*.

Despite their entangled boundaries, La Romanée (0.84 hectares giving 27 hl) and Romanée-Conti (1.8 hectares, 52 hl) make up a single vineyard or *climat*. A small part of the vineyard was bought before the Revolution by the Prince de Conti and was named after him.

Soils along the Côte and Hautes Côtes, level with Vosne-Romanée.

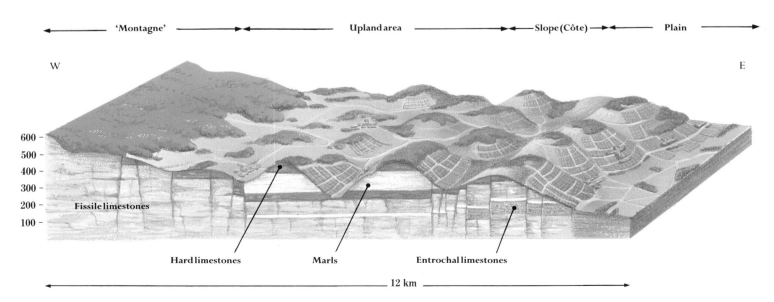

Romanée-Conti was famous everywhere by the eighteenth century and slightly overshadowed La Romanée. Both *appellations* are quite remarkable, with ideal sites and stunning wine. La Romanée grows on rather more sloping ground and it is perhaps this that gives the *appellation* its distinctiveness.

Romanée Saint-Vivant (9.4 hectares, 250 hl) takes its name from the monastery that owned it before the Revolution. Its situation is rather different from that of the other *grands crus* in the village: on marl in the higher portion, then lower down on soils like those of Romanée-Conti and Richebourg. The wines here are

astringent, with a substantial quality, which ages well. The aromas have a slight animal note as they develop.

Higher up the slope, the other *grands crus* are grown on hard limestone strata and shallow, pebbly soils. In Richebourg the aspect is slightly north-east. These are aristocratic wines, accessible when

young, but with the structure to mature well.

Vosne also has several remarkable *premiers crus*: Suchots, Beaumonts, Malconsorts and La Grand Rue, between Romanée and La Tâche. The Vosne-Romanée *appellation* overlaps with Flagey-Echezeaux but has a more varied character.

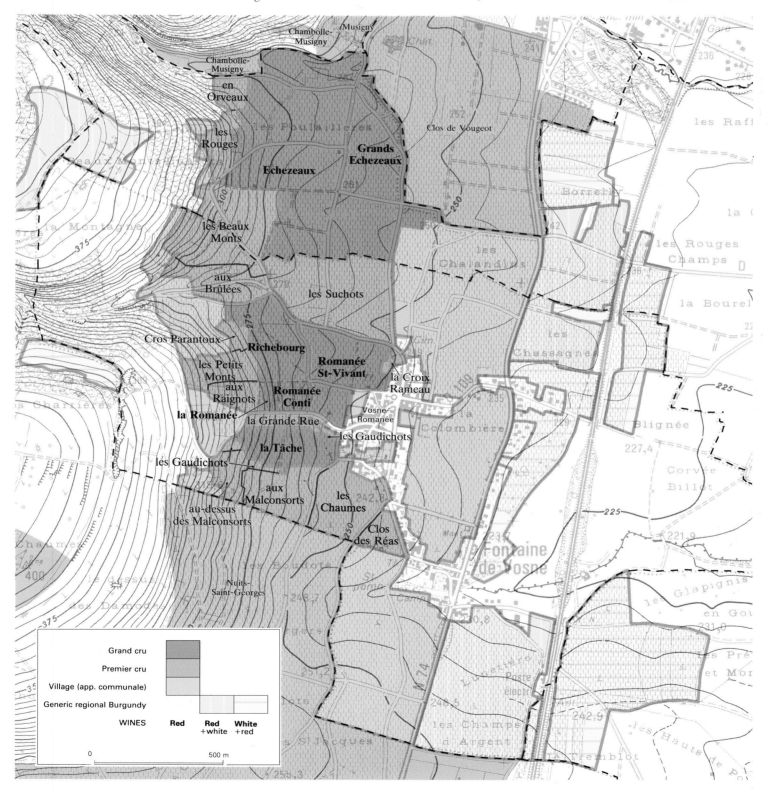

NUITS-SAINTS-GEORGES

THE seventeenth-century bell-tower of Nuits-Saint-Georges looks down on the busy *négociants*' offices in a town of 5,000 inhabitants and an expanding economy. The river Meuzin flows down from the Hautes-Côtes through the attractive Combe de la Serrée, though its course is almost hidden by buildings. As you go out towards Beaune, the handsome Château Gris can be seen perched up on the side of the hill.

The vineyards are north of the village, on a site similar to Vosne-Romanée: a steep hillside ending in a gentle slope down to the main road. The geographical character is the same from Gevrey-Chambertin onwards, but further south the slopes begin to face slightly east-south-east. Good soil becomes less common, the area of vines diminishes and the main road forming a boundary for fine wines edges closer to the vine-slopes. The bare hilltops of Vosne and to the

north of Nuits are now replaced by woodland. In the village of Premeaux, which is part of the Nuits-Saint-Georges AOC zone, the *appellation* includes a series of *clos* bordering the main road.

In 1892 Nuits added the name of Saint-Georges. Like Beaune, it is an important centre for *négociants/éleveurs* and a number of related activities, such as the production of sparkling wine (Crémant de Bourgogne) and fruit juices, and the packing and labelling of wine.

With Nuits the main centre for local people, and with the cultivation in the Hautes-Côtes nearby of soft fruit such as raspberries and blackcurrants, the manufacture of fruit liqueurs, especially crème de cassis, has grown up in the town. The maturing and marketing of brandies such as Marc and Fine de Bourgogne is another important local industry.

FINE *PREMIERS CRUS*

THE wines of Nuits have all the great Burgundy characteristics. They are generally firm and long-lasting, with a certain hardness in youth. There are no *grands crus* but a number of *premiers crus* (100 hectares, 3,000 hl), which in breeding are only just behind Côte de Nuits *grands crus*, particularly Les St-Georges, Les Vaucrains and Les Cailles. Differences in soil, aspect and situation between vineyards in the north and the south of the area mean some fairly diverse wines.

The vineyards at Nuits-Saint-Georges.

In the north Les Damodes, Aux Boudots, La Richemone, Aux Chaignots, Clos de Thorey, Aux Murgers and Aux Vignerondes grow on the same hillside as Vosne-Romanée, and their style almost merges with their neighbour's. There are still layers of marl here, giving the wine a certain astringency, which will ensure that it ages well. The light, shallow soils higher up the slope add slightly more refinement. There are scattered patches of waste land where arable soil necessary for vine-growing

---

THE SAINT-GEORGES MOON CRATER

IN Jules Verne's 'Journey Round the Moon', *the hero celebrates 'the union of Earth and its satellite' by drinking a bottle of Nuits. On 25 July 1971 this gesture was repeated when the Apollo XV space crew officially baptized a lunar depression as the Saint-Georges Crater. The inhabitants of Nuits gave the same name to a square in the town and the American astronauts came to the opening ceremony in 1973. So Nuits is justifiably proud of having the only wine known on both the Earth and the Moon.*

has been eroded. In some places the rock has been crushed so that vines can be grown, but a ban on bringing in soil from elsewhere restricts new planting.

ONE VILLAGE, MANY WINES

IN the southern sector, Les Pruliers, Les Procès, Rue de Chaux and Roncière give elegant wines, delicious to drink young, although, like all the Nuits-Saint-Georges *appellation* (170 hectares, 4,500 hl), they also age very well. It is from the Premeaux pink limestone that Les Porrets gains its wild, greeny pear flavour, while Les Vaucrains, Les Cailles and Les St-Georges, a *cru* that goes back to AD 1,000, derive their strength and maturing potential from the scree brought down from the little valley nearby. Above these are Les Perrières, Les Crots and Les Poulettes, growing directly on rock.

Premeaux-Prissey (42 hectares of *premiers crus*, giving 1,800 hl) is Clos territory: Clos des Forêts Saint-Georges in Les Forêts; Clos des Corvées, Clos des Corvées Pagets, Clos Saint-Marc, all near the church in Aux Corvées; Clos des Argillières, Clos des Grandes Vignes and Clos de L'Arlot on such a steep slope in the middle of Premeaux that part of it can only be worked by hand; and finally Clos de la Maréchale with its splendidly uniform red earth.

Apart from a couple of holdings, the whole of the Nuits-Saint-Georges *appellation* is confined to this one village. It is not completely consistent. The wines from the southern part of the village, on scree which has come down from the plateau above, are different from the wines from the north where, like the village wines of Vosne-Romanée, they grow on later, Oligocene rock. Nuits-Saint-Georges also has a regional *appellation* wine called Côte-de-Nuits-Villages.

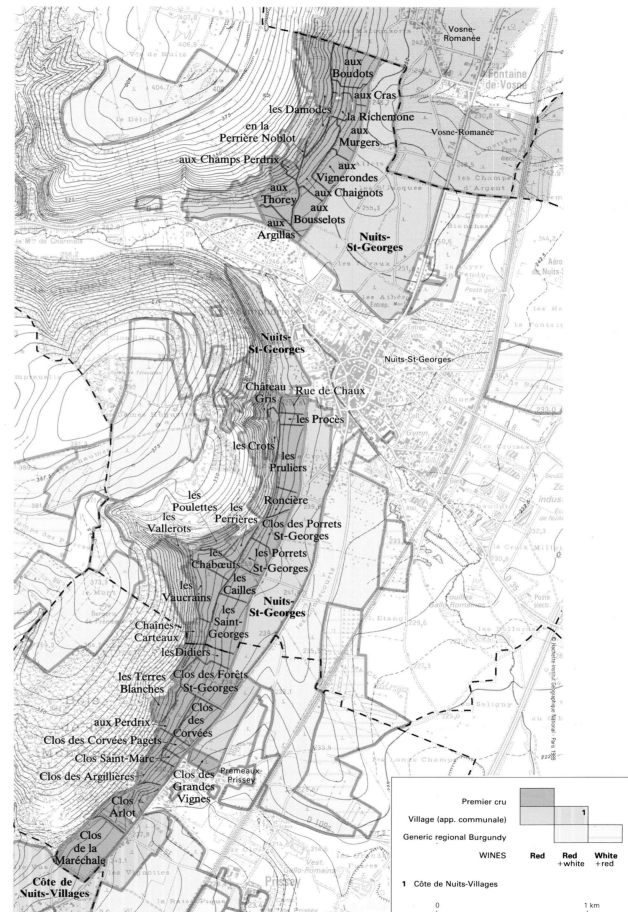

	Premier cru		
Village (app. communale)			1
Generic regional Burgundy			
WINES	Red	Red +white	White +red

1 Côte de Nuits-Villages

0   1 km

CÔTE DE BEAUNE AND HAUTES CÔTES DE BEAUNE

SHORTLY after Corgoloin it is possible to see all along the Côte de Beaune from the hill at Corton right up to the pyramid-shaped mound of Camp de Chassey opposite Les Maranges. There is a distance of about 20 km between these two vineyards. At this stage, the Côte opens out and becomes less steep, there are deep valleys and an endless sea of vines. Geology here has shaped the landscape to much softer effect.

UNIFORMITY AND DIVERSITY

IN Burgundy an appearance of uniformity never rules out differences, and within a short space the flanks of the Corton hill provide every possible kind of site. Hillsides are entirely covered with vines except for woods of oak or pine at the very top. The soils are of deep marl sloping out for some distance into the plain. The foot of the slope consists of harder limestone and gradually merges with the alluvial deposits of the Saône valley. On this terrain, covered with scree brought down from the plateau, village and regional *appellations* are grown in a wider variety of situations than in the Côte de Nuits.

This part of the Côte consists of a succession of hills and broad valleys. With such variable soil types and aspects the choice of grapes now includes Chardonnay, which is very rare in the Côte de Nuits. Perhaps white wine grapes prefer these 'white' soils? This is true for Charlemagne and Saint-Romain, but there are excellent red wines here, such as Volnay and Pommard, which are also grown on light soil. Meursault and Montrachet wines are cultivated on different soil. While Côte de Nuits red wines need long keeping, those of

Côte de Beaune can come to life much earlier.

Beaune is the uncontested wine capital of Burgundy. The shady heights of the Montagne de Beaune rise above the town, which in the early nineteenth century had almost as large a population as Dijon. Until recently, it chose not to extend beyond its circle of ramparts and to stay faithful to its one industry. The wine trade remains centred in Beaune, where there are a large number of offices and cellars belonging to firms of *négociants/éleveurs*.

All the wine from this part of the Côte used to be called Beaune. *Appellations* are now much stricter. Red wines of all the village *appellations* in Côte de Beaune, except for Aloxe-Corton, Beaune, Pommard and Volnay, are now sold as AOC Côte de Beaune-Villages, so there is an obvious difference between this and the comparable Côte de Nuits *appellation*, which is restricted to five villages (see p.136). However, the *appellation* does not apply to the 50 hectares of Côte de Beaune in Beaune itself (see p.154). These rules may seem tortuous but the wines of Burgundy cannot be fully understood without mastering a maze of complications.

THE REVIVAL OF THE HAUTES CÔTES

THE Hautes Côtes de Nuits on their well-defined plateau between the Côte itself and the valley of the river Ouche have an austere beauty of their own. The Hautes Côtes de Beaune have a bolder appearance. In an area about 30 km long by 5 or 6 km wide, there is now a landscape full of surprises with valleys leading in unexpected directions. Vines cover the hillsides everywhere up to 300 or 400 m and sometimes higher. The geology here is also unlike that of Hautes Côtes de Nuits, and Lias formations begin to appear.

Wine has been grown here for centuries and there is a local story that Meloisey wine was drunk at the coronation of Philip-Augustus (1180–1223). As in the Hautes Côtes de Nuits, immense damage was caused by the phylloxera epidemic and later problems of overproduction, by competition with wines from Languedoc and Algeria, the slump in wine sales, the 1914 war and depopulation. But a revival is taking place, with great help from the recently founded Hautes Côtes cooperative. This region, which had never had an AOC, in 1961 was granted the *appellations* Bourgogne-Hautes Côtes (de Nuits and de Beaune) for its improvement in quality. In 1914 there had been 3,000 hectares of vines in the Hautes Côtes; in 1963 there were only 700. The area is gradually being extended and has now reached 1,000 hectares. Strict specification of the best *terroirs*, replanting on the best exposed slopes, the use of Pinot Noir and Chardonnay with some Gamay and Aligoté, the enthusiasm of young growers who have staked everything on staying on the land: all these factors have contributed to the development of this wine region. The wines produced are full of fruit, are very pleasant to drink young, and have the firmness needed for ageing.

The château of La Rochepot.

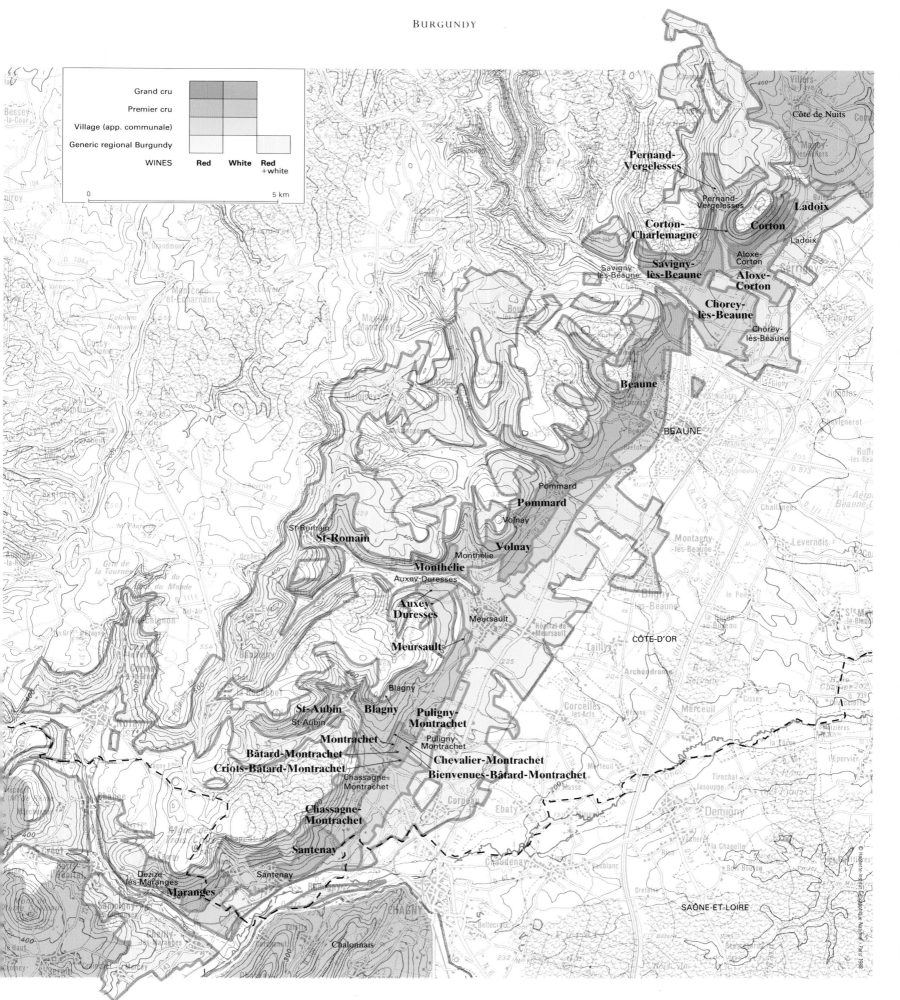

Grand cru
Premier cru
Village (app. communale)
Generic regional Burgundy

WINES   Red   White   Red +white

0   5 km

Pernand-Vergelesses
Côte de Nuits
Pernand-Vergelesses
Ladoix
Corton-Charlemagne
Corton
Ladoix
Savigny-lès-Beaune
Savigny-lès-Beaune
Aloxe-Corton
Aloxe-Corton
Chorey-lès-Beaune
Chorey-lès-Beaune
Beaune
BEAUNE
Pommard
Pommard
Volnay
Montélie
Volnay
St-Romain
St-Romain
Monthélie
Auxey-Duresses
Auxey-Duresses
Meursault
Meursault
Blagny
Blagny
St-Aubin
St-Aubin
Blagny
Puligny-Montrachet
Montrachet
Puligny-Montrachet
Bâtard-Montrachet
Criots-Bâtard-Montrachet
Chevalier-Montrachet
Bienvenues-Bâtard-Montrachet
Chassagne-Montrachet
Chassagne-Montrachet
Santenay
Santenay
Dezize-lès-Maranges
Maranges
Chalonnais
SAÔNE-ET-LOIRE
CÔTE-D'OR
Montagny-lès-Beaune
Levernois

THE so-called 'Montagne' of Corton forms a landmark in the north of the Beaune region and from its south-east and south-west side looks out over this gentle, rounded landscape. The site is perfect for vines, which stretch out over the plain and into the valleys, without any loss of quality. Instead of being neatly lined up along the Côte, the villages may be anywhere: in the plain, like Chorey-les-Beaune, set in a valley, like Savigny-les-Beaune, or on the valley side, like Pernand-Vergelesses.

LADOIX-SERRIGNY

SERRIGNY is an agricultural hamlet in the plain and Ladoix is the principal village *appellation*, given especially to red wines (135 hectares, 2,200 hl). The name comes from *douix*, an old word for 'spring', here referring to the little river Lauve which emerges at the base of the Corton hill. However, the hamlet of Buisson is the real place for vines. This is the gateway into the Côte de Beaune and is an authentic little wine village with narrow streets winding between the houses. The hard

Above, wine harvest at Aloxe-Corton.

limestone of Côte de Nuits is here covered with layers of Corton marl.

Wines grown beneath Bois de Mont share the vibrancy and charm of Côte de Nuits. The remaining wines are grown at the base of the Corton hill and on the northern extension of the slope. Based on Pinot Noir they have quite a different character – harder and needing longer to mature. At the foot of the Combe de Magny, the soils consist more of clay, with abundant flints. (*Chaille* means 'flint': hence the vineyard name, Les Chaillots.)

The slope which forms an extension of the red Corton zone has some excellent red wines, a number of which are classed as *premiers crus* (Le Bois Roussot). The marls higher up

give some good-quality white wine, such as Les Grêchons, but the recently promoted *premiers crus* from the parts of Basses and Hautes Mourottes not used for *grands crus*, and particularly from La Corvée, are quite remarkable for their different styles.

ALOXE-CORTON

THE best vineyard areas in the village are used for both *grands crus* and *premiers crus* and consist of layers of marl and thinly covered limestone. The lower section is more varied and is covered mainly with quantities of flint and deposits brought down from the Combe de Pernand.

The wines here are of the same sort of style as Les Chaillots at Ladoix: hard in youth and needing time to mature. At Les Boutières the soils are fairly leached clay and the wine is of less high quality. Marl from Bresse just edges into the Aloxe-Corton AOC on the Ladoix boundary, high up on the Côte near the fine chapel of Notre-Dame du Chemin, protectress of travellers.

Below, château of Corton-André.

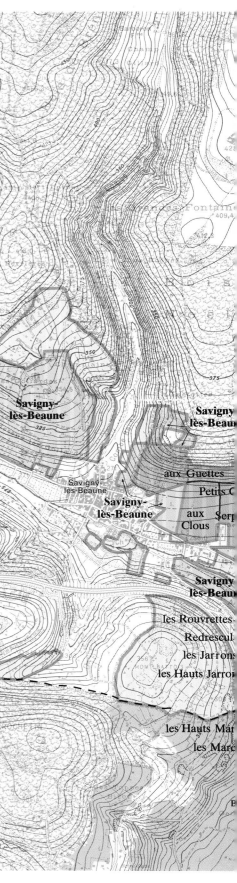

ORTON

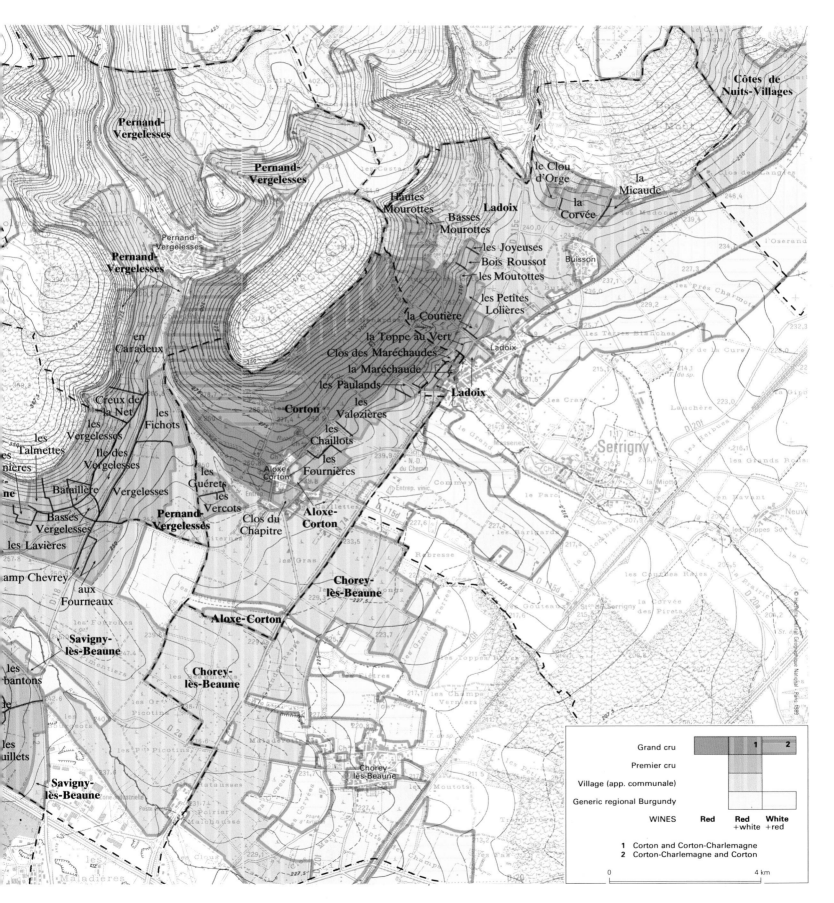

Côtes de Nuits-Villages

Pernand-Vergelesses

Pernand-Vergelesses

le Clou d'Orge

la Micaude

Hautes Mourottes

Ladoix

la Corvée

Basses Mourottes

les Joyeuses

Bois Roussot

les Moutottes

Pernand-Vergelesses

Buisson

les Petites Lolières

la Coutière

la Toppe au Vert

Ladoix

en Caradeux

Clos des Maréchaudes

la Maréchaude

les Paulands

Ladoix

Creux de la Net

Corton

les Valozières

les Chaillots

les Fichots

les Vergelesses

les Talmettes

Île des Vergelesses

les Fournières

Aloxe-Corton

Serrigny

Bataillère

Vergelesses

les Guérets

les Vercots

Basses Vergelesses

Clos du Chapitre

Aloxe-Corton

les Lavières

Chorey-lès-Beaune

amp Chevrey

aux Fourneaux

Aloxe-Corton

les bantons

Chorey-lès-Beaune

Savigny-lès-Beaune

Chorey-lès-Beaune

Savigny-lès-Beaune

les uillets

	WINES	Red	Red +white	White +red
Grand cru			1	2
Premier cru				
Village (app. communale)				
Generic regional Burgundy				

1 Corton and Corton-Charlemagne
2 Corton-Charlemagne and Corton

0   4 km

Mis en bouteille par
LOUIS LATOUR, Négociant à Beaune (Côte-d'Or)

PERNAND-VERGELESSES

YOU have to climb up the side of the valley to reach this village, which looks almost like a painting for a stage set. The big house overlooking the road was the home, from 1925 until his death in 1949, of Jacques Copeau, a theatrical innovator and the founder of the Théâtre du Vieux-Colombier in Paris. He had hopes of turning it into a French Bayreuth.

Pernand-Vergelesses shares ownership of the Corton massif, on the south-western side of which are the *grands crus* of Corton-Charlemagne and Charlemagne. Various parts of the same site are also entitled to produce red AOC Corton, AOC Aloxe-Corton and red and white AOC Pernand-Vergelesses.

There are 195 hectares in the village, producing 3,500 hl, of which 2,000 hl are red wine. On the slopes there are some reputable Aligotés, which used to be grown right into the heart of the Charlemagne zone. These have often been replaced by Chardonnay and Pinot Noir and some excellent white wine and greater quantities of red are being made. The village *appellation* gives peasant wines in the best sense of the word: solid and sturdy in youth, but with enough character to age well.

SAVIGNY-LES-BEAUNE

PERNAND and Savigny-lès-Beaune together share the site of Les Vergelesses, which is supposed to have inspired Charlemagne's pun '*Vin je bois, verre je laisse*' (literally 'wine I drink, glass I leave'). The *premier cru* is grown in both villages but the best examples come from an island in the middle of this sea of vines: the Ile des Hautes Vergelesses. The wines from this site are very feminine, but with the charm and elegance of a mature woman.

The Rhoin flows down from Bouilland, a picturesque village in the Hautes Côtes. The shoulder of land between this river and the Pernand valley is covered with vines almost as far as the village of Chorey-lès-Beaune down in the plain. As far as vine-growing is concerned, this is the widest section of the Côte. The wines produced here on scree deposits have remarkable lightness of character, but Savigny's main reputation comes from the *premiers crus*, which all possess great refinement. To the south,

Vergelesses is followed on the lower part of the hillside by Les Lavières. The so-called lava here – small blocks a few centimetres thick of coarse-grained limestone – produces airy, elegant wines (375 hectares, 11,500 hl, of mainly red wines).

On the other side is the '*montagne*' of Beaune and below the motorway are the vineyards of Les Narbantons and Les Jarrons, which give fresh, firm wines, both white and red. The wine from Les Marconnets is closer to that of Beaune.

CHOREY-LES-BEAUNE

AS one moves eastwards away from the Côte and nearer the Bresse region, the soils become richer and the wines less delicate. At Chorey-lès-Beaune, there are two different types of wine: in the south the wine comes from limestone scree probably funnelled down the valleys of Pernand and Bouilland and is similar to the Savigny *appellation*; in the north it is produced on a mixture of clay and flint and is like the neighbouring Aloxe-Corton (140 hectares, 5,500 hl of red wines).

CORTON AND CORTON-CHARLEMAGNE

THE Corton wood is a majestic culmination of the finest wine-growing area on the Côte. The hill at Corton is described as a *montagne* although it does not rise above 400 m. This splendid region is divided between Aloxe-Corton, Pernand-Vergelesses and Ladoix-Serrigny and is the only region to have both a red and a white *grand cru* (Corton and Corton-Charlemagne).

The wood comes within the village area of Pernand-Vergelesses and is long and thin like a French bean. It occupies the best-exposed side of the hill on a low cliff forming the upper boundary of the vines. Since the soil is fine, compacted chalk (upper Oxfordian) there is insufficient nourishment here for vines and their grapes. The altitude is also rather too high for *grands crus*.

Lower down, the better-exposed sides of the hill are covered with vines. The aspects go from east-facing through full south and round to west-north-west. Vines are cultivated at levels from 250 to 350 m on an almost continuous slope, which is rather unusual on the Côte.

The geology is fairly consistent and has had a direct influence on the choice of grape varieties, types of wine and *appellations d'origine*. Just below the wood, the upper part of the hillside is based on thick marl consisting of almost 45 per cent chalk, and on a deep layer of fine quartz sands.

Top, the typically Burgundian village of Pernand-Vergelesses.
Above, Corton: the hillside where perfect Chardonnay can be grown.

WHY CHARLEMAGNE?

THE emperor Charlemagne owned an estate planted with vines between Aloxe and Pernand, and in AD 775 offered it to the church of Saulieu. Hence the vineyard name of En Charlemagne. He chose a white wine to avoid staining his luxuriant beard!

A number of vineyards are named after families: Chambertin comes from the Bertin family, La Boudriotte from Boudriot, La Commaraine from the lords of Commarin and Les Bressandes from Bressand, to name but a few.

These whitish-looking marls are almost on the surface and are interspersed with thin bands of chalk. Chardonnay here gives very high-quality white wines.

A little lower, just below the 300 m contour line, the hill becomes less steep and we come onto more compact layers of less eroded limestone. The upper, fairly shallow layers are of sandstone marl. Lower down is an iron-rich yellow or red oolitic layer (oolitic ironstone) visible on the southern slope, then limestone known as 'mother-of-pearl' because of all the fossil shells it contains. This limestone is often covered with colluvial deposits and is very suitable for Pinot Noir.

The choice of grapes is not necessarily as clear-cut as the distinction between marl and hard limestone. On the upper slope, for example, Pinot Noir is grown alongside Chardonnay, but lower down the reverse does not occur.

Pushing down the 'cap' which forms on top of the fermenting must.

Soils based on marl are often rather shallow (grey rendzina) and, as they are also colder, Chardonnay ripens better than Pinot Noir. Chardonnay can grow on brown limestone but the wines would probably then be too soft and insufficiently acid.

However, Pinot Noir can ripen very well on these thin surface layers and derives from them all the aromatic refinement of great Burgundy. Deeper layers of marl give not just simple tannin, but fullness, body and mouth-filling astringency, so that a youthful wine has the slight

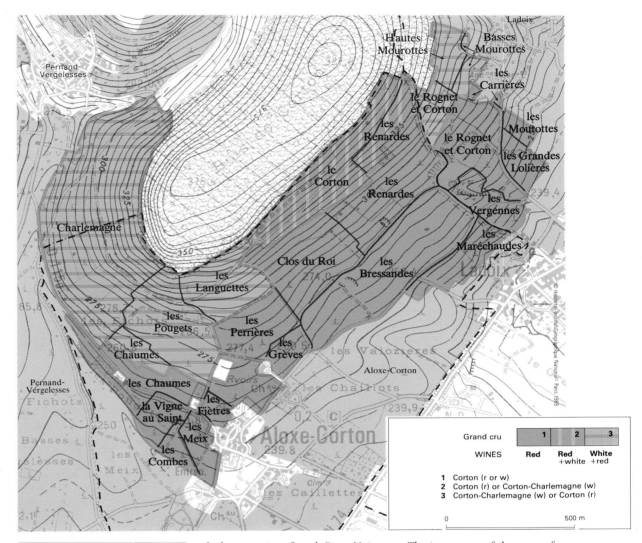

A fire of vine-prunings.

roughness of clay. In Burgundy all the red wines grown on clay-rich soils like these have similar characteristics and develop aromatic hints of game and undergrowth as they age.

There are redder soils on the shallow, fissured limestone with a fairly high proportion of marl. Pinot Noir here gives some very distinguished wine.

The Corton hill has only one kind of great white wine but several varieties of red. Several *appellations* have traditionally existed. The main one, especially for reds, is Corton (160 hectares, 3,000 hl). The best-known white is Corton-Charlemagne (72 hectares, 1,300 hl), but there was also the *appellation* of Charlemagne, now no longer used. These *appellations* probably all derive from the Pernand vineyard site known as *en Charlemagne*, which had soil and exposure suitable for white wine. Until 1948, the Charlemagne *appellation* could be applied to the Aligoté-based wine produced there.

Since red wines can differ so much, growers now commonly put the name of the locality, or *lieu-dit*, after the Corton AOC. This is not to be confused with a brand-name added after the *appellation*.

The importance of the name of a vineyard site or *climat* attached to the Corton AOC varies according to the site and the type of wine produced. Red wines from the *lieux-dits* Les Languettes, Clos du Roy, Le Corton and Les Renardes in Aloxe-Corton are more substantial and develop quite differently from wines grown in the *climats* Les Perrières, Les Bressandes and Les Maréchaudes in Aloxe-Corton, and Les Vergennes and Les Lolières in Ladoix-Serrigny.

BEAUNE

BEAUNE is situated at the junction of a number of motorways and, as the wine capital of Burgundy, it has inevitably become a magnet for tourists. With its ancient ramparts and fortifications, its quiet streets, wrought-iron gates and high walls covered in wistaria and ivy, Beaune continues to live and work above cellars teeming with bottles of wine.

The town has managed to resist over-modernization and new suburbs such as Saint-Jacques have had to expand into the plain. The Paris–Lyon motorway, carving its way round Beaune from Savigny, has not had the destructive effect once feared, and the town and its hill have retained their charm. The broad slope overlooking the town has no *grand cru* but the largest area (320 hectares) of *premiers crus* on the whole Côte and also 130 hectares of Beaune AOC. In all, 12,000 hl of wine are produced,

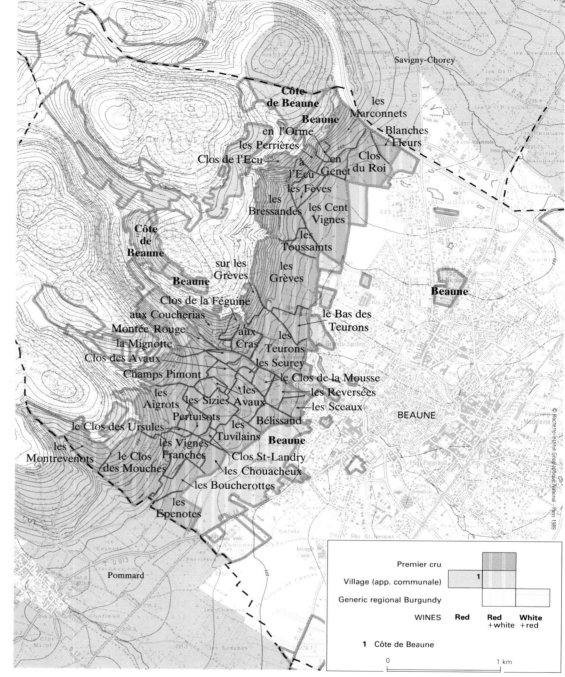

The Hospices de Beaune.

most of which is red.

Beaune wines all have a very distinctive character. The whites suggest honey, acacia, honeysuckle and roasted almonds, in a style reminiscent of Pernand or Savigny. The reds have great aromatic complexity, with a gamey note on top of the classic Burgundy soft fruit. There are very clear differences between some of the *premiers crus*, and some much lighter wines are produced on the sandy soils of Les Grèves, for instance. This is the site of the Vigne de l'Enfant-Jésus,

which once belonged to the Carmelites. The Clos des Mouches (*mouches* means flies) takes its name from the presence of the wasps and bees there.

The Côte de Beaune AOC (50 hectares, 220 hl) is classed as neither a regional nor a village *appellation*. It grows at the top of the slope at Les Mondes Rondes and La Grande Châtelaine, ripens late because of the height and produces wine similar to the village AOC. Côte de Beaune cannot at present be sold under the name Côte de Beaune-Villages.

AUCTIONS AT THE HÔTEL-DIEU

THE Hôtel-Dieu was built as a charity hospital in 1443 by Chancellor Nicolas Rolin and is Burgundy's single most representative building. The flamboyant Gothic style, the polychrome roof, Rogier van de Weyden's 'Last Judgement' altarpiece, the *grande salle* or great chamber for the poor all epitomize the

region and its golden age as a Duchy. The Hospices de Beaune wine auction takes place on the third Sunday in November and is now a world event.

The estate covers 58 hectares, all in Côte de Beaune except for a vineyard in Mazis-Chambertin. The different *cuvées* all bear donors' names. The auctions take place in the traditional way, while a candle is burning down, and often reach astronomical levels which bear no relation to actual market prices.

POMMARD

POMMARD is on the road from Beaune to Chagny and was once known for a ford that was rather difficult to negotiate. This market-town is situated 280 m up the side of a hill. The little river Vendaine runs into the Dheune here and causes a great deal of damage when it floods.

The Pommard was developed by monasteries at the height of the Middle Ages. It produces red wines which are firm and tannic, often a fine deep red in colour and more robust than the Beaune wines. With their plum-like bouquet, which hints of leather, the wines have a fresh, clean taste and keep well. The village has no *grands crus*, but the *premiers crus* of Les Epenots, Les Rugiens, Clos de la Commaraine, Clos Blanc and Les Chanlins are all excellent wines, as well as the village *appellation*, Les Noizons. Altogether there are 350 hectares, including 125 of *premiers crus*, and a yield of 10,500 hl of red wine.

Vines are grown right up to the base of the pine woods on top of the Côte. The soil contains more clay than at Beaune and is often coloured red by iron oxides (the reason for the vineyard name, Les Rugiens). The rich earth gives these wines their backbone. Locations vary with the way sites are aligned on each side of the Vendaine valley; Les Charmots, Les Arvelets and La Chanière, for instance, all face full south, whereas elsewhere on the slope, sites face south-east. The enclosure walls often prevent air from circulating freely but probably cause the vinous warmth and richness of Pommard wines.

Château de Pommard, with its *clos* of vines in one continuous mass, covers about 20 hectares, unique for the Côte d'Or. It is working to promote the village *appellation*. The buildings contain antique wine-making equipment.

The Château de la Commaraine has cellars dating back to the twelfth century.

The traditional wine-press in the cave coopérative *at Pommard.*

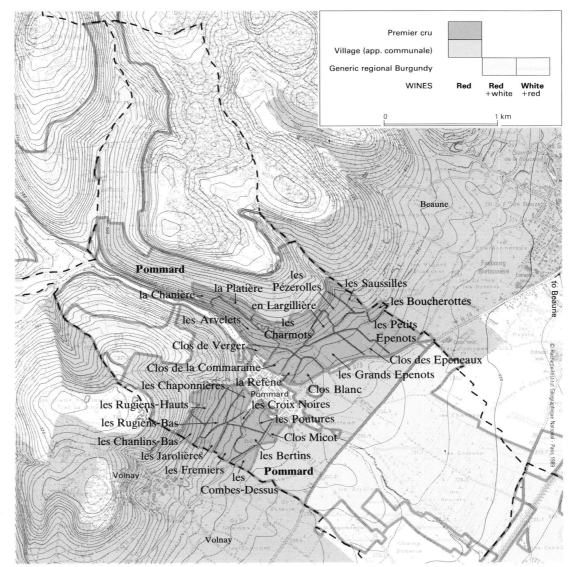

Premier cru

Village (app. communale)

Generic regional Burgundy

WINES | Red | Red +white | White +red

0   1 km

Pommard

la Chanière
la Platière
les Pézerolles
les Saussilles
en Largillière
les Boucherottes
les Arvelets
les Charmots
les Petits Epenots
Clos de Verger
Clos des Epeneaux
Clos de la Commaraine
les Grands Epenots
les Chaponnières
la Refène
Clos Blanc
Pommard
les Rugiens-Hauts
les Croix Noires
les Rugiens-Bas
les Poutures
Clos Micot
les Chanlins-Bas
les Jarolières
les Bertins
les Fremiers
Pommard
les Combes-Dessus

Beaune

Volnay

Volnay

to Beaune

© Hachette/Institut Géographique National - Paris 1989

POMMARD-CLOS DE VERGER
PREMIER CRU

APPELLATION POMMARD CONTRÔLÉE

Domaine BILLARD-GONNET
PROPRIÉTAIRE A POMMARD, COTE-D'OR, FRANCE

MIS EN BOUTEILLE AU DOMAINE

75 cl

VOLNAY

MOST Côte de Nuits villages spread down into the plain from their valleys while those of the Côte de Beaune are often set up on the hillsides. Volnay is one of these: perched up on a steep, narrow site, it huddles against the side of the Chaignot hill. It is a real wine village, like Pernand.

Most of its vines are grown facing south-east on deep layers of limestone marl. Large areas of this are overlaid with various pebbly or sandy-looking formations, which is probably the reason why Volnay is thought to produce some of the most refined wine in Côte de Beaune. They can be compared with wines from Chambolle-Musigny in the Côte de Nuits. One has to be careful about such comparisons, however, as both

sites and weather can vary in the two vineyards, and there are a number of differences in the way the land is cultivated in Volnay. The latter has 220 hectares, including 114 of *premiers crus*; in all 7,400 hl of red wines.

The northern part of Volnay has some distinctive red-coloured, lightish clay, is fairly uniform and in all respects similar to Pommard (Chanlin and Fremiets). In the lower sector, pebbly clay/limestone debris from the valley covers the entire slope from north to south. Volnay *appellation* wine is produced mainly on this type of brown limestone soil. Between these two areas, on outcrops of marl at the edge of the village, are Pitures-Dessus and Clos des Ducs, both well-constructed, full-bodied *premiers crus*.

In the south more red clay is the site for the following *premiers crus*: Les Caillerets (including Clos des 60 Ouvrées), Champans and, just above

the road to Autun, the lower parts of Taille-Pieds and Clos des Chênes, all producing wines similar to Chanlin. The upper parts of Taille-Pieds and Clos des Chênes are made up of clay formed *in situ* and of fairly thick pebbly deposits over clayey marl. Wines from here have ageing potential, with aromas that can develop earthy tones of undergrowth, like those of Les Renardes and some other Cortons.

Les Santenots is produced in the Meursault village area but classed as AOC Volnay. It is very like Les Caillerets, with similar characteristics to Clos de la Bousse d'Or, Clos de la Barre and Les Angles.

AROUND SAINT-ROMAIN

DRIVING south from Beaune on the N74, the D973 road to Autun passes through Pommard and Volnay, and then comes to Monthélie. On the other side of the saddle of hard limestone is the Combe de Saint-Romain, where there is now Chardonnay growing instead of Pinot Noir. The landscape here is more varied and it is sometimes thought that the first vines in Burgundy were grown here.

On each side of the Anay valley the vines at the western edge of Monthélie merge into Auxey-Duresses. This was once two hamlets, Auxey-le-Grand and Auxey-le-Petit, which later adopted the vineyard name of Les Duresses.

Monthélie is on the west side of the Volnay slope and in sites such as Sur la Velle and Les Vignes Rondes produces wine resembling that from Clos des Chênes in Volnay. Les Champs Fulliot is distinctly chalky lower down and gives bottles with immense finesse rather than body. Altogether there are 140 hectares, including thirty-one *premiers crus*, and a yield of 2,850 hl of mainly red wine.

The best section of the Auxey-Duresses *appellation*, on the south-east side of Montagne du Bourdon, consists of Les Duresses and Climat du Val, both on the same slope south of the valley. Le Val is on a thick layer of pebbles in a natural well-exposed dip, and produces wines of great breeding. There are 170 hectares, thirty-two of these *premiers crus*, and an overall yield of 1,050 hl, three quarters of which is red.

On the north-west slope, clinging to the cliffside, are the little Hautes-Côtes wine villages of Saint-Romain, Orches, Evelle and Baubigny. Only the first of these is entitled to a village *appellation* for its high-quality white wine. As often happens in Burgundy, Saint-Romain has two wine-growing areas: in the west, Lias terrain with thick scree over cold clays, where regional *appellations* are produced if the aspect is suitable. This terrain runs in a trench from Le Bouilland to

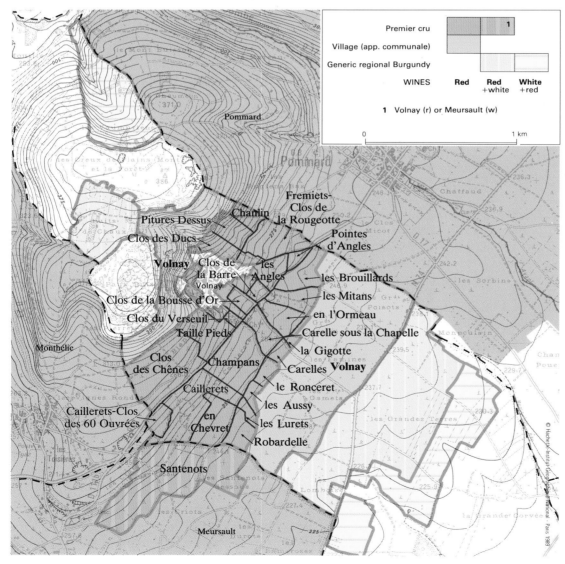

Premier cru			**1**
Village (app. communale)			
Generic regional Burgundy			

WINES   **Red**   **Red** +white   **White** +red

1   Volnay (r) or Meursault (w)

0   1 km

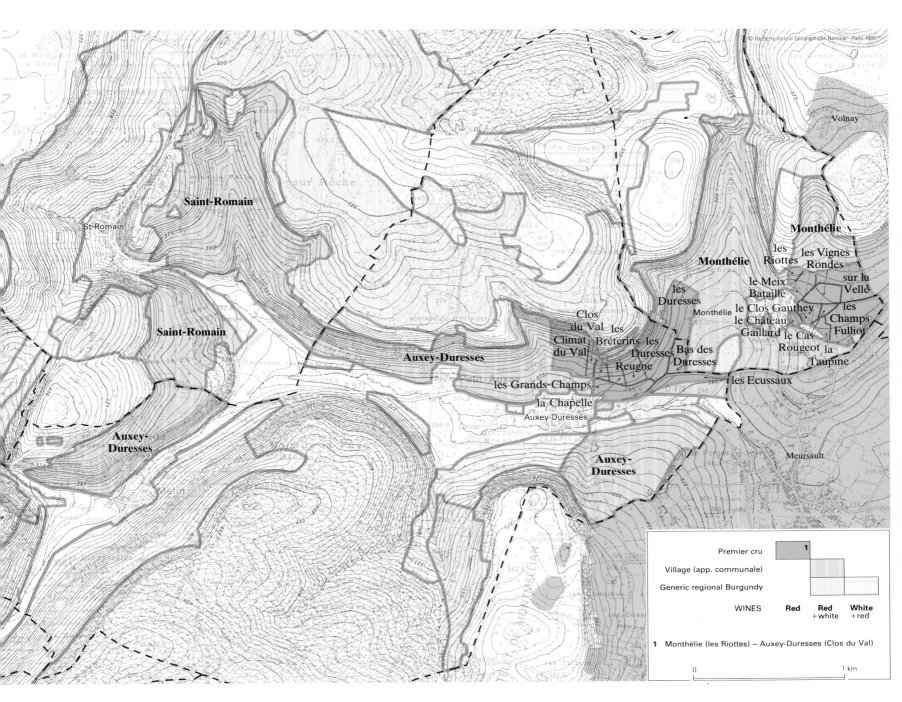

Premier cru **1**

Village (app. communale)

Generic regional Burgundy

WINES **Red** **Red**
+white **White**
+red

1 Monthélie (les Riottes) – Auxey-Duresses (Clos du Val)

0   1 km

Left, detail from a tapestry by Lurçat (Wine Museum, Beaune).

Right, winter in Saint-Romain.

Nolay. In the east there is Jurassic soil, with marls which are very suitable for growing Chardonnay. This gives genuinely distinctive, rather crisp and fruity dry wines (135 hectares, 190 hl, half red, half white).

Back towards Auxey-Duresses and closer to Meursault, is a gently sloping area of vines with a northeast aspect. This produces white wine that has a good deal in common with the wines of its illustrious neighbour.

157

MEURSAULT

THE Côte de Beaune is full of little hamlets clustered round a church, but there are some more extensive villages, such as Gevrey-Chambertin and Meursault. The latter has spread to the size of a town in an assortment of lanes and broad streets, cramped cottages and prosperous family houses, a château with splendid cellars, and everywhere vines, orchards and gardens. All this is dominated by the miraculously slender fifteenth-century church spire, which is 53 m high.

Before even the Clos de Vougeot existed, the Abbey of Cîteaux had vines at Meursault. In 1831 Dr J. Morelot wrote that the vineyards here 'owe their centuries of fame to white wine'. In the middle of the last century, white wine was of course their main business, and a very celebrated one, but wine-making diversified soon after this and now red wines too are grown in Meursault, although the best are not known by this name.

BETWEEN THE REDS AND THE WHITES

THE N74 at this point gradually leaves the Côte behind. On the river Cloux slightly east of the road, Meursault straddles the valley extending from Auxey-Duresses and forming a boundary between the red wine zone in the north and the white in the south. Les Santenots (30 hectares) follows on from the Volnay vineyards and grows the best Meursault red wines. In 1855 Les Santenots du Milieu received the top classification as *tête de cuvée* signifying that it produced the best among this particular batch of wines. After a decision in 1924 by the Beaune Tribunal, they acquired the right to the name Volnay Santenots instead of Meursault.

The tradition of cultivating Pinot Noir continues here. Wine not classed as Volnay Santenots is entitled to the AOC Meursault Côte de Beaune. The small plot of Les Caillerets and the *lieu-dit* called Les Cras in the area extending from Les Caillerets into Volnay should normally also have been

Top right, the château at Meursault.
Right, barrel-making.

entitled to the AOC Volnay, as the wines produced there are so similar.

The southern slope consists of two levels divided by low cliffs formerly used as stone quarries. Comblanchian stone from the Middle Jurassic appears again here after disappearing underground at Buisson (Ladoix-Serrigny), forming a synclinal fold with its median at Volnay, according to geologists. The limestone has changed slightly from hard calcareous 'marble' to dolomitic limestone. Dolomite was used locally in the manufacture of glass.

Above these cliffs, Chardonnay grows very well at heights between 260 and 270 m right up to the bare or wooded top of the Côte, on fissured marly limestone of varying degrees of hardness. The soil here is shallow but adequate and gives regional *appellation* wines of good quality and some elegance and subtlety, particularly Les Chevalières and Les Luchets. At Les Tillets, vines are grown in terraces on marly limestone. This is the *appellation* boundary and at this point grapes are growing too high for quality.

THE IDEAL SITUATION

THE finest wines are grown above the quarry area, on marly terrain alternating with brown surface soil which has developed on top of the parent rock, or on debris washed down from the cliffs. Soil and shelter from wind give the ideal combination for producing immensely seductive wines.

Les Perrières has the most distinctive blend of refinement and charm, with full rich wines, which manage to be dry and luscious at the same time. In good years they reach full maturity after about ten years. Les Genevrières-Dessus, the upper parts of Le Porusot-Dessus and of Les Bouches Chères, now called Les

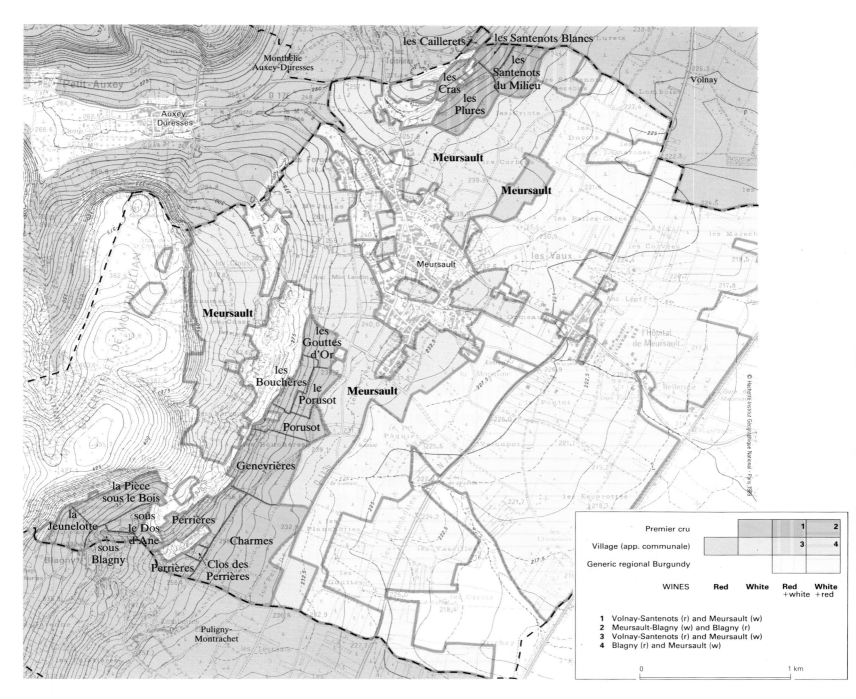

Premier cru

Village (app. communale)

Generic regional Burgundy

			1	**2**
			3	**4**

| WINES | **Red** | **White** | **Red +white** | **White +red** |

1 Volnay-Santenots (r) and Meursault (w)
2 Meursault-Blagny (w) and Blagny (r)
3 Volnay-Santenots (r) and Meursault (w)
4 Blagny (r) and Meursault (w)

0   1 km

Bouchères, all have similar characteristics.

Lower down there is sloping, pebbly terrain making for more delicate wines, more elegant and less full-bodied in the upper parts of Les Charmes, Les Genevrières-Dessous and Le Porusot. Further north, Les Gouttes d'Or and the lower part of Les Bouchères are on shallow soils which encourage drier wines with good backbone and a fat 'buttery' quality. Les Petits Charrons and Les Grands Charrons are not classed as *premiers crus*, but still give very good quality wines.

At the foot of the slope, the land then gently flattens out towards the east and vines grow almost up to the busy N7. There are limestone blocks and pebbles in large quantities at the bottom of the hill but, on the flatter ground, these are replaced by clay. In all there are 130 hectares of *premiers crus*.

The Meursault village *appellation* is neatly placed above the road to Puligny, except where it spreads out a little just below the village, at Sous la Velle. Some respectable Burgundy regional *appellation* wines are grown near the village.

BLAGNY

BLAGNY is a hamlet of a few houses, above the quarries between Meursault and Puligny, and quite close to Montrachet. The stone for the steps of the Hôtel-Dieu in Beaune came from here. The vines at Blagny grow on a broad terrace of marl with a full south aspect, sheltered from north and west winds by a cliff and a screen of trees. The area has its own microclimate.

The Blagny *appellation* is restricted

to red wine (54 hectares, including 44.4 hectares of *premiers crus*, and an average yield of 260 hl). These wines can be rather hard, intensely perfumed, with the occasional very individual and earthy hint of game. They are some of the most sought after on the Côte de Beaune.

White wines are sold either as Meursault followed by the *climat* name, or as Puligny-Montrachet. Pièce sous le Bois, Sous le Dos d'Ane and La Jeunelotte are the best known of the *climats*, producing red wine as well as white, all with a very distinctive personality.

MONTRACHET

IN the eyes of the world Montrachet has always been the supreme dry white wine, yet it is produced on an insignificant-looking hill with short grass and a few stunted bushes at the top. In the past this was called Mont-Rachat ('the bald hill'). The stone gates leading into the *clos* are just wide enough for pedestrians and have none of the grandeur of Clos de Vougeot.

The villages of Chassagne-Montrachet and Puligny-Montrachet share the *Grand Cru*, which, unlike many *clos*, has never been owned by one village only. It was founded in medieval times and became famous in the seventeenth century. The plot owned by the Marquis de Laguiche is one of the few in Burgundy to have been in the same family for centuries.

The present boundaries of Montrachet (a little under 8 hectares) were defined by the Beaune Tribunal in 1921. The *appellation* was granted to a half hectare in the plot near Les Dents de Chien, below the service road to the west, as well as to the historic *clos* itself.

The areas of the other *grands crus* (Chevalier-Montrachet with 7.3 hectares, Bâtard-Montrachet with 11.8, Bienvenues-Bâtard-Montrachet

Top, Bacchus figurine (Château de Tanlay museum).

Centre, Clos de la Pucelle vineyard at Puligny-Montrachet.

with 3.6, and Criots-Bâtard-Montrachet with 1.6) were defined in 1938, when the AOC system was set up. The first two *appellations* had been known since the eighteenth century, but the others were a compromise between various local claims. A section of Le Cailleret (called Les Demoiselles after the owners, Adèle and Julie Voillot, two nineteenth-century ladies from Beaune) was included in Chevalier-Montrachet at the insistence of *négoce/éleveur* firms in Beaune, who produced longstanding commercial usage and authenticated deeds as evidence of their entitlement. The idea of a Blanchots-Bâtard-Montrachet was discarded. Finally, in 1974, another section of Le Cailleret was incorporated into Chevalier-Montrachet by the INAO.

It is not known how the names Chevalier and Bâtard came about.

They have been in common use for a very long time, probably to show where these vineyards stood in relation to Montrachet itself. After all, Montrachet is still called '*le*' Montrachet – *the* Montrachet.

THE SUCCESS OF CHARDONNAY

HOW is it that Chardonnay is so remarkably successful on this ordinary-looking, rather unpromising land? The natural features of the site are in fact very advantageous. The position facing east and south-east gives ideally sunny conditions and, because of the semi-Mediterranean climate, snow always melts first here. Chevalier-Montrachet, in Puligny, is the highest of the group, growing at

levels between 265 and 290 m, on a steep regular 20 per cent gradient, and on shallow soils. Precious soil has even had to be scraped off the summit and spread on the hillside where vines are grown. Montrachet grows at about 260 m on a more gradual 10 per cent gradient, almost flattening out lower down. The aspect shifts completely to the south-east at the southern edge of the *clos*. It is often claimed that differences of situation make for different tastes in the wine, but this has never been proved at tastings.

There is no slope in Bâtard-Montrachet on the left of the road to Chassagne-Montrachet, nor in the lower section of Bienvenues-Bâtard-Montrachet in the village of Puligny-Montrachet. On the other hand, Criots-Bâtard-Montrachet has a south-south-east aspect at 240 m on the hillside extending into the Bâtard area.

Chevalier-Montrachet and Montrachet are both grown on a base of Bathonian limestone, but on different soils. Chevalier is grown further up, on alternating layers of marl and limestone containing some of magnesium. These are absent in Montrachet, where the lower section beside the road is grown on brown limestone soil over compacted debris.

In Bâtard-Montrachet the debris soils close to the road are similar to those of Montrachet. However, in Bienvenues-Bâtard-Montrachet and the rest of Bâtard, as in Chailles, there is a higher proportion of clay and silt. The deep soils here are less rich in permeable limestone pebbles and carbonates, and drainage is not as good.

'ON THE RIGHT HAND OF THE LORD'

MONTRACHET is not a wine whose qualities are instantly obvious. The wine of any year has breeding, richness and length in the mouth sufficient to give it a place, according to legend, 'on the right hand of the Lord'. The green-gold colour is allied to elegance, power and amazing aromatic complexity. It can be kept for years. Chevalier has a strong structure but seems more accessible as the light shallow soil on which it is

grown produces stunning scent and refinement when it is still young.

Bâtard sometimes seems 'thicker', with plenty of charm but slightly more earthiness. These characteristics come from heavier soil but also give it an astonishing ability to age for years. Criots and Bienvenues are very alike, with a slightly drier character in the first and more lightness in the second.

In all, the *grands crus*, on scarcely more than 30 hectares, produce 850 hl, including 230 in Montrachet.

Left, fine white Burgundy maturing in a cellar at Chassagne-Montrachet.

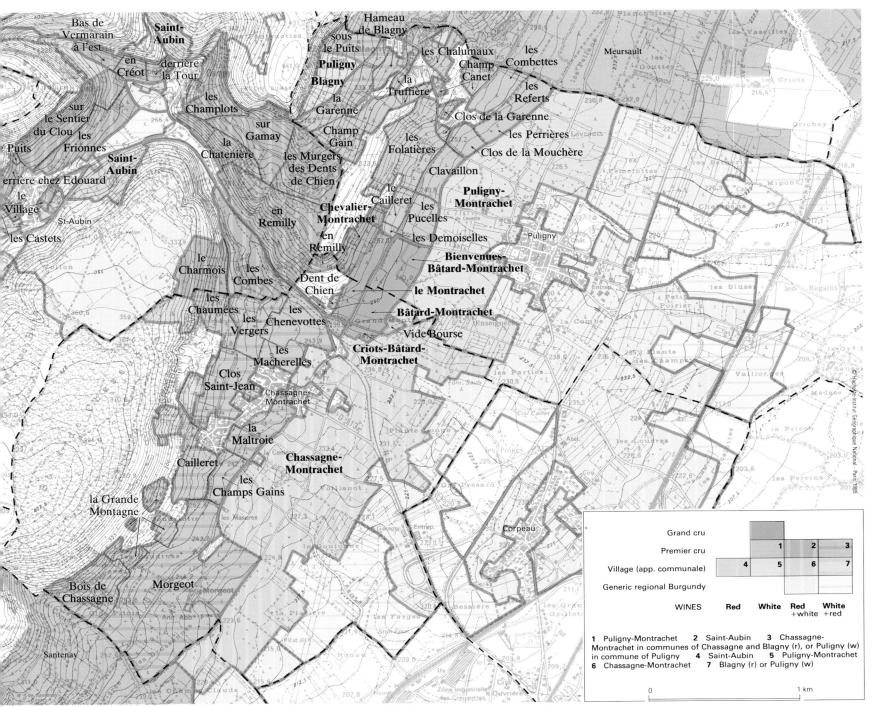

PULIGNY-MONTRACHET AND CHASSAGNE-MONTRACHET

Above, the Thénard domaine at Montrachet.
Below, Chassagne-Montrachet – the village.

WHEREAS Puligny grew mainly red wine in the last century, it now concentrates almost entirely on white. The *premiers crus* (100 hectares out of the 215 under vines) are grown in ten or so sites situated on the slope between Meursault and the Montrachets. Some of these wines, such as those from Les Combettes, Les Pucelles and Le Clavoillon, have great finesse, and at Les Folatières an almost ethereal quality. Le Cailleret borders on the Montrachet vineyards. Champ-Gain, Champ-Canet and La

Garenne all give excellent reds. Like the hamlet of Blagny on its ridge, Chassagne-Montrachet also produces both red and white wines.

The enclave of great white burgundies extends a short way beyond the village, where the hillside has similar characteristics. Les Grandes Ruchottes, En Virondot and Les Caillerets are special territory for white wine, which shows all the delicacy of Chardonnay. There is another extremely successful site for white wines near Morgeot, between Chassagne and Santenay, on what remains of a vineyard belonging to the Abbey of Maizières.

The rest of the region is better suited to red wines, as at Morgeot. Clos Saint-Jean produces some very refined wine from colluvial soil

deposits, which are sometimes quite deep.

The village used to cultivate the Beurot grape and, like Santenay, has adopted a pruning method quite different from the *taille Guyot* method used elsewhere on the Côte. Vines are often spur-pruned and trained horizontally according to the Cordon de Royat system, which encourages a better long-term build-up of reserves within the individual plant. The technique has some effect on the quality of the wine.

SAINT-AUBIN, SANTENAY AND LES MARANGES

THE village of Saint-Aubin occupies a position to the back of the Côte, slightly higher up than Chassagne and Puligny-Montrachet, and with a colder, drier climate. Vines are in the course of being replanted over an area of more than 150 hectares producing 2,800 hl. Les Murgers des Dents de Chien and La Chatenière are close to the Montrachet *grands crus* and give some excellent white wine. Saint-Aubin is strong and supple with a highly characteristic walnut flavour.

Above the hamlet of Gamay, from which the grape is supposed to have received its name, there is terrain suitable for red wines similar to those from Blagny – full-bodied but with rather more warmth. Up behind Saint-Aubin, a pleasant hillside with good soil and shelter from cold winds produces some good wines, including some respectable Aligoté.

There are three villages on the south side of the Montagne des Trois Croix, but tectonic movements have produced different geological formations in each. Jurassic marly limestone gives way to Liassic marl containing more clay, which is therefore colder. This drawback is balanced by an excellent south aspect and perfect drainage on a steep slope. Wines here are in a different style, more astringent and needing a few years in the bottle to reach their full maturity.

The three villages of Dezize-lès-Maranges, Cheilly-lès-Maranges and Sampigny-lès-Maranges intend to amalgamate under the single *appellation* of Les Maranges. At Sampigny-lès-Maranges you can see a huge eighteenth-century wine-press and some traditional galleried wine-growers' houses.

Santenay is best known for hot springs with a few patients and a casino with rather more gamblers, but has some good wine too. The village consists of three parts: Santenay-le-Haut, Santenay-le-Bas and Saint-Jean. There is a continuation of the varied soils beginning at Chassagne-Montrachet and a foretaste of the hilly Côte Chalonnaise on the other bank of the river Dheune. In all, there are 375 hectares giving 10,200 hl of mainly red wine.

Santenay red seems rather retiring at first, with a certain hardness. In the long run it will be extremely pleasing, but is far from being a light wine to drink quickly, so let it age for a while. Do the same with Beauregard and La Comme, which are also rather hard in youth, but unexpectedly charming after the ageing required by their robust character. Pinot Noir gives these wines scents of strawberry and other soft fruit and a slightly astringent aftertaste. The last glass of Santenay is always the best. The best plots, they say, are east of the church, at Les Gravières, and at Clos de Tavannes, which borders on Chassagne and produces a full firm wine. Its elegance comes from growing on a thick layer of pebbles over marl. On the hillside behind Santenay, Beaurepaire and La Maladière are on fissured limestone and thin layers of marl. .

The village of Remigny is set in the side of the hill and has a part share in the Chassagne-Montrachet and Santenay *appellations*.

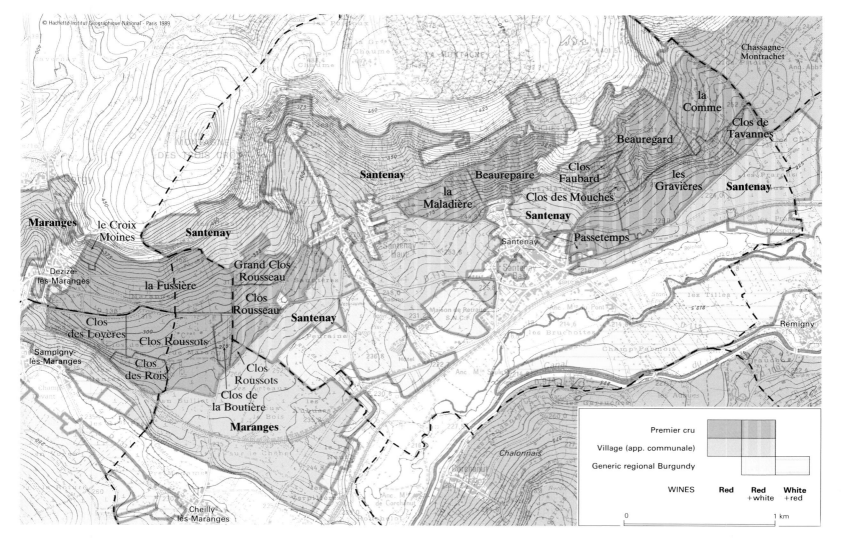

THE CÔTE CHALONNAISE

ON the other side of the river Dheune everything immediately looks very different. There is still a regular chain of hills continuing along the same line as the Côte, but the countryside is much less uniform and turns into a closely set patchwork of different landscapes.

The Côte Chalonnaise wine region occupies a narrow strip of sedimentary terrain between Chagny and Saint-Gengoux-le-National. As far north as Chalon-sur-Saône, there are faulted rocks of hard limestone overlying Trias and Lias sands and clays. The landscape has been shaped by considerable faulting and in this way provides varied situations for vine-growing. There are outcrops of the metamorphic rock that forms the base of the Massif Central. A great variety of different formations occur: sandy clay over granitic rocks, pure and mixed sands over Trias sandstone, marl containing different proportions of clay and limestone, and limestone formed into cliffs or slopes.

Local weather patterns are equally varied, with stronger Mediterranean tendencies further south. With all this diversity behind it, wine-growing here is very adaptable. Pinot Noir and Chardonnay are grown, as well as Gamay and Aligoté.

The port of Chalon, on the Saône, used to have an important shipping trade. The term 'Côtes Chalonnaises' was first used at the beginning of this century, though later replaced by the Bourgogne *appellation*. There is now a movement to revise this in about forty villages and to add on the name Côte Chalonnaise. The region now demanding recognition is known mainly for the four village *appellations* of Rully, Mercurey, Givry and Montagny.

Nothing about wine is ever simple, and administrative boundaries often fail to coincide with those of wine-growing areas. Four villages in Saône-et-Loire and close to the Côte d'Or are a logical part of the Hautes Côtes de Beaune. These are Créot, Epertully, Change and Paris-l'Hôpital, all producing wines with the same tannic quality as that of Nolay. They should not be drunk too young.

Vines are also grown in the area round Couches, west of Chalon. The five villages south of the Hautes-Côtes formerly produced some good '*grand ordinaire*' wine intended for the mining towns of Epinac and Montceau. Some decent burgundy is produced nowadays from clay-limestone soils, and soils with a higher clay content produce solid wines which lack refinement in youth but which develop well later. Gamay is very successful for lighter wines when grown on sandstone soils over the metamorphic bedrock.

Overlooking the vines at Rully: though much restored, the château has twelfth- and sixteenth-century buildings.

BOURGOGNE ALIGOTÉ BOUZERON

ALIGOTÉ was popular early this century and in the pre-phylloxera period, and was used for everyday carafe wines. Even in famous vineyards, it was sometimes grown instead of Chardonnay for its fresh, lively taste. Nowadays it is cultivated in the plain, in the Auxerre region to some extent, in the Hautes Côtes, and in Bouzeron, a little village near Chagny. Brown limestone soils here cover the base of hard Jurassic limestone, which forms a slope each side of a valley running north to south. Aligoté grows so well here that this has become the only village with an

appellation entitling it to use its own name after Bourgogne Aligoté (Bourgogne Aligoté Bouzeron, 1,000 hl).

RULLY

MEDIEVAL castle towers, an elegant church spire, peaceful houses and tree-filled gardens give Rully a look of settled permanence. Yet, before it became established on the hill where it is today, the village had occupied a number of different sites.

The wines of Rully are said to convey suggestions of cool polished marble. They certainly have an immediately recognizable style of their own, with their dry, subtle fragrance and unaffected charm.

The Rully wine area covers almost 520 hectares both in Rully itself and to a small extent in Chagny. Development has taken place very recently and production has grown from around 500 hl in 1955 to the present level of 10,000 hl of village *appellation* wines and almost 2,000 hl of *premiers crus*. Equal areas of Chardonnay and Pinot Noir have been planted.

The land here is of Middle and Upper Jurassic formation and consists of fissured oolitic limestones and marls. Aligned north to south are a number of longitudinal faults which cut up the area where vines can be grown. The soils are fairly uniform, mainly of the brown chalky type, and give the wine a pleasingly consistent quality. The variation is caused more by different situations and altitudes. The east face of the hill looks out over the Saône plain and this is certainly the best side, where vines are cultivated at heights between 230 and 300 m. There is a good deal of Pinot Noir, which gives straightforward full, fleshy wines on a level with the best Côte de Beaune. A few vineyard sites have even acquired a *premier cru* reputation, particularly Les Saint-Jacques and Les Cloux. Because sites are often

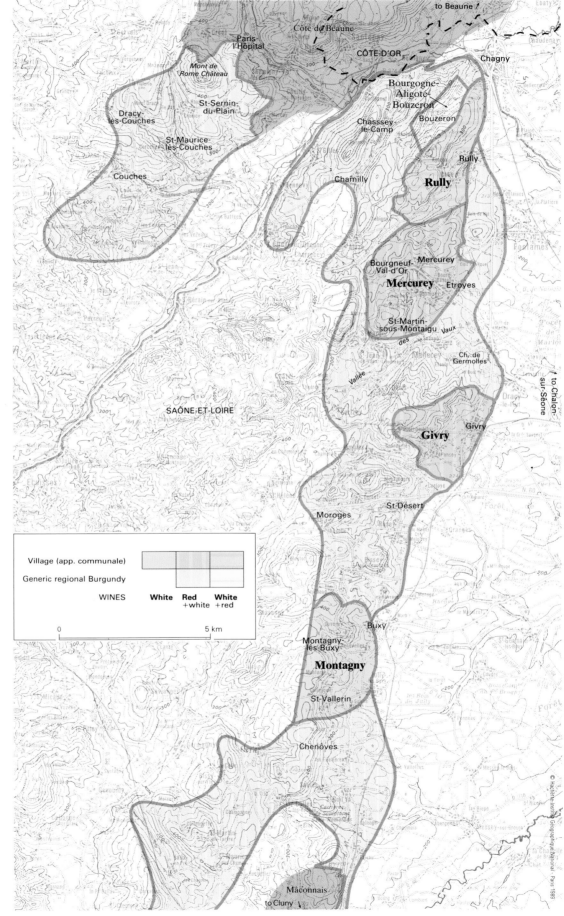

at heights up to 370 m, and on ridges with varying aspects and marly soils, Chardonnay tends to be used for any new planting. Rully white wines are pleasingly crisp and pure with a fragrant bouquet similar to that of wines from the Chassagne-Montrachet region.

A number of firms specializing in making sparkling wine by bottle fermentation became established in the area and white wines used to be grown locally for this purpose. Since the well-deserved success of the Rully still white wines, these firms now make mainly Crémant de Bourgogne based on supplies from nearby villages.

villages of Mercurey (since 1971 also including Bourgneuf-Val d'Or) and Saint-Martin-sous-Montaigu. Mercurey is not much larger than Rully, but owes its greater importance to several large-scale *domaines* and to an old and active tradition of wine-growing.

Soil and microclimates here produce wine with a less individual style than Rully's, although the geology in both villages is very much the same and the same rock formations stretch from Rully into the more hilly terrain north of Mercurey. These formations suit Pinot Noir, which here produces some high-quality red wines, elegant and well-structured where the

In the southern sector and in the village of Bourgneuf-Val d'Or, the aspect is again less good, often facing towards the north. Past the hamlet of Touches there are more favourable east-facing slopes extending into Saint-Martin-sous-Montaigu, where vines grown near the old castle have an ideal site. South of this village the soils are Lias marl and the wines are consequently less refined. Finally, on the eastern boundary at Etroyes, Bresse-type Pliocene formations in the plain produce a more ordinary wine some way from typical Mercurey.

The wine-growing society Confrérie des Compagnons de

the castle of Germolles. The village is finding it difficult to withstand pressure from the expanding town of Chalon-sur-Saône, although some growers are trying hard to maintain Givry's vitality.

The village has a remarkable situation and almost ideal consistency of soil and aspect. The small sector of Champs Pourot has slightly different terrain from the rest of the *appellation* and there are also differences in the small island of vines at Russilly, where the southern aspect makes up for any disadvantages. As a rule, the Argovian layer of marl and limestone favour red wines (5,000 hl), round and fragrant, with plenty of tannin and a bouquet suggesting wet woodland. A small amount of white wine is also produced (less than 500 hl).

MONTAGNY

MONTAGNY is the southernmost Côte Chalonnaise *appellation* and produces only white wines in four village areas: Montagny-lès-Buxy, Saint-Vallerin, Buxy and Jully-lès-Buxy. Vines are grown over 100 hectares, producing 6,000 hl, but this area could be extended. From Montagny, down in the valley, you can see practically all the vine-growing area spread out over hills varying in height from 250 to 400 m.

MERCUREY

AT an altitude of 250 to 300 m, Mercurey spreads down from the top of the hills into the Val d'Or, the well-named Golden Valley. This large village of 2,000 inhabitants, within sight of the Morvan hills on one side and the Saône valley on the other, has wine-growing as its livelihood, and is very much a local centre. The tourist route takes visitors from the *cave de dégustation* (tasting cellars) up to the orientation table, passing on the way the charming church at Touches, the château of Montaigu, which rises above the village of Saint-Martin, and the statue of the Virgin of Mercurey.

This is the best known of the Côte Chalonnaise *appellations*. There are 630 hectares of vines producing about 25,000 hl of red wine and 1,000 of white. The *appellation* covers the two

situation is good, powerful on limestone and more supple on clay. Classification of the *premiers crus* is not yet completed, but among the best wines, those grown in Les Champs Martin, Clos l'Evêque and the Petits and Grands Voyens should certainly be mentioned. In this northern sector some less favourable sites, as at Les Montelons, give crisper wines, which are only really good in years when the grapes can ripen sufficiently.

Above left, Château of Chamirey.
Above, a glass of Mercurey.

Saint-Vincent et Disciples de la Chanteflûte, was founded in honour of the local wines and of the pipette or *Chanteflûte* used at official tastings. The *Chanteflûte* is used as a seal of approval, like the *tastevin* elsewhere in Burgundy.

GIVRY

FOR a long time Givry was the principal wine village on the Cote Chalonnaise. Wine from here had an excellent reputation in the Middle Ages and King Henri IV is said to have had a weakness for it, as he also did for Gabrielle d'Estrées, the lady of

The general aspect goes from northeast to south-south-west, with east predominating. The soils are very different from those in the other Côte Chalonnaise villages, and consist of Lias and Trias marls and marly sandstones. Montagny can in fact be regarded as the gateway to the Mâcon region.

A good Montagny is very dry with some reserve and reticence but a delicate bouquet. The Buxy Cave Cooperative, the most important in the northern half of Saône-et-Loire, is very active in promoting the local wines.

THE MÂCONNAIS

BETWEEN Tournus and Mâcon, France begins to look Mediterranean. The houses have flattened roofs, curving southern tiles and often a verandah along the front, a covered terrace with wooden pillars and a cellar underneath where the vats and wine-press are stored. There are not many vines where the Côte Chalonnaise comes to an end, but they reappear round Mâcon.

The poems of Lamartine (1790-1869) are full of references to this region. He was brought up in the village of Milly, and the châteaux of Pierreclos, Saint-Point and Monceau are particularly associated with him. As the river Saône flows past the foot of the Mâconnais hills before joining the Rhône at Lyon, it slows down and often causes floods in the region. The river is a vital element in Mâcon's importance. For a long time the town has been a centre for trade and administration on the edge of the Charolais and Bresse regions and an important focus for the wine industry. Wine sold and sent out from here was known in the past simply as Mâcon wine.

On the map the Mâconnais region forms a rectangle 50 km from north to south and 15 km from east to west, with the river Grosne marking a clear boundary to the north and west, and the flat Bresse countryside to the east. In the south yet another wine region begins with the metamorphic rocks of Beaujolais.

There is a repeated formation consisting of three monoclinal chains of

Chasselas in the Mâcon region, a typical local house.

hills inclined eastwards and bordered by longitudinal faults running north-north-east/south-south-west. The varying hardness of rock outcrops is visible in the landscape, with a repeating pattern of diverse-looking hills and valleys. Lias marl, and in particular marl of the upper Jurassic, have formed broad east-facing slopes which are very suitable for vine-growing. Western slopes have a less advantageous climate and often consist of much steeper, hard limestone formations, with less growing space for vines. Woods on the hilltops provide useful weather protection. Often the south-facing sides of valleys hollowed out by small rivers are planted with vines.

Gamay is grown on metamorphic bedrock with a sandstone covering (acid sands and granite arenaceous rocks), and on clays. Elsewhere there is mainly limestone and here Chardonnay and Aligoté are cultivated

on the more marly terrains, and Pinot Noir on shallow, chalky soils.

Although there are distinct Mediterranean influences, southern Burgundy still has a continental climate. The prevailing winds are from the north, especially the *bise*, the bitter wind, and from the south, a soft wind brings rain. Vines are grown up to heights of 350 and 400 m.

Vines here are less densely planted than in the Côte d'Or, at a density of 7,000 rather than 10,000 root-stocks per hectare. There is also a different pruning technique as, because of the climate, fruiting is more regular on long canes. The Mâconnais method is known as *taille à queue*: one long stem is arched over the middle wire support and is tied by the tip to the wire below.

MÂCON

THERE are several *appellations* with this name, although Mâcon itself has no vines. Mâcon and Mâcon-Supérieur reds and rosés, also Mâcon followed in certain cases by the village name, are based essentially on Gamay or sometimes Pinot Noir.

Wines of this *appellation* vary according to where they are produced, and can be Burgundy or Beaujolais in type. About 70,000 hl are produced, with a rustic character and good tannin.

For white wines only Chardonnay is grown. There are two *appellations*: Mâcon and, within this, Mâcon-Villages, where the term 'Villages' can be replaced by the name of the village producing the wine. Cooperatives have become well-established in the region, controlling 80 per cent of production, and have contributed to the popularity of these light, fragrant wines, with their occasional muscat flavours. The best Mâcon-Villages grow on the Upper Jurassic marl trench between Hurigny and Viré, east of the Mâconnais hills. Lugny, Prissé and Cruzille are other villages with an excellent reputation. The production of white Mâcon-Villages totals 120,000 hl.

POUILLY-FUISSÉ AND SAINT-VÉRAN

THE dramatic outlines of Solutré and Vergisson, their limestone cliffs rearing up above a sea of vines, make an unexpected contrast to the quiet landscape round Mâcon 8 km to the east. The prehistoric Solutréen period around 20,000 BC was called after the rock of Solutré, at the foot of which piles of horse bones 2 m deep and covering almost 4 hectares were discovered. Tens of thousands of horses were driven over the cliff here by hunting tribes moving their flocks from the Saône valley up to the hills. As you wander through today's vineyards you are more likely to meet goats, whose milk is made into excellent Mâconnais cheese.

Local houses often have attractive verandahs, called *galeries*, and their almost flat roofs slope as gently as the hills around them. Pouilly-Fuissé, Pouilly-Loché and Pouilly-Vinzelles are produced in the villages of Fuissé, Chaintré, Vergisson and Solutré.

Above, the château at Chasselas with its three medieval towers.

Left, the rock of Solutré.

The Pouilly-Fuissé production area extends over 750 hectares and produces about 40,000 hl each year. Not to be confused with wines from Pouilly-sur-Loire, these wines are based on Chardonnay, green-gold in colour, dry, with great refinement and distinction. They have a pleasant,

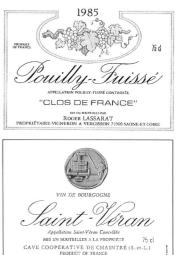

natural bouquet and aromas of toast and hazelnuts from the time spent in wood. Variations in soil produce some very clear differences, however. The eastern slope of Vergisson-Fuissé is made up of limestone and marly limestone, while Chaintré further south is only partly on these soils from the Middle and Upper Jurassic. In the section furthest west are clays overlying the granite bedrock. On the hillside running from west to east are layers of marl and Lias formations, overlapping with Trias clay and sandstone levels.

Pouilly-Loché is minute, consisting of only 15 hectares in the village of Loché. These fairly uncommon wines can also be called Pouilly-Vinzelles

(60 hectares), the *appellation* granted to the villages of Loché and Vinzelles. The two *appellations* are a close relative of Pouilly-Fuissé.

SAINT-VÉRAN

THE Saint-Véran AOC dates only from 1971 and is an amalgamation of several villages round Saint-Vérand, which has lost its 'd' in the process.

These are two distinct zones on each side of the Pouilly-Fuissé *appellation*. In the north are the villages of Davayé and Prissé; in the south

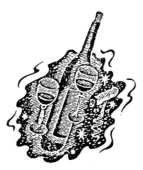

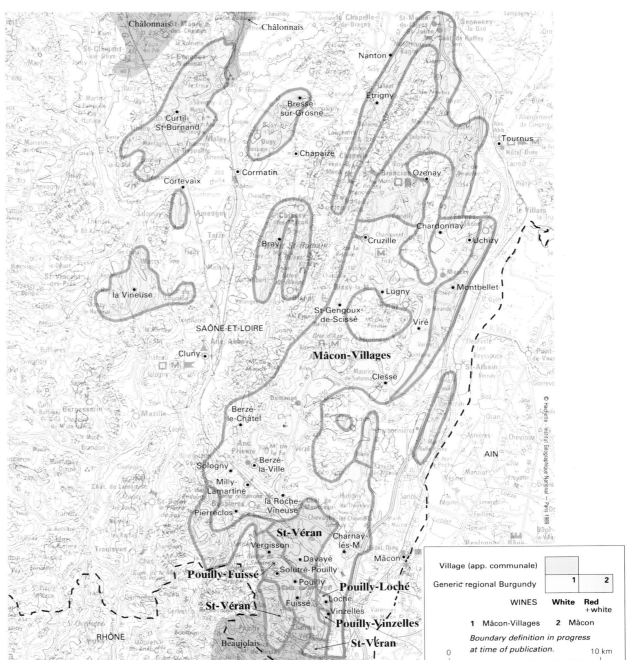

Top left, weighing the grapes.

Left, the church at Fuissé.

Chânes, Chasselas (either the grape variety was called after this village, or vice versa), Leynes, Saint-Amour and Saint-Vérand. Only chalky soils are classified for this *appellation*, thus giving very homogeneous white wines (25,000 hl) based on Chardonnay, rather reminiscent of Pouilly-Fuissé, though with perhaps a little less length on the palate. There is no doubt that Saint-Véran has a worthy place among Mâconnais wines.

BEAUJOLAIS

THE only Beaujolais most people know about is Beaujolais nouveau. This type of wine was recognized in 1951 and for over thirty years has been the universal symbol for a young, good-natured, undemanding thirst-quencher. There is general impatience for it to emerge from the wine-press and the Beaujolais Race to London or San Francisco is now a world event.

A few weeks after the harvest, more than half the crop is nowadays turned into Beaujolais nouveau – 65 million bottles of it. It is a *primeur* wine (made to be drunk young) and has to wait until mid-November for its first appearance. There is a short period of fermentation, and the Beaujolais vinification process allows the young fruity aroma to develop, sometimes almost to excess.

The present-day image of Beaujolais unfortunately means that the public is unaware of the variety and longevity of Beaujolais wines.

Beginning south of Mâcon and stretching some 50 km to the outskirts of Lyon, Beaujolais really belongs to the wine region of Burgundy (according to a Dijon edict of 1930). However, its character and the size of its output (an area of 20,500 hectares in the Rhône *département* and 1,600 hectares in Saône-et-Loire producing 1,300,000 hl or 170 million bottles) make it a complete region in itself.

Beaujolais is the eastern part of a wedge of hills bordering the Massif Central. Rivers flowing down to the Saône have scoured valleys, such as the Ardières valley, which joins the Saône and Loire by way of the Echarmeaux Pass. The highest point is Mont Saint-Rigaud (1,012 m). The tops of the hills are thickly wooded while the slopes up to 500 m are covered with vines. They flourish on the eastern side, well shielded from the west wind (the Traverse blowing from the Loire) and exposed to the rising sun. Châteaux, houses and *cuvages*, as the buildings used for winemaking are called, are almost buried in the vines clinging to these generously rounded hills.

At Villefranche-sur-Saône, a road

Near Juliénas.

forms the boundary between Beaujolais's two geological zones. To the north, the very old rocks of the Hercynian folding consist of granite debris, porphyry and schist, with no limestone, and have produced a gentle landscape with rounded hills and a wine-making tradition going back to the tenth century. Vines are grown on the hills, and meadowland covers the valley floors, partly filled with granite sand from decomposed igneous rock. To the south, the Jurassic limestone-clay soils, and in particular the entrochal limestone, called *pierre dorée* (or 'golden stone'), from the erosion of the Hercynian series in the Mesozoic era, have resulted in a more varied landscape, with meadows and coppices.

The climate is temperate, with little very cold weather. The last hard winter frost was in 1956 when it killed 10 per cent of the vines. A particular advantage is the orientation towards the valley of the Saône, which moderates the effects of heat and sunlight. Rainfall is average but hail can sometimes ruin the crops.

DOMAIN OF THE GAMAY GRAPE

EXCEPT for a few small areas planted with Chardonnay (Beaujolais white wine is pleasant but little known), Gamay Noir à Jus Blanc is the dominant grape. It distinctly prefers the acid soil of Haut Beaujolais where the *villages* and *crus* are situated. The saying is that wine is a rich crop on poor soil. A special vinification process using whole grapes produces

wines with rich flower and fruit aromas: violet, iris, peony, peach, banana and soft fruit such as raspberries. The grapes are not crushed or destalked and no machines are used for harvesting. These *primeur* wines owe their fresh, spontaneous character to this process. Even the local houses, with their low-pitched roofs, have been influenced by the demands of winemaking. The *cuvage* (process of fermentation) often takes place on an upper floor so that, as they are brought in from the vines, grapes can fall by gravity into the vats and the wine can flow naturally from vat to cellar. The wine is stored in *pièces*, casks holding from 214 to 216 l, according to the *appellation*.

The Beaujolais region is like the wine – warm and with a characteristic earthiness. The name comes from the lords of Beaujeu who held it, almost independent from the rest of France, until 1400. François I later annexed it for the Crown. Beaujolais is quite different from Burgundy: it slopes down towards Villefranche and Lyon rather than towards Beaune and so has a more southern and light-hearted outlook than the less extrovert country between Mâcon and Dijon. Economic difficulties (before the *primeur* fashion) and the attitudes resulting from them led to the foundation of twenty or so cooperatives, for the most part very active. *Caveaux* (tasting cellars) are another Beaujolais speciality but have taken much longer to get going in Burgundy.

BEAUJOLAIS WINE

ALTHOUGH seventy-nine communes in the Rhône and eleven in the Saône-et-Loire *département* can produce Beaujolais, the *appellation* is particularly important for the fifty or so communes to the west and south of Villefranche-sur-Saône, between the River Nizerand and the Azergues. The 610,000 hl of wine produced from an area of 9,700 hectares are essentially reds, with some incidental rosés, made almost exclusively from

Gamay Noir à Jus Blanc. To the north, Chardonnay is grown on the more calcareous soil in the canton of La Chapelle-de-Guinchay, and supplies almost three quarters of the 6,000 hl of white Beaujolais.

The method of pruning most often used is the *taille Guyot*. The picked grapes must be kept whole, so there is no machine harvesting, and vines less than four years old cannot claim AOC status.

The definition of the *appellation* Beaujolais Supérieur applies to red, rosé and white wines. The wines are not limited to specific areas but must have an alcohol level slightly higher than plain Beaujolais. Around 10,000 hl of this wine are declared annually.

A SPRIGHTLY WINE

BEAUJOLAIS has the colour of rubies, tinged with violet. The bouquet suggests fruit and flowers and is lively, fresh, sprightly and straightforward. It can be drunk from a *pot*, a heavy-bottomed 46 cl carafe used since 1846 by Boules players, and in all the little taverns and restaurants of Lyon. Villefranche-sur-Saône, with 30,000 inhabitants, is in fact the economic capital of this wine area, and after 1530 had replaced Beaujeu as the capital of the whole small region. The inhabitants of Villefranche are known as Caladois, a name taken from the broad paving-stones or *calades* in front of the church of Notre Dame des Marais. The numerous but narrow shop windows in the Rue Nationale can be traced back to a former tax based on the width of the shop-fronts. Every year, at the end of January, the Fête des Conscrits takes place. The streets swarm with men dressed in dinner-jackets, top-hats and white gloves, and carrying bouquets of flowers, as they take part in ten-yearly commemorations of their military service.

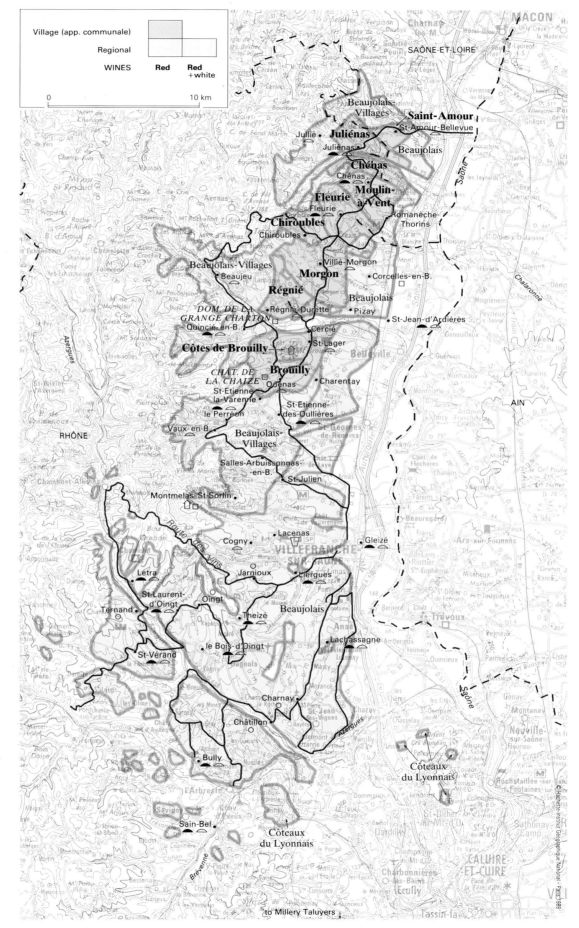

BEAUJOLAIS-VILLAGES

BEAUJOLAIS is a landscape of hills and valleys, with the constant green background of vines. The 6,200 hectares north of Villefranche-sur-Saône are a transitional zone between ordinary Beaujolais and the *crus* growing on lime-free granite sands. There are thirty-seven communes altogether, including eight in Saône-et-Loire and the others in the Rhône *département*. The reputation of these wines was recognized in 1946 when permission was given to add the name of the commune producing the wine to that of Beaujolais. In 1950 this was simplified so that the 350,000 hl of the regional *appellation* could be sold under the label of Beaujolais-Villages. There is only a tiny amount of white wine, so the label refers to reds and rosés where pruning and production have followed the same rules as for the *cru* wines. The quality of these wines gives a foretaste of the *crus*, but the lighter soils also produce wines popular as *primeurs*.

Above, Beaujeu, the Temple of Bacchus.

Top, Gamay Noir à Jus Blanc; this variety grows to perfection on Beaujolais soil.

Once the capital of Beaujolais, Beaujeu is now just a small town of 2,500 inhabitants. Before AD 1000 it had a fortress defending the road which joins the Rhône corridor and the valley of the Loire. In early times, the lords of Beaujeu made it clear that they would not be dominated by their powerful neighbours, the Count of Mâcon, the Abbot of Cluny or the Archbishop of Lyon, who all owned vines in the nearby countryside. In the town of Beaujeu there is a statue in honour of Gnafron, like Guignol a character in the Lyon puppet theatre and a great lover of Beaujolais. The Hospices de Beaujeu, dating back to the twelfth century, holds its traditional wine auction on the second Sunday in December and, as in Beaune, the wine is sold by candlelight.

Left, Anne de Beaujeu.

SAINT-AMOUR AND JULIÉNAS

Centre, golden stone in southern Beaujolais.

THE BEAUJOLAIS CRUS

WITH Beaujolais *primeurs* being sent all over the world, the local *appellations* or *crus* tend to be eclipsed. Although the latter are excellent, very individual wines, you have to be patient to appreciate their quality as it takes more than just a few weeks for this to be revealed.

At present there are ten *crus*, with the addition in 1988 of Régnié to Saint-Amour, Juliénas, Moulin-à-Vent, Chénas, Fleurie, Chiroubles, Morgon, Brouilly and Côte de Brouilly. These are red wines only, based on Gamay Noir à Jus Blanc, although Pinot Noir and Pinot Gris are allowed in Côte de Brouilly. In each of these *appellations* it is permissible to add 15

per cent of wine from white wine grapes (Chardonnay, Aligoté and Pinot Blanc), but this practice no longer occurs.

The most usual pruning technique is known as *gobelet* pruning ('goblet' because of the shape of bush this method produces), with a maximum of twelve buds to each plant. Long stems, as in *Guyot* pruning, are not allowed. Training into a fan shape is permitted but rarely practised.

The *cru* region stretches for some 20 km. Smaller localities and *climats* may sometimes be included in the *appellation*.

SAINT-AMOUR

'*ON peut mourir d'amour, mais il faut ressusciter au Saint-Amour.*' This enthusiastic comment means that you may die of love, but come to life again with a bottle of Saint-Amour. Saint-Amour succeeded in obtaining its *cru appellation* in 1946, the last to do so until Régnié thirty years later. North-east of Juliénas, on the border between Mâcon limestone and Beaujolais granite, the 280 hectares of this *appellation* are situated in the commune of Saint-Amour-Bellevue (Saône-et-Loire).

The village name is said to come from a Roman legionary, a Christian convert, whose statue stands near the church at the corner of the Salle des Fêtes. The vineyards, which were owned for many years by the canons of Mâcon, spread over the eastern side of the Montagne de Bessay (478 m) and the Colline de l'Eglise (310 m), and cover the east and south-east facing hillsides which slope gently down to the slow waters of the Saône, although most of the vines grow at a height of about 250 m. Planted on granite and siliceous clay, shingle and layers of schist, they produce an annual 16,000 hl of crimson-coloured wine. This has a fruity bouquet, with suggestions of soft fruit, apricot and peach, and its elegance and charm live up to the name of Saint-Amour. Although supple, it is often firm in structure and contains

hints both of its *terroir* and of the wine-making techniques which now favour youthful wines.

The tasting cellar dates from 1965 and has decorations by Nicolas Janin, an artist from Lyon. There are frequent Swiss visitors, who buy about half the local output. Along the road to Juliénas, the hamlet of Les Thevenins is a reminder of the Mâcon canons who stored their wine there and often came back for restorative visits.

JULIÉNAS

CURVING round the Mont du Bessay from the south-west to the southeast, the Juliénas *appellation* consists of 600 hectares in the communes of Pruzilly (Saône-et-Loire), Emeringes and especially Jullié and Juliénas (Rhône), which are said to be the oldest in Beaujolais and claim to go back to Julius Caesar's time.

Maison de la Dîme at Juliénas, one of the sixteenth- and seventeenth-century buildings where tithes were collected.

This is a transitional zone with granitic soil of volcanic and sedimentary origin, and also more recent alluvial soil which is deeper and more clayey. As a whole, the 32,000 hl of wine from this *appellation* are characterized by a firm, robust structure as well as a certain tautness and fleshiness. Juliénas has been popularized by the Lyon food-writers and perhaps has the unfortunate reputation of being an 'easy', rather down-to-earth wine. In fact, it has both vigour and character and after two or three years has plenty of body to go with its aroma of raspberries and cherries.

Once the property of the Beaujeu family, the château of Juliénas has splendid cellars to store the wine crop from their lands. The château of Bois de la Salle is a former priory dating from 1660. It now houses the Cave coopérative, which started up there in 1960 and processes almost a third of the *appellation* wines. A disused church in the middle of the village, the Cellier de la Vieille Eglise, has been turned into a tasting cellar decorated with Bacchus paintings by Basset and Monier, from Lyon. On the second weekend in November this ancient building is devoted to celebrations in honour of the wine of Juliénas.

CLOCHEMERLE-EN-BEAUJOLAIS

THE village of Vaux-en-Beaujolais was the inspiration for Gabriel Chevallier's well-known novel Clochemerle, with its racy picture of local cares and delights, all the moods and stormy disputes which have made Clochemerle into a symbol of parish pump squabbling. Chevallier wrote of the wine of Beaujolais: 'The more you drink of it, the more you have the feeling that your wife is charming, your friends loyal, the future hopeful and mankind in general tolerable.'

MOULIN-À-VENT AND CHÉNAS

MOULIN-À-VENT

A windmill surrounded by vines and visible for miles is a landmark for this *cru*. It was built 300 years ago for the peasants to grind their corn and now, minus its sails, it is classified as a historical monument. However, since 1957 the other local windmill, built beside the N6 road at La Maison Blanche, has provided all the amenities of a cellar for *dégustation*.

The subject of frequent wrangling between the Abbey of Tournus, formerly overlords of Romanèche-Thorins, and the Barons of Beaujeu, overlords of Chénas and Fleurie, this *terroir* finally received authorization from a 1924 Mâcon tribunal to use the name Moulin-à-Vent instead of Thorins, a right confirmed by decree in 1936. Moulin-à-Vent is not in fact the name of a commune. The production area extends over 640 hectares on the boundary of two *départements* (Romanèche-Thorins in Saône-et-Loire and Chénas in the Rhône).

The vines grow on eastward-facing hillsides, at a height of 250 to 280 m and on a very gradual slope. The soil is shallow: at most 1 m depth of 'gore', a salmon-pink sandstone originating in the decomposing granitic rock beneath it and rich in manganese. This mineral was exploited in the eighteenth and nineteenth centuries and mined right up to the middle of the village square.

Moulin-à-Vent produces 36,000 hl of a deep ruby, sometimes almost garnet-coloured wine. The nose is a blend of soft fruit, violets and roses. It is a full and well structured wine, with a good balance of taste, and can often be kept for ten years. With age it acquires heady flavours of truffle, wild boletus mushrooms and venison. Wines showing traces of manganese can be very robust and individual in style.

In October every year the village of Romanèche-Thorins celebrates the memory of Benoît Raclet (1780–1844), who discovered a way to destroy the moth pest *Pyralis* by scalding the vine stocks with hot water. There is a little museum devoted to him in what was once his house. The Guillon Museum contains works by the Compagnons du Tour de France. There is also a nicely arranged zoo in the village.

Make your way through Les Guillates, Les Gimarets, Les Bruyères, Le Champ de Cour, past densely regimented vines on their little hills of pink sand, and end up at the *caveau* by the old mill. Here you can sample the wine while admiring the panoramic view over the Saône valley, from Mâcon to Belleville.

Chénas, some of the remaining oak trees.

CHÉNAS

IN Chénas there are no longer many of the oak trees after which the region was named (*chêne* means oak), as vines have taken over since medieval times. Wines from the village had a good reputation as far back as the seventeenth century, when Louis XIII ordered them to be served at his table. The vineyards run west to east, on slopes overhanging Moulin-à-Vent, which also occupies land in the commune of Chénas itself. Chénas has about a third of its 200 hectares of vines here, growing at around 250 m on the eastern and southern faces of two little hills, the Cabane des Chasseurs and the Pic de Rémont, which allegedly appeared after the giant Gargantua relieved himself here.

The other sector of Chénas vines is up at about 210 m in the commune of La Chapelle-de-Guinchay, spreading over slopes and terraces that face across the Saône valley. The soil changes from pure granite sand in the west to silt and granite sand mixed with gravel and shingle.

The *appellation* dates from 1936. The wines have many points in common with Moulin-à-Vent: deep red colour, aromas of fruit and flowers, with just the occasional hint of peony spiciness. They are solidly built and age well. The average crop is about 13,000 hl.

The Chénas coopérative, since 1934 in an outbuilding of the Château des Michauds, makes about 40 per cent of the *appellation*. The cellar, with its sixteenth-century vaulted roof, houses an immense number of oak barrels and casks. The commune includes several scattered hamlets.

Moulin-à-Vent; the windmill here dates from the seventeenth century.

FLEURIE AND CHIROUBLES

FLEURIE

LEAVING Chénas southwards by the D68, we very soon see the Chapel of the Madonna, built in 1875 in thanksgiving to the Virgin Mary for protecting the vines against German invaders. This building is situated at a height of 425 m, on top of a hill completely covered in vines. The Fleurie *appellation* extends over 810 hectares.

A 1744 milestone, on the N6 in the hamlet of La Maison Blanche, shows that Fleurie was once a boundary village between the provinces of Mâcon and Beaujolais. Over the centuries, the Fleurie vines were the cause of endless quarrelling, especially the vineyards belonging to the convent of Arpaye, a dependency of the Abbey of Cluny.

The *appellation* boundaries coincide with those of the commune. The vines grow at a height of about 300 m, on slopes exposed to the east. They climb steeply westwards on a type of granite (large-crystal biotite) common in Beaujolais and called Fleurie granite. The soils here are fairly shallow, 30 to 50 cm thick, and are made up of granite sands which are very thin and dry and need constant feeding with humus. The disappearance of cattle-farming has caused problems with manure supply. The less hilly sector of Fleurie is situated on an alluvial cone with a broad southeastern aspect. Here the soil consists of shingle of crystalline or volcanic origin, together with a generally clay-rich matrix of sand and gravel.

The sandy terrain extending into Moulin-à-Vent produces wines with delicacy and finesse, while the shingle gives more strength and colour. The annual tasting at the beginning of November provides a chance to enjoy all the scents of iris, violet and amber in Fleurie, a lively, fruity wine which lives up to the charming promise of its name. It is often presented as the most 'feminine' of the Beaujolais *crus*.

After Brouilly and Morgon, Fleurie is the third highest in output of the *crus*. The wine cooperative, built in 1932 in the centre of the village, produces a third of the *appellation*. There are also two local tasting cellars and, for larger groups of visitors, a basement reception area with ceramic wall decorations. Both cellars offer a whole range of wines from evocatively named vineyards: La Rochette, La Chapelle des Bois, Les Roches, Grille-Midi, La Joie du Palais. One of the best is Les Moriers, a most attractive wine.

A local celebrity is Marguerite Chabert, a colourful character whose family invented the famous sausage dish of Andouillettes au Fleurie.

CHIROUBLES

THE land west of Fleurie has all the problems of cultivation in the mountains. If you follow the vines up these steep hills you come upon a splendidly commanding view over Beaujolais. After the Fût d'Avenas, at a height of 700 m, there is the little village of Avenas on an old Roman road or, if you stay up in the hills, there's another panoramic view – this time over the vines of Chiroubles. An orientation table there shows where you can see eighty different church spires.

This *appellation* was created in 1936 and covers 350 hectares of sometimes steep hillside at heights between 300 and 480 m. The soil here is almost uniformly made up of granite sands from the Fleurie massif. The sunshine

Overlooking the vineyards of Fleurie, the chapel of the Madonna.

A traditional wine-press at Fleurie.

on this natural amphitheatre is ideal for vine-growing, although there have been difficulties with clearing and maintaining the land, and particularly with erosion problems. The local dry-stone walls are known here as *rases*.

The output of Chiroubles consists of 18,000 hl annually. This wine is instantly recognizable, with its fairly light colour, supple freshness and strong scent of violets. Chiroubles is still unfamiliar outside France, but can be the most charming and ethereal of these *crus*. The area was once also famous for its turnips, but these are now no longer grown.

In the church square there is a bust of Victor Pulliat (1827–96), a grape expert who had at least 2,000 vine varieties growing at Tempéré, his *domaine* along the road to Villié-Morgon. In the fight against phylloxera he pioneered grafting and the use of American vine-stocks.

About 15 per cent of local production is made into wine by the Maison des Vignerons, the smallest cooperative in Beaujolais. Wine-lovers are drawn to Chiroubles every spring by the Fête des Crus du Beaujolais et du Mâconnais.

LYON'S THIRD RIVER

IT has been said that Lyon has three rivers: the Rhône, the Saône and then the Beaujolais, which never dries up. The wine was popularized in the thirties by Lyon writers and journalists, and later by the Paris press, in Lyon from 1940 to 1942. After the war the satirical paper, Le canard enchaîné, *ascribing its own raciness to Beaujolais, gave it even more of a reputation.*

MORGON AND RÉGNIÉ

MORGON

BY following the D18 westwards from the terraces of Chiroubles to Villié-Morgon, one in fact goes through much of the Morgon vine area. The coppices and meadows along the upper section of road give way at St-Joseph, the highest point in the commune of Villié-Morgon, to the 1,040 hectares of vines. These spread down the hillsides facing east and south-east, sloping gradually from heights of 450 and 235 m down to the feudal keep of the château of

Pizay, with its famous *cuvage* (building housing wine-vats) and topiary gardens.

The best Morgon wine comes from the Montagne de Py. Rising above a sea of vines, a single tree grows on the top of this perfectly shaped hill. Throughout this *appellation,* created in 1936, the vines grow in soil known as *pourri* ('rotten'), derived from volcanic sediment (basaltic rocks mixed with pyritic schist impregnated with ferrous oxide and called *morgons*). This soil

Above, formal gardens at the Château de Pizay.

Left, the Compagnons du Beaujolais hold an enthronement ceremony.

gives 60,000 hl of wine deep in colour, rich in dry matter and of a quality to age well. With the virile quality of Burgundy, Morgon has an unexaggerated firm and solid structure, and plenty of characteristic body. There are often expansive aromas of raspberry and kirsch and a deep, dark garnet colour.

To the east and on less steeply sloping ground, the wines are different. Shingle from crystalline or volcanic rock is predominant here, together with siliceous rock over clay-rich sand and gravel. To the west and north are granite sands similar to those of Fleurie and Chiroubles.

The name of the little town of Villié-Morgon comes from the fusion in 1867 of the two villages of Villié and Morgon, and there is a history of wine-growing going back to the tenth century. In a park in the middle of the town is the present *caveau*, the first in Beaujolais, which was built in 1953 below the walls of the eighteenth-century château of Fontcrenne.

Three roads run south to Brouilly and Côte de Brouilly: the D9 through Régnié-Durette, past its church with two towers; the D68 round the east side of the Montagne de Py; and the D18 to Cercié by way of Pizay.

RÉGNIÉ

SINCE 1988 Régnié has been the tenth Beaujolais *cru*, but has had to battle for years for justifiable promotion to this AOC and for recognition of its genuine and consistent quality.

Régnié-Durette, a fusion in 1973 of two separate communes, is wedged between the Morgon AOC area to the north and west and Brouilly to the south. Its 800 hectares of vines, at a height of 350 m, face south-east towards the Montagne de Brouilly, and are planted on soils of decomposed granite from the Fleurie massif. They dominate the Ardières valley and the road running from Belleville-sur-Saône to Beaujeu through plantations of *crus* and Beaujolais-Villages. From the seventeenth century on, this road and the Canal de Briare provided easier transport for Beaujolais wines, especially towards Paris. The solid granite buildings in the hamlet of Les Dépôts show how important this road once was for the local wine-trade.

The church of Régnié-Durette is a mid-nineteenth-century building in the style of the Fourvières basilica in Lyon, and its two towers make the village visible from some distance. The Domaine de la Grange Charton, close to the church and the D9 road, was bequeathed in 1806 to the Hospices de Beaujeu. The immense *cuvage* and other buildings are used for making and storing the *domaine* wine from the 63 hectares of vines managed by eleven different growers. As at Beaune, the Hospices de Beaujeu sell their wine by auction every year. The 1988 vintage (35,000 hl) is the first for this new AOC, with its seductive ruby colour and flavour of fruit. Its elegance and softness are reminiscent of Brouilly, its robustness sometimes more like Morgon.

WINE CONFRÉRIES IN BEAUJOLAIS

THE wine-growers' fraternity, Compagnons du Beaujolais, live up to their motto: 'Vuidons les tonneaux' ('Drink the casks dry'). This confrérie, founded in 1948, has a cellar for its meetings at Lacenas near Villefranche-sur-Saône. The members go all over the world to popularize Beaujolais. They also organize the Grumage, similar to the Tastevinage in Burgundy: official tastings to determine the wines best for laying down, such wines being known as vins grumés. The confrérie called the Grappilleurs de Pierres dorées was founded in 1968 and the Gosier Sec in 1961.

Brouilly, Côte de Brouilly and Lyonnais

BROUILLY

WITH its 1,200 hectares, the 1938 *appellation* of Brouilly is the largest of the Beaujolais *crus.* Bisected in the north by the Ardières valley, the traditional Beaujolais–Paris trade route, it envelops Mont Brouilly, which is 484 m high, and spreads over the communes of Odenas, Saint-Lager, Charentay, Cercié, Quincié and Saint-Etienne-la-Varenne. Brouilly is not itself the name of a village. Going from north to south there are three distinct geological zones. First there

Above, Mont Brouilly.

Top right, designs for fans, 1830 (Arts Décoratifs library, Paris).

are the soils of Fleurie-type granite in the area west of Mont Brouilly, which is itself made up of hard, compact rock (*cornes*) of a characteristic blue-green. In the east, near the former river terraces of the Saône, there are faults cutting into and breaking up what formerly was a fairly homogeneous alluvial zone.

The same diversity can of course be found in the wines of Brouilly. The 70,000 hl produced here are sometimes pleasant for early drinking, but can also age well. Those grown on granite have plenty of fruit and are enjoyable in their youth. Those from the central schistous area are more intense in colour and have serious keeping qualities. In the fringe areas,

with their varied soil, everything depends on the grower's skill. Brouilly contains suggestions of bilberries (blueberries), apples and blackberries.

Along the route des Vins between Belleville-sur-Saône and Cercié there are a number of places of interest, such as St Ennemond's chapel, standing guard over the harvest, the vineyard called Pisse-Vieille – the pride of the Hospices de Beaujeu – and at Saint-Lager the tasting-cellar for Brouilly and Côte de Brouilly.

All along the route there are châteaux: the eighteenth-century Sermezy; Arginy, a twelfth-century Templar castle; La Chaize near Odenas, built in the seventeenth century and containing a 110-m-long cellar, the largest in Beaujolais.

CÔTE DE BROUILLY

THE AOC Côte de Brouilly completely encircles Mont Brouilly and covers 300 hectares in the communes of Odenas, Saint-Lager, Cercié and Quincié. It is often quoted as a perfect example of geological uniformity: granite and very hard greenish-blue schist, which is known here as *cornes vertes*. From the tree-covered heights of Mont Brouilly one can see over the Saône valley, the plateau of La Dombes and south to the outskirts of Lyon. There is a chapel built in 1857 and dedicated to Notre Dame du Raisin as a record of the grim battle against oïdium.

The *appellation* dates from 1938, and was the object of impassioned debate among the local growers. Some wanted to safeguard the name of Brouilly itself, others to achieve a volume of production entitling them to a special denomination. Planted on terrain with aspects varying according to their position round Mont Brouilly, the vines produce 17,000 hl of intensely coloured wine, deep purple with delicious scents of soft fruit such as redcurrant, raspberry or even bilberry (blueberry). They have backbone, a certain longevity and, because of strong sunshine on the slopes, a higher degree of alcohol than any of the other Beaujolais *crus.*

La Chaize, the château.

COTEAUX DU LYONNAIS

WINE-growing in the Lyonnais hills originated in the Middle Ages with encouragement from religious houses as well as rich merchants in Lyon. The wine had had a good reputation in the sixteenth century, but the vines, which covered 12,000 hectares in the second half of the nineteenth century, gradually disappeared. Now they survive only on two isolated sites: one on the fringe of Beaujolais, north-west of Lyon; the other in the Rhône valley, south-west of the city. The vines occupy east-facing slopes and are thus protected by the Massif Central from extremes of Atlantic weather. They

also benefit from sub-Mediterranean influences from the Rhône valley.

Apart from the clayey and limestone soils of the Monts d'Or region, the soils are light and permeable. Gamay Noir à Jus Blanc, grown at between 200 and 500 m, produces 13,000 hl of red and rosé wine of the same family as Beaujolais. There is a small output (400 hl) of white wine based on Chardonnay and Aligoté.

JURA

THE JURA WINE REGION

THE Jura is a region of little villages full of steeply roofed houses and churches with onion domes. It is a proud land, which belonged to Burgundy and Spain before returning to France under Louis XIV, and is still fiercely independent. Its Revermont wine region extends over faulting separating the Bresse plain from the first plateau in the Jura mountains. It runs north to south like a long chain about 80 km long by 10 km wide from Salins-les-Bains to Saint-Amour, not to be confused with the similarly named place in Beaujolais. Closer to Lons-le-Saunier steep

The thirteenth-century vaulted cellar at the Cellier des Chartreux, Montaigu.

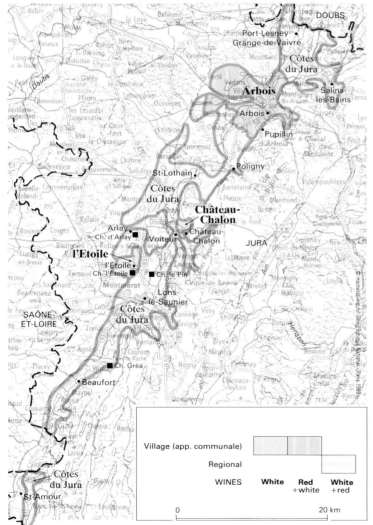

Village (app. communale)

Regional

WINES | **White** | **Red** | **White**
| | +white | +red

0   20 km

hanging valleys (*reculées*) slope up like rocky, tree-covered steps between the piedmont area and the plateau. They give great individuality to this harsh, stern landscape where the only softening features are the hillsides planted with vines.

Vine-growing here goes back to the distant past: even Pliny the Younger wrote in praise of the local wine. In the last century there were more than 20,000 hectares but today there are hardly more than 1,500, with an output for the *appellation* of around 41,000 hl. Vineyards are situated between the 220 and 380 m contours, usually with a western aspect but sometimes south-west or south, depending on the direction of the valley. The terrain is fairly flat near the river Ain but soon becomes more undulating, especially from Château-Chalon up to Arbois. Above Salins the Poupet bridge marks the end of the vineyard region.

The climate is often very harsh, but this is balanced by long periods of sunshine. The terrain is of Mesozoic formation, with very complex geology: wine-coloured red marl and clays of Triassic origin on which the reds and rosés are grown, and Liassic blue marl overlaid with limestone on which whites do very well. Various grape varieties are cultivated:

Ploussard or Poulsard, Trousseau and Pinot Noir for the reds; Chardonnay (sometimes called Melon d'Arbois or Gamay Blanc) and Savagnin or Naturé for the whites. The very definite local characteristics of these grapes and the unique soil they are grown on give the wine a strongly individual accent, like the Jura people. The red and rosé wines have a clean taste of fruit and flowers with just enough body to be able to expand with age. The rosés here are in fact pseudo-reds, since they are vinified with a long fermentation period like true reds and the rosé colour comes from the rather pale Poulsard grape. They do have red wine character and take on terracotta tints as they age. The white wines are dry, with nutty flavours – walnut, hazel and roasted almond – and have a unique character, a kind of yellowness, which has more to do with taste than colour. There are also some excellent sparkling wines.

CÔTES DU JURA

THE AOC Côtes du Jura is produced all over the region in some sixty communes, with the Arbois, Château-Chalon and L'Etoile *appellations* sandwiched among them. There is an output of 15,000 to 30,000 hl from vines planted on some 600 hectares.

Among interesting places to visit are: the Château d'Arlay; the perched village of Montaigu, the birthplace of Rouget de Lisle, author of the Marseillaise; and the small town of Poligny which produces both wine and Gruyère cheese. Other interesting places are Le Vernois where, unusually in France, the wine-growing area has been completely redefined; and of course Château-Chalon and Nevy-sur-Seille.

ARBOIS

THE Arbois *appellation* has 780 hectares of vines producing wine in a delimited area of 2,700 hectares spread over thirteen communes. Arbois itself is on the river Cuisance, a charming, small ochre-coloured town piled up round the yellow sandstone church tower and completely surrounded with vines. It was in at the beginning of the Jura wine trade and is now its main centre. A third of the vines belong to the firm of Henri Maire, which also buys in grapes from 800 growers. On the first Sunday in September is the Biou festival, when a gigantic bunch of grapes is carried in a procession in honour of Saint-Just, the patron saint of Arbois. The great man of this town is of course Louis Pasteur, whose house and laboratory can be visited.

Drying grapes for vin de paille.

The annual output varies between 20,000 and 40,000 hl (three fifths of this is red or rosé, the rest white) and is much influenced by weather conditions. Since 1970 the name Pupillin, for wine produced there, can be added to the Arbois *appellation*.

L'ETOILE

THIS *appellation*, for white wines and *vins jaunes* only, is produced on Liassic marl on very well exposed slopes in the communes of L'Etoile, Plainoiseau and Saint-Didier. The name comes from the star shapes of the crinoid fossils found on the

ground here. Chardonnay and Savagnin give elegant wine with a lot of character and ageing potential. About 3,000 hl are produced on around 55 hectares.

CHÂTEAU-CHALON

IT is a truth universally acknowledged that this is one of the great white wines of France. White is not the right word, however, since this 1936 *appellation* is restricted to the *vin jaune* produced in the communes of Château-Chalon, Ménétru, Domblans and Nevy-sur-Seille. There are scarcely 40 hectares producing up to 1,000 hl annually, so this wine is rare and expensive. The growers have formed a union, which determines the potential yield of each plot – an arrangement unique in France. The yield is often quite low and they sometimes decide to make no wine at all when the grapes do not ripen adequately, as happened in 1974, 1980 and 1984.

Château-Chalon is an ancient village perched up on a rocky escarpment, looking down on hillsides with woods at the top and vines lower down. On the steeper slopes there is

The St-Vernier festival at Château-Chalon.

limestone scree mixed with Liassic marl, then more homogeneous marl terrain. The river Seille has scoured a steep *reculée*, which shelters the vines from the north wind and ensures plenty of sunshine from the south and south-west.

Savagnin, or Naturé, the only grape authorized for this *appellation*, is historically rather puzzling. It is not the Tokay grape brought from Hungary in the tenth century by the Abbesses of Château-Chalon. It is unlikely to have come from Jerez in the period of the Spanish occupation of Franche-Comté. It might possibly be a direct descendant of the wild vine (*Vitis labrusca*), which once grew in north-east France. Whatever the truth may be, Savagnin is very closely related to the Traminer of Alsace.

The grapes are generally harvested at the end of October or the beginning of November. The wine is vinified according to classic white wine

Poulsard grapes.

techniques and is then matured for six years in oak casks. These have to be the right kind for the yellow colour to 'take'. The cask is not completely filled and there is no topping up, so that nothing disturbs the thin surface film, a veil of live yeasts, which by a slow complex process is responsible for the colour of *vin jaune*. The wine may or may not respond to this process. Finally it is put into special bottles, *clavelins* holding 63 cl, which correspond to 1 l of the wine harvested six years earlier. At this point the wine is indestructible and can age for 100 years without the slightest deterioration.

The growers say that this wine should be drunk not cold, but at ambient temperature, and opened some time beforehand to let it aerate and develop its subtle green walnut flavours. It has tremendous body, and with age its colour may deepen to amber.

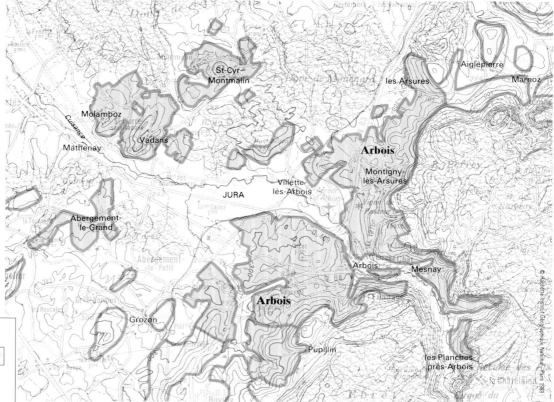

Village (app. communale)	1
Regional	2
WINES	**Red** +white	**White** +red

1 Arbois   2 Côtes du Jura

0   5 km

SAVOIE

THE Savoie wine region extends across mountainous country between Lake Geneva and the right bank of the river Isère. With a background of picturesque lakes and snow-covered peaks, it occupies the most favourable aspects in the valleys and lower slopes of the Alps. The wine it produces is crisp and fresh like the mountain air.

The vineyards arch round in a curve whose southern tip forms a tight loop at the base of the Bauges mountains. Vines are grown principally near Lake Geneva and the Lac du Bourget and on land near the Rhône and Isère, on south-east and south-west facing slopes sometimes up to heights of 500 m. The mountainous barriers formed by the Bauges and the Chartreuse massif, and the presence of lakes and rivers, have a moderating effect on the continental climate. All this gives good ripening conditions, especially as the region has around 1,600 hours of sunshine annually and fine autumn weather.

Above, the Chignin wine region.
Above right, the Abymes vineyards alongside the lake of Saint-André, with the Belle Jounc range in the distance.

This is an area of small-scale vineyards: 1,200 of them on 1,500 hectares of *appellation* territory. The highest proportion (1,100 hectares) is in the *département* of Savoie, the rest in Haute Savoie (160 hectares), Isère (90 hectares) and Ain (80 hectares). Seventy per cent of production is made up of white wines, which in Savoie find good growing conditions on chalky soils, mixed with some marl or clay. The glacial morains in Haute Savoie also provide a favourable environment and dry white wines are successfully grown on the clay, silt or alluvial deposits brought down by glaciers.

DIVERSITY OF WINE

THE largest wine-growing district is south of Chambéry on rubble from Mont Granier. It is made up of 500 hectares covering the *crus* of Apremont and Abymes and takes in the villages of Apremont, Les Marches, Myans and Saint-Baldolph as well as Chapareillan in the Isère *département*. Jacquère, the basic grape variety for Savoie white wine, gives 35,000 hl of wine made by a process of slow, cool fermentation and allowed to mature on fine lees. These wines, sometimes very slightly sparkling, are fresh, fruity and light.

The huge thirteenth-century rock-fall from Mont Granier, like that of the Abymes de Myans, forms a considerable landmark in this changeable landscape.

Between Montmélian and Albertville on the right bank of the Isère and alongside the Bauges massif, the vineyards of Arbin, Cruet, Saint-Jean-de-la-Porte, Saint-Pierre-d'Albigny and Fréterive produce 17,000 hl of red, rosé and white wines, with predominant use of Mondeuse, the red grape variety most typical of Savoie. The best known *cru* is Arbin, certainly a wine for keeping. This region has many wine nurseries, as Savoie is the second most prolific of the *départements* specializing in young vine plants.

South-east of Chambéry, and close to the Bauges, Chignin has some remarkable whites based on Jacquère, and on Roussanne (known locally as Bergeron) for Chignin-Bergeron. The towers of an ancient ruined castle rise up above this very old vineyard.

On the side of the La Charve Mountain, on the Rhône banks west of Lac du Bourget, is the well-organized wine district of Jongieux, which covers more than 180 hectares in the villages of Lucey, Jongieux, Billième, Saint-Jean-de-Chevelu and Yenne. Here are the excellent Roussette wines from Marestel and Monthoux. On the northern tip of Lac du Bourget, Chautagne from the Ruffieux Cave Coopérative is based on Gamay and is one of the best Savoie red wines.

Chasselas is grown beside Lake Geneva and makes some distinctive and pleasant dry whites, as well as the slightly sparkling Ripaille at Thonon, Marignan at Sciez, and Marin in the village of that name. The same grape is used for Crépy, from a miniature version of the Swiss Valais wine district, producing 4,000 hl on 70 hectares. It has been said that this is the most diuretic of French wines.

Ayse, in the narrow Arve valley near Bonneville, produces 1,000 hl of sparkling white wine, made either by the *méthode champenoise* or by the local method of spontaneous bottle fermentation. Frangy, at the confluence of Les Usses and the Rhône, makes 500 hl of a much appreciated wine, a Roussette based on the Altesse grape.

SEYSSEL

THE Seyssel AOC was set up in 1942 and is the oldest in Savoie. It produces 3,000 hl on 65 hectares of land extending along both banks of the Rhône between steep hillsides cut by ravines. This is where the Altesse grape originated, giving Seyssel its distinctive supple wines with their elegant blend of aromas. Their violet scent reminds one that for a long time the perfume-makers of Grasse had Florentine irises grown here and in fact derived a violet scent from these flowers. Sparkling Seyssel (1,000 hl) is based on a different grape selection, Molette, and sometimes a good white (Chasselas), mixed with a minimum of 10 per cent Altesse. The still wines produced in Savoie should be drunk fairly quickly.

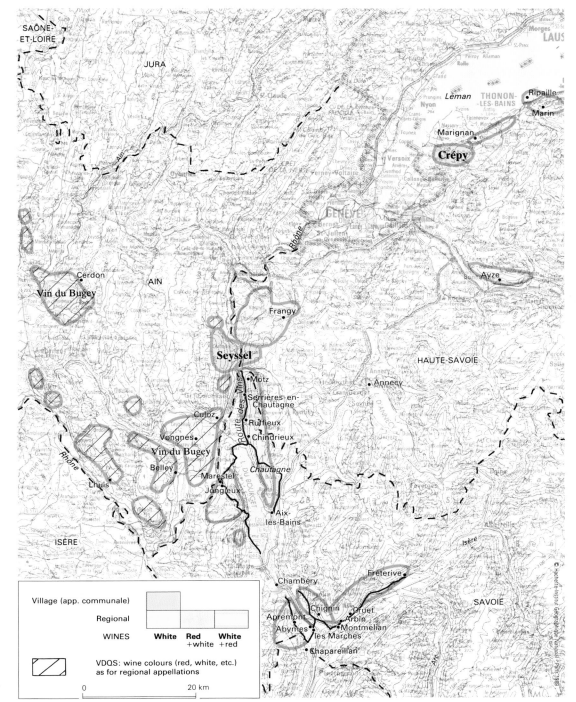

Village (app. communale)

Regional

WINES **White** **Red +white** **White +red**

VDQS: wine colours (red, white, etc.) as for regional appellations

0   20 km

BUGEY

BECAUSE of its abbeys, the Bugey wine district in the Ain *département* was once of some importance. It is now much diminished, with only 250 hectares giving 14,000 hl of VDQS

Below, a peasant hut, or sarto, *near Apremont.*

wine. Historically, Bugey was once attached to Burgundy. The land is of Jurassic formation, with a great variety of marl and clay soils at the foot of the hills and limestone on the slopes. The climate is basically maritime, with a certain amount of Mediterranean and continental influence.

The politician and gourmet Brillat-Savarin (1755–1826) was a native of Bugey and the region has certainly not lost its tradition of gastronomy. As in Savoie, everyone is very

hospitable and the kitchen is the real heart of the house. A number of grape varieties are grown here: for red wines Poulsard from the Jura, Mondeuse from Savoie, Pinot and Gamay from Burgundy; for white wines Altesse and Jacquère from Savoie, Chardonnay and Aligoté from Burgundy, as well as Molette, which is the only authentic regional variety and has been used for more than a hundred years to make sparkling wine.

THE RHÔNE VALLEY

THE Rhône valley vineyards run in and out between the hills, perching on terraces and precipitous hillsides, and forming a splendid green contrast to the sun-mellowed rooftiles of the houses. This wine region is a world in itself, but is not really a single region. In the north, downstream from Vienne, vines have to grow discreetly, tucked behind clear boundaries which they are not allowed to cross; but in the south they make up for this by erupting in all directions and occupying all available space. This area gives a foretaste of the vast expanses of vines in Provence and Languedoc. Here they stretch as far as the eye can see, even onto the slopes of Mont Ventoux and the high plateau of the Ardèche.

CHARACTER

The dual character of the wine region, north and south, is a reflection of the natural environment. The Rhône valley, in the 200 or so kilometres between Vienne and Avignon, has a far from uniform appearance. Throughout its length the river has to carve its way between the Alps

and the Massif Central, and this is particularly true in the north, below Lyon, where the mountains press in and constrict it. Sometimes there is scarcely room along the valley for the river, the main road and autoroute, and the line for the modern high speed train. Gorges and open valleys alternate as the Rhône sweeps down to the south. Massive alluvial deposits from the Alps have been washed down onto the eastern bank facing the steep, chestnut-clad slopes of the Vivarais. Then, at Vienne and Tournon, the river changes once more, cutting gorges through the middle of the primitive massif. In the river valley downstream from Valence vinegrowing stops, but makes a sudden reappearance near Donzère about 30 km further south, perhaps because of less harsh conditions in the vast lowland area round Orange. The clear

light and the type of crops on the gently sloping Coteaux du Tricastin begin to look like Provence, but still with a hint of austerity. The Alpilles hills are a final obstruction forcing the river to run close against the Gard foothills. The wide expanses of the Camargue appear at last and the Rhône can meander gently into the Mediterranean.

GEOLOGY

THE geology of the Rhône valley is both complex and simple: complex because all kinds of formation, from Precambrian to Quaternary, can be found; and simple because these all derive from one phenomenon – the relative movement, at times violent, between the young Alpine chain to the east and the ancient bedrock of the Massif Central. In the Mesozoic era the latter had already been formed into an imposing mountain mass, while the Alps were still a vast sea, in the depths of which large quantities of calcareous sediment were piling up, although as yet only the Pelvoux and the Mercantour massifs had emerged. At the end of the Mesozoic and Tertiary eras, the plate forming present-day Italy was drifting towards north-west Europe; in the course of this it pushed up millions of years of sedimentary deposits, folding them and driving them against the almost stationary mass of the Massif Central. Between these two masses, one stationary and the other active, the narrow course of the Rhône was already being traced. In the Miocene and Pliocene, sea flowing in from the south took this route, and the first influx deposited much of the soil forming the left bank of the southern Côtes du Rhône. Finally, in the Quaternary era, the young Alpine massif was strongly eroded by rivers, which washed down and deposited large quantities of pebbles. These were polished and rolled over hundreds of kilometres and were eventually to form broad flat terraces excellent for growing vines, as at Crozes-Hermitage, further south at Donzère and Les Granges Gontardes bordering the Tricastin region, and also in the Visan-Valréas basin, the Plan de Dieu, and especially at Châteauneuf-du-Pape, Tavel, Lirac and Roquemaure.

NORTH AND SOUTH

THE local geology is a result of impacts between east and west, while the climate is a confrontation between northern, continental influences and those from the Mediterranean. One element connects the entire valley and that is the Mistral. This wind can blow violently through the whole region or more gently, as a result of slight changes of temperature or pressure, but it is always there, and the landscape is punctuated with trees and bushes leaning away from the wind.

Despite its Mediterranean latitude, the north of the valley has a continental climate. The winds and the enclosed nature of the valley contribute to a wide temperature range, with hot summers and severe winters. Coming south from Lyon, a traveller will often see grey skies suddenly giving way to intense blue by the time he or she reaches Donzère. At this point you cross into the Mediterranean sector of the valley, noted for its pure air and limpid light; the Alpilles form a distinct barrier here and have a moderating effect on the climate.

Such diverse influences in both weather and geology were likely to encourage the production of a variety of wines, but natural factors are not a complete explanation. The birth and development of wine-growing in the region owe a great deal to history, for example the establishment of the Papacy in Avignon in the late Middle Ages.

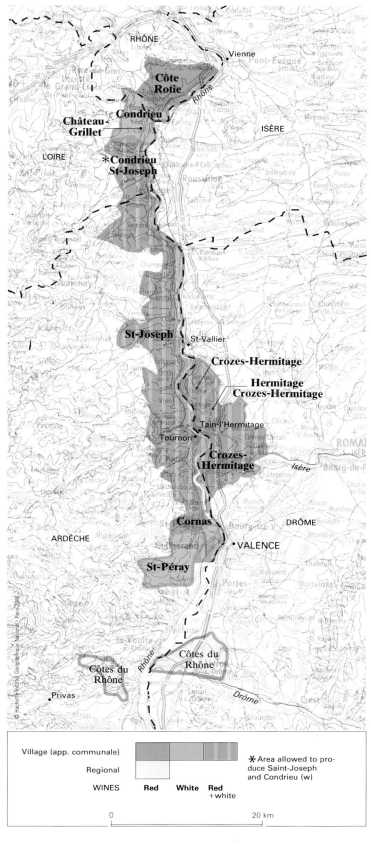

Village (app. communale)				*Area allowed to produce Saint-Joseph and Condrieu (w)
Regional				
WINES	Red	White	Red +white	

0   20 km

Left hand page, top, Condrieu, high above the Rhône.

Bottom, treading the grapes, from mosaic showing seasonal occupations, early third century AD (Saint-Romain-en-Gal).

This page, steep granite slopes at Saint-Joseph.

183

PAPAL VINEYARDS

ALL wine-growing in France owes much to the medieval clergy, but it is only the Rhône valley that can boast of direct Papal influence.

However, the impact of wine on the Rhône valley population came much earlier than the Popes. It began once again with Greece, by way of Massalia (Marseille), where the Greek colonists set up trading posts. It was therefore through the Greeks that the local inhabitants became accustomed to drinking wine, although it was the Romans who taught them how to grow it. Curiously enough, it seems that the first vineyards were in the north rather than the south of the valley.

Vienne is a garrison town and a historic centre built on stepped terraces above a loop in the river. It became a focus for the wine industry, perhaps just by chance when the Romans stopped here, because of the natural beauty of the riverbanks downstream, or just because of a lucky guess by some pioneering tribe. For whatever reason, and with the help of toiling legions from across the Alps, vines were established in the area, which was to become the northern Côtes du Rhône. From the very beginning, the region acquired a fame that it was never to lose, and developed a flourishing trade, as shown

by recently excavated bas-relief carvings and inscriptions.

As elsewhere in the West, barbarian invasion caused vineyards to be destroyed and trade routes dislocated. Although in the Middle Ages the valley was divided between the Kingdom of France on the right bank, and the Empire on the left, vine-growing began to come back to life. Religious orders, such as the Carthusians and Cistercians, played an important part in redeveloping northern vineyards. In the south, the impetus was a result of the establishment of the Papal court in Avignon in 1305. Church dignitaries and their followers were not satisfied with importing wine from Burgundy, but also planted their own vineyards, especially at Châteauneuf where the Pope had a castle and some land.

After the return to Rome of the Papacy, the Rhône wine region

continued to grow, in both size and reputation, until the Revolution of 1789. Unlike areas such as Burgundy and Bordeaux whose closeness to England and Paris provided favourable trading conditions, the Rhône valley had a more laborious task. Expansion was also held back for some time by taxes affecting the wine trade. The seventeenth century brought the abolition of these taxes and the development of important communication routes such as the Canal du Midi.

IN the two centuries before the Revolution there was a fashion for wine from this area, the Gard side of the river north-west of Avignon. Its rapid growth resulted from an amalgamation of growers from Tavel Roquemaure, Lirac, Chusclan and places nearby. They first attempted to ban wine coming from less prominent neighbouring parishes. After an unfavourable Royal Edict of 1729, they later succeeded in making it obligatory

---

BEAUMES DE VENISE AND RASTEAU

THE terrain and situations of these two villages make them particularly well suited to the production of vin doux naturel. *Beaumes de Venise, south of the Dentelles de Montmirail has a wonderfully evocative name, suggesting warmth and honey and flowers. The name (which has nothing to do with either balm or Venice) comes from* baoumo, *Provençal for cave, and from* Comtat Venaissin, *the old name for this region.*

The appellation zone faces south and is well sheltered from the Mistral. Only one grape variety is grown on this varied terrain: Muscat à Petits Grains, on which is based the delicate Muscat de Beaumes de Venise. This should be tried the year after the harvest. It is not over sweet but has a rich and complex bouquet suggesting lemon and citronella with a faint aftertaste of roses.

To the north-west of Gigondas, Rasteau lies in a sheltered situation among small hills between the river Aygues and the Ouvèze, where Grenache Noir achieves a high natural sugar level. Rasteau can be white, turning amber as it matures, or red if the grapes have been kept longer on the skins. They have a rich and complex bouquet, with dominant soft fruit aromas.

Soils in the southern Côtes du Rhône.

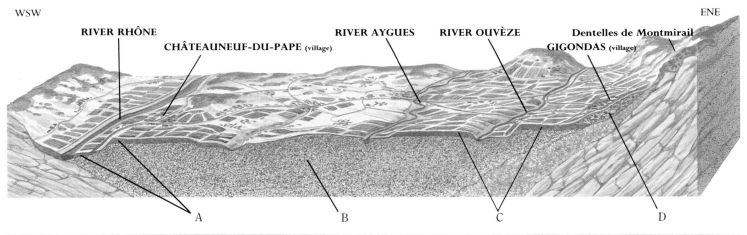

Soil surface (importance for heat)	Quartzite pebbles	Calcareous sands	Calcareous pebbles and flints	Clay/pebbles
Subsoil (importance for water supply)	Thick layers of clay/pebbles	Sandy	Shallow layers of clay/pebbles	Clay/pebbles

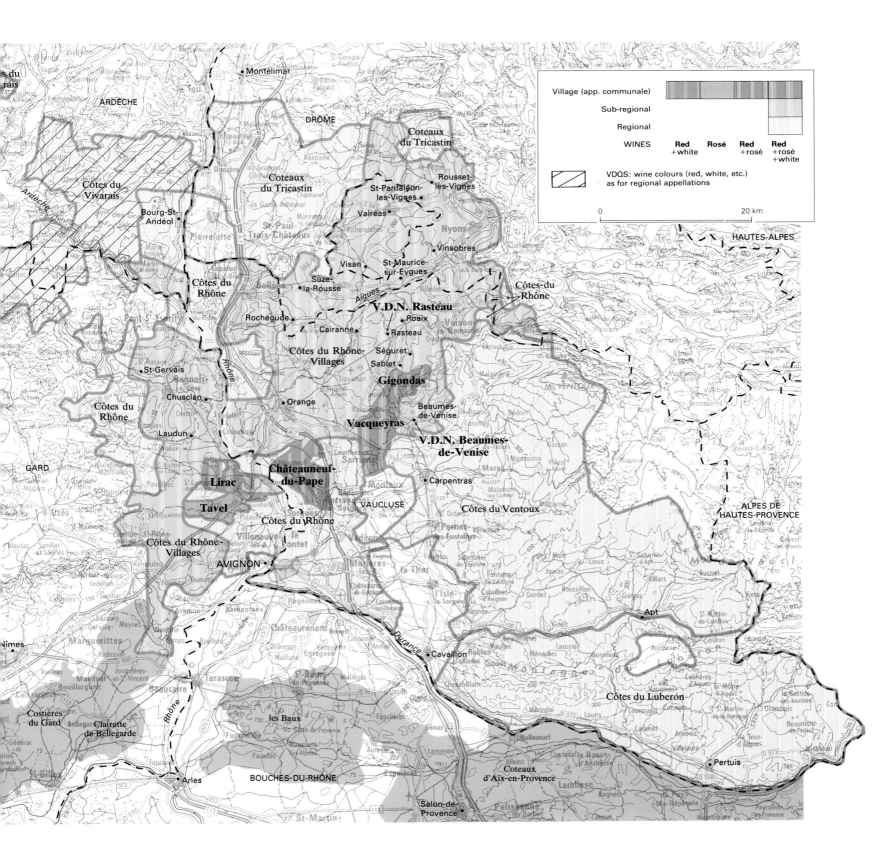

to brand casks with the letters CDR (Côtes du Rhône). This surprisingly modern organization then devised a whole series of protective measures for quality wines produced in these villages. Wines from the Côte du Rhône Gardoise were widely sold in the eighteenth century, especially in Great Britain, Germany, Holland and Flanders.

Wine from the left bank was less successful. Expansion was small because of competition from market-gardening and fruit trees, and in particular from olives, which grew on slopes and shallow pebbly terraces now occupied by the most reputable *crus*. Apart from Châteauneuf-du-Pape, there were only isolated pockets of vines, at least until the twentieth century when, thanks largely to Baron Leroy de Boiseaumarie, Côtes du Rhône were able to regain their status and identity.

CÔTES DU RHÔNE

THE Rhône valley consists of a patchwork of *appellations*, including Château-Grillet, one of the smallest in France. It also has the largest regional *appellation* after Bordeaux, as the Côtes du Rhône area extends through 163 villages and six *départements* (Rhône, Loire, Drôme, Ardèche, Gard and Vaucluse).

THE REALM OF WINE

THE size of the *appellation* makes it understandable that it should be confused in the public mind with Rhône valley vineyards as a whole. This is not in theory such an absurd idea as sites entitled to the *appellation* go all the way south from Vienne to Avignon. In practice almost the entire production of Côtes du Rhône, apart from a miniscule 1,000 hl, comes from the southern sector alone. The northern vineyards are devoted almost exclusively to regional *appellations*.

The southern Côtes du Rhône occupy a gigantic basin spreading over four *départements* (Drôme, Vaucluse, Gard and Ardèche) between the towns of Bollène and Avignon. Wine is the one subject of conversation on both sides of the river and is as dominant in people's lives as vines are in the countryside. The two sides of the river are linked in this way but each side has its own distinctive personality.

On the Gard side of the river, vine-growing is concentrated on a number of gently rolling hills rising between

Saint-Joseph, a recently terraced vineyard.

the river to the east and the Ardèche and Gard plateaux to the west. These low plateaux of hard, dense limestone lead on to the majestically harsh mountains of the Cévennes.

This wild country of plunging narrow ravines is in complete contrast to the more gentle vineyard region, where softer rock formations have allowed rivers to spread in broad valleys on their way to the Rhône. Vines flourish in the sunshine here, on soils consisting of sand or sand and marl, and grow up the sides of hills as high as 250 m, after which the hilltops are mainly covered with resinous Mediterranean trees. On the right bank the Rhône and its tributaries have left only small quantities of

Above, the village of Aiguèze, at the entrance to the Ardèche gorges.
Right, a detail from a carving in the castle chapel Université du Vin, Suze-la-Rousse.

pebbly alluvial deposits, except in two more southerly places round Tavel and Lirac, and again near Domazan and Estézagues.

This hilly landscape on the Languedoc side is offset by wide unchanging horizons on the other, in the flat basin round Valréas, Sainte-Cécile-les-Vignes, Orange, Travaillan and Avignon. A few clumps of trees in the gardens of big estates give a single note of contrast in the endless flat-lands. However, high country is never very far away and these basins are themselves framed by hills. The east bank is dominated in the north-east by the Lance mountain overlooking the sheltered Nyons area and its famous olive groves, and in the east by Mont Ventoux, well known to Tour de France cyclists, forming a protective barrier between most of the vineyards and the cold weather of the Alps. This barrier makes it possible for vines to grow quite happily at heights up to 450 m, as at Vinsobres, although they really prefer to be down in the basin area. Here they are cultivated on light sandy soils overlying the Miocene bedrock and on huge quantities of pebbles washed down from miles away in the Alps by

the Rhône, the Lez, the Aygues and the Ouvèze. These rivers have gradually built up the broad terraces at Valréas, Suze-la-Rousse and Plan-de-Dieu, as well as the *garrigue* areas at Vacqueyras, Sarrians and Châteauneuf-du-Pape. The soils here are ideal for vine-growing as they consist of layers, often very thick, of rounded pebbles mixed with red sandy clay.

MEDITERRANEAN INFLUENCES

VINEYARDS on both banks of the river are filled with the scent of thyme and lavender, and remind us that the southern Côtes du Rhône are in a very Mediterranean part of the world. The Alpilles chain of hills has a special effect on the climate, however, and

spring and autumn rainfall is lower here than on the coast. In summer, the ripening period for grapes, there is also greater divergence between day and night temperatures.

GRAPE VARIETIES

THE Côtes du Rhône region stands out from France as a whole because of the vast number of grape varieties from which growers can choose. In theory there are some twenty-three varieties, although in fact not more than ten of these are used. For red wines, the main variety is, of course,

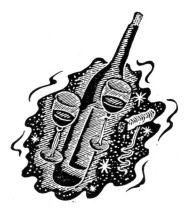

Grenache, which gives wine strong in alcohol and with full-bodied, powerful aromas. Cinsault, which is particularly important in rosés, has a fruity bouquet of great elegance and refinement, but a low yield. Syrah's resistance to oxidation makes it complementary to Grenache, and it is also valuable for its aromatic complexity and ability to age. There are similar qualities in Mourvèdre, but its Spanish origins demand a very warm, well-exposed situation. Other red varieties include Carignan and Counoise.

In white wines, the grapes most often used are Clairette, Bourboulenc, Picpoul and Grenache Blanc.

THE VILLAGES OF THE CÔTES DU RHÔNE

IN an area as extensive as the Côtes du Rhône there are all sorts of nuances separating the different vineyards. These variations have been skilfully exploited and have resulted in longer keeping wines, a development rewarded in 1966 by the *appellation* Côtes du Rhône Villages. This covers 81 communes divided into two groups, the first entitled to the *appellation* alone, the second to the addition of the commune name. The latter group has greater prestige and covers 25 communes, with 16 recognized names: Rochegude, Rousset-les-Vignes, Saint-Pantaléon-les-Vignes, Saint-Maurice-sur-Eygues, Vinsobres, Chusclan (5 communes), Laudun (3), Saint-Gervais, Cairanne, Beaumes-de-Venise (4), Rasteau, Roaix, Sablet, Séguret, Valréas and Visan.

These villages are scattered throughout Côtes du Rhône territory and are varied in both situation and in the wine they produce. Their reputation has made them the official choice at important events such as the Roland-Garros tennis tournament and the Cannes Film Festival. To a greater degree than basic Côtes du Rhône, these are powerful, robust and heady wines and need less Grenache and a higher proportion (at least 25 per cent) of Syrah, Mourvèdre and Cinsault in their make-up. The best known are the full and fleshy reds of Vinsobres Cairanne, the fruity Chusclan rosés and the fresh, elegant whites of Laudun.

The rich variety in these Côtes du Rhône Villages vineyards is even more apparent in the regional *appellation*, where differences in soil, subsoil, exposure and microclimate all combine to produce a great number of very distinctive ecosystems.

Top right, vines growing above the village of Beaumes-de-Venise, with the crags of the Dentelles de Montmirail in the background.

Above left, Marsanne grapes; above right, Grenache grapes.

Far right, the banner of grapes. St. Vincent wine fraternity at Visan, Côtes du Rhône.

A ROMAN CELLAR

THE historical importance of the Rhône valley makes it a favourite place for archaeologists, who have even extended their research to wine. At Donzère one of the largest and oldest wine cellars ever found has been excavated, and the extent and variety of its wine-making equipment shows how large local vineyards must have been. This cellar, for instance, must have been built to process a crop from about 50 hectares.

CÔTE RÔTIE

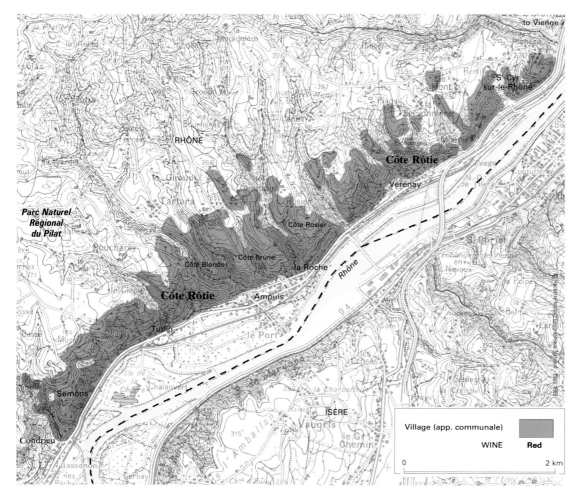

IT is impossible not to notice, a few miles south of Vienne, the extraordinary vineyards clinging to the slopes which rise so impressively above the right bank of the Rhône.

VERTICAL VINEYARDS

MORE than anywhere else, this place makes one realize the importance of the human factor in wine-growing. For vines to be established on these steep slopes, men had to remedy nature and enclose the soil in dry-stone walls called *cheys*. On the precipitous Landonne sites on the Côte Rozier, the only machine that can be used is a winch. Little paths stagger down the sides of the Côte Brune and the Côte Blonde, apparently landing on the rooftops of the village of Ampuis.

According to the legend, Maugiron, the great lord of Ampuis, had twin daughters, equal in both beauty and virtue. Only their hair was different, one daughter being dark and the other fair. Unable to decide which of the two should inherit his land, Maugiron bequeathed the Côte Brune to one and the Côte Blonde to the other.

Is the Côte Rôtie the oldest vineyard in France, as some producers claim? It may be. Certainly, by the first century BC, it already ranked high among the wines of Vienne. Since that time, the wine from these sheer hillsides has always been of excellent quality. This could hardly be otherwise considering the conditions in which it is produced. With a yield of barely 4,000 hl, for a long time it was known only to a few devotees, and was mainly sold abroad, but since the late seventies, its fame has increased much faster than the yield and prices have soared.

One look at a map of the area helps to explain how this exceptional quality is achieved. When the Rhône reaches Vienne, it loops round and starts flowing in a south-westerly direction, so that the right bank as far as the hamlet of Semons has an ideal south or south-east exposure. However, there is a subtle difference between the Côte Brune and the Côte Blonde.

The rocky matrix of mica schist formed from two sorts of mica has begun to break up on the surface into a pebbly soil known locally as *arzelle*. Some people think there are slight variations in soil texture or composition between the two côtes. In fact, the difference probably lies in the choice of grape.

The Côte Rôtie produces only red wine based on one variety, Syrah, but it was once customary to add 10 to 15 per cent of Viognier to make the wine more balanced and agreeable. Nowadays, however, Syrah accounts for 95 per cent of the total production of grapes in this region. Owing to improvements in vinification, a number of growers no longer use Viognier as they are now able to produce a suppler-tasting Côte Rôtie of 100 per cent Syrah than in the past.

As it happens, Viognier is grown to a large extent on the Côte Blonde but hardly at all on the Côte Brune. Experts find that the Côte Blonde wines are exceptionally soft, elegant and refined, whereas those of the Côte Brune have more toughness and backbone, and rather more ageing potential.

The Syrah vines are trained on rows of props, fixed in the ground in pairs like an upturned letter V. In vineyards further south these props are used singly and fixed upright.

The Côte Rôtie wines can be tasted in cool cellars hollowed out of the rock. The bouquet has suggestions of violets, spice and soft fruit, and acquires exceptional balance and breeding as it matures.

In some years, wines from one plot, such as La Mouline or La Turque, are especially remarkable. This is probably the most appropriate reward for growers who have to cultivate their vines by hand in this particularly steep part of the Rhône valley.

Drystone walls, known as cheys, *at Côte Rôtie.*

CONDRIEU AND CHÂTEAU-GRILLET

Château-Grillet: a famous appellation with a tiny output.

produce these wines – wines that are both delicate and mellow, with scents of honey and acacia.

CHÂTEAU-GRILLET

CHÂTEAU-GRILLET is exceptionally small in size (only 2.5 hectares), and belongs to one owner with an estate dating back to Roman times and medieval cellars restored during the Renaissance. The *appellation* is in the middle of Condrieu territory and is based only on Viognier which, as at Condrieu, has ideal granite soils here. Château-Grillet would be almost exactly like Condrieu, except that it grows in a very precipitous and well exposed corrie, instead of at the outfall of a valley like its neighbours. This may seem a small detail, but it is one that makes the wine quite distinctive. Only 50 to 70 hl are produced each year, so it is for the privileged few.

CONDRIEU

THE Condrieu vineyard is on the right bank of the Rhône, 11 km south of Vienne, and historically is joined to that of Côte Rôtie. Both of them date back to Roman times and to Vienne's period of grandeur. Condrieu was possibly more extensive then, although only a bare 22 hectares are in production today. Whatever the truth of this, it is amazing that a vineyard should survive through twenty centuries.

The beauty of the old city, with its ancient houses and look of a small Mediterranean port, is evidence that Condrieu has always been an important place on the Rhône. It was originally a ford, which was unusual on this otherwise impassable section of the river, and an ideal site for a port. So for centuries, until the building of the railways, Condrieu was a junction for

the regional economy and a centre for the river boatmen, who were known as *culs de piau* because of their leather breeches. It had always been a double intersection, with routes going north and south, as well as east and west. It was therefore easy to acquire wealthy customers and also plenty of labourers who could work part-time in the vineyards.

These conditions can be found in other wine regions and do not fully explain Condrieu's special character. The distinctive features of Condrieu are that it produces only white wines; that it includes only sites that are really suitable for Viognier, the single authorized variety; and that these clearly demarcated sites cover only 20 hectares, in a narrow strip 16 km long going through seven communes (Limony-en-Ardèche, Chavanay, Malleval, Saint-Michel-sur-Rhône, Saint-Pierre-de-Boeuf, Vérin and Condrieu).

To reach its full potential Viognier needs plenty of warmth and very particular sites, such as the south-facing slopes of little valleys carved in the granite by streams from the top of Mont-Pilat. It also needs complete shelter from north winds.

In addition to all this, there are slopes as steep as at Côte Rôtie and terraces so narrow that just a few rows of vines can be planted. These are vines, too, which only start producing after six or seven years and the yield is low, on average 20 hl to the hectare. Growers certainly have to be very hard-working and persistent to

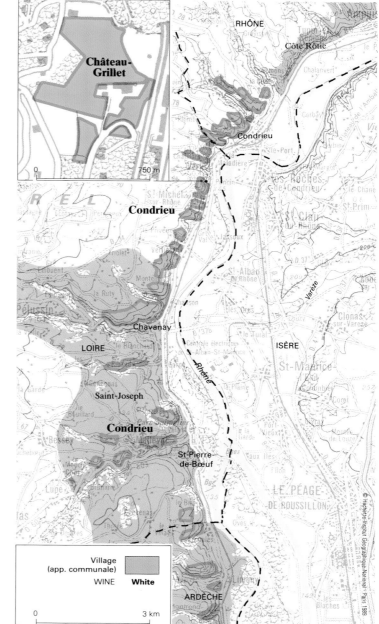

HERMITAGE

NOWADAYS the autoroute makes a detour of some miles round the town of Tain l'Hermitage, but anyone used to the railway or the old N7 road will know the magnificent hillside with its conspicuous white stripes and the names of important *négociants* such as Jaboulet and Chapoutier.

The Romans arrived here between 120 and 100 BC and were soon aware, as at Côte-Rôtie, of the possibilities of this steep slope and its warm, southern aspect. It is almost certain that wine from these vineyards helped to make the reputation of Vienne wines; Hermitage as a name appeared very much later. The Romans certainly built a temple to Hercules at the top of the hill here, but this had no connection with vine-growing. The temple was probably destroyed by invading barbarians and rebuilt as a chapel of Saint Christopher, from whom the hill got its name. According to local legend, in 1224 the knight Henri Gaspart de Sterimberg returned exhausted from the Crusades, and was allowed by Queen Blanche of Castille to retire and live a life of peaceful contemplation in a hovel by the chapel. He is said to have cleared and cultivated the land on this hillside.

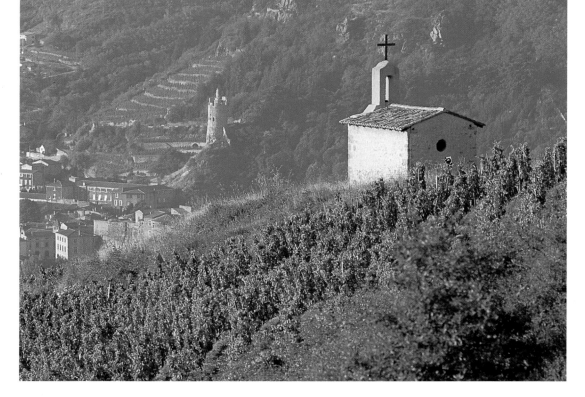

THE HERMITS AND THEIR WINE

AFTER the death of Henri Gaspart de Sterimberg, the place was occupied by hermits. The chapel enjoyed a good position as a stopping-place between Lyon and the Mediterranean for any travellers wanting to rest and pray, and also to taste the hermits' increasingly famous wine. This was the origin of the name of Hermitage. The fame of this wine soon spread beyond France, and in the seventeenth century it was known in England and as far away as the court of the Tsars. In the past, Hermitage was also blended with Bordeaux to give the latter more colour and alcohol. This wine was then exported via Bordeaux to Great Britain as 'Bordeaux Ermitage'. The chapel still exists today, on top of the magnificent hill which stands guard at the entrance to the valley. Strangely enough, the Hermitage hillside is not as splendidly uniform as the right-bank vineyards, although this certainly has no effect on quality.

DISPLACED ROCKS

THE western side of the hill, the higher section where the chapel is built, consists of a mass of porphyritic granite; the only outcrop of this on the left bank and derived from the edge of the Massif Central. It continues on to form the Saint-Joseph hillside and is the site of the famous vineyard plot called Les Bessards.

In fact this granite block acted as a sort of bridge pier at the period when the Rhône was depositing large quantities of pebbles washed down from the Alps. Layers of pebbles several metres thick accumulated behind this rampart and now form the whole eastern side of the hill (in Méal, Chante-Alouette, Les Murets and Rocoules). Cultivation is difficult here because of the slope, and also because of this dense mass of pebbles, which has become cemented into a conglomerate.

The Hermitage *appellation* produces red and white wine. As with neighbouring *appellations*, only Syrah is used for making red wines. It is planted mainly on the granite western slopes, giving wines of a deep rich red, with an intense fragrance in which violets, blackcurrants and strawberries all play a part. Each plot, or *quarter*, has its own special variations, some with more violets, others with more spice in the bouquet. With age, the early asperity softens and the wine acquires a splendid richness and balance. White wines are based on Marsanne and a little Roussane, and exude scents of flowers and green coffee-beans. Roussane was the variety most often cultivated in the past, although less so now because of its vulnerability to parasites and to oxidation. Hermitage white wines, like the reds, have the ability to mature over several years or even decades, after which they acquire a honeyed, waxy bouquet of marvellous intensity.

Production consists of about 3,300 hl of red and a little less than 1,000 hl of white wine.

CROZES-HERMITAGE

Fantasy costume: a vine-grower from the seventeenth century (Musée Carnavalet, Paris). Left-hand page, Hermitage: above, the chapel; below, the vineyards.

THESE wines have always been overshadowed by those of the more celebrated Hermitage. Although Crozes-Hermitage territory completely encircles its neighbour, there are clear differences between them in spite of similar geological formations. A large part of the zone, especially the part where most improvement has taken place in recent years, lies on the southern, Würmian terraces. This is a large, relatively flat area, triangular in shape, with soils consisting of rounded pebbles in a matrix of red clay vulnerable to drought. Only a few years ago this area was dominated by fruit trees, particularly peaches, but now vines occupy as much space as the peach trees.

AN EXPANDING INDUSTRY

THE *coteau* of Les Pends, situated slightly further north with an ancient ruined tower looking down over its western edge, produces some excellent wines, whites especially, which have made the name of the village of Mercurol. The zone consists of Riss scree terraces and is a continuation of the Hermitage slope. The western

villages are separated from the southern area by the Bouterne valley containing the autoroute, and include several different zones. From the east, there is first a Mindel pebble terrace covered with loess, with no vines on the cold soils along the edge, where it is ideal for growing apricots. The village of Larnage on the edge of this plateau has some rather distinctive white wines produced on white sandy soils (Eocene kaolins). Vines here are grown only on these soils.

Further west is Crozes, from which the *appellation* took its name, and slightly further north, lying along the Rhône valley, is the Gervans slope producing some good white wines on loess-covered granite.

So Crozes-Hermitage is not so much a consistent wine-region as a collection of individual sites, which can all be rather different. The wines too are fairly varied, although they have a family likeness to Hermitage wines, being based on the same grape varieties: Syrah for reds, Marsanne and Roussane for whites. These are grown on less steep slopes and produce wines without the deep colour of Hermitage. The reds mature more quickly but retain all the characteristic bouquet and refinement of Syrah from this area. The whites are less complex and intense, but have a fresh quality, which makes them delicious to drink.

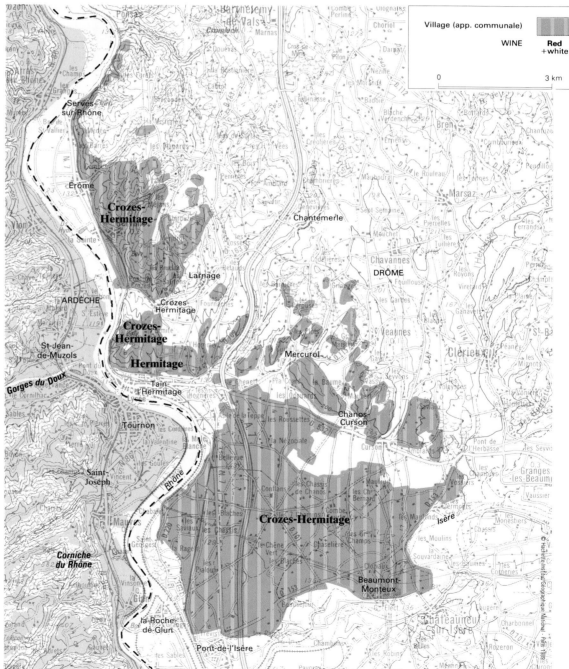

SAINT-JOSEPH, CORNAS AND SAINT-PÉRAY

THE Saint-Joseph *appellation* is a narrow strip some 60 km long winding between Chavanay and Guilherand, and linking Condrieu and Côte-Rôtie in the north with the Valence region in the south. The Saint-Joseph slopes are part of the ledge bordering the Massif Central, and have a view over to the jagged peaks of the Alps, and in fine weather even to the majestic mass of Mont-Blanc.

MAUVES WINE FROM SAINT-JOSEPH

THIS *appellation* has not always covered such an extensive area. Medieval French kings appreciated the refinement and elegance of these wines, then called *Vins de Mauves*. They had a great reputation and were produced between Tournon and the village of Mauves, on a granite escarpment forming a continuation along the right bank of the Rhône of part of the Hermitage slopes.

Even today, the best Saint-Joseph vines grow on these slopes: on the Saint-Joseph hill at Tournon, and on Sainte Epine at Saint-Jean-de-Muzols, further north, near the entrance of the picturesque river Doux gorges.

In the last twenty-five years local wine-growing has developed round these two important pockets of

Above, Saint-Joseph and the church of Notre-Dame-de-Vion.
Below, the statue of Saint Joseph, high above the town of Tournon.
Right, wine maturing in a Cornas cellar.

granite. The middle sector of the *appellation* used to be on the softer gneiss terraces but fewer vines are grown here now.

Saint-Joseph wines, mainly red and based on Syrah only, are delightfully soft and delicate and ready to drink after only two or three years. The whites, from Marsanne with some occasional Roussane, have breeding and a predominantly floral bouquet.

CORNAS

IN the diverse northern Côtes du Rhône, Cornas is yet another variation on the theme of Syrah and granite. The village has a superb situation by the Rhône, in a kind of amphitheatre encircled by vineyards on steeply climbing terraces.

To explore Cornas properly, take the road from the centre of the village to the Chapelle de Saint-Pierre and the village of Saint-Romain de Lerps. On the harsh plateau, where the road becomes less steep and sheep and conifers soon take over from vines, take the track to Tezier and a house gently collapsing in ruins among the cedar trees.

The view from this point is quite magnificent. Below are terraces of vines cascading right down to the village with its tall church spire, 52 m high and apparently almost within touching distance. On the left, the great Jurassic limestone mass of the Arlettes hills forms the northern end of the amphitheatre, giving protection from cold winds. On the right is the castle of Crussol, the home of the fifteenth-century Counts of Uzès, towering majestically over the Valence plain, with the Vercors, the forest of Saou and the Alps all visible in the background.

Syrah is the only grape variety grown here. Further north vines are grown on pairs of props, but the technique here is to train them on single supports pointing upwards like rows of bayonets. The soils are similar to those at Saint-Joseph a couple of miles north, but the vines seem to react quite differently. Saint-Joseph is soft and delicate, rather feminine in character; Cornas, on the other hand, begins harsh and tough, with a tannic quality giving a certain virility, and needs a few years before it softens and produces a well-structured, deep-coloured wine.

SAINT-PÉRAY

A few hundred metres further down river, Syrah astonishingly disappears

altogether, leaving only the Marsanne and Roussane (called Roussette here) which go into the white wines of Saint-Péray.

There is a change in the landscape too: the Saint-Péray vineyards spread up both sides of the Mialon valley, which follows the former course of the Rhône. The bottom of the valley is filled with Pliocene deposits, and is dominated to the north by the granite edge of the plateau of Saint-Romain de Lerps and to the south by a hump-backed ridge of Jurassic limestone crowned by the lofty ruined castle of Crussol.

The landscape here consists largely of pasture, with woodland along the plateau edge. Vines have to be concentrated in a few special plots and even there have difficulty standing up to creeping urbanization from the

direction of Valence. Saint-Péray used to be a naturally sparkling wine, but is made with a second fermentation in the bottle now that the Champagne method has been introduced at the Château de Beauregard. It has a combination of sparkle and substance, produced by the granite subsoil, and unusual in French sparkling wines. There is also a tiny production of still white wines, which have a firm dry quality like the Crozes-Hermitage whites.

GIGONDAS

GIGONDAS is in the southern Côtes du Rhône, unlike the other local *appellations*, and has a spectacular situation next to the extraordinary Dentelles de Montmirail. These are limestone crags crowning a group of hills and eroded into lace-like ridges, needles and saw-tooth formations.

The old fortified village lies at the foot of the Dentelles des Florets, overlooked by a ruined castle, and has always had vineyards. Pliny the Elder mentions the place, and on the Saint-Cosme estate cellars dug into the Miocene sands show that vines were grown here in Roman times.

Other estates in the village, once part of the area ruled by the Princes of Orange, have an interesting history. Vine-growing became particularly important in the nineteenth century, when new methods were introduced by Eugène Raspail. Competition from olive-growing prevented further expansion, as Gigondas, well away from the main trade routes, was a symbol of the authentic Provence and its 'silver sea' of olive trees. The village was famous, not for its wine, but for purgative waters from the medicinal spring of Montmirail. It

was not until after the great frosts of 1929, 1940 and especially 1956, when the olives were finally destroyed, that vines were grown in their place throughout the region.

This is an area where the sun's heat produces high alcohol levels and not enough freshness of taste. For this reason, white wines are not grown and the entire production is devoted

Above, the village of Gigondas.
Right, Caryatid supporting the façade at
Château Raspail, Gigondas.

to rosé and especially red wines. As well as the Grenache Noir which grows so well here, a higher proportion of Syrah now goes into these wines. Mourvèdre is used to a lesser extent, but is slightly susceptible to dry conditions on the slopes. Cinsault was also grown for some years but rightly abandoned; it is now used mainly in the production of rosés.

Gigondas wines have a high level of alcohol, 14° to 14.5°, and an assertive sappiness and strength. They have a complex bouquet suggesting ripe fruit and spices, and an aromatic woodland aftertaste. They round out well as they mature, but retain their firm backbone.

Map legend:
- Côtes du Rhône-Villages
- l'Ouvèze
- VAUCLUSE
- CH. RASPAIL
- LE COLOMBIER
- Gigondas
- LES BOSQUETS
- **Gigondas**
- Dentelles de Montmirail
- Vacqueyras
- Côtes du Rhône-Villages
- CH. DE MONTMIRAIL
- Vacqueyras
- to Beaumes-de-Venise

Village (app. communale)

WINE — **Red** +rosé

0 ————— 5 km

EUGÈNE RASPAIL

EUGÈNE Raspail, a nephew of the scientist and politician François-Vincent Raspail, also became involved in politics, and both he and his uncle were exiled from Paris. Eugène received an amnesty on returning to manage Le Colombier, the estate bought by his father, and in 1866 built the present Château Raspail, a handsome Provençal house with remarkable caryatids. By bringing in scientific modern methods to replace traditional practices, he contributed a great deal to the development of wine-growing in the region.

CHÂTEAUNEUF-DU-PAPE

not been John XXII, the second of the Avignon Popes, reigning from 1316 to 1334. Many of his successors liked to visit the Pope's castle, even after the Palace at Avignon had been finished.

The presence of the Papal court in Châteauneuf encouraged wine-growing, even though John XXII, despite his Cahors origin, usually drank Beaune wine. However, he had the idea of planting a small vineyard, from which some excellent wine was harvested. The wine acquired a reputation, encouraged others in the region, and a few centuries later even inspired one of Alphonse Daudet's short stories. Most of Châteauneuf's typical great *domaines*, almost all belonging to old families, seem to have developed very little until the mid-seventeenth century, when they very rapidly began to reach today's heights.

It was around 1750 that wine-growing expanded most here. The village grew rich round the Pope's castle and other fine châteaux were built by grand aristocratic families. In 1769 the elegant château of Vaudieu was built by Jean-Joseph de Gérin, Lieutenant-Général de l'Amirauté at Marseille, and a descendant of the Florentine Gerini family; a few years later the Domaine de la Nerte was

THIS is the most prestigious *appellation* in the Mediterranean wine area and from its position, 120 m high, it dominates the whole plain of the Comtat Venaissin. Châteauneuf-du-Pape has always represented wine-making at its most strict and authentic, and in this it is an example for other French AOC wines.

time called Château Galcornier. It is claimed that there had not been much vine-growing here before the thirteenth century, as growers had no means of acquiring tools strong enough to work soils full of enormous pebbles. It seems strange that the Popes chose this place for their summer residence.

and looked as though he had only a few months to live, but for sixteen more years his dynamic character drove him on to build a château more like a fortress than a palace. All this would be unimportant if the man had

Above, Châteauneuf-du-Pape. Below, Château des Fines Roches.
Left, a steel mould with the coat of arms for Châteauneuf bottles.

It is probable that vineyards were established in this exceptional position in the period of the Avignon Popes. They may have existed earlier but very few documents have come down to us on the history of Châteauneuf-du-Pape, where in any case the main village was for a long

POPE JOHN XXII

THE destiny of this corner of Provence was much altered when a 72-year-old man decided to live there. The old man was short, thin and pale

altered to look as it does today; and in the early nineteenth century the Marquis Fortia d'Urban, a descendant of the Kings of Aragon, built Château Fortia.

In the last century these *domaines* had such prestige that their names were mentioned more often than that of Châteauneuf, but this name also had very sound connotations, and this was to become even more apparent in 1929, when Châteauneuf set an excellent example. Instigated by Baron Leroy de Boiseaumarie, proprietors decided to make a sustained effort to improve quality and codify production conditions. Like the nineteenth-century Provençal poet Mistral, the Baron was to be honoured by having a bust dedicated to him in his own lifetime.

The production area extends over five communes (Châteauneuf-du-Pape, Orange, Bédarrides, Courthézon and Sorgues), on a hill rising to 124 m. Geologically the area consists of Villafranchian terraces with often thick layers of large quartzite pebbles mixed with a sandy red clay. Châteauneuf is renowned for these pebbles, which are essential for the way they store heat during the day and give it out to the vines at night. Other geological formations are present: the bedrock of the hill is composed of Miocene sandy marl overlying a mass of limestone to the west. These marls have been covered by the Villafranchian terraces, and by other deposits and terraces (from the Riss and Würm glaciation periods), still pebbly, but without the exceptionally thick pebble layers of the Villafranchian.

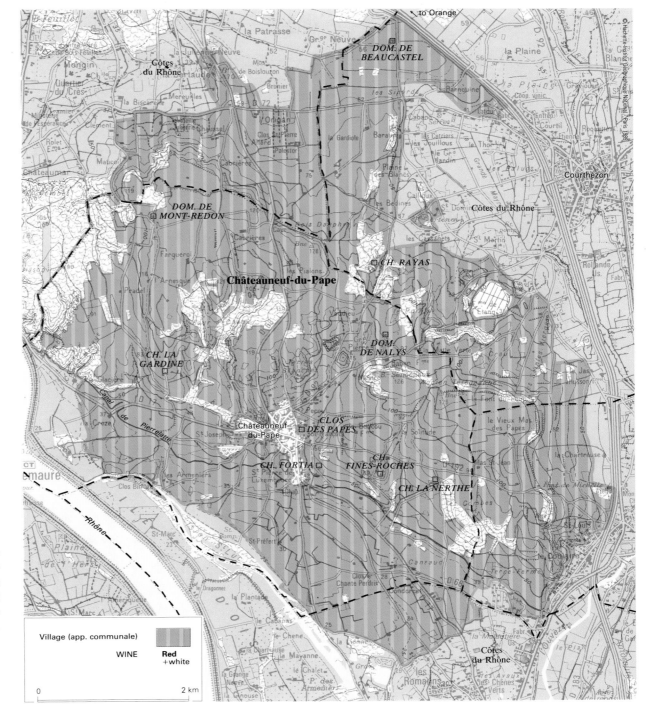

Wine storage at the eighteenth-century Château La Narthe.

On these very individual soils, the *appellation* is entitled to grow no fewer than thirteen grape varieties, principally for red wines, but for some whites too. There are six dominant varieties: Grenache, Clairette, Mourvèdre, Picpoul, Terret and Syrah. The seven subsidiary varieties are Counoise, Muscardin, Vaccarèse, Picardan, Cinsault, Roussane and Bourboulenc. Despite problems of soils and geology, the grapes growing on this sea of pebbles give a firm and powerful red wine of intense colour; a wine that needs to be matured. White wines were in the majority in Papal times, but a white Châteauneuf is now fairly unusual in spite of its remarkable aromatic complexity.

LIRAC AND TAVEL

Good wine has been produced for centuries at Tavel (above) and Lirac (below).

and Lirac were very much the focus of this whole area.

TAVEL, A ROYAL ROSÉ

TAVEL is a large wine village encircled by the Gard forest, and well known for its attractive light-coloured stone, the so-called Tavel marble, but of course it is particularly famous for its wine, the 'finest rosé in France', according to a luminous sign visible to anyone driving to Nîmes on the *Languedocienne* autoroute.

The fame of Tavel rosé goes back many years. Louis XIV used to drink it at Versailles in the seventeenth century, which was a period of expansion for this region. However, there were abuses, and to avoid any compromise of quality it became necessary to restrict further planting and to introduce fines for fraud. The success of these measures meant that in the eighteenth century Tavel was able to export great quantities of its wine throughout Europe. At that time wine was almost the main source of income for the villagers. Their wines were praised in the nineteenth century by Balzac and Brillat-Savarin and they were able to maintain their success until the time of the phylloxera crisis. The effects of this were

catastrophic, with the area of vines reduced from 700 to a meagre 50 hectares. This stagnation persisted and even just before the Second World War only 200 hectares were under vines.

Today the area of vines is equal to that in pre-phylloxera times. The *appellation* zone, extending through the Tavel commune and slightly into Roquemaure, consists of two distinct geological areas: north-west of the village fine river sands are covered with a Villafranchian terrace of round pebbles mixed with fine sandy clay from the forest of Clary; on the western edge of the plateau, there are more recent plantings of vines on splinters of limestone.

Only rosé is permitted here, but what a magnificent rosé this is! Nine different grape varieties are allowed. Of these the two most important are Grenache for its warmth and mellowness, and Cinsault for elegance and refinement. Nowadays, too, Syrah and Mourvèdre are being used more and more to give fruit and breeding as well as better keeping qualities. Tavel is slowly changing for the better: the 'onion-skin' colour traditionally preferred, the iridescent ruby and topaz partly caused by the Grenache oxidizing, is now being replaced by stronger tones of pink, and the wine also has more fruit and body. Tavel is now exported throughout the world.

AS with literature and art, it can be very difficult when making wine to gauge what will work. Success and failure may be no more than a hair's breadth apart.

A good wine can be delightfully evocative of sunshine and holidays, especially a wine from this part of Provence. Lirac and Tavel are on the right bank of the Rhône facing Châteauneuf, and enjoy a privileged position by virtue of both nature and history. The vineyards are exceptionally well sited: from the Vivarais region limestone plateaux project towards Avignon, and Tavel and Lirac are at the end of these, beyond the wooded areas of Saint-Victor and Malmont.

PAST IMPORTANCE

TAVEL and Lirac, in addition to this favourable situation, have the advantage of being near the river. Also nearby are the castles of Roquemaure and Lers, standing guard on each side of the Rhône, a reminder of the past importance of this area. These two fortresses, solidly ensconced on their rocky pinnacles, form a barrier at one end of the valley and protected the port of Roquemaure when it was a centre for the river trade. In the eighteenth century it was from here that wine from the Côte du Rhône Gardoise was despatched, and Tavel

LIRAC

THE Lirac *appellation* is shared by four villages, including Saint-Laurent des Arbres, where the diocese of Avignon owned land on which vines were cultivated. These surround the castle and its conspicuous keep, and in the sixteenth century produced enough wine to send a tithe of five full boat loads across the river. The quality of the wine was already famous and vine-growing was becoming the main employment of the local population, especially in the eighteenth century. As a way of guaranteeing quality at this period, the town authorities, the 'consuls' of Lirac, used to inspect the vines before deciding on the harvest date. Anybody harvesting earlier would be fined on behalf of the poor, his crop confiscated by the community and his wine-making equipment burnt in the market-place.

The natural situation here is like that of Tavel, with the same soils, the same types of plot, the same weather and the same history, yet Lirac has taken a different path. Besides being more extensive (spread over the four villages of Lirac, Roquemaure, Saint-Laurent des Arbres and Saint-Génies de Comolas), Lirac produces red, white and rosé wine. The best known are the rosés, more substantial than Tavel and more like Chusclan in character. The reds are typical of the region, powerful, generous and well balanced, but still underestimated. The whites are based mainly on Clairette and Bourboulenc; these are graceful, scented wines, with considerable finesse, and appropriately enough go very well with seafood from the nearby Mediterranean.

Tavel: the actor Jean Le Poulain is enrolled in one of the many local wine fraternities.

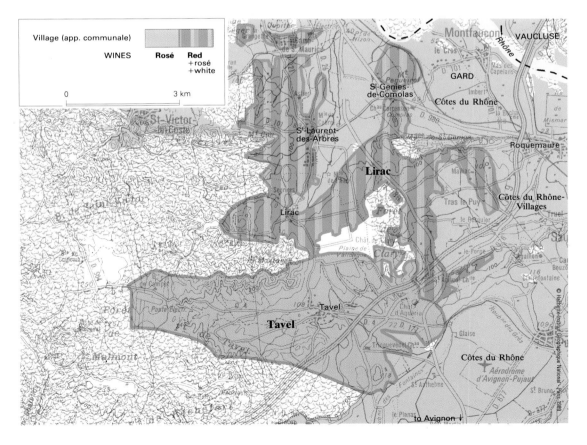

197

BETWEEN DIE AND THE LUBERON

attractive fruity reds are made from a combination of Syrah and Pinot grown on the one pebbly slope rising above the village.

CÔTES DU VIVARAIS

THIS is an area on the right bank of the Rhône, overlooking the narrow stretch of river at Donzère. Like the Coteaux du Tricastin, it tends to be overshadowed by the gigantic region of southern Côtes du Rhône, a situation rather more damaging than useful. Yet this VDQS is very different from Côtes du Rhône and originates in an area which has nothing in common with the Rhône valley. This is where the Ardèche gorges cut their way through the plateaux of Saint Remèze to the north and Orgnac l'Aven to the south. Like the deep swallow-holes or *avens*, the gorges were hollowed out by the action of water on rock, in this case very hard limestone. These uplands have very shallow soils and meagre *garrigue* vegetation, but vines can be grown where the surface rock has

Above, vineyards between Mont Ventoux and the Luberon hills. Below and left, nineteenth- to twentieth-century carvings re-used on a Carpentras house.

VINES flourish throughout the Rhône valley and are still to be found even on the higher land away from the river. Between Die and the Luberon hills, all round Côtes du Rhône territory, are a number of areas producing wines quite comparable with those of their larger neighbour.

CLAIRETTE DE DIE AND CHÂTILLON-EN-DIOIS

THE most northerly of these areas is round the town of Die, on the slopes of the Upper Drôme valley between Luc-en-Diois (500 m) and Aouste-sur-Sye (160 m). The region upstream from Crest is shared between two *appellations*: Clairette de Die in the west, and Châtillon-en-Diois in the east.

The Die region is a high valley on the fringe of the Alps, sheltered by cliffs edging the Vercors plateau. This is a geologist's paradise, full of rocks that have been split and folded and then laid bare by erosion in the course of the formation of the Alps. Downstream from Espenel, in the middle of the *appellation* area, are the famous 'black lands', Jurassic schistous soils,

which are excellent for vines and have helped to give the area its reputation. The climate here is colder and damper than in the Rhône valley and ideal for white wines.

This must have been evident in very early days as, in the first century AD, Pliny's 'Natural History' mentions 'Aiglencos', a sparkling *vin doux naturel* made here by the indigenous Voconces people. These days two kinds of sparkling wine are made. The first is based on Muscat à Petits Grains and is made by the traditional Die method: the wines are bottled without added yeast and sugar when they are only partly fermented, and it is the natural grape sugars that produce the sparkle. The second kind is based on the Clairette grape and acquires its sparkle from a second fermentation in the bottle.

In the upper valleys of the Drôme and the Bez are vineyards producing the still wines of Châtillon-en-Diois. The light fresh whites are based on Chardonnay with some Aligoté. The

ANTIQUE REFRIGERATION METHODS

PLINY COMPARED 'genuine' vin doux naturel with adulterated versions made with honey and other additions. He also explained how the Gauls managed to cool down the must while making this wine: 'To prevent it from overheating and turning into ordinary wine, the must was taken from the vat and put into casks which were then plunged into the icy river until they were completely frozen.'

---

weathered, when there is more of the typical red clay soil over white chalky rubble. South of Orgnac, the Bernas white limestone is different geologically but has similar soils.

This area is both cooler and wetter than the Rhône valley and Grenache here is combined with Carignan, and more frequently now with Syrah, to give reds and rosés of great freshness and refinement, with a predominant soft fruit bouquet. They all need to be drunk young.

COTEAUX DU TRICASTIN

THIS region is south of Montélimar and looks across to the Côtes du Vivarais from the left bank of the Rhône. It consists of a hard limestone massif carved into valleys of varying breadth and with an east-to-west alignment, which reduces the effect of Mediterranean weather. For this reason the valleys are used mainly for mixed farming, with vines only in a few well-sheltered, south-facing sites. Most of the vines are in fact grown on the outer fringe of the massif, on Villafranchian weathered alluvial soils consisting of red clay and pebbles. The best example of this can be seen in the plot called Bois des Mattes, on each side of the autoroute near the perched village of La Garde Adhémar.

Red wines based on Grenache Noir, Cinsault and Syrah can be robust but elegant, rather less warm in character than Côtes du Rhône. A small amount of white and rosé is also produced here.

CÔTES DU VENTOUX

THE *appellation* covers the basin containing the villages of Malaucène and Entrechaux in the north, the Carpentras basin in the centre and the northern side of the Apt valley in the south. Côtes du Ventoux may at first seem a rather diverse area, but all these areas have a common denominator in the Vaucluse plateau and in Mont Ventoux. The so-called 'Giant of Provence' is white all the year round – in

Vines and olives growing in the Côtes du Luberon.

winter with snow and in summer with bare limestone scree. Masses of cold or simply cooler air pour down the slopes from the 1909 m summit and tone down the extreme Mediterranean heat. Because of this, the sandy Malaucène basin, the pebbly terraces round Carpentras and the slopes of sand or sandy marl in the Apt region all have harsher winters with more rain; they also have more rain in summer and cooler nights following the torrid heat of the day. Although the region came later to wine-growing than its neighbours near the river, it now has extensive vineyards on the lower slopes of Mont Ventoux. These concentrate almost exclusively on red and rosé wines, less powerful and heady than Côtes du Rhône but with an excellent balance between fruity freshness and refinement, especially when young.

CÔTES DU LUBERON

FOR many years the Luberon hills, the enchanted land of Henri Bosco's novels, were simply abandoned to the cicadas. This secret mountain country

has now become a home for many artists, craftsmen and writers, drawn here by the blue dawn light, the limpid air and the scent of upland herbs. The high hill villages include Oppède-le-Vieux, now brought back to life by craftsmen, Lacoste with the ruined castle of the Marquis de Sade, and Bonnieux on its stepped terraces. There is Lourmarin too (where Albert Camus is buried), Cucuron (the 'Cucugnan' of Daudet's delightful short story), and the beautiful village and château of Ansouis. Vines could hardly be left out of all this, although, as in the Ventoux area, they came late and faced competition from table grapes and market-gardening.

Lower Cretaceous limestone forms the backbone of the region although, except where there is suit-

able limestone debris at the foot of the hills, this is not important for vine-growing. Most of the wine terrain in fact consists of Miocene sands, overlaid in places by pebbly terraces.

There are some excellent flowery, fruity red wines produced here, based on Grenache and Syrah. The area is unusual for its white and rosé wines, of which there are better examples here than in the rest of the Mediterranean region. These come from Ugni Blanc and Clairette grown mainly on the southern flank of the Luberon, and are elegant, mellow, flower-scented wines, which manage to be both rich and refined.

COTEAUX DE PIERREVERT

THIS is a VDQS *appellation* and is one of the highest wine regions in France, in the Alpes de Haute Provence north-east of Luberon. Its official area includes forty villages, but because of the harsh natural environment only ten or so actually produce the red, rosé and white wines much appreciated locally for their fresh, lively character.

PROVENCE

THE landscape of Provence is patterned with vines. Almost half its 10,000 or so hectares of cultivated land are planted with them. They run beside the rocky Mediterranean coves and beaches between Marseille and Nice, threading their way along the valley of the Arc and the Argens between sunburnt rock and the scents of rosemary and thyme, coming to a stop only where fragrant pine-woods form a natural barrier.

Wine history begins here with a love story, as told by the Roman historian Pompeius Trogus. Around 600 BC, Phocaean sea-traders from Greece were building a settlement on the site of present-day Marseille. They are said to have been invited to a feast by the king of the local tribe, who wanted a husband for his daughter Gyptis. In the course of the banquet, Gyptis indicated her choice by offering a cup of wine to Protis, the Phocaean leader, who subsequently married her. The story shows that wine must have existed here before the arrival of the legendary Greek

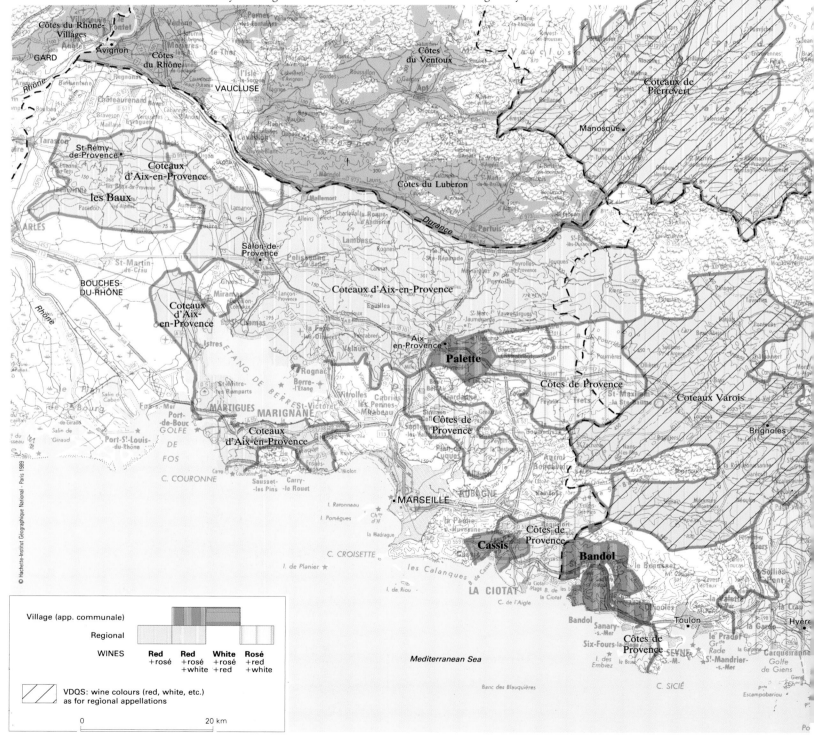

Village (app. communale)			
Regional			
WINES	**Red** +rosé	**Red** +rosé +white	**White** +rosé +red	**Rosé** +red +white

VDQS: wine colours (red, white, etc.) as for regional appellations

0   20 km

Mediterranean Sea

© Hachette-Institut Géographique National - Paris 1989

traders, who later taught the native people the technique of vine pruning.

When the Romans arrived here in 125 BC, they found vineyards already flourishing. Colonial officials took to the local wine, and retired Roman legionaries began growing vines on plots of land granted by the Empire. From the port of Marseille it was then sold throughout the Mediterranean world. The great villa of Pardigan at Cavalaire consisted of stone buildings with vats for crushing grapes, presses and fermentation vessels, and around the year 50 BC was producing about 1,000 hl of wine.

In Provençal harbours, at Toulon in particular, archaeologists excavating second-century strata have recently discovered bundles of vine twigs and numbered amphorae containing fine wine and stamped with a merchant's name. At this period, Marseille, Toulon and Fréjus were important as export centres for Provençal wine, as well as for oil and purple dye.

At the beginning of the third century wine production and distribution was seriously disrupted by barbarian invasion. It was the Church, and the establishment of the Papacy at Avignon, that restored and upheld the Provençal wine-growing tradition. Local wine even achieved success at the first international wine festival organized in 1214 by King Philippe-Auguste of France. Eleanor of Provence, the wife of Henry III of England, boosted the reputation of wines from Provence, just as her mother-in-law, Eleanor of Aquitaine, had done for those of Gascony.

In the fifteenth century King René of Anjou, Count of Provence, owned a small vineyard just outside Aix, where he grew a very good Palette wine similar to that still enjoyed today. He encouraged the production and sale of wine by turning Marseille into a free port, and also introduced methods for making *clairet* and rosé.

Madame de Sévigné was recommending Provençal wine at the end of the seventeenth century, in letters to her aristocratic friends. And even the governor of Burgundy sent for wine from Cassis. Throughout the eighteenth century, growers from this district close to Marseille went on giving gifts of wine to curry favour with the Bishop of Marseille and with Aix lawyers. Nineteenth-century Provence was well known for its robust red wines based on Mourvèdre, with elegant qualities described by wine specialists such as Guyot, Julien and Pélicot.

REVIVAL OF A TRADITION

PROVENCE has a wine tradition going back 2,600 years; a tradition which is being thoroughly rejuvenated today. There are now six AOC wines, including three small-scale *appellations* on the coast: Cassis, Bandol and Bellet. The Cassis AOC was granted in 1936 and applies to the

King René of Anjou, statue by the nineteenth-century sculptor David d'Angers (Aix-en-Provence).

whole area of the commune, in a limestone valley running down to the sea. The Bandol *appellation* dates from 1941. Vines are grown on limestone and sand terraces buttressed by dry-stone walls, the choice of grape varieties is meticulous and there are long hours of sunshine: these conditions all contribute to exceptional wine. The Bellet *appellation* also dates from 1941 and covers an area within the boundaries of Nice.

The OAC districts of inland Provence are more varied in size. The largest is Côtes de Provence, which forms a continuous strip running from Toulon to Draguignan with small offshoots to the west, near Cuges-les-Pins and Gardanne. The

vineyards of Coteaux d'Aix-en-Provence lie between the Durance valley and the Mediterranean. Lastly, just outside Aix, is the tiny district of Palette, granted an AOC in 1948.

Besides these, there are the VDQS wines such as Coteaux Varois, grown on limestone in the area round Brignoles. There are a number of *vins de pays* named after the district producing them, such as Argens and Mont-Caume in the Var *département*, and Petite Crau and Golfe du Lion in Bouches-du-Rhône.

The present output from the Provençal wine region reaches almost 4 million hl, and between 700,000 and 800,000 hl of this come from the six AOC areas.

The poet Mistral, statue by Théodore Rivière, 1909 (Arles).

FAVOURABLE CONDITIONS

THE climate and soils of Provence are very favourable for vine-growing. The AOC districts are all on sites sheltered from cold north winds such as the Mistral and the Tramontane, and exposed to milder maritime influences in the south and south-east. Weather conditions determined by aspect and topography are typical of much of the Var *département*, as in the Massif des Maures and round Draguignan.

Soils, whatever their age, derive their mineral content from massifs of ancient crystalline rock (the Massif des Maures is a remnant of these) and have evolved according to drainage in the rock formations underlying them. Drainage is particularly important in Provence because of the extreme variations between wet and dry seasons. The hard, rocky soil has been

patiently shaped into terraces as an essential means of withstanding the torrential autumn storms. On the other hand, the permanently sunny aspect also causes slopes to dry out very quickly.

The great diversity of this wine region is reflected in its thirteen different grape varieties. Grapes for reds and rosés include the following

Above, a capital in the cloisters of Saint-Paul-de-Mausole monastery.

Top, the old harbour at Toulon, detail of painting by Claude Vernet, 1756 (Musée de la Marine, Paris).

Grape varieties: above, Clairette; below, Mourvèdre.

BEHIND THE CYPRESSES AND PLANE TREES

GROWN on the crumbling granite and schist of the Maures and Estérel foothills between the Alps and the sea, these wines develop great firmness and refinement. Wine estates lie tucked away between villages, behind rows of cypresses and avenues of tall plane trees. Visitors can go down into the deep vaulted cellars to taste wonderful rosés, some of the first wines in history according to Theban fresco paintings; reds for long keeping and less common, but often surprisingly good, white wines.

Muscat wines were a Provençal speciality in pre-phylloxera days but have now disappeared. Today there are a number of wine *confréries*, such as the Ordre Illustre des Chevaliers de Méduse, which promote the wines of Provence, as the medieval troubadours did in their day.

Left, the fountain at the very fine Cistercian abbey of Le Thoronet.

Below, Montagne-Sainte-Victoire.

Above, Grenache; below, Syrah.

varieties: Cinsault, for its light colour and smooth fragrance and fruit; Grenache for warmth, generosity and aromatic intensity; the spicy Mourvèdre used in Bandol; the strong colour and firmness of Carignan; the light fruity freshness of Tibouren; the classic keeping qualities of Cabernet Sauvignon; Syrah, brought to Provence by the Romans, with its scents of cherry and violet; and finally some Barbaroux.

White varieties include Ugni-Blanc, which gives a sharp wine for early drinking; Clairette for finesse; Bourboulenc, rustic and strongly alcoholic; Rolle, on which the reputation of Bellet is based; and the distinctive smokiness of Sauvignon.

This is a region of small properties, and for this reason, except in the large *domaines* near Aix and Draguignan, which bottle their own wine, more than half the crop is processed in *caves coopératives*. A hundred of these exist in Var alone.

SOME FAMOUS WINE-GROWERS

THE most celebrated wine-grower in Provence was certainly King René of Anjou (1409–80). Count of Provence, who owned a vineyard in the present district of Palette where he made an excellent Muscat vin cuit. He also introduced clairet and the famous local rosé. In the eighteenth century, trade in wine was encouraged when the port of Bandol was founded by Boyer de Foresta. The period of the late nineteenth and early twentieth centuries was the time when Marcel Ott began resuscitating forgotten grape varieties and planting all sorts of new ones throughout Provence. There were champions of other varieties too, such as Jean Rougier for Clairette, Lucien Peyraud for Mourvèdre, and Mari for Folle Noire. A final example in this impressive list is Emile Bodin, who replanted his vineyard of Mas de Calendal and revitalized the wine of Cassis. He was also a passionate defender of local tradition and of the Provençal language.

CÔTES DE PROVENCE

THE Côtes de Provence vineyards, granted an AOC in 1977, make up almost 80 per cent of the Provençal wine region. They produce 700,000 hl from 18,000 hectares in the Var and Bouches-du-Rhône *départements*, with a small extension into the Alpes-Maritimes at Villars. Thirteen grape varieties are cultivated of which the most commonly occurring are Cinsault, Grenache, Carignan, Mourvèdre, Tibouren and Syrah for reds and rosés, and Ugni, Sémillon, Clairette and Rolle for whites.

Côtes de Provence was once known best for its rosé wines, which form 60 per cent of the total production, but growers now concentrate on producing firm reds, which mature well (35 per cent), and dry, fruity whites of some breeding (5 per cent).

Vineyards are perched on terraced hillsides with dry-stone walls or half-hidden among pine trees, in a varied geological environment. The three main areas are the coastal district of the Massif des Maures, the Permian basin and the Triassic plateau. The first lies between Toulon and Saint-Raphaël, and consists of ancient granite and schist. Vines grow here on light-coloured micaceous schist and on a combination of dark, slaty phyllite and a hard, opaque white quartz. The soils contain almost no limestone and are mainly given up to forests of pine and cork oak, and plants such as heather and large-flowered lavender.

Wine-growing plays an important part in the commercial life of Gassin, a small fortified town behind Saint-Tropez, with several well-known wine estates such as Château Barbeyrolles and Château Minuty. This could be the starting point for a brief wine tour round to La Croix-Valmer, a winter resort which in the last century used to promote its healthy climate, but now specializes in a grape 'cure'.

The Permian basin curves between Toulon and Saint-Raphaël, north of the Massif des Maures, and the dark red of its rocks and soil make a striking contrast to deep green pine trees and greenish-grey olives. The terrain here is Permian sandstone, seen in most spectacular form on either side of the railway between Gonfaron and Le Luc. The basin divides siliceous soils from limestone. Its own soils are sand and clay, sometimes rich in salt, and these give very distinctive scents and flavours to the wine. In the central Var area are a number of wine villages, such as Le Luc (Domaine de la Bernade) in a charming green valley, and Vidauban on the right bank of the Argens.

Triassic limestone predominates on the attractively rugged plateau, where vines are grown mainly in terraces. Dry-stone walls have been built to retain the pebbly red earth as it slopes down over layers of limestone sometimes several hundred metres deep. The rolling plain south of Draguignan has become an important production area, with a number of famous estates such as Sainte-Roseline and Saint-Martin. You will come across typical Provençal farms (*mas*) and splendid sixteenth- and seventeenth-century *bastide* houses as you make your way through this landscape of vines and olive trees,

with the ubiquitous rusty sound of cicadas in your ears. An excursion through this glorious countryside could fittingly end at the Maison des Vins Côtes de Provence, which has exhibitions devoted to wine cultivation and to the history of wine in Provence.

Left, a hamlet near Saint-Antonin-du-Var.

Below, vineyards at Les Maures.

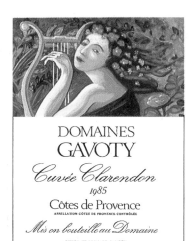

DOMAINES
GAVOTY
Cuvée Clarendon
1985
Côtes de Provence
APPELLATION CÔTES DE PROVENCE CONTRÔLÉE

Mis en bouteille au Domaine

PIERRE ET BERNARD GAVOTY
PROPRIÉTAIRES A CABASSE ET FLASSANS
VAR · FRANCE
Produce of France
75cl

BELLET

THE tiny wine district of Bellet was planted by Phocaean settlers in the fourth century BC, and consists of 30 hectares among olives and fruit trees in the hills west of Nice. Grape varieties which are rare or unknown elsewhere in Provence (Folle Noire, Braquet, Rolle and Chardonnay) are used to make about 1,200 hl each year of an unusual, much sought after wine, most of which is sold and drunk locally.

red, and 30 per cent each of rosé and white wine. All have an alcohol content of 12 per cent and can be aged for anything from 10 to 30 years.

There is some good distinctive red wine, with a sumptuous cherry bouquet, made from the local Fuella and Braquet varieties. The deep ruby wine from the imposing Château de Crémat is outstanding, and was very popular in Turin in the days when Nice belonged to the Kingdom of

Left, the château at Bellet. Below, detail from 'Double Portrait with Wineglass', by Chagall, 1917 (Musée d'Art moderne, Paris).

Bellet wine has great refinement and delicacy. These qualities come from growing on terraces of pudding-stone overlaid with siliceous limestone soil, and from a very sunny climate with sea breezes alternating with winds from the Alps. An AOC was granted as early as 1941, and production consists of 40 per cent

Sardinia. Braquet grapes are used for some fresh, silky rosés, scented with broom and honey. White wines are dry but have plenty of body, with a delicious fragrance of lime blossom and vine flowers; their character comes from Rolle, a Nice speciality, and from the Chardonnay which does so well at this altitude.

BANDOL

BANDOL wines have a reputation for their perfume of vanilla and raspberries and for their sombre depth of colour. It is interesting to consider whether these qualities come from the moderating climatic effects of the Mediterranean, from soil rich in fossil shells or from the predominant grape, the powerful Mourvèdre. All these elements probably have some effect. Bandol certainly has an exceptional situation – an immense amphitheatre buttressed to the north by a bare plateau (the Camp du Castellet, famous for its Formula 1 racing circuit) which screens it from cold north winds. The *appellation* produces 1,000 hl in the eight villages of Bandol, Sanary, La Cadière-d'Azur, Le Castellet, Evenos, Ollioules, Le Beausset and Saint-Cyr.

The terrain in the centre of this amphitheatre is particularly rugged. The tectonic movements that pushed up the Alps in the Tertiary era affected even this region and huge flows of drift material were swept far to the south. At Beausset-Vieux in the middle of the region, for instance, there is a hill known all over the world as a geological oddity because its oldest strata occur at the top.

MAGICAL LANDSCAPE

A visit to the chapel at Beausset-Vieux is essential for the astonishing panoramic view, a magical distillation of the Provençal landscape, including the two hilltop villages of La Cadière and Le Castellet against the background of the Saint-Beaume range in the north, and a glimpse of the sea beyond the hills above Bandol in the south.

The high quality of Bandol wine is due in part to 3,000 h of sunshine and in part to the choice of grape. White wine is based on Ugni-Blanc, Clairette and Bourboulenc. Cinsault, Grenache and Mourvèdre yield glowing rosés and tannic reds whose predominantly spicy bouquet has traces of cherry and mulberry.

These wines have been famous since Greek and Roman times. Their medieval name was La Cadière and it was in the eighteenth century, after a local nobleman called Boyer de Foresta set up a port at Bandol to encourage trade, that they acquired their present *appellation*. They were exported to America, Brazil and the Indies in casks stamped with the letter B. In the early nineteenth century 1,200 vessels were putting into port at Bandol and were shipping out more than 60,000 hl every year.

Left, the village of La Cadière-d'Azur.

Below left, cellar at the Château de Pibarnon.

Below, Les Baumelles.

After the phylloxera disaster, Bandol wines began a second upward surge just before the Second World War, when energetic expansion by some local growers led to an AOC in 1941. Today the annual production of 35,000 hl (5 per cent red and 40 per cent white) is sold all over the world.

CASSIS

THE small harbour town of Cassis, with its delightful colour-washed houses, lies between Marseille and La Ciotat, at the foot of some of the highest cliffs in France. Behind the town 200 hectares of vineyards rise in tiers over the hard white limestone and produce an annual crop of 4,700 hl, two thirds of which is white wine. Cassis wine was granted an AOC in 1936, but was already well known in the twelfth century when the Abbey of Saint-Victor and the Chapter of Marseille Cathedral, both powerful bodies, had to call on the Pope to settle a dispute about land.

It was not until the twentieth century that Cassis began to recover from the effects of phylloxera. The *vigneron* poet, Emile Bodin, helped to establish definitive Cassis grape varieties at his Calendal vineyards. These include the classic Sauvignon,

Cassis landscapes: sea and hills.

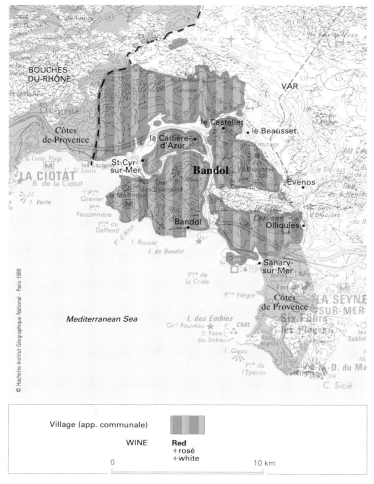

Clairette and Ugni-Blanc as well as the much less familiar Doucillon, Pascal-Blanc and Marsanne, with their subtle scent of lime blossom. The AOC area coincides with that of the village.

Cassis today is famous for a dry white wine with a heady fragrance. The Provençal poet Frédéric Mistral (1830–1914) described it in these words: 'The bee makes no sweeter honey than this wine, as clear as a diamond and scented with the rosemary, heather and myrtle growing on these hills'. Visitors can enjoy these wines on the sunny terraces of the Col de la Belle Fille high above Cassis. The delicious cool flavours are said to come from the constant sea breezes from the Mediterranean.

Village (app. communale)

WINE   **Red**
        +rosé
        +white

0   10 km

© Hachette-Institut Géographique National · Paris 1989

COTEAUX D'AIX-EN-PROVENCE AND PALETTE

THE vineyards of Coteaux d'Aix-en-Provence are scattered among woods and scrubland between the Durance valley and the Mediterranean. They cover 3,000 hectares, well sheltered from the mistral in the country west of Aix-en-Provence, a city famous for its architecture and museums and once the capital of Provence. The *appellation* has three zones: the Coteaux d'Aix and the districts of Les Baux and L'Etang de Berre.

patterned with olive and almond trees and with vineyards producing wine which has to try hard to live up to the olives and olive oil from the dramatic fortified village of Les Baux. There are about a dozen *domaines*, including the Mas de la Dame once painted by Van Gogh.

Grape varieties here include Grenache, Cabernet Sauvignon, Mourvèdre and Syrah for reds, Ugni-Blanc, Clairette, and Sauvignon for whites.

an area of great beauty. Contrasting with the region's red soil, the black spindle shapes of the cypresses, the olive groves, the vines and the pines have inspired generations of painters. There, on the banks of the river Arc, Cézanne found the setting for one of his best-known paintings, *les grandes baigneuses*.

Hemmed by a forest-fringed hill range which shields them from the winds, the vineyards extend across

the vineyards belong to two *domaines*, including the renowned Château Simone, from which it derives the aristocratic cachet of its *appellation*. Nestling at the foot of a hill and facing north, Château Simone, with its park of lime trees, is a haven of tranquillity. It is in its centuries-old vaulted cellars that the Palette wines develop their originality and powerful aroma. The red wines, dark and with a good structure, have a bouquet of violet

Above, the sixteenth-century Château de Fonscolombes: the name goes back to King René's time in the previous century.

The dry, rocky hills rising above the alluvial valleys of the Rhône and the Durance are a striking contrast to the lush gardens and sweet-smelling orchards round Aix. Every patch of green seems to hide a *mas* or *bastide*: these were once aristocratic houses and they still have a look of unpretentious refinement in their box-hedged gardens. Nearer the Luberon hills to the north-west, there are grander estates with fountains and long avenues of plane trees where some well-known wines are produced.

The western side of the region is occupied by the Alpilles range, a mass of jagged stone under the legendary Provençal sky. These slopes are

Red wines produced on the mainly clay/limestone soils are firm and well structured, with a subtle, animal bouquet if Mourvèdre is predominant, or fruity, floral scents with Syrah. White wines are uncommon here, but can be fresh and aromatic.

THE DISTINGUISHED VINEYARDS OF PALETTE

PLANTED by the Carmelites of Aix-en-Provence 500 years ago, the vineyards of Palette (15 hectares, 600 hectolitres) are situated in the immediate surroundings of the town in

the boundaries of the communes of Aix, Meyreuil and Le Tholonet and are dominated by a mountain, Sainte-Victoire. Until recently, some of their produce was used to make the famous mulled wine traditionally drunk at Christmas as an accompaniment to the Provençal thirteen desserts.

Growing on the geological shelf typical of Langesse limestone, today

Above, vines at Les Baux, an important place in Provençal history.

and pine resin. As for the rosé wines, and particularly the white wines, which constitute 40 per cent of the production, they have great complexity and mature exceptionally well. The principal grape varieties are Grenache and Cinsault for the reds and a rich Clairette for the whites.

COTEAUX VAROIS

A pleasant wine district has grown up round Brignoles, the former summer residence of the medieval Counts of Provence. The Coteaux Varois, recently granted VDQS status, are wedged in among Côtes de Provence and Coteaux d'Aix vineyards, although there are a number of differences between them. The terrain here consists of limestone only, and the region is cooler as it is shielded from maritime influences by the Sainte-Baume range and the hills round Toulon.

The principal grape varieties are Carignan, Grenache, Cinsault and Syrah, with the addition of some Tibouren and Cabernet Sauvignon. These give some attractively soft red and rosé wines, which are best drunk young.

CORSICA

IT was the Genoese who brought wine growing to Corsica in the sixteenth century and vineyards have grown up near the prehistoric stone figures at Filitosa. Today the wine region covers around 10,000 hectares, including 2,400 hectares for AOC wines, and produces 70,000 hl, 10 per cent of it white. There had been 9,000 hectares of vines in Corsica before the phylloxera epidemic, but it was not until 1957 that local persistence brought about a fresh expansion in wine growing. Vineyards were re-established on steep hillsides

Round the perimeter of the island all sorts of slight variations appear according to the soil type or the proportions of different grapes used. The names of these small districts can be

Below, vines beside the Mediterranean on the east coast of Cap Corse.

grown there. Niellucio is one of these: it is not unlike the Chianti grape Sangiovese, with a predominantly tannic character which does very well on limestone. This is the principal variety for Patrimonio, a miniature enclave of limestone which extends east and south of the Gulf of Saint-Florent. Here you find sump-

tuous, long-lasting reds, with a bouquet of venison and violets and remarkable persistence in the mouth.

The chamomile-scented Malvoisie or Vermentino is the same variety as the Provençal Rolle, and contributes 75 or 80 per cent of the grapes for the pale gold AOC white wines.

The Ajaccio *appellation* wines are grown on granite soils all over the hills above the old port. The crisp-skinned Sciacarello is the principal grape here, yielding long-lived red wines scented with raspberries, coffee and toasted almonds.

which had been abandoned to chestnuts and *maquis* scrubland vegetation.

Granite is the most common type of soil throughout the south and west of the island. In the east, schistous rock has given rise to dark, firm soils. The south and the area round the Gulf of Saint-Florent in the north is on limestone. All these soils will allow good wine to be produced. The climate is Mediterranean, but less extreme because of the closeness of the sea.

The Vin de Corse *appellation* applies to the whole island, but the majority of wines are produced firstly in the eastern plain between Bastia *coopératives*, and secondly in the foothills of the mountains, beneath enchantingly named hilltop villages.

hyphenated with the Vin de Corse *appellation*: Coteaux du Cap Corse, for the steeply terraced vineyards in the extreme north; Calvi, in the north-west; Sartène; Figari; and Porto-Vecchio, for the area round the southern cape. The top local *appellations* are those of Ajaccio and Patrimonio.

THE ISLAND WITH FORTY GRAPE VARIETIES

THERE are forty or so grape varieties particular to Corsica and still

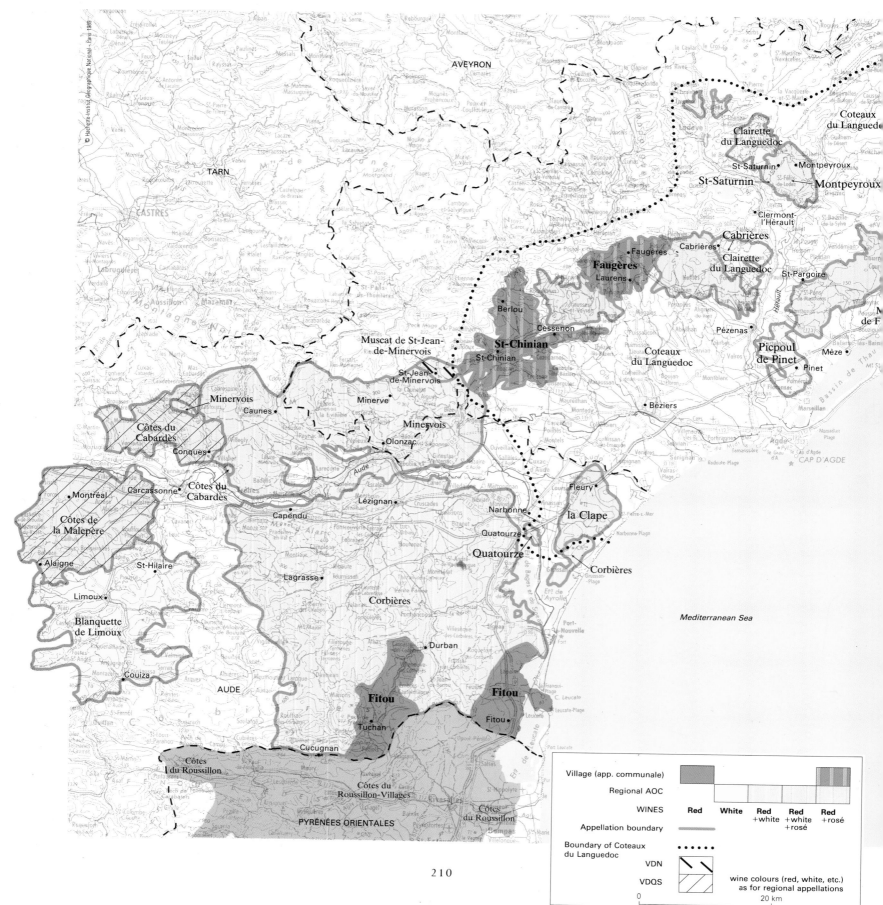

AVEYRON

TARN

CASTRES

Coteaux
du Languedoc

Clairette
du Languedoc

St-Saturnin • Montpeyroux

St-Saturnin — Montpeyroux

Clermont-
l'Hérault

Cabrières

Faugères
Faugères Cabrières Clairette
du Languedoc
St-Pargoire

Laurens

Berlou

Cessenon Pézenas

Muscat de St-Jean-
de-Minervois

St-Chinian
St-Chinian

Coteaux
du Languedoc

Picpoul
de Pinet

Mèze

St-Jean-
de-Minervois

Pinet

Minervois

Caunes

Minerve

Minervois

Béziers

Olonzac

Côtes du
Cabardès

Conques

CAP D'AGDE

Carcassonne Côtes du
Cabardès

Montréal

Fleury

Aude

Côtes de
la Malepère

Lézignan

Narbonne

la Clape

Alaigne

St-Hilaire

Quatourze

Quatourze

Limoux

Corbières

Lagrasse

Corbières

Blanquette
de Limoux

Mediterranean Sea

Couiza

AUDE

Durban

Fitou

Fitou

Fitou

Tuchan

Cucugnan

Côtes
du Roussillon

Côtes du
Roussillon-Villages

PYRÉNÉES ORIENTALES

Côtes du
Roussillon

		Red	White	Red +white	Red +white +rosé	Red +rosé
Village (app. communale)						
Regional AOC						
WINES						
Appellation boundary						

Boundary of Coteaux
du Languedoc · · · · · ·

VDN

VDQS

wine colours (red, white, etc.)
as for regional appellations

0   20 km

ROUSSILLON

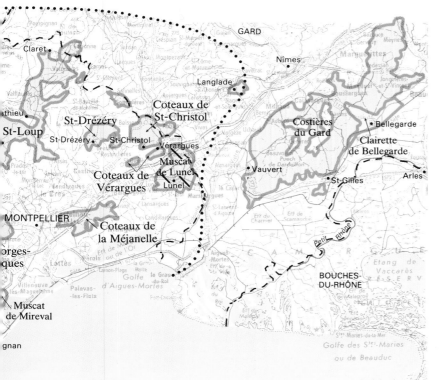

THE remarkably distinctive landscape of the Languedoc plain is a vast sea of vines in varying tones of green. Vines are everywhere, pushing back the frontiers of the natural scrubland, competing for space beside holiday beaches, creeping along the edge of the coastal lagoons opposite the curious island town of Sète, encroaching on human habitations in towns and villages. The image of monotonous, all-enveloping vines is so strong that one tends to forget how diverse the wine industry actually is in this region.

THE LAND OF RED WINE

VINES have in fact taken over one third of the plain in the Gard *département* and are continuing to expand in the south-west, where they occupy up to two thirds of the land in the lower valleys of the Hérault and Aude rivers. This is certainly the kingdom of red wine: more than half of all French table wine comes from this region. The grape varieties used are principally Carignan and Aramon, although relatively less Aramon is grown now that an attempt is being made to raise standards by going back to traditional Languedoc varieties such as Cinsault, Grenache Noir, Syrah and Mourvèdre, and by introducing aromatic varieties such as Merlot or the Cabernets.

The Languedoc riots in 1907, the sight of huge container-wagons of wine from Narbonne and Béziers, and the enormous size of the local *coopératives* have all helped to convey the idea of this region as a mass producer of wine. For further evidence of the essential role of wine in this area, you have only to visit Montpellier at the time of the wine-fair, wander round the typically Mediterranean town of Béziers, or listen to songs about wine by the well-known singer Georges Brassens, a native of the Languedoc town of Sète.

Mass wine-growing in the region does not in fact go back very far. When Jefferson visited the south of France in 1787, he noted that the Béziers countryside consisted of hills with olive trees, sainfoin, pastureland and a few vines and mulberries. Vine monoculture dates from the middle of the nineteenth century, when railways opened up new markets and vine-growing moved down from the hills, a tendency reinforced by the phylloxera epidemic and the need for low-lying ground that could be flooded.

It was in the early twentieth century that legends grew round the local wine industry, with the 1907 riots and the Great War issue of '*un quart de pinard*' ('a quarter litre of plonk') to men about to go over the top. Local wine subsequently began to suffer a recession, which became particularly marked in the fifties. Various redevelopment projects, such as fruit-growing, were set up to deal with this slump. The loss of Algeria and its wine industry caused some improvement, but the inauguration of the EEC then brought new competitors from elsewhere in the Mediterranean. The crisis became so serious that there were violent confrontations in the mid-seventies between Languedoc wine-growers and the police. The solution undoubtedly lies in the use of improved grape varieties and hillside planting.

Fontfroide, Abbey of Sainte-Marie.

Red wine production here covers more than 310,000 hectares, making this the largest mass-producing wine region in the world. However, although the plain is dominated by the wine industry, some *appellations* have taken to the hills in the interests of fine wine production. The landscape of Languedoc and Roussillon is incomparably rich and varied: the gently rolling Costières du Gard in the east are a complete contrast to the rugged Corbière hills and the cliff-like slopes at Banyuls. The vineyards of the region grow in varied countryside with equally varied geology and soil structure. Soils may consist of schistous rock from the Precambrian massif, of Mesozoic sandstone, as well as of rounded pebbles from the Quaternary era. Erosion by the very dense network of waterways continues to carve the landscape into hills and valleys.

The best wine is grown on pebbly soil containing a high proportion of solid matter, well drained to avoid waterlogging but deep enough not to dry out. The soil has to be loose enough for the vine roots to find their way down through it in all directions.

In spite of the region's great geological complexity, a certain unity comes from the schistous rocks on the one hand and the red pebbly soils on the other. The other unifying factor is the Mediterranean climate. After Corsica, the Languedoc and Roussillon region is the hottest in France, with average annual temperatures between 13.5°C and 15°C. Rainfall tends to occur as torrential storms but the actual number of wet days is very small. Winds are very drying when they come from inland, like the Mistral, the Cers and the Tramontane, but winds from the sea moderate the heat and bring beneficial moisture.

This combination of soil and weather is very favourable for high-quality wine-growing, especially for

the *vins doux naturels*, which are so much at home in Roussillon. A great many different grape varieties can reach their full potential here, and blending can produce wine of great richness and balance. The principal varieties are Carignan, Syrah, Mourvèdre and Grenache for red wines, and Grenache Blanc, Clairette, Picpoul, Maccabéo, Carignan Blanc, Ugni Blanc and Terret Blanc for whites.

With such a variety of sites and of grapes, Languedoc is no longer simply the largest producer of table and country wines in the world, but, in volume of *appellation* wine produced, is now third in France after the Rhône valley and the Bordeaux area.

An eighteenth-century altarpiece with a carving of the wine god Silenus (church of Saint-Julien, Vinça).

THE Coteaux du Languedoc extend in a huge crescent through 121 villages between Nîmes and Narbonne and look down on a sea of vines growing in the plain. Although the Coteaux yield more than 300,000 hl per year, these are not mass-producing prairie-type vineyards. They consist of a series of small plots scattered throughout the hilly scrubland. Eleven individual red and rosé and two white *crus* are entitled to the AOC Coteaux du Languedoc: these are La Clape, Quatourze (in the Aude *département*), Cabrières, Montpeyroux, Saint Saturnin, Pic-Saint-Loup, Saint-Georges d'Orques, La Méjanelle, Saint-Drézéry, Saint-Christol and Vérargues (in Hérault); and, for white wines, La Clape and Picpoul de Pinet.

BLENDING GRAPE VARIETIES

BECAUSE of weather conditions, it is necessary to blend several grape varieties in order to obtain a balanced wine. Red and rosé wines should be based on Carignan, Grenache, Cinsault, Syrah and Mourvèdre. Carignan, which came originally from Carinea in Aragon, is the principal variety grown and gives good results in hillside locations. It is happy in hot dry areas and on schistous soils, where it gives deep coloured, tannic wines whose astringency and lack of aroma can be counteracted by the use of carbonic maceration. Cinsault, which is also adapted to a dry environment, produces supple, elegant, rather light wines and is particularly suitable for rosés and all sorts of *primeur* wines. At present, not more than 50 per cent of the vines grown should consist of Carignan and Cinsault, and in 1992 this will be reduced to 40 per cent, thus allowing a greater proportion of Syrah, Mourvèdre and Grenache. The latter variety is vigorous and drought-resistant, but has a tendency to pollination failure (*coulure*) and inconsistent fruiting. Wine from this grape has a full, generous character, rich texture and good aroma. Syrah, which comes from the Rhône valley, is also a grape for quality. It ripens early so growers have to watch out for over-ripeness. Vinified

Typical landscape with vines in Languedoc.

at temperatures between 11°C and 12.5°C, it produces strong-coloured wines with fragrance and good structure. Mourvèdre, a late-ripening variety, has to be grown in warm locations such as pebble terraces not too much affected by drought. This too gives colour, structure and scent. At least 10 per cent of both Syrah and Mourvèdre have to be grown, and a minimum of 20 per cent of Grenache.

White wines are based on varieties which include Grenache Blanc, Picpoul, Clairette, Bourboulenc, Marsanne, Roussane and Rolle.

Area and yield of Languedoc Roussillon wine region		
	Area (hectares)	Yield (hl)
Table wines	300,000	18,000,000
Vins de pays		7,000,000
AOC	51,500	2,600,000
VDQS	628	35,000
VDN	29,150	604,000

ANGUEDOC

VÉRARGUES AND MÉJANELLE

THE easternmost section of the Coteaux du Languedoc is the Vérargues region, best known for its *vin doux naturel*, Muscat de Lunel. It is also proud of its supple, fruity red wines, about which Rousseau once wrote an admiring letter to D'Alembert.

The area contains three *crus*, the actual Coteaux de Vérargues, Saint-Christol, and Saint-Drézéry, shared between eleven villages, and has excellent red soils over a pebbly Lower Pleistocene stratum.

The Château de Castries, known as the Languedoc Versailles, stands between the Coteaux de Vérargues and the Méjanelle plateau running eastward to Montpellier. There are thick, pebbly soils here, rich in red clays and with gravel ridges very suitable for growing vines. This plateau was formed in the era when the Rhône flowed into the Mediterranean near Montpellier. On it now are a number of eighteenth-century houses and large farms hidden in impressive pine-woods.

Saint-Georges d'Orques, a little to the west of Montpellier, has a reputation going back a very long time. Wine from here was recommended by Jefferson as an alternative to the grain spirit which gave rise to so much alcoholism at that period. As early as the first half of the eighteenth century, the consuls of the town ordered casks to be stamped with the trade-mark of a knight slaying a dragon, as a guarantee of the quality and authenticity of their wine. Saint-Georges produces red and rosé wine on sites consisting of red scree from the Lower Pleistocene and scattered limestone pebbles washed down from the garrigue-covered massif.

Although it is no more than a hill 658 m high, the Pic-Saint-Loup nevertheless dominates the surrounding countryside. The hills are a favourite place for gliding because of the thermals they create: they also attract huntsmen and walkers interested in the rich variety of wild flowers. The wooded slopes of the peak are surrounded by low hills on which vines can be grown on an area about 30 km long by 15 km wide. There are favourable soils here, consisting of compacted or sandy limestone, scree and deposits of alluvial soils, as well as terraces of red pebbly soil.

Distance from the sea and an average altitude of 150 m combine to create a slightly more continental climate, with a cooler spring and autumn than can be expected for the rest of the region. This has some effect on the red wines produced, giving them a light and fruity, rather delicate character. In the future, it may well be that white and rosé wine will also seem suitable for growing here.

THE GARRIGUE

AT the foot of the arid Larzac plateau, with its scents of thyme and lavender, the villages of Saint-Saturnin and Montpeyroux are wedged in the fault between the red Lodève clays and the causse plateau of Viols-le-Fort to the east. The Hérault, emerging from the limestone plateau of Saint-Guilhem-le-Désert, has formed huge terraces of pebbles mixed with red clay which slope gently down towards the river. These slopes are almost covered with vines and produce red and rosé wines of long-standing reputation.

Some 10 km to the south-west of Saint-Saturnin, the vineyards of Cabrières are situated down in a deep corrie or *cirque* of schistous rock between four massifs covered in dense woodland. Red wines and a rosé are produced here in the shelter of these remote hills.

SEASHORE VINES

THE winds previously mentioned all come from the foothills of the Massif Central, whereas Pinet grows by the sea, or rather on the shore of the Thau coastal lagoon. This dry white wine shows its affinity with local food by growing practically in the turquoise water of the oyster beds. The grey and whitish soils, consisting of clay and a pebbly mixture of limestone splinters and fossil shells over a layer of marl, are very suitable for the Picpoul grape, which gives a dry, fragrant wine, excellent with shellfish.

The hill of La Clape lies between Narbonne and the sea. This rocky mass of limestone, once called the 'Lake Island', has a seashore graveyard where the peaceful atmosphere is in poignant contrast with the deaths at sea commemorated here. Summer tourists may come here now, but La Clape has been a vineyard for many years. The combination of poor soil (marly limestone, cliffs of hard limestone and Quaternary alluvial deposits) and the lowest rainfall in France favours the cultivation of some excellent wine. The reds are generous and fruity, with a tannic quality needing some years to mature. The whites, based on Bourboulenc, are fresh and supple, and also have a good reputation.

The vineyard of Quatourze is also just outside Narbonne and close to the sea. This is a very homogeneous area, consisting of terraces of pebbles mixed with Lower Pleistocene red clay, and with a covering of rust-coloured soils gleaming with white quartz. These give powerful wines with plenty of body and warmth and with spicy, woodland aromas which intensify with maturity. Unfortunately, this vineyard is threatened by urban development.

Detail from a seventeenth-century Flemish tapestry (from a collection at the Château de Flaugergues).

FAUGÈRES, SAINT-CHINIAN, COSTIÈRES DU GARD

THE Coteaux du Languedoc also include, besides the vineyards previously mentioned, the *crus* of Faugères and Saint-Chinian, both with their own *appellation*.

Faugères lies in rugged country, perched up in the foothills of the Cévennes and looking down towards Béziers in the plain, where the richer life has attracted many growers from the mountains. Vines in this rough hill country are certainly more a vocation than a business, but a determination to stay and do battle with stone and drought often brings its reward. These very uniform schistous soils have a small yield of powerful, heady wine, with a bouquet of soft fruit, liquorice and spice.

Saint-Chinian too has a small yield, 88,800 hl on 1,800 hectares, but is larger and more varied than Faugères. The northern sector round Berlou and Roquebrun is predominantly schistous terrain. In the south, round Saint-Chinian itself, are limestone and red clays and also Lower Pleistocene terrace formations. There is the same microclimate throughout the region: remarkably limpid air and enough warmth for mimosas and orange trees to be able to grow easily.

The variety of sites in the Saint-Chinian region obviously has some influence on the wines produced. These are both rich and delicate when grown on schist, and more powerful and complex on clay.

THE COSTIÈRES REGION

IN the north is the great Roman city of Nimes; in the east, Beaucaire, which for centuries had an immense July fair; in the south, Saint-Gilles, the finest example of a Romanesque church in the Midi; and in the west, the famous prehistoric site of Nages. The Costières du Gard seems to have

Above, Italic amphora, first century BC and right, amphora from Massalia (Marseille), 350–150 BC (both from Musée Archéologique, Ensérune).

famous places as its frontier posts. In 1986 it finally acquired its right to an AOC.

The Costières region consists of a group of slopes and plateaux, in all about 40 km long and 15 km wide. In spite of its size, the region is remarkably uniform. There is a single soil type derived from Lower Pleistocene terrace formations which consist of pebbles in a matrix of various sorts of sand, and of chalk washed away in some places and forming a crust in others. The more friable

Château de Laurens

FAUGÈRES N° 93421
AOC APPELLATION FAUGÈRES CONTRÔLÉE 75 cl e
MIS EN BOUTEILLE PAR
LES PRODUCTEURS RÉUNIS · 34480 LAURENS · FRANCE

pebbles have been degraded and the clay freed to give the typical red soil colour of the region. Pebbles also play an important part in local wine-growing as they store heat during the day and give it out again at night.

CLAIRETTE DE BELLEGARDE

CLAIRETTE de Bellegarde is produced on pebbly soils in the south-eastern Costières between Beaucaire and Saint-Gilles, and was classed as AOC in 1949. It is a dry white wine with a very characteristic bouquet, and a yield of not more than 3,000 hl per year.

ABBEY VINEYARDS

SITES like these were exploited very early on and the history of this wine region is both ancient and honourable. Vines were first grown here in the Graeco-Roman period but it was in the Middle Ages that wine-growing became really important. After the founding of the Abbeys of Saint-Gilles and Psalmody in the eighth century, Benedictine monks began the process of clearing the land and planting vines. They also tried to discover the soils most likely to produce good wine and to determine the best methods of cultivation. They were almost certainly responsible for introducing Mourvèdre, which is known locally as the 'Saint-Gilles' vine. The region had a good enough reputation by the sixteenth century for the agriculturist Olivier de Serres (1539–1619) to recommend the wines of Saint-Gilles. He describes them in his 'Théâtre d'agriculture' as 'lusty, dark-seeming wines, firm and spirituous withal'.

At the present time the *appellation* has a yield of about 200,000 hl of red and rosé wine, together with around 4,000 hl of white. Reds and rosés are based on a maximum of 50 per cent Carignan and Cinsault, a minimum of 25 per cent Grenache Noir, and a minimum of 15 per cent Syrah and Mourvèdre. Different areas produce a different style of wine. The southern sector facing the sea gives red wines of some strength and backbone, while further north, looking over the Nîmes *garrigue*, a much more supple and fruity wine for easy drinking is produced.

Pebble soil in the Costières du Gard.

MINERVOIS

'MINERVE has the most fantastic situation in the whole of France,' according to a southerner, the Duc de Levy-Mirepois. His slight exaggeration may have been inspired by the name Minerve, which is thought to have classical connections, as well as by the village's dramatic perch on a promontory joined to the bare plateau only by a narrow strip of land. In historical times, Minerve was also important for the part it played in the Cathar story.

MEDITERRANEAN INFLUENCE

THE village of Minerve is not just a tourist spot, however. It is the centre of a wine *appellation* established in a huge amphitheatre of land at the foot of the Montagne Noire. There are vineyards here producing 240,000 hl of white, rosé and, in particular, red wines, grown on a series of terraces running down to the river Aude. Because of the size of the region, which extends over almost 60 km and through sixty-one villages, there are considerable differences in weather and hence some varied sub-regions.

The eastern sector consists principally of gently rolling limestone hills and the distinctive ridge called the Serre d'Oupia. In the easternmost part there are also broad terraces of pebbles washed down by the river Cesse. The area as a whole has a markedly Mediterranean climate and is strongly affected in summer by moist sea breezes. The basic grape for red wines is Carignan, together with Grenache and Mourvèdre. Whites are based mainly on Bourboulenc and Maccabéo.

On the other side, west of the Laure Minervois hills, the climate is still Mediterranean but moderated by north-west winds bringing Atlantic influences. The terrain is essentially molasse sediments interspersed with beds of sandstone and puddingstone, as well as several levels of terraces laid down by the rivers Clamoux and Orbiel. At this meeting-point of two weather systems, Carignan probably reaches the limit of its potential.

The village of La Caunette, in the heart of the Minervois wine region.

Lying between these two sectors, the Minervois heartland is relatively well sheltered from the effects of both Atlantic and Mediterranean. There are extremely hot dry summers and less rain than elsewhere in the region. It is a very uniform sector consisting partly of vast terraces of pebbles brought down by the river Argent-Double and the Ognon, and partly of a very distinctive landscape of so-called *mourrels*, precipitous flat-topped hills made up of layers of rock capped with sandstone or puddingstone. These hills with their sparse Aleppo pines are separated by slightly undulating depressions of limestone molasse, and it is here that vines are grown. Prehistoric standing stones and ancient chapels make this a very evocative landscape. It is still mainly Carignan which is grown here, together with Grenache on marl, Cinsault on sandstone, and also Syrah and Mourvèdre. Lastly, the jagged southern edge of the Montagne Noire has

soils consisting largely of limestone pebbles. Low-lying areas are very hot, but higher up the cooler air means later ripening and a chance for grapes to benefit from brilliant dry autumn weather. This is especially advantageous for the Muscat grown at Saint-Jean de Minervois, which with Minerve itself is a focal point of the region.

The Minervois countryside is criss-crossed with delightful roads, including a *route des Vins* past a number of *dégustation* cellars. For some years now growers have been endeavouring to produce wine with elegance and breeding, and are therefore beginning to plant better grape varieties and to make wine with whole, uncrushed

grapes. To highlight this achievement, they have now produced a specially engraved bottle reserved for estate-bottled wine at the top of their range.

CÔTES DU CABARDÈS AND DE L'ORBIEL

THESE VDQS areas, set on the side of the Montagne Noire, are a western continuation of the Minervois. The Cabardès fortresses on their high pinnacles made an impregnable refuge for the Cathars in the early thirteenth century. The region has a distinctive climate at the junction of Atlantic and Mediterranean systems and can grow grapes adapted to both; Grenache and Syrah as well as Merlot and the Cabernets. Soils vary according to altitude: schist above 400 m, a middle area of limestone plateaux, and clayey limestones and sandstones at the lowest level. The wines all have a very marked personality.

CÔTES DE LA MALEPÈRE

THE VDQS region of Côtes de la Malepère lies south-west of Carcassonne between the Limoux area and the Canal du Midi. This also has a transitional weather pattern exaggerated by the particular characteristics of certain slopes and the presence in the middle of the area of the Malepère massif. Conditions like these are ideal for grape varieties adapted to an Atlantic environment. Two types of landscape are evident: a border zone of Quaternary gravel terraces; and everywhere else mainly limestone hillsides interspersed with sandstone and puddingstone. From this area there is an annual yield of about 10,000 hl of robust, fruity red and rosé wine.

MUSCAT DE SAINT-JEAN DE MINERVOIS

THESE vineyards are on limestone in hilly scrubland at a height of 200 m. The altitude means that Muscat grapes here are harvested three weeks later than Muscat elsewhere. The wine produced is refined and deliciously scented, with very distinctive floral notes.

CORBIÈRES

CORBIÈRES AND FITOU

PERCHED high on their limestone crags, the fortresses of Peyrepertuse, Puilaurens, Quéribus, Termes and Aguilar, known as *'les cinq fils de Carcassonne'* ('the five sons of Carcassonne'), are a reminder of less peaceful centuries in the Corbières region. The time has gone when the frontier between France and the Iberian peninsula passed somewhere between Narbonne and Perpignan, and when these mountains were darkened by the tragedy of the Cathars. Nowadays these ruined castles serve only as a memorial of those days and their only assailant is the wind over the *garrigue*.

Above, the Tauch hills, in the Corbières range. Centre, the castle of Aguilar.

This sparse scrubland, together with rocks, mountains and heathland, occupies 80 per cent of the surface area, and vines have to make do with whatever is left. Vines are clearly the most suitable plants for these arid conditions and cultivating them gives a sense of pride and independence to local growers who have to battle with this harsh land. They fight erosion by building little walls round cultivated fields, as the soil here is no longer held together by the roots of the original oak forest.

Over the years, wine growers also have to come to terms with the almost perpetual wind, blowing violently for 300 days in a year, and causing changes of weather in the prevailing Mediterranean climate. The Cers blows from the west,

bringing drought and destruction, where the moist Marin subdues the extreme summer heat and brings heavy rain in spring and autumn. With vineyards cut off from each other by the hilly terrain, and with the extreme diversity of soils, it is very difficult to define the Corbières region. However, the different sub-regions undoubtedly owe their special character to the winds.

FROM THE MEDITERRANEAN TO THE MONTAGNE D'ALARIC

THE coastal section of the Corbières consists of a series of hills running from north to south, forming a homogeneous group of limestone slopes with consistent weather. This is the driest part of France, with less than 400 mm of rain some years, but the sea is close enough to moderate temperatures and provide the minimum of moisture needed for growing grapes.

The high Corbières region in the south is sheltered from extremes of weather by the high peaks surrounding it. In this dramatic environment vines are grown on the precipitous sides of a series of little basin-like depressions, the only areas where it is possible to grow anything among the heath and scrubland. Soils consisting of schist or of clay and limestone give powerful, full-bodied wines which improve as they mature.

The very densely cultivated wine region of the central Corbières has been established in the Orbieu basin, on Quaternary river terraces and also on a number of limestone or sandstone hills in this rather more gentle landscape. The microclimate of the area is particularly hot and dry in summer.

The north-western corner of the *appellation* is dominated by the Corbières d'Alaric vineyards surrounding

Château de Lastours
Corbières
Appellation Corbières Contrôlée

PRODUCE OF FRANCE — Mis en bouteille au Château par le C.A.T. producteur/éleveur à Portel (11490) — 75 cl e

the Montagne d'Alaric itself. Slight variations in the climate here have made it possible to develop a whole spectrum of wines differing with the site on which they are grown. For instance, the lower part of the south-east face has an extremely hot climate, whereas Atlantic influences are discernible on the western side.

Like other Languedoc regions, the Corbières wine industry, with a yield of 600,000 hl of red, rosé and white wine, has benefited from considerable financial investment as well as from improvements both in techniques and choice of grape. Syrah and Mourvèdre are now planted beside the old Carignan, which after 1990 will not be allowed to exceed 60 per cent. The Corbières region acquired its AOC in 1985 and, without losing their special character, the wines have certainly become more diversified, with more finesse and aromatic intensity.

FITOU

FITOU is included in the Corbières wine region and is unusual in having the right to produce VDN Rivesaltes and Muscat de Rivesaltes as well as having the oldest red wine AOC in Languedoc-Roussillon. It is also extraordinarily divided as it consists of two pockets of vine-growing separated by a limestone plateau. The first is at Fitou itself, where vines alternate rather oddly with coastal resorts; the second is centred on Tuchan, about 30 kilometres further west, and encircled by the rugged Corbières mountains.

The vineyards near the sea are established on hard limestone, overlaid with warm, shallow and pebbly soils. In the high Corbières sector it depends in which village the vineyards are situated, and soils can be either schistous, or a mixture of limestone, sandstone and schist. Carignan and Grenache, the principal grape varieties, reach their full potential on all these sites. Fitou produces about 80,000 hl of distinctive fat, well-structured wines, deep ruby in colour and capable of maturing. These are a good example of traditional Languedoc wines extending both their market and their reputation.

LIMOUX

SOME towns seem to turn their backs on their surroundings. Limoux certainly makes the most of its green valley on the river Aude and its outskirts are a pleasing mixture of town and country. The local people have a reputation for enjoying life. This is clear even in the museum, where carved and painted fruit and flowers seem to have come straight out of late nineteenth-century paintings of delicious, enchanted gardens.

The town also holds some spectacular festivals. Every year there is a masked carnival for Mardi Gras, the legacy of a time when millers would run through the narrow streets scattering sweets to symbolize the sharing

running north to south alongside two hills. These are in turn cut through by small streams which are most important for wine-growing in the area. Further up the valley, north of a line running from Castelreng to Magrie and Saint-Polycarpe, the country is gently rolling, with heights of less than 400 m. Altitude increases as you go south and the landscape begins to look more rugged. In spite of these contrasts and the complex local geology, the soils are in fact very homogeneous, based mainly on sandstone, fairly compacted limestone and marls. Alternating layers of hard rock and friable clay/limestone marl have resulted in a characteristic *cuesta*-type escarpment.

At this meeting-point of the Mediterranean, Atlantic and Pyrenean weather systems, the exposure

with more than 3,000 hectares shared by forty-one communes.

The region is unlike its neighbours in having good distribution of rainfall and a regular water-supply. It is also unusual in its choice of grapes adapted to the locality, a policy which has encouraged the cultivation of three varieties unknown elsewhere in Languedoc.

None of the varieties used for Blanquette is used in any other Mediterranean *appellation*. The most traditional is Mauzac, which has leaves with whitish felting on the back – hence the name Blanquette. This is the basic grape and has to contribute an obligatory minimum of 70 per cent. It gives a fragrance of apple and potential for the nose to develop further. This is a late variety like Chenin, which contributes

sugar to reactivate fermentation, is added and the wine undergoes secondary fermentation in the bottle, which is then stored on special wooden shelving called *lattes* for at least nine months, according to the classic *méthode champenoise*. Then come the *remuage*, turning the bottles to shift the sediment, the *dégorgeage*, or 'disgorgement' of the yeasty deposit, and the final topping up with *liqueur d'expédition* consisting of some extra sugar and wine. The Blanquette then quietly matures in the cellar,

of wealth. Even without the millers, today's processions of masked dancers are aware that this is not just a bit of folklore for tourists but an intensely significant manifestation of local pride.

Limoux has splendid natural surroundings. The town lies in a wide bowl between the foothills of the Pyrenees and the Malpère and Corbières mountains, surrounded on all sides by hills isolating it from its neighbours.

In the heart of the Limoux territory, the river Aude forms a boundary

of the vineyard is what counts most. Slopes facing south and terraces where there is little natural vegetation are the most suitable for vines.

CELEBRATION WINE

LIMOUX seems to express its own capacity for enjoyment through its famous Blanquette, a *vin de fête* like all sparkling wine. This is the only exclusively white *appellation* in Languedoc,

essential fruit and acidity but is fragile and needs some care. Unlike the two previous varieties, Chardonnay ripens early and brings unmistakable smoothness and a fat, expansive quality, with a more complex bouquet.

The grapes are picked into boxes and are kept whole until they reach the press. After running off the lees, the must, consisting of 100 l for every 160 kg of grapes, ferments at low temperature for two or three weeks. It is then clarified and the wine to be included in the blend is selected by an expert. The *liqueur de tirage*, yeast and

Left, bottling the sparkling Blanquette de Limoux.
Above, Limoux.

before becoming one of the 7.5 million bottles sold every year.

The Limoux AOC also applies to a dry white wine, of which 900 hl are produced every year, but this very individual region is best represented by Blanquette de Limoux and by the small hand-produced wine known as 'old-fashioned' Blanquette, which gets its first fermentation directly in the bottle.

ROUSSILLON

IN its amphitheatre of mountains barred to the north by the towering fortress walls of Salses, Roussillon (the French Catalan region) could seem a harsh place, but there is charm both in its natural situation at the extreme south of the mainland and in the orchards and vineyards which men have added. The sight of delicate peach blossom in spring or of the vines growing round the castle of Salses is enough to convey an atmosphere of peaceful, civilized living.

Vines here have very favourable growing conditions. The soil, deficient in organic matter and very diverse in colour and geology, often provides an ideal *terroir* consisting of pebbles mixed with red clay. The dry, sunny climate, accentuated by the Tramontane, the dominant northwest wind, is particularly good for *vins doux naturels*, a regional speciality which includes all the immense range of Banyuls, Rivesaltes, Maury and Muscat de Rivesaltes. However, this is not all the region can offer. Its 56,000 hectares produce the reds, whites and rosés of the two *appellations* Côtes du Roussillon and Côtes du Roussillon Villages.

although with a yield of less than 20 hl to the hectare. Vine-growing is spreading into inland valleys exposed to a maritime climate, and creeping up mountainsides to a height of 400 m. In Roussillon, where water-management has been familiar since the Middle Ages, the vineyards are criss-crossed by an ingenious system of drainage channels. Banyuls certainly suffers extremes of weather. Violent storms occur after periods of summer drought and can cause considerable damage.

These terraced vineyards are beautiful to look at but not at all easy to manage. There is not a single tractor. Mules, with old wooden tubs strapped to them, still carry all the crops to the cellars. The growers' own hands are in constant daily contact with the vines and the soil. Perhaps because they do not mind hard labour themselves they subject some of the more robust wines to some harsh processes, exposing them in demijohns and half-barrels to all kinds of weather. The wine seems to develop very well in these conditions, not unlike those on the boats that used to carry the wine of Collioure (sometimes called Spanish wine) to the tables of the great European courts in the days before the Pyrenees Treaty of 1659 when Roussillon still belonged to Spain.

For the Banyuls Grand Cru *appellation* the wine has to be matured in wood for at least thirty months.

· BETWEEN THE MEDITERRANEAN AND THE PYRENEES: A PROBLEM AREA

THE vineyards of the Côte Vermeille are spectacular in the way they encircle the ports of Banyuls and Collioure and plunge steeply down into the Mediterranean. They need to be seen from the coast road between Argelès-sur-Mer and Cerbère. Further along the extraordinary twists and turns of this road is Collioure, one of the most picturesque of Mediterranean ports, the city of the kings of Majorca and of many famous artists, such as Matisse, Braque and Dufy. After this you come to Port-Vendres and Banyuls, where the sculptor Maillol was born.

To most people the Côte Vermeille simply suggests holidays. To the vine-growers it means a *terroir* won over with immense difficulty. It probably would not have become a wine-growing area if sailors from Corinth had not once anchored in sheltered creeks along the rocky coast and planted the first vines there. Nor would its vineyard exist today without the laborious replacement of the rocks washed down from the terraces after every storm. The vines, on stocks lacking vigour, grow on bare schistous rock the colour of terracotta, their roots poking through the terrace walls. Grenache Noir is the main variety, a particularly drought-resistant, rustic type which gives grapes with high sugar content

Above, Salses, the castle.

Centre, the drainage system on the hillsides at Banyuls.

Barrels of vin doux naturel *maturing in the sun, where the wine develops a much prized aroma.*

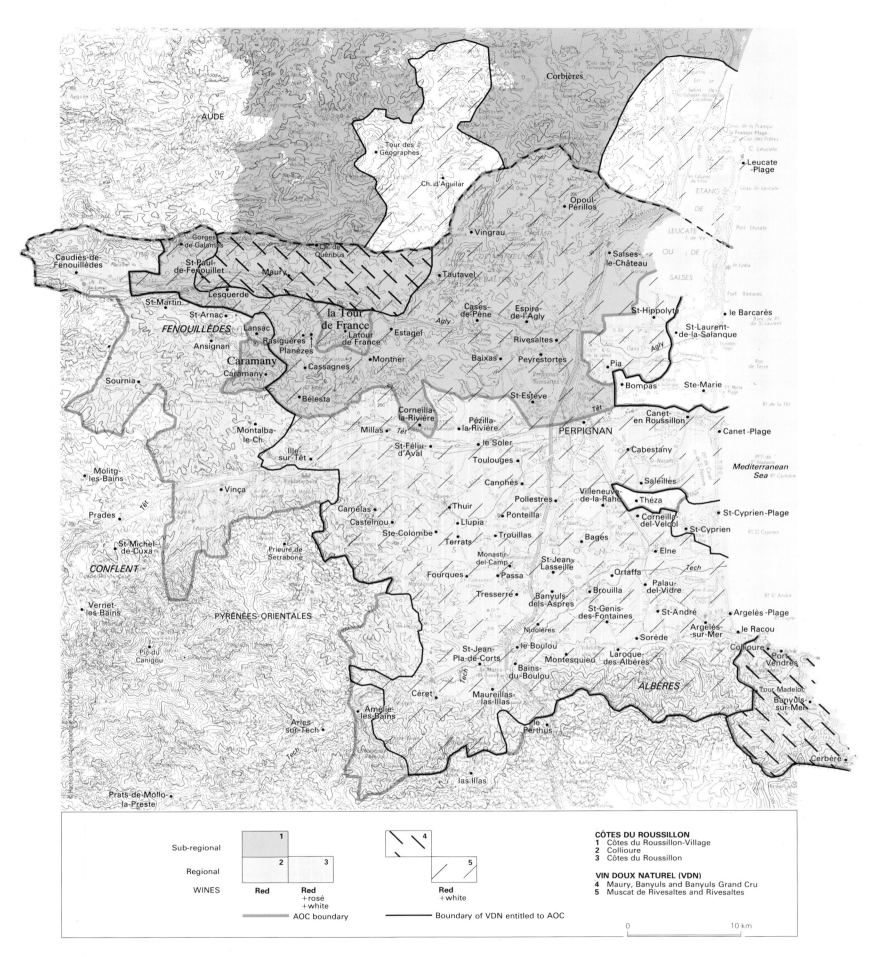

Sub-regional

Regional

WINES

1		
2	**3**	

Red | Red +rosé +white

Red +white

4	
5	

AOC boundary

Boundary of VDN entitled to AOC

CÔTES DU ROUSSILLON
1 Côtes du Roussillon-Village
2 Collioure
3 Côtes du Roussillon

VIN DOUX NATUREL (VDN)
4 Maury, Banyuls and Banyuls Grand Cru
5 Muscat de Rivesaltes and Rivesaltes

0   10 km

Banyuls wines have remarkable longevity. They are ruby-coloured when young but with age acquire tones of mahogany and terracotta together with a fragrance of cooked fruit, prunes and coffee.

A small amount of dry wine with a Collioure *appellation* is also produced in Banyuls. Grenache Noir, with the addition of Carignan, Syrah and Mourvèdre, produces robust red wine, with plenty of warmth and juiciness.

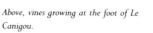

THE ASPRES REGION

BETWEEN Perpignan and the Albères chain, Mont Canigou looms over a harsh, dry countryside of occasional Romanesque chapels and vines growing with holm oaks, with a few cork oaks on less arid slopes. The superb medieval village of Castelnou looks down on the Aspres region and the town of Thuir, once the centre of the local wine industry and still containing *caves*, which can be visited.

This region is divided between Côtes du Roussillon and some Rivesaltes and Muscat de Rivesaltes. The first are grown on clay/pebble soil lying over a Pliocene substrate, and consisting of elements derived from the Canigou massif. These bleached and decalcified soils are often very acidic. The Rivesaltes and Muscat de Rivesaltes occupy a few terraced patches classed as VDN land, by the small rivers Canterrane, Réari and Tech. In the twelfth century the Templars settled at Le Mas Dieu, near Trouillas, and restored vineyards which had been ruined by Visigoth and Saracen invasion. There are also vines on the Albères piedmont terrain in the eastern Pyrenees, the region of the famous Col du Perthus crossed by Hannibal and his elephants.

Nowadays Côtes du Roussillon is derived from at least three grape varieties: Carignan, an old Catalan grape variety with healthy root-

Above, vines growing at the foot of Le Canigou.

stocks, gives backbone; from the Grenache comes fruity fullness and warmth; and from the Syrah delicate hints of iris and cherry. Apart from the Syrah, these vine are shaped *en gobelet*, to produce a compact wind-resistant bush, and pruned down to spurs bearing two buds.

White Grenache is used here for Rivesaltes wine. Finally, there is some Maccabéo with soft felted leaves (another typically Catalan variety) which is beginning to appear in the Aspres region. On the dry hillsides this is used to make Rivesaltes scented with broom and wild honey; on cooler ground it is turned into white wine with a fruity freshness delicious for drinking young.

RIVESALTES

AT the foot of Mont Canigou lies the vast pebbly expanse of the plateau of Crest, which slopes gently down towards the coastal lagoons and the sea. The region has traditionally produced strong, sweet wines and the 'capital' of this local industry is Rivesaltes, the birthplace of Maréchal Joffre. The town has given its name to a VDN *appellation* formerly restricted to the

Above, the port of Collioure.

Top right, 'La bouteille banyuls' ('Bottle of Banyuls'), painting by Juan Gris, 1914 (Musée des Beaux-Arts, Berne).

immediate area but now extending over a large part of the Roussillon wine region and into nine communes of the Aude *département*. These wines are based on Maccabéo, white and red Grenache and, where there is an unusual amount of sunshine, on Malvoisie. Rivesaltes is strong and sweet, with a luscious richness and a flavour so individual that it is bound to provoke strong reactions in people lucky enough to taste it.

Muscat vines were planted in the Rivesaltes area and were responsible for the Muscat de Rivesaltes

appellation, now authorized throughout Roussillon. Only two Muscat varieties are permitted: Muscat à Petits Grains, imported by the Greeks and giving wine with a refined and delicate bouquet; and Muscat d'Alexandrie (or Muscat romain) which was introduced later. With its late ripening and concentrated fragrance, Muscat needs a very warm environment. It flourishes in Roussillon, where you can admire the grapes turning deliciously golden in the sun.

CATHAR COUNTRY

THE valley of the river Agly between Rivesaltes and Le Fenouillèdes (a district of Languedoc before the French

---

BANYULS AND COLLIOURE: SEA INFLUENCES

IT was not by chance that vineyards grew up near these two ports. Vines were planted by settlers from Massalia (now Marseille) and from the very beginning, in classical times, wine was exported in great round amphorae called Marseillaises. In the Middle Ages, too, the ports of Roussillon, especially Collioure, sent wine by sea to the Balearics, Sardinia, the Levant, the Byzantine Empire, North Africa and, of course, Flanders and England.

Revolution) is entirely given up to vines. The local *vins doux naturels* were formerly called Côtes d'Agli but are now part of the Rivesaltes *appellation*. There is also some Côtes du Roussillon Villages, strong red wine (at least 12° alcohol) with solidity and decent ageing potential.

In this rather arid and rocky *garrigue* environment, with its complex geology, very diverse wines can be produced. The lower Agly valley consists of stepped terraces covered with scree from the Villafranchian era and overlying a Pliocene clay/silt substrate. All these terraces are classified as VDN and Côtes du Roussillon-Villages and give a fairly small yield of heady, well-structured wines. The substrate, often on a slope, is visible between two levels of terracing and its deeper, cooler soils provide a more suitable terrain for Maccabéo vines. They also suit the Syrah and Mourvèdre used for Côtes du Roussillon. At the edge of these terraces, close to the foothills of the Corbières, the more or less calcareous, red Mediterranean soils start to appear at Calce, Baixas and Espira, and provide an ideal terrain for Muscat à Petits

weather and soil conditions, as recent studies of ancient cultivation show that they did.

In the middle valley of the Agly the bedrock is the base for an extraordinary medley of soils: schist at Montner and Rasiguères, gneiss at Caramany, granite sands and limestone at Tautavel. Each *terroir,* even within the same commune, gives different wine so that individual *caveaux* have tended to specialize: Rasiguères, for instance, has a Côtes du Roussillon rosé, made exclusively by the *saignée* method

RANCIO

THE traditional practice of making VDN in half barrels exposed to the weather and with no topping up produces after a number of years that very individual wine known as rancio. In the course of this process, wines that were once white become amber and then dark amber in colour; red wines lose their colour and are tinged first with terracotta and finally amber. In this way, after at least eight to ten years, both red and white wines become the same dark amber colour with a characteristic greenish hue. The nose is evocative of dried fruit and green walnut skins. Every grower cherishes this 'special' cask of rancio and, as in the solera system of Southern Spain, each time wine is taken from the cask it is replaced with a small amount of younger wine.

Grains and its deliciously aromatic wines. It is amazing to think that wine-growers from Greece and Rome were able to adapt their vines to local

(from the first free run juice that comes out of the bottom of the vat when the grapes are first put in but not crushed). Caramany and Latour de France are the only communes entitled to use the village name as well as the Côtes du Roussillon Villages *appellation*.

At Latour de France old vines planted on these very sunny hillsides yield long-keeping wines. On the gneiss soils at Caramany the Carignan grape gives supple, fruity, very fragrant wines with hints of spice in some years. These are traditionally vinified by carbonic maceration, a process that gives the Carignan an air of

VINS DOUX NATURELS

THESE are the great speciality in Roussillon, which makes 90 per cent of the whole French output. This can be attributed to an exceptional combination of soil and weather conducive to grapes with a specially high sugar level. To be entitled to the VDN appellation, the must has to have a sugar content of 252 g per litre or 14° of alcohol. The Roussillon area has made these sweet VDN for a very long time. A thirteenth-century Catalan called Arnau de Villanova is supposed to have discovered the mutage process, the addition of grape spirit or eau de vie to grape juice. Nowadays the appellation calls for a regulated addition of alcohol during the fermentation period.

There are various VDN possibilities, according to the grapes from which they are made. Amber-coloured wines come from the Grenache Blanc or Gris, from Maccabéo and from Malvoisie de Roussillon. Reds and tile-reds are based on Grenache Noir. Colours and aromas change as the wines mature, often in large casks, and may end up as rancio, the ultimate stage of the wine-making process. Muscat de Rivesaltes, based on Muscat à Petits Grains and Muscat d'Alexandrie, is for drinking young.

breeding and which has progressed a good deal since the Côtes du Roussillon *appellation* was created. This is why in these regions the picked grapes are very carefully kept from being crushed. Depending on the length of fermentation, this technique can also create *nouveau* and *primeur* wines, which are some of the earliest to appear in France.

Nowadays more and more Syrah and Mourvèdre are used here in red wine production. Mourvèdre tends to be planted in the warmest areas in the lower part of the valley, as higher up only Syrah ripens successfully.

Tautavel is one place deserving special mention since it is here, in the cave called Caune de l'Arago, that relics of France's earliest inhabitants have been discovered: a *Homo erectus* skull 500,000 years old and traces of human occupation going back 1,200,000 years. Beneath its high limestone cliffs, Tautavel also produces from long-ripened grapes wines that mature well; VDN as well as Côtes du Roussillon Villages.

FENOUILLÈDES AND MAURY

THE mountainous region of Fenouillèdes, once a remote part of the Languedoc frontier, has vines growing on bare rock with no fine topsoil at all. The town of Montalba was a frontier post between France and Spain before the Pyrenees Treaty and now has a museum of local wine traditions. The area as a whole differs from nearby *garrigue* in its vegetation

Demijohns of sweet wine maturing out of doors at Maury.

(holm oaks) and, owing to the altitude, in its relatively cooler weather. The Saint Martin sector produces some excellent white wine from the Maccabéo grape and also red wine, with a very refined nose, which needs to be drunk young.

With the legendary Cathar citadel of Quéribus looming over it on a pinnacle of rock, Maury on its weathered black schistous soil stands out among vineyards in the Languedoc fringes of the Roussillon wine region. *Vins doux naturels* with the Maury *appellation* are made here, almost exclusively from Grenache Noir. These are wines for long keeping, distinguished by their ruby and mahogany colouring and their mingled scents of cooked fruit, cocoa and coffee.

THE SOUTH-WEST

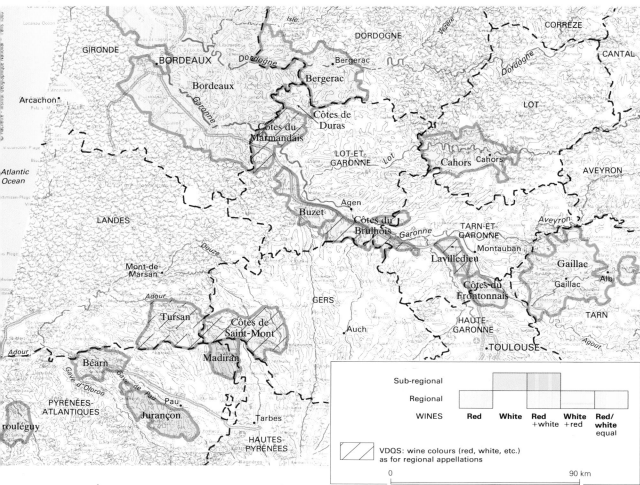

	Red	White	Red+white	White+red	Red/white equal
Sub-regional					
Regional					

WINES

VDQS: wine colours (red, white, etc.) as for regional appellations

0   90 km

on trade with France during the Napoleonic Wars.

The wine industry in this region had still not achieved real expansion at the time of the phylloxera catastrophe, which proceeded to tear it apart. Even today it is much fragmented, although roughly centred in two areas: one near the Garonne and its tributaries, the other in the foot-hills of the Pyrenees.

The area of the Garonne, the Tarn, the Lot and the Dordogne, was in turn a vassal and a rival of Bordeaux. The Pyrenean region, with many small areas of vine-growing between the river Adour and the Pyrenees, had always had the port of Bayonne as an outlet for its export trade to the rich Dutch market and later to North America. From these steep vineyards the snow-covered peaks of the Spanish frontier are visible, the core of this very distinctive wine region that continues on the Spanish side with the wines of Txacoli, Navarre and Rioja. Similarities in the grapes grown show

Below left, Montaigne's château, with the tower where he wrote the 'Essais'.
Below, cross used as emblem for the wine growers of Marcillac (church of Saint-Austremoine).

ALTHOUGH part of a single administrative group, each of the South-west wine regions has a character of its own: the Basque region with the town of Irouléguy as its centre, Béarn (centred on Jurançon), Périgord (Bergerac), and lastly the region round Cahors. The wine map

here, as varied as the local countryside and its accents, forms a complicated jigsaw, which only stays joined together because of the unending struggle over the centuries with neighbouring Bordeaux and its powerful and protectionist wine trade.

Bordeaux's strong geographical position allowed it to block shipping on the Garonne and to act as a departure port for trade with English-speaking countries. It also enjoyed various privileges conferred on it by the Plantagenet ruling dynasty and defended by the aldermen of the city; privileges that the French monarchy dared not question, even after the end of the Hundred Years War.

The people of Bordeaux held fast to the guarantee that no wine from outside the city should be allowed within the Port de la Lune before the Gironde harvest was sold, so cargoes of 'up-country' wine sometimes had

to wait until Christmas for permission from the city courts and were often blended with mediocre wine from the Bordeaux marshes.

A HARD-EARNED REPUTATION

BY a strange paradox, it was the Wars of Religion in the late sixteenth century that finally produced ambassadors for these wines: the refugees driven out of France by poverty and intolerance spread their reputation throughout Europe and across the Atlantic. When the dispensations granted to Bordeaux were finally swept away by the French Revolution, it was unfortunate that wines from the South-west should then find themselves up against the English embargo

that there must often have been exchanges *'tras los montes'* ('across the mountains').

This region remains determined to be different. Local growers are firm individualists who have hung on to local grape varieties which are now museum pieces: Manseng, Tannat, Barroque, Arrufiat, Mauzac, Duras, Auxerrois, Mansoi, Négrette and Folle Noire are some of the most surprising survivals. The wines too, have retained the strong local accent and authenticity valued by lovers of *vins de terroir*.

THE GARONNE REGION

BETWEEN Toulouse and the Gironde, many large centres of wine production have sprung up on the banks of the Garonne, and the river route is immensely profitable to both growers and boatmen. This centuries-old symbiotic relationship with the river has given the area a very distinctive character. The uniform weather and soil conditions on the slopes and terraces mean that the region can be viewed as a whole. There is a difference, however, in the choice of vines: the growers upstream tend to choose Négrette, whereas downstream they prefer varieties more typical of Bordeaux.

THE FRONTONNAIS AREA

THE extremely poor soils (gravel and *boulbène* – stony silt and clay) on the three terraces going down to the Tarn provide suitable growing conditions for the unusual, rather fragile and delicate Négrette. Two former VDQS (Fronton and Villauric) have joined together to form a single AOC which produces very individual, supple and fragrant wines from the area between Toulouse and Montauban. These are also given character by the range of soils on which they are grown and by the use of complementary vines, including Cabernets, Gamay and Syrah, giving added scent, refinement and liveliness. The Côtes du Frontonnais, often called Toulouse wines, include fragrant, fruity rosés, and reds which are light and supple or big and powerful, depending on the grapes and soil involved.

LAVILLEDIEU

THE VDQS area of Lavilledieu is a continuation of Frontonnais and occupies terraces between the Tarn and the Garonne. On poor soil

The eighteenth-century 'petit château', next to the château of Duras.

consisting of leached *boulbène*, vines such as those of Frontonnais give red and rosé wines of some fruitiness and character, all made in tiny amounts by a single *coopérative*.

BRULHOIS

THIS new VDQS revives the name of the region once known as the Comté de Brulhois and occupies both banks of the river below Agen. The vines are on slopes continuing those of Moissac, with its famous Chasselas grapes, and the last hills of Gascony. Some respectable red and rosé wines are produced from Tannat, Cabernet, Merlot, Fer and Malbec grapes.

BUZET

THE wine region of Côtes de Buzet lies halfway between Agen and Marmande, between the left bank of the Garonne and the fringes of the Landes forest, in hilly countryside cut into by the rivers Baïse, Gélise, Lourbise and Galaup. With its varied soils (*boulbène*, a heavy clay known as *terrefort*, and gravels) providing ideal growing conditions for Aquitaine vine varieties (Cabernet Sauvignon, Cabernet Franc, Merlot and Malbec), Buzet was for many years included in Bordeaux. There were considerable problems after the phylloxera crisis and its new identity as Côtes de Buzet should be credited entirely to a single *coopérative*, which from the beginning has been working for quality. The wines are based on a rigorous selection

of grapes and are raised in wood in accordance with Médoc tradition. With their classical style and breeding, they are excellent examples of the wide range produced in the South-west.

CÔTES DU MARMANDAIS

THIS is a VDQS zone situated at the entrance to the Gironde on a natural extension of the southern gravel soils and the Entre-Deux-Mers plateau. The slopes of Cocumont (on the left bank of the Garonne) and Beaupuy (on the right) are planted with Bordeaux-type vines and give fresh, fruity white wines and supple, fragrant reds and rosés, all of real quality.

CÔTES DE DURAS

THE Duras area is dominated by the magnificent castle (twelfth to seventeenth century) perched on its high rock overlooking the Dropt valley. This is a transitional wine region, bordering on the Dordogne vineyards to the north and those of the Garonne to the south. It is part of the Guyenne hill region and is separated from its neighbour in the Gironde only by an administrative boundary. The land is hollowed out by the rivers Dropt and Dourdèze and consists of limestone hilltops where white grape varieties are grown, and stony clay and limestone slopes more suitable for Cabernet, Merlot and Malbec. White wine used to be mainly sweet and there is still some Sémillon and a small amount of Muscadelle, Ondenc and Pineau de la Loire grown in the area. Now white wines are principally made from Sauvignon, with ideal growing conditions here. They are fresh and scented, with much liveliness and breeding, and quite able to stand comparison with the other great Sauvignon regions. The red wines are often based on individual grape varieties: they have strong colour and meatiness, or can be light and fragrant when made by the carbonic maceration process. There are a few good keeping wines, aged in oak casks.

The sixteenth-century château of Buzet, with thirteenth-century tower.

CAHORS AND GAILLAC

THE two great tributaries of the Garonne, the rivers Lot and Tarn, run through a series of secret gorges and delightful, deep valleys. It is here that the two historic wine regions of Cahors and Gaillac have grown up and established their special identity over the centuries. The greater extremes of weather here where Atlantic and Continental systems meet and the difference in the vines grown all make this region seem very unlike its neighbours in Aquitaine.

CAHORS – LAND OF CONTRASTS

THE Cahors vineyards are all round the city itself, on isolated plateaux along the twists and loops of the Lot gorges, and interconnected by few roads. There are many separate levels in this rather fragmented area. The valley floor close to the river consists of recent alluvial deposits of fertile silt not used for vine-growing, which begins on the older alluvial soils formed into terraces and gentle slopes. These thin soils are made up of quartz pebbles, siliceous gravel mixed with red clay, and ferruginous sands over an imperme-able ironpan subsoil: all this means a good water supply for the vine roots. These alluvial deposits are mixed with Causse scree and patches of the limestone substratum are also visible.

At the top of the sometimes very steep hillsides overhanging the valley there is the Causses area, where vines once flourished before being devas-tated by phylloxera. There have been some attempts to replant these ancient vineyards, especially round the charm-ing château of Haute-Serre; and here and there on this stony plateau with its little eroded valleys, vines do manage to grow among great stretches of wilderness and occasional oak trees, which harbour Quercy's other main gastronomic treasure: truffles. Grapes ripen well on these warm, shallow soils but the permeable limestone subsoil gives no protection against drought. In winter, the cold here is extreme and the frosts much to be feared. The valley area, however, has its own favourable microclimate: the sides of the valley concentrate the sun's heat and shelter the lower part from cold air, which remains trapped on the Causses. Plots which face the south-east provide the best conditions for ripening.

Left, Puy-l'Evêque.

Below, Bastide house at Cahors.

THE AUXERROIS GRAPE

IN Quercy there is endless argument about whether the best Cahors wine comes from the valley or the Causses, from old or new vineyards. At least it is agreed that the wine inherits its principal character from one grape – the Auxerrois, usually called Côt, or Malbec in Bordeaux, Pressac in Libourne, Pied-rouge in Lot-et-Garonne, Grofforin in the Charentes region, and Grelot in Tours. The terrain here suits it very well and allows the wine to achieve all its potential colour, fragrance and structure. There may be additions of Jurançon Noir (or 'Folle Noire'), which grows very well on the Causses, of Tannat or of Merlot, but Cahors is the only red wine *appellation* in the South-west to withstand the temptation to grow Cabernet Sauvignon. This is how Cahors has succeeded in remaining so individual and close to its regional roots.

CENTURIES OF TURMOIL

THE wine of Cahors was drunk by Roman emperors, chronicled throughout the centuries, and certainly used as communion wine by the Orthodox Church. In England it was known as 'black wine'. There have been splendid periods in the history of Quercy and some disastrous times as well. With vines first ravaged by phylloxera and then annihilated by frosts in 1956, the Cahors wine industry became almost extinct. Fortunately, the energetic managers of the *cave* at Parnac, which has previously had some large estates, and also some remarkably self-reliant proprietors, have together been determined enough to re-establish its former reputation. This has been made easier by the strong personality of the local growers, often as colourful as their own wine and immensely attached to the province of Quercy. Recently, the Comte de Montpezat, the Grand Master of the Confrérie des Vins de Cahors, has brought the whole image of wine-growing into the public

eye. His daughter-in-law, the Queen of Denmark, has also contributed to local prestige by acquiring the Château de Caïx in this area.

The Cahors *appellation* consists of a single wine, diverse though this is. With their deep, intense colour, Cahors wines are fruity and substantial in youth. For two or three years they stay rather austerely closed up, but their powerful tannic qualities ensure that they age well and come into bloom as round full-bodied wines. The miraculous partnership between Cahors and truffles is not just poetic imagination. The flavours of this mysterious fungus are enhanced by the spicy fragrance of this ancient wine of Quercy.

GAILLAC

'ERO *piquant et sautabo dins lou veyre*', ('It sparkled and danced in the glass'). In the sixteenth century, 150 years before Dom Pérignon invented Champagne, the Languedoc poet Auger Gaillard was celebrating the

sparkling wine of Gaillac. This shows how prosperous the region was. It was one of the first wine regions to have what in effect was an *appellation contrôlée* when, in 1221, a charter issued by Count Raymond VII of Toulouse protected local wine by enforcing the marking of casks and forbidding foreign imports.

Gaillac is situated in the Albi region and is a patchwork of vineyards centred on this little port on the river Tarn. The wine industry was

influenced by the presence of the small industrial area of Graulhet and production has reflected social and economic conditions in the region. In the past, with the Carmaux mine nearby, this meant wine for everyday local consumption, but industrial change has recently encouraged a swing back to growing higher quality wine on the hillsides.

With its intermediate position between the Atlantic and the Mediterranean, the crossroads character of the Gaillac wine region is evident in the variety of its *domaines* and the diverseness of soils and grape varieties. The *appellation* divides into five distinct parts: on the left bank of the Tarn are terraces of gravel and round pebbles and, slightly separate, the Cunac clay and gravel zone suitable for red grapes; in the plain only the old alluvial deposits are used for wine growing; on the right bank, well-exposed molasse slopes with superficial sand and gravel deposits are sites favoured for white grapes; north of these are well-defined clay and limestone hillsides; finally, the Cordes area, backed up against the forest sheltering it from north winds, has saddles of limestone very suitable for dry white wines. With its damp springs and long dry autumns, the Gaillac region seems to waver between Atlantic, Mediterranean and mountain climates. There seems to be similar indecision about choice of grapes and methods of production. Cahors produces a single wine – Gaillac seems to have them all! Local grapes, which over the centuries have given wines a particular style (*Len de l'el*

Gaillac: above, the abbey of Saint-Michel, and below left, vines round Château Camille Portes.

– *Loin de l'oeil* or 'far from sight' – Ondenc and Mauzac for white wines; Duras, which gives the *appellation* much of its distinctive character; Braucol and Fer Servadou for red wines), have suffered from fashions in replanting and have been joined by Cabernet Franc and Cabernet Sauvignon, Merlot, Sauvignon and Sémillon. These show the powerful attraction of Bordeaux a long way to the west, but there are also Négrette, Muscadelle and Jurançon Rouge from nearby Fronton, and even Syrah and Gamay from further east.

In such conditions it is understandable that local wines are extremely varied in style and character. They range from the slightly sparkling 'Moustillant' (not included in the *appellation*), which brings back fond memories of the 'rough' new wine once common in bars at harvest-time; classical red wine for keeping, with a spicy nose and good backbone; dry white wines (Perlés and sweet); rosés, red *primeurs* and finally sparkling wines, made either by the *méthode champenoise*, or by a local method in which the sparkling quality is produced by allowing residual natural sugar to ferment in the bottle. A series of rackings stops the first fermentation and the wine still contains some yeasts when it is bottled. This small-scale, so-called Gaillac method is comparable with the method for Blanquette de Limoux, a rival for the title of the oldest sparkling wine.

THE DORDOGNE

THE province of Périgord can boast three magnificent produces – truffle, cep (edible boletus fungus) and *foie gras* – and three traditional districts – Périgord Noir, Vert and Blanc.

At Castillon every summer the famous battle of 1453 is re-enacted, which drove the English out of Aquitaine. Upstream from here the Périgord wine region is an extension of the Libourne vineyards and everything – weather, soil and grapes – has an obvious family likeness to its western neighbour. The Dordogne valley with its terraced hillsides and undulating plateaux is one of the finest in the South-west. Brilliant sunflower

fields, castles and manor-houses, quiet old abbeys and villages form a tranquil landscape in which men have lived since prehistoric times.

From the Gironde boundary east of Castillon-la-Bataille to Saint-Pierre d'Eyraud, the *appellation* covers only the right bank and its older alluvial terraces (thin leached soils with a plateau of sand and gravel to the north). Further upstream, on the north bank there is an area of gravel hillside; on the south bank some clay and limestone slopes and plateaux of

stony clay and silt. The weather is a cross between the Continental and Atlantic systems and grape varieties typical of Aquitaine are able to ripen in the autumn sunshine. The still predominant white wine is based on Sauvignon for dry wines, and Sémillon and Muscadelle for sweet, together with a small amount of Ugni Blanc, Ondenc and Chenin. The red wines, made from Cabernet (Sauvignon and Franc), Merlot and possibly some Malbec, have a Gironde flavour with variations according to the soil.

Bergerac wines have remained rather distinct from others in this upland region and have lived on better terms of coexistence with Bordeaux. The river Dordogne flows into the Gironde estuary beyond Bordeaux, making it possible to avoid the Port de la Lune. After the Revocation of the Edict of Nantes in 1685, there were a great many Protestant refugees from Périgord. They reinforced trading links with their countries of exile, especially Germany and The Netherlands, and encouraged the buyers' taste for sweet wines. For a long time this influenced the kind of wine produced in Périgord.

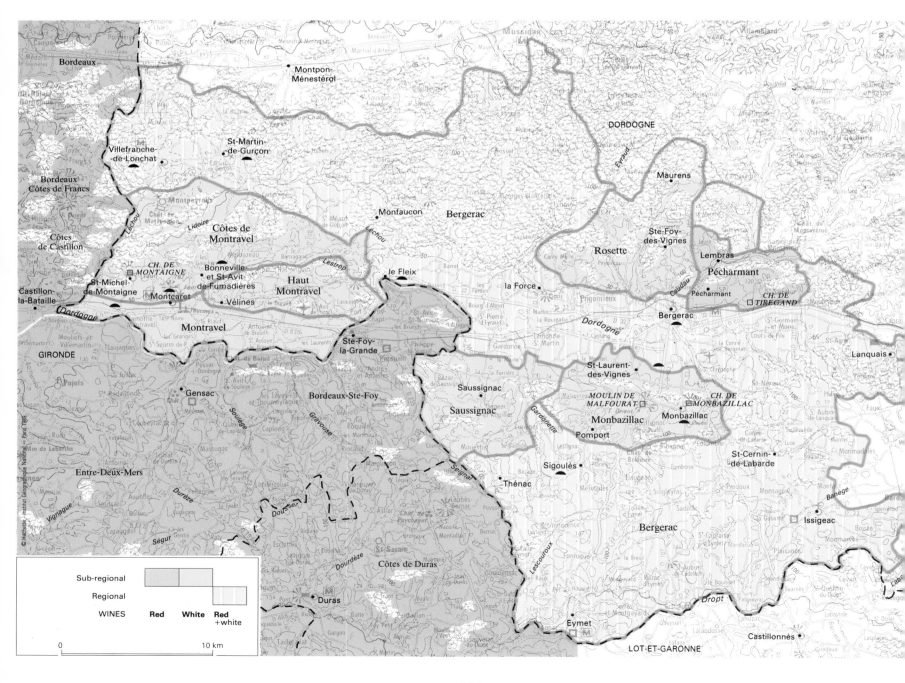

BERGERAC AND CÔTES DE BERGERAC

THE Bergerac regional *appellation* covers all ninety-three communes in the Bergerac district. The hillsides on the whole are left to other AOC, and Bergerac is grown on plateaux extending each side of the river behind other local *appellations*. The reds are best drunk young and are usually supple, light and fragrant; the whites are lively and fruity (based on an increasing proportion of Sauvignon); and the rosés have a supple fruitiness.

Côtes de Bergerac are more robust, deep-coloured red wines than the plain Bergerac and have better ageing potential. The whites are sweet and light with just a hint of sharpness and make delicately scented apéritif wines.

MONTRAVEL

ON the very edge of the Gironde, the AOC Montravel gets its name from the delightful village of Lamothe-Montravel. The *appellation* is subdivided into Montravel, Haut-Montravel and Côtes de Montravel. The first of these is grown on the plain alongside the Dordogne and consists of dry white wines of firmness and refinement. From the slopes to the north come the elegant, well-balanced sweet Côtes de Montravel. Between the two is Haut-Montravel, where the more calcareous soils give sweet wines of great charm and breeding. These wines have just the right balance of lusciousness and vivacity, and with age take on a marvellous golden colour and scents of honey and warm fruit.

SAUSSIGNAC

THE small Saussignac *appellation* from the left bank of the Dordogne is well known for its smooth, sweet wines. These are very scented and elegant, halfway between Bergerac and Montravel on the one hand and Monbazillac on the other. They are fresh when young and fatter and more substantial as they mature.

The Renaissance château of Monbazillac.

PÉCHARMANT AND ROSETTE

THE small, enticingly named red wine *appellation* of Pécharmant to the north of Bergerac consists of 180 hectares on clay and gravel slopes with a very favourable southern aspect. There is here a very distinctive subsoil known as *tran*; this is strongly ferruginous and in the first few years produces characteristic rustic tastes which balance and harmonize very well as the wine matures. Of all the Dordogne wines, the Pécharmant is the most worth keeping. Deep-coloured, strong and substantial, it has an edge of tannin, which benefits from ageing four to six years in the bottle.

Rosette straddles the Pécharmant and Bergerac districts and is an *appellation* for a light sweet wine. There is some reticence about the volume of wine produced.

MONBAZILLAC

THE splendid château of Monbazillac rises out of the vines on hills above the Dordogne valley. It is now owned by the local *coopérative* and has become the symbol for the most famous Dordogne *appellation*. On clay and limestone slopes with a northern aspect, the five communes of Monbazillac, Pomport, Saint-Laurent des Vignes, Colombier and Rouffignac de Sigoulès produce from 2,700 hectares one of the oldest sweet dessert wines in France. In the district between the Dordogne and the Gardonette, the morning mists in autumn set off the noble rot (*Botrytis*

cinerea), which softens the skin on the grapes and allows the juice to evaporate and concentrate in the afternoon sun until the 'roasted' scent typical of this sort of wine appears. The grapes at this stage look like candied fruit, with little juice but a high sugar content.

As with Sauternes, the grapes are harvested in batches as they reach this stage of roasted ripeness. The must often reaches a level of 16° of alcohol and only part of the sugar is fermented off; the rest contributes to the natural liquorous texture of the wine.

These are deep golden, full-bodied wines with little acidity, powerful and long on the palate, with hints of honey and hazelnuts and toasted fruity aromas. Monbazillacs are classic 'liqueur' wines, capable of lasting

Conques, the abbey church of Sainte Foy.

years. It is unfortunate that they have sometimes been relegated to the rôle of dessert wines and have been hit by the fashionable dislike for *vins liquoureux*. They have rightly been reinstated in new gastronomic partnership with *foie gras* or *poularde à la crème* (chicken in rich cream sauces).

AVEYRON WINES

AT the foot of Mont Aubrac, the so-called 'meat mountain', with its summer pastures and herds of pale golden cows, are the picturesque, small-scale *appellations* of the province of Rouergue. In this mountainous landscape, on the narrow, rocky terraces carved out of the hillside, the vineyards of Marcillac, Entraygues and Estaing are relics of a local wine industry which owed its former prosperity to the monks of the Abbey of Conques. Even the houses look different from those in the other wine regions of the South-west, and stone and slate here take the place of brick and Roman tiles. The Aveyron vines introduce a touch of lightheartedness to this majestic, but sometimes harsh and austere setting.

At Marcillac, in a natural basin with its own favourable microclimate, the Mansoi vine (the local name for Fer Servadou) produces very individual raspberry-scented tannic red wines (VDQS). This is an instantly recognizable wine, to be drunk with *tripoux de rouergue* (tripe with sheep's trotters). Scarcely 20 hectares cling to the steep hillside on narrow terraces, which often have only two rows of vines: these are the VDQS vineyards of Entraygues and Fel, which produce substantial, fruity red wines (based on Fer, Cabernets and Gamay) on the schistous Fel soils, and sappy, scented white wines (based on Chenin) on the clayey siliceous soils called *barènes*.

At Estaing (VDQS) on the so-called *adrechs*, minute terraces with one or two rows of vines which manage to catch the reluctant sunshine, some characterful peasant wines are produced from a medley of local grapes. Abouriou, Moussaygues and Gamay are some of those used for fresh and fruity reds; and Chenin and Rousselou for the crisp, fragrant whites.

THE PYRENEAN WINE REGION

WHETHER in the Basque country or Gascony, every little village in the Pyrenean foothills has wanted to produce its own wine. Perhaps it was a pretext for drinking with travellers, who may be called tourists today but were formerly pilgrims on their way to Santiago, about to enter the alien world of high mountain valleys. The wine-growers here have a strong sense of regional identity. They may express this by wearing a 'pancake' (a beret worn flat on their heads), by their tough and cheerful characters, and by strong attachment to the old *appellations*. The wine slopes, produced here by Tertiary glaciation or deposits from mountain torrents, are huddled against the mountains, with forests and pastures on the hillsides above and maize fields and orchards further down. Vines here are not predominant, but they continue to be cultivated according to the historic traditions laid down by their founders, the abbeys and hospices along the path of Saint James of Compostella.

JURANÇON

THE vineyards of Jurançon owe their fame to the royal house of Navarre, which became that of France under Henri IV (1553–1610), but they seem to be hidden away south of Pau as if reluctant to be seen by the visitor in a hurry. Behind a rocky ridge, on the sunnier sections of very precipitous hillsides, there are fragments of vineyards belonging to Monein, Lasseube, Lahourcade, Gan and Jurançon, the latter with

the famous crest of La Chapelle de Rousse.

Enjoying a weather system influenced by both the Atlantic and the Pyrenees, the vines are cultivated on espaliers 1.70 m high to escape the spring frosts, a custom surviving from the time when they were trained up fruit trees. The wine region certainly vies with Roussillon and Corsica for the title of the most southerly in France, but enjoys weather more like that in some northern wine areas. The scree soils are clay and limestone or clay and siliceous with a high proportion of pebbles. Three local grape varieties contribute to the very individual Jurançon wines: Gros Manseng, Courbu and Petit Manseng. According to one story, there is an example of the latter vine at the château of Pau, brought from Fontainebleau where Henry IV had planted it at a time when he was anxious to keep near him a piece of his beloved land of Béarn.

The Petit Manseng is not very productive but is known for the way the grape skin allows *passerillage* (the lengthy concentration of juices in the grape), a process which can last until the late harvests, sometimes even until the first snow. This is the variety for the best sweet wine, smooth with scents of honey and exotic fruit, and a touch of green to give a light airy character. These wines age well and can be classed with the greatest wines.

Gros Manseng will give dry fruit-scented white wines, some of which will keep. Lastly, Courbu contributes to the very distinctive balance of these wines, which are still greatly underrated.

Above, the Jurançon region.
Below, Irouléguy.

IROULÉGUY

THE wine of Irouléguy is grown in the Atlantic climate of the Pays Basque, on the south-facing lower slopes of the steep valleys of Baïgorry, Irouléguy and Anhaux. This *appellation* is all that is left of an ancient wine region once stretching as far as Bayonne, and still indicated by the name Ardantz (meaning 'vine' in Basque) on a medieval house. The vineyards here produce the *vin basque* which is drunk all over the world by exiled members of that nomadic race.

BÉARN

MOST of the Béarn AOC territory is in the pleasant hills of the Entre-deux-Gaves region, round the town of Salies-de-Béarn and downstream from Orthez on the left bank of the Pau river.

This rather divided *appellation* also includes two fragments in the

Madiran and Jurançon zones. It produces some very aromatic white wines based mainly on Raffiat de Moncade; the lively, delicate rosés and the robust, full-bodied reds come from the same grape varieties as the Madiran wines.

MADIRAN

THE Madiran wine region spreads into the *départements* of Pyrénées Atlantiques, Hautes Pyrénées and Gers and is situated on hills overlooking the Adour valley, on clay and limestone and also siliceous soils, mixed with fine-particled gravels. Tannat, the predominant grape, produces inky-coloured, virile and tannic wines. Its solid framework is rounded out with the complementary scent and suppleness given by Cabernet Sauvignon, Bouchy (or Cabernet Franc), Pinenc or Fer Servadou. Some traditional Madiran wines are raised in wood and can be kept, but there are lighter, fresh and fragrant wines for drinking at once. Madiran's tannic qualities bring out the smooth sweetness of *confit d'oie* (preserved goose) and its distinctive regional character is just right for the taste of the local *salmis de palombe* (a rich wood-pigeon stew) and *magrets rôtis* (roasted duck fillets).

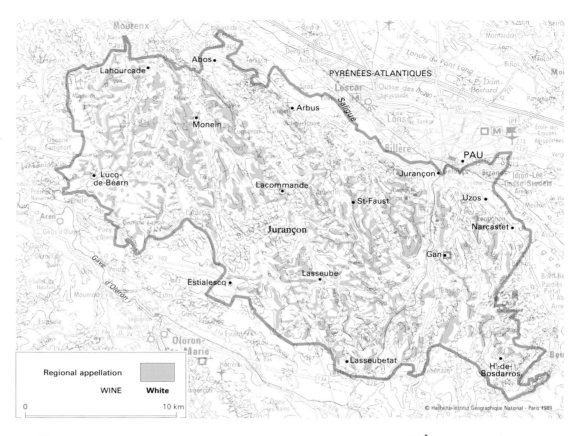

Left, Tannat grapes.

Right, one of the mosaics found in 1868 and 1911 at the Gallo-Roman villa, Séviac-Montréal.

PACHERENC DU VIC-BILH

THIS AOC has a curious and uninformative name: 'Vic-Bilh' means 'old country' in the Béarnais language, but it overlaps with that of Madiran and includes the lines of hills in northeastern Béarn. The wines that come from here are very individual whites based on Arrufiat, Manseng, Courbu, Sémillon and Sauvignon. Sweet or dry, these are full, substantial wines with aromas of dried fruit and the potential for several years' ageing.

TURSAN

THE small Tursan VDQS area, with its perched villages, extends northwest of Madiran, in the softer hills of the Chalosse region. Here a distinctive grape variety known as Baroque is used for some characteristic local white wine. There are also some solid and virile reds and rosés based on Tannat, Pinenc and Cabernet.

CÔTES DE SAINT-MONT

THE VDQS Côtes de Saint-Mont continue on from Madiran on hills alongside the river Adour and upstream from Aire-Sur-Adour. This area uses the same vine varieties as its neighbours and produces some characteristic well-balanced red wines of considerable roundness and warmth, and some lively, fragrant dry whites. They have more suppleness than the Madiran wines, but still a unique local character.

'OUR HENRY'

THE wine of Jurançon entered history in 1553 at the baptism of Henri de Navarre, lord of Béarn, who was later to ascend the French throne as Henri IV. The people of Béarn have always regarded him as their particular king – 'lou nouste Henric' ('our Henry'). To make the baby strong and vigorous, his grandfather, Henri d'Albret, decided to rub his lips with a garlic clove and then gave him a few drops of Jurançon to take the sting away.

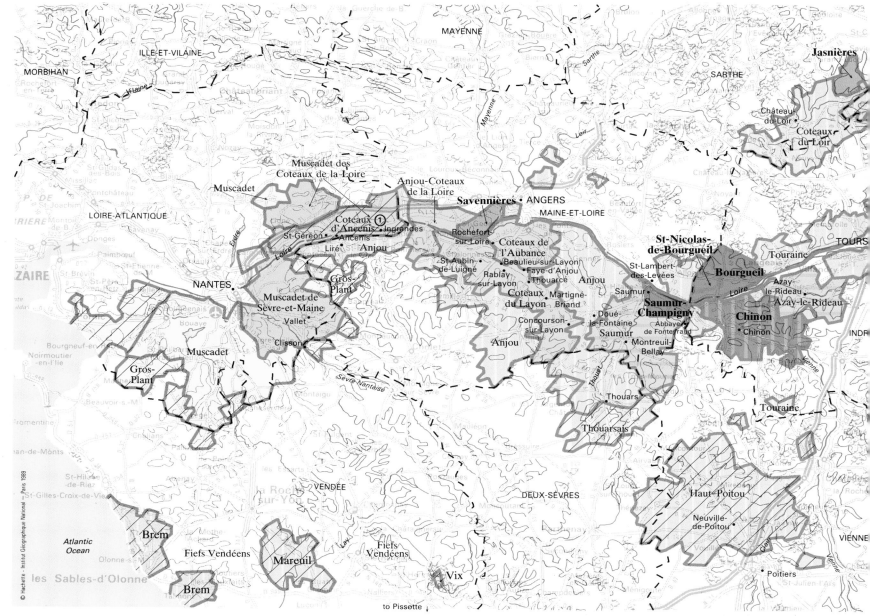

Pineau d'Aunis.

THE Loire Valley, famous for its mild climate and magnificent Renaissance châteaux, produces fruity, delicate wines with the luminous clarity of the local skies. Nowadays most of the production is spread over four large AOC regions: the Pays Nantais (Muscadet: 600,000 hl), Anjou and Saumur (800,000 hl), Touraine (500,000 hl), and the Sancerre and Pouilly region (130,000 hl), all on choice sites bordering the 'royal' river and its tributaries.

THE TWENTY LEAGUE EDICT

IN the Middle Ages various wine areas had their moments of fame, but, in the sixteenth century, uncontrolled wine-growing began encroaching even on the outskirts of Paris. Both as a public health measure and as a check on sales and taxes, the Paris Parlement in 1577 issued an edict forbidding merchants and innkeepers to obtain their supplies of wine within a 20 league (88 km) perimeter drawn round Paris. In effect, this gave a monopoly to the Orléans region, encouraging unscrupulous practices and mediocre grape varieties. Although this edict was rescinded in 1789, high-quality wine production in the Loiret and Loir-et-Cher *départements* was to be held back for many years.

VALLEY

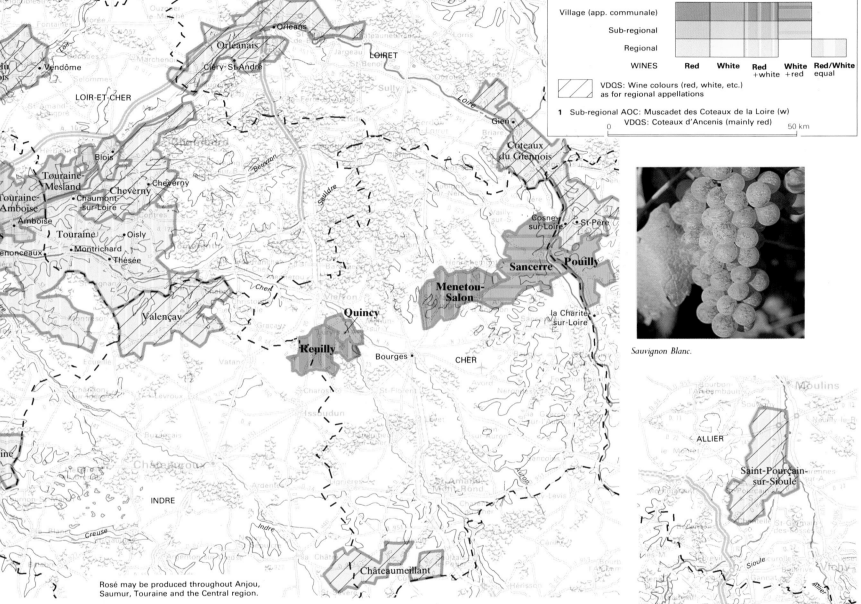

Sauvignon Blanc.

Rosé may be produced throughout Anjou,
Saumur, Touraine and the Central region.

Chenin.

HISTORY

UP to the last century, the Loire and its tributaries formed a major navigable waterway. The sixteenth century was a golden age for the region, both in the arts and in political and economic life, although all this came to a brutal end with the Wars of Religion.

The wine trade had been active since the Middle Ages. From the time of the Plantagenet kings, the English aristocracy had been buying wine in Anjou and the Loire Valley, as far up-river as Saint Pourçain near Vichy. This was then shipped out from Nantes, after payment of customs dues at Ingrandes, then a border town between France and the province of Brittany. Right up until the Revolution, wine destined to be exported overseas from Anjou and Touraine had

to compete with wine from Nantes, and needed to be good enough to sell in spite of the additional taxation. This to compete with wine from Nantes, and needed to be good enough to sell in spite of the additional taxation. This explains why the provinces upstream pursued a tradition of quality, whereas the Nantes region in the seventeenth century began growing common grape varieties.

A FAVOURED CLIMATE

THE Loire vineyard sites are all on the eastern face of hills, which draw down excessive moisture from the prevailing Atlantic winds, giving the valley a rainfall of less than 600 mm per year and a mild, sunny climate. The Anjou wine region, sheltered by the Mauges hills, and the Sancerre region, sheltered by hills of around 400 m, are perfect examples of this configuration. Most of the good wine areas are on tributaries where Atlantic influences can cut across.

VARIED GEOLOGY

THESE are the northernmost limits for growing vines. Consequently, they can flourish only on carefully selected soils.

As a rule, vines grow on slopes turned away from the north, or on river terraces with a favourable climate. In the Nantes region, in Anjou as far up as Ponts-de-Cé, and in the Britanny massif, vine-growing soils lie

Left, 'La Cène' ('The Last Supper'), one of Jean Fouquet's paintings for the Etienne Chevalier Book of Hours, around 1446 (Musée Condé, Chantilly).
Below left, the month of September, from a late fifteenth century Book of Hours (Bibliothèque d'Angers).

over granite, gneiss and particularly schist, with patches of volcanic rock in some exceptional sites. From Blois as far as Ponts-de-Cé, the Loire makes its way past cliffs of tufa and old quarries form galleries where sparkling wine is made. Where rock forming the upper part of the cliffs is not covered with silt, it provides excellent warm sites for vines. The flinty, so-called *perruches* soils are especially suitable for white grapes, as at Vouvray. Turonian chalk, rich in mica and glauconite, forms clayey limestone slopes particularly favouring red wines. The Aubuis terrain, on chalky tufa, is less suitable.

The old terraces of sandy gravel known here as *varennes*, are valuable sites for red wine. In the Orléans area, wine-growing has survived only on the narrow strip of gravel terraces along the river Loire and the Loiret. Between Sancerre and Pouilly, the Kimmeridgian marl soils are similar to those at Chablis in Burgundy. Continuing up the valley to Saint-Pourçain, at the confluence of the Sioule and the Allier, there are old gravel terraces, Tertiary limestone soils, and soils (like those of

Beaujolais) overlying the Precambrian crystalline bedrock. Soil and climate here are both remarkable and help to explain the popularity of this wine area in medieval times.

Loire wines are principally whites or *clairets*, light-coloured wines produced by the brief maceration of fruity red grape varieties. There are four categories of classic grape varieties.

GRAPES ORIGINATING IN THE LOIRE REGION

CHENIN Noir, or Pineau d'Aunis, is the oldest Loire variety; it makes a delicious, characterful rosé but is uncommon now in Anjou or Touraine. It is agreed that selection from Chenin Noir produced the white variety known as Pineau de la Loire or Chenin Blanc, the principal grape of Anjou and Touraine. This is a grape that ripens late, in the first cold autumn weather, and develops an inimitable flavour when grown on the exceptional sites of Coteaux du Layon, and at Savennières, Vouvray and around Saumur. Although Chenin Blanc is the

◄——————— ANJOU ———————►◄—— TOURAINE ——►

◄—— Anjou 'noir' ——►◄—— Anjou 'blanc' – Saumur region ——►

SW

NE

CHOLET   CONCOURSON   SAUMUR   ST-NICOLAS-DE-BOURGUEIL

River Layon   River Thouet   River Loire

200 m

100 m

Tufa chalk

Granites and granitic rocks   Fault   Senonian   Recent alluvial deposits   Old alluvial deposits   Lower Turonian

Briovenian schists   Carboniferous   Miocene shell-marl   Secondary sands and marls

predominant variety in these areas, it is dwindling elsewhere because of cultivation problems.

Sauvignon also comes into the first category of grapes grown in the Loire, although there is some argument about whether it originated there or in the Bordeaux region. Recent research has shown that Chenin and Sauvignon are in fact related. This strongly aromatic white grape was fairly widespread throughout the Loire valley and the south-west as late as the seventeenth century, although its use subsequently declined. Now it is popular and is the only variety permitted for the white wine of Sancerre, Pouilly-Fumé, Quincy, Menetou-Salon and Reuilly. It is also predominant in Touraine.

SOUTH-WESTERN VARIETIES

THESE include the Cabernet varieties from Bordeaux and the Côt from Cahors. There is also the Négrette from Fronton, still grown in the Vendée and Poitou.

The Cabernet varieties undoubtedly originated in the Bordeaux area. In the Loire Valley, however, Cabernet Franc acquired the name Breton, since it arrived by way of Nantes in Britanny. It gives elegantly fruity and long-keeping red wines, grown on the *varennes* and chalky slopes of Bourgeuil, Chinon and Saumur-Champigny. Elsewhere it does less well, except in the Layon valleys and in the Brissac region of Anjou, where it produces distinguished AOC Anjou-Villages and some velvety rosés.

The Côt grape is susceptible to frost damage, so growing it is rather troublesome, but it was once the principal variety of the Indre and Cher valleys in Touraine, and also of the Poitou region. After the phylloxera disaster it was supplanted by coarser varieties, although it is now being cultivated again in Touraine.

Folle Blanche, the Gros Plant of the Nantes region, is an important variety used for distilling the finest Cognac and Armagnac *eaux-de-vie*, although it has disappeared from the place where it originated because of its susceptibility to oïdium and mildew. In the cool conditions of the Pays Nantais it is possible to cultivate it, but it is a very productive variety, difficult to turn into a dry wine. In fact, it has another name, *Enrageant*, meaning infuriating.

BURGUNDY VARIETIES

IN the Middle Ages, Pinot Noir and Gris Meunier, together with Chardonnay, had already been introduced to Saint-Pourçain. From there they found their way to Touraine and the Orléans region, where they are still known as Auvernat Noir and Auvernat Blanc. Pinot Noir remains the official variety for red and rosé wines in the Sancerre region; its use is also expanding in the AOC and VDQS areas of central France. Chardonnay too is more widely cultivated, especially as a basis for the sparkling Crémant de Loire in Anjou and Touraine.

The variety called Melon de Bourgogne, now practically unknown in Burgundy, came to rest in the eighteenth century in the Sèvre and Maine valleys of the Pays Nantais, where it acquired the name Muscadet.

NEW VARIETIES

THESE are principally the Grolleau and the Gamay Noir à Jus Blanc. Grolleau originated at Cinq-Mars in the Touraine at the beginning of the nineteenth century and has since then spread almost to excess. The heavy crop gives a pleasant carafe rosé and is used to make Loire and Anjou rosé wines.

The family of Gamays is enormous. They are used mainly for the *vins ordinaires*, which were blamed for the decline of the Loire and Burgundy wine regions in the eighteenth and nineteenth centuries. However, the cultivation of Gamay Noir à Jus Blanc in the classic Beaujolais manner dates from the middle of the nineteenth century, when the Princesse de Croy's success with it contributed to the reputation of this *appellation*. In the last twenty years it has been planted in the Cher valley of eastern Touraine, where it gives a well-rounded wine when blended with Côt or with Cabernet.

Other local grape varieties still survive in limited areas, such as the Romorantin at Cheverny and the Tressalier at Saint-Pourçain.

THE LOIRE TODAY

THE controls of the AOC system have ensured the progress in quality of the Loire wines. Between 1955 and 1985 the AOC area of Touraine has doubled and that of Sancerre has more than tripled. The Anjou wine region has remained static but, with the decline in sweet white wine, has undergone major replanting. The area

The Grolleau Gris grape variety.
Chinon: the town and castle.

of Chenin has decreased from 9,000 to 4,500 hectares in thirty years, replaced mainly by Cabernet Franc. Muscadet continues to gain in reputation and is one of the Loire Valley's great successes. Overall, during this period, the Loire *appellation* vineyards have increased from 29,000 to 40,000 hectares, and their wines now make up 12 per cent of French AOC wines. Most of these are white wines, particularly important in the export market and the region is now fourth in importance in the export trade.

The Loire wine areas include three main regions:

The lower Loire consists mainly of the Nantes wine region, based on sites in the Britanny massif. The weather here is the most subject to Atlantic influence and the choice of grape varieties owes much to particular factors in Breton history.

The middle Loire from Angers up to Blois covers the wine regions of Anjou, Saumur, Touraine and peripheral sites in Poitou and the valley of the Loir. Chenin, or Pineau de la Loire, predominates for white wine; Cabernet for red. The latter is particularly successful at the confluence of the Vienne and the Thouet, giving the wines of Bourgueil, Chinon and Saumur-Champigny. The middle Loire is also the area where Pineau d'Aunis and Grolleau are grown to produce the majority of rosés. The Rosés de Loire and Crémants de Loire areas overlap with those of the Anjou and Touraine *appellations* and are based on the same grape varieties.

Lastly, the small and scattered wine areas of central France occupy some varied sites where the Loire cuts across the geological strata of the Paris Basin.

scattered throughout this huge area, do not really amount to an autonomous wine region. Gros Plant gives a very crisp wine, which goes well with seafood. It has certainly been successful but could decline slightly due to regional marketing limitations.

Muscadet and Gros Plant are, subject to certain controls, the only French wines entitled to use the description *sur lie*. This refers to a special wine-making method in which the wine is not drawn off directly after fermentation, but remains on the lees or sediment. This is a refined technique which intensifies both flavour and freshness but requires healthy crops and very careful vinification.

The area of VDQS Coteaux d'Ancenis covers that of Coteaux de la Loire, with a few additional villages. It includes about 300 hectares, mainly planted with Gamay and Anjou grape varieties. The principal producers are at Oudon, Saint-Géréon and Le Cellier on the right bank, and at Liré, Champtoceaux and La Varenne on the left bank. The Ancenis *coopérative* has greatly helped this *appellation*.

The VDQS Fiefs Vendéens is not actually in the Pays Nantais, nor in the Loire basin, but could be included alongside the wines of Brittany. This wine was recognized as a VDQS in 1984, rewarding growers for their efforts in maintaining the wine-growing traditions of these medieval church lands or *fiefs*. Their existence can be documented from the early seventeenth century. This 300 hectare wine region is divided into four small pockets of land around Mareuil, Brem, Vix and Pissotte. Red wine is the main production, based especially on Gamay and Pinot, but rosés and white wines (mainly Chenin) produced in the Vendée coastal area can also be interesting.

Vallet, in central Muscadet. France's largest wine fair takes place here in March.

THE NANTES REGION

A visit to the Nantes wine region, situated south-west of the city of Nantes along the valleys of the Sèvre and the Maine, makes it clear why sixth-century Breton invaders decided to settle there. It is a delightful area and vines also seem to feel at home in these river valleys. The boundaries of the present Loire-Atlantique and Maine-et-Loire *départements* coincide with the former frontier between Brittany and France.

There are no visible traces of any wine-growing undertaken by the dukes who once ruled Brittany. In the sixteenth century, Brittany was united with France but retained her former trading rights. This privilege was a disaster for high-quality wine-growing, as the Nantes region held the monopoly in the seventeenth century for supplying *vins ordinaires* to Dutch shippers buying wine and brandy for export. It was their influence that allowed vineyards to be taken over by Folle Blanche (Gros Plant). The seventeenth-century statesman Colbert was amazingly cogent in expressing his disquiet that northern consumers should be misled in this way about the authentic taste of French wine.

After the great frost of 1709, however, the cultivation of Muscadet or Melon, brought in from Burgundy in about 1639, spread throughout the best sites in the Pays Nantais. After the Second World War there were still barely 4,000 hectares of Muscadet under cultivation.

Because of the complexities of the past it is difficult to achieve uniformity among present-day growers, and a map of the Nantes wine-growing areas looks very complicated.

AOC Muscadet covers two sub-regions of unequal importance. Muscadet des Coteaux de la Loire (500 hectares) is grown on slopes of schist or granite, and is divided between the villages on the north bank of the Loire up to Varades and on the south bank up to Saint-Florent-le-Vieil, spreading across into Anjou. Muscadet de Sèvre-et-Maine is grown over 9,000 hectares in twenty-three villages and forms the core of the wine region.

Straight regional AOC Muscadet (800 hectares) occupies some forty villages in an area, mostly west of the Sèvre-et-Maine region. These are mainly scattered vineyards, on Miocene sandy gravel soils over the bedrock of the Armorican massif.

The VDQS Gros Plant du Pays Nantais (3,000 hectares), with a production area entirely overlapping that of Muscadet, also extends down through the Pays de Retz towards the Atlantic. The plots of Gros Plant,

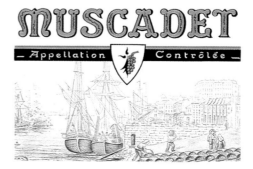

MUSCADET DE SÈVRE-ET-MAINE

MUSCADET is produced in a pleasant environment of cheerful, well cared for villages and seems to reflect this in its fragrance of fruit and flowers, and its elegant, smooth, mouth-filling qualities. The success of this wine is not just a fashion but a tribute to consistent achievement. The best-known villages are strung out on both sides of the river Sèvre, between Vertou and Clisson, where the vines grow on the schistous soil of undulating valleys. There are attractive roads leading through La Haie Fouassière and to the Maison des Vins at the highest point of the region (65 m). Saint-Fiacre, on the confluence of the Sèvre and the Maine, is often regarded as the local capital. Châteauthébaud, Maisdon-sur-Sèvre, Monnières and Gorges all have inviting wine cellars for visitors to wander around. The wine region comes to an end further south, giving way to the granite soils of Vendée woods and meadows. At Le Pallet you can look around the Pierre Abélard Museum of wine and local history,

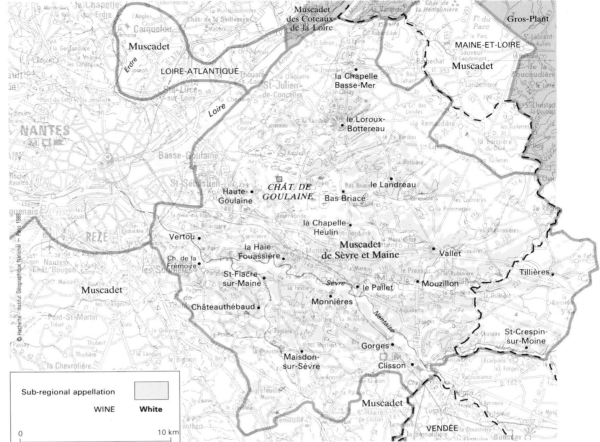

before going on to the small town of Vallet, a centre of Muscadet production, with an important March fair. The soils of this area, especially at Mouzillon, lie over ancient crystalline rock, the dark gabbros of Le Pallet.

AT THE BRITTANY BORDER

THE Sèvre-et-Maine wine region extends along either side of the Goulaine marshes. The Renaissance château of Haute-Goulaine is the last in the Loire Valley and the first in Brittany, and is built of a combination of tufa and granite. Gneiss and granite

Left, an eighteenth-century wine-press at La Haie Fouassière.

Right, Château du Coing at Saint-Fiacre.

soils reappear near the Brittany border, on the slopes near Le Loroux-Bottereau and La Chapelle-Basse-Mer.

Muscadet has a promising future as a traditional wine with solid professional backing. Eighty per cent of it is sold through specialized and energetic marketing concerns. An indicator of its success is the fact that 40 per cent is sold abroad. In France, too, the main buyers are from the Paris region, the north and the west, showing that Muscadet is no longer just the local wine it once was. Trade is particularly bustling during the many winter wine fairs.

The Confrérie des Bretvins wine fraternity, which meets in the Château of Goulaine, is one of the oldest in France and claims the fifteenth-century duchess Anne de Bretagne as its patroness.

ANJOU AND SAUMUR

THE Anjou wine region covers only a small part of what was once a powerful royal province on the borders of Normandy, Brittany and Poitou. The region is edged to the west by the valleys of the Maine and the Layon and has a mild climate sheltered from Atlantic influence by the wooded Vendée plain. The average annual rainfall of the Layon valley at Brissac is about 500 mm, making it one of the driest regions outside Mediterranean France. It is in the area of Anjou with a reputation for quality of life – or *douceur angevine*, as the sixteenth-century poet Du Bellay described it – that wine-growing is concentrated. More than 75 per cent of Anjou vineyards lie in a strip 50 km long and 10 km wide running southeast from Savennières to Les Verchers-sur-Layon.

Above, Coulée de Serrant: the enclosed vineyard.
Above right, 'Breton' vines near Brissac. Below, the Château de Fesles.

THE WINES OF ANJOU AND THEIR HISTORY

ANGERS is the principal city in this region and in medieval times was the centre of an important wine area. The

vineyards of Anjou were first cultivated between the eighth and twelfth centuries by large monasteries, and especially by the great Breton and Norman abbeys such as Mont-Saint-Michel. When the Count of Anjou, Henry Plantagenet, was crowned Henry II of England in 1154, the English aristocracy took to drinking white wines and *clairets* from the king's homeland. Even today, the United Kingdom is the principal export customer for Anjou wine. When in 1214 the French King Philippe Auguste finally wrested Anjou from King John at the battle of La Roche aux Moines, near Savennières, he ensured the support of the inhabitants mainly by giving up to them all feudal rights connected with the wine trade. The last Count of Anjou, who was also Count of Provence and King of Naples, was the legendary King René (1434–80). A poet, patron of the arts and an inspired and peaceful administrator, he turned Anjou after the Hundred Years War into the richest and most beautiful province in France. Through him, the fame of Anjou wines spread as far as Provence and Italy. The royal account books estimated wine production in Anjou at 300,000 *pipes* (1,300,000 hl) per year; more than is produced today.

During the seventeenth and eighteenth centuries, the constant wars with England and Holland and the ever-rising customs charges payable at the border town of Ingrandes caused a reduction in exports. At the end of the eighteenth century, there was a crisis in high-quality winegrowing. During the Revolution, the

Vendée wars devastated the vineyards and there were difficulties for the export trade under Napoleon. However, it was the Empress Joséphine, with her love of Coulée de Serrant wine from Savennières, who helped to reinstate Anjou wine in Paris.

Before the phylloxera epidemic, Anjou produced some 800,000 hl per year, an output very close to that of quality AOC today. Later replanting, with the introduction of hybrids and coarser grape varieties, was a threat to the classic varieties. Between 1950 and the present day the overall area under vines fell from 30,000 to 20,000 hectares, although the area under classic varieties remained stable at around 15,000 hectares. However, the proportions of white and red varieties have been transposed: Chenin used to cover 9,000 hectares, but now has only 4,500. Grolleau has also decreased and now covers only 3,000 hectares; on the other hand, Cabernet (more than 90 per cent of it Cabernet Franc) has increased

to more than 5,500 hectares.

It could be argued that it is now time for Anjou to stop diverging from its tradition of white Chenin wines. There has been much work on both sweet and dry white wines and on reds from carefully restricted sites. In October 1987 the new *appellation* of Anjou-Villages was recognized, which is made entirely from Cabernet Franc and Cabernet Sauvignon. The former rather undistinguished image of ubiquitous Anjou rosé will gradually fade with the introduction of these more refined wines.

In Angers the Hôtel de la Godeline, the city's first Hôtel de Ville in the fifteenth century, has been restored and is now the meeting place for the Conseil Interprofessionnel des Vins d'Anjou and for the Confrérie des Chevaliers des Sacavins. A specimen vine can be seen growing within the walls of the castle, and there is a wine museum and a Maison des Vins for tasting all the regional wines in the grounds of the former Hôpital Saint-Jean, where the well-known modern tapestries of Jean Lurçat (the 'Chant du monde'), are also exhibited. The magnificent fourteenth-century tapestries depicting the Apocalypse are on show in the castle.

SAVENNIÈRES AND THE COTEAUX DU LAYON

THE vineyards of Anjou have special features resulting from their situation at the juncture of Precambrian terrain from the Armorican massif and the Mesozoic sedimentary sites in the Paris Basin.

Vines are grown on the rocky corniches of the Layon valley and on slopes near Saumur. The Savennières vineyards face south-east, downstream from where the Maine runs into the Loire, and extend over four principal slopes, in a narrow strip between Epiré and the village of Savennières. This is very pleasant countryside and the dry wine of AOC Savennières is refined and elegant. The vineyard at Coulée de Serrant and La Roche aux Moines are well worth a visit. At this very significant spot in the Loire valley, on the local schist veined with volcanic rock, Pineau de la Loire makes some marvellous wine, which was regarded by Curnonsky (the writer on gastronomy) as some of the finest in the world. As well as Coulée de Serrant and La Roche aux Moines, there is excellent wine from Epiré, from the Clos de Papillon and from Coulaine, west of Savennières, along the road to Saint-Georges-sur-Loire.

The Coteaux du Layon begin south of the river, at Rochefort-sur-Loire. Along the Corniche Angevine there are outcrops of schist containing seams of hard rock such as spilite, rhyolite, jasper and phthanite. A geological fault on the left bank of the Layon river has produced superb slopes visible after the Moulin Guérin at Saint-Aubin-de-Luigné. This fault extends in a line south-east from Rochefort-sur-Loire as far as Concourson-sur-Layon and Les Verchers-sur-Layon. Growers here have concentrated on producing grapes of concentrated ripeness, and each individual site or vineyard can achieve wonderful nuances of flavour, according to the year or batch of grapes. After Chaudefonds-sur-Layon and Saint-Aubin-de-Luigné, Chaume becomes visible from La Soucherie. The vineyards are situated on gravel soils over carboniferous puddingstone, and their south-eastern aspect gives them shelter from both Atlantic influences and north winds. The wine here is remarkable, particularly Quarts-de-Chaume. These are certainly the finest sweet wines of the Loire valley.

The second Layon *grand cru* is AOC Bonnezeaux, produced at Thouarcé in vineyards extending over slopes on the right bank, here dissected into tiny valleys by dried up springs. The iron-rich water which gave Bonnezeaux its name has disappeared, but schist with hard veins of coloured minerals such as phthanite has formed steep slopes. Some of the hills are capped with windmills, among them the restored mill at La Montagne. Bonnezeaux wine is comparable in quality to Quarts-de-Chaume, with delicious softness and fruit. For a long time now the owner of the château of Fesles has been producing one of the best Bonnezeaux and other growers are following after him. Rablay-sur-Layon and Champ-sur-Layon also produce excellent wines and those from Maligné and Chavagnes-les-Eaux, near Martigné-Briand, have been well known since the eighteenth century. There is a wine museum which can be visited in the village of Saint-Lambert-du-Lattay.

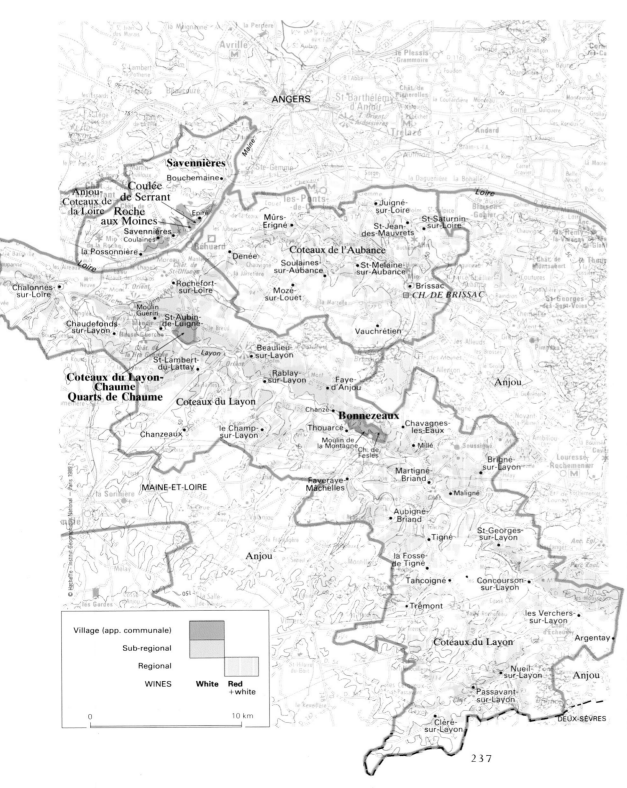

Village (app. communale)		
Sub-regional		
Regional		
WINES	**White**	**Red** +white

0   10 km

AUBANCE AND BRISSAC-QUINCÉ

THERE are some good vineyards on slopes and on the Denée plateau, stretching out towards Mosé-sur-Louet, Saint-Melaine-sur-Aubance, Vauchrétien and Brissac-Quincé, and as far as Chauvigné. Red wine producers here belong to the Confrérie des Echansons de Brissac wine fraternity, which holds a wine fair in mid-September at Brissac-Quincé. There are also reputable wines from the limestone slopes at Charcé, Grézillé, Coutures, Blaison-Gohier and from Angers-type schistous soil at Saint-Jean-des-Mauvrets and Juigné-sur-Loire.

THE UPPER LAYON VALLEY

ALTHOUGH these sites are some way from main roads and railways, they do not deserve to be neglected. Sweet wines are produced here which are as remarkable as some in the Coteaux du Layon, and in this extreme southern corner of Anjou the red wines often have a fuller, smoother quality. The best are probably from Concourson-sur-Layon, but there are good wines too from Tigné, La Fosse-de-Tigné, Saint-Georges-sur-Layon, Les Verchers-sur-Layon, Passavent and Cléré-sur-Layon. The old town of Doué-la-Fontaine has a number of quarries and cellars. In those belonging to the Touchais firm there is the largest store of old Layon wine, which is kept for ten years before being sold.

SAUMUR AND SAUMUR-CHAMPIGNY

SAUMUR had now become the focus of the Anjou wine trade. At the end of the sixteenth century, in the reign of Henri IV, it was a centre of Protestantism, under the influence of the king's counsellor Duplessis-Mornay, known as the 'Protestant Pope'. During the seventeenth

Above, the castle of Montreuil-Bellay.
Right, the cellar at the Château de Brézé.

century, when the Dutch were shipping the best Loire wines overseas, Saumur was probably the main trading centre for the wine of the region. Most of the Anjou wine businesses, even today, are in or around Saumur, and some still have Dutch or Huguenot roots.

The vines of the Saumur region grow in scattered pockets on chalk tufa hills or on outcrops of Senonian or Eocene rock, as at Brézé, Le Coudray-Macouard and Epieds on the right bank of the Dive, or Le Puy-Notre-Dame and Le Vaudelnay on the left bank of the Thouet. The low hill at Argentay forms the southwest boundary of the Saumur region.

A plateau of Senonian sands and slopes of glauconitic chalk overlying the chalk tufa provide a good situation for the vineyards of Saumur-Champigny.

The area was once as well known as Vouvray, mainly for its white wines, but the vine-stocks able to resist chlorosis on this chalky soil did not allow Chenin grapes to ripen sufficiently. Cabernet Franc, the Breton variety, had been doing very well for some time round Champigny and Chaintre, and the Champigny red wine vineyards were successfully extended into nine defined village areas, from Montsoreau to Dampierre-sur-Loire and Saint-Cyr-en-Bourg.

The wines of this *appellation* have been well known for centuries, and are light, fruity and well balanced. A pioneer in this region was Père Cristal, a friend of Clemonceau. His influence can still be seen in the curious layout of the Clos Cristal. At Chaintre there is a seventeenth-century Oratorian priory, surrounded by a vineyard.

SPARKLING SAUMUR

THE production zone for sparkling Saumur is more extensive than that of still red and white wines. It coincides with part of the Coteaux du Layon, as far as Martigné-Briand and Vihiers,

The interesting Clos Cristal vineyard is now owned by the Hospices de Saumur.

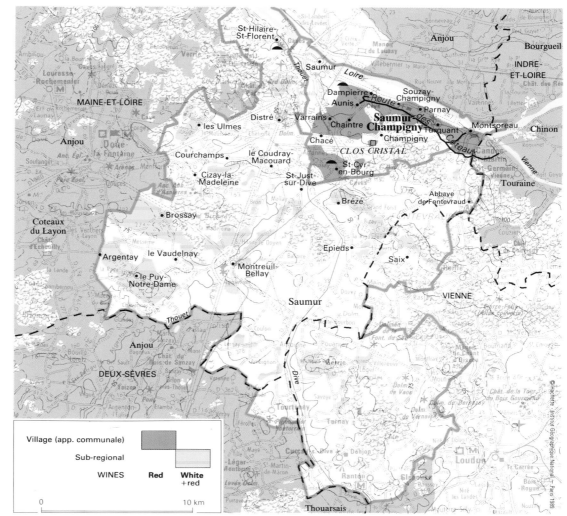

then with the Aubance area up to Grézillé and Coutures, corresponding in fact with the sites where Chenin is cultivated on a limestone subsoil. Most of the best sparkling wine producers are at Saint-Hilaire – Saint-Florent, north-west of Saumur. There is also the wine-making *coopérative* of Saint-Cyr-en-Bourg, with cellars in a series of stone galleries cut more than 25 m down into the tufa.

The Château of Montsoreau.

TOURAINE

THE number of vineyards in Touraine, in the middle valley of the Loire, almost equals the number of famous châteaux and, besides the Touraine *appellation*, local wine labels often include the name of some historic royal or aristocratic estate from the banks of the Loire and its tributaries.

VARYING MICROCLIMATES

THE regional *appellation* dates only from just before the Second World War, although vine-growing here obviously began in the distant past, as shown by the eleventh-century wine-press at Cheillé and by documents going back to the seventh century. It is even said that the first vines ever to appear in Touraine were planted at Vouvray by Saint Martin in the year 380.

The temperate climate of this region is less maritime in character than that of Anjou, although there are obvious gradations as you travel from west to east. Furthest west, the Chinon/Bourgueil area on the confluence of the Vienne and the Loire is only 150 km from the sea, and maritime influences are still discernible here in the broad valley sheltered from north winds by wooded hills. The favourable climate makes this part of Touraine very suitable for growing Cabernet Franc.

Further east, at Vouvray and Montlouis, there are regular slopes facing south over the Loire and the Cher. Autumn here is warm, sunny and damp enough to allow the late variety, Chenin Blanc, to be grown on to a very ripe stage and, one year in three, to produce the concentrated sweetness of *pourriture noble*.

Above, painting of Saint Martin, 1450 (Musée des Beaux-Arts, Bâle). Top, carving by Raymond Mason, 1982 (Marlborough Gallery, London).

In the eastern sector near Blois the climate becomes definitely continental, with severe winters and late springs. These are suitable conditions for the grape varieties of central France: Gamay Noir à Jus Blanc, Pinot Noir, and Sauvignon in the Sancerre region.

ST MARTIN, THE APOSTLE OF WINE

ST Martin, who brought Christianity to western Gaul, founded the abbey of Marmoutier in 372 and, according to legend, liked to visit the monks tending the vines there. He left his donkey browsing on the vines one day and it was discovered at harvest time that there were finer grapes on the chewed stems than on those left to grow long. So the monks of Marmoutier came to realize the advantages of pruning, and the rest of the world followed suit.

SOIL CONDITIONS

THE late Mesozoic subsoil of Touraine consists of fairly soft chalk, known as tufa, in which huge caverns were once carved out to quarry the stone for houses and châteaux and for the embankments beside the Loire. These caverns are often very deep, with a constant temperature of around 11°C, and are used today for storing and maturing wine.

The tufa is close to the surface on certain slopes. The best Côtes de Vouvray grow where these have a thin covering (to a depth of about 40 cm) of warm and well-drained pebbly clay/limestone soil. The intermediate valley slopes are covered with Mesozoic clay-with-flints and are naturally well drained. The many surface flints are useful in helping the grapes to ripen, as at night they give out heat stored during the day.

Tertiary sands from the Massif Central were deposited in Sologne but have overflowed into eastern Touraine, near Oisly and Mesland. The light soils formed in this way produce some very refined wine based on Sauvignon and some well-structured reds.

Lastly, there are Quaternary deposits of alluvial gravel which the Loire, the Vienne and the Cher have built up into terraces. Excellent wine can be grown where these have a favourable aspect, as at Bourgueil, Chinon and Montlouis.

SUITABLE GRAPE VARIETIES

FACED with such a range of different weather and soil conditions, growers through the centuries have had to look for the most suitable grape varieties. Some, such as Côt and Cabernet, were brought from the south-west; others, like Pinot and Gamay Noir à Jus Blanc, came from the eastern-central region. Pineau de la Loire (Chenin Blanc), either alone or blended with the related Arbois or Menu Pineau, is typical of the Loire Valley itself. Since it ripens late, the grower often needs to blend in an earlier variety such as Sauvignon or, to a small extent, the Chardonnay from Burgundy.

Although the Touraine regional *appellation* was recognized in 1939 it was only in the fifties that it started to develop a clear-cut identity. The basic

grape varieties have not changed but are now grown in distinctly different proportions. Pineau is now used principally in the manufacture of sparkling wines. Arbois is practically extinct. Sauvignon has taken the place of both and now makes up almost 70 per cent of all white varieties.

Gamay Noir à Jus Blanc is the most widely grown of the red varieties, followed by Cabernet Franc on the

Top, the Château of Chenonceau.

Above, turning the bottles to shift deposit in sparkling wines.

Left, a meeting of the wine fraternity in the Abbaye Saint-Julien, Tours.

best slopes, and by Côt. The latter is spreading now that more fertile versions have been developed. Subsidiary varieties such as Grolleau, the local Pineau d'Aunis and Cabernet Sauvignon are also grown fairly widely.

Seventy villages are entitled to produce AOC Touraine, although many make no use of this right. There are 5,000 hectares, producing 300,000 hl of wine, with slightly

more red than white. Attempts are being made to develop a distinctive Touraine-type red based on Gamay and Côt, as well as a Touraine Primeur.

AMBOISE, AZAY-LE-RIDEAU AND MESLAND

THE network of rivers cuts up the landscape of Touraine into a number of different sectors. Three of these zones are allowed to add their own names to the basic Touraine regional *appellation*: Amboise and Azay-le-Rideau, close to Balzac's château of Saché, in the Indre-et-Loire *département*; and, in Loir-et-Cher, the vineyards of Mesland. They were planted in the eleventh century by the Abbey of Marmoutier on the sunny right bank of the Loire, and are mentioned by Charles d'Orléans, the poet imprisoned for twenty-five years after his capture at Agincourt.

Minute differences in microclimates or variations in soil and rock have all contributed to the character of wines with names which conjure up a landscape or a famous château. The Amboise and Mesland regions both have a distinctive Loire quality. It would be amusing to trace the links between wine and architecture. The elegant refinement of Touraine-Azay-le-Rideau rosé, based on Grolleau, seems a perfect reflection of the château of Azay. The ample solidity of the Touraine-Amboise reds and rosés

own to the local tourist industry by adding to the prestige of this magnificent region.

MEMORABLE VINEYARDS

THE history of the Loire valley can hardly be dissociated from the vineyards planted throughout the region, in cities, castles and monasteries. These sometimes supplied the local market or were used by the owner for direct or indirect profit, and some of them acquired considerable fame. Throughout the region from Haut-Poitou to Orléans, ranks of vines line the valleys of the Loire and its tributaries. Vineyards exist which have a long and continuous

Above, left, Grolleau Noir.
Above, right, an illustration for Rabelais's Gargantua, *by Adrien Leroy 1913 (Bibliothèque Nationale).*
Below, an eighteenth- to nineteenth-century wine-press (Cave de la Dive Bouteille, Bourgueil).

certainly suggests the handsome façade of the castle above the Loire. And Chenonceau is not just a splendid château bridging the waters of the Cher but the name of a flowery white, a supple red and an ethereal rosé.

With their strong Loire character, these Touraine wines are fresh, distinctive and easy to drink. They make a considerable contribution of their

history and which are still famous today; others are mentioned in history but have disappeared for economic and social reasons rather than for intrinsic lack of quality.

Not far from Poitiers, which was a city in Roman times, there are vineyards producing Haut-Poitou wines based on Gamay and Chardonnay. The officially delimited area is rather too large but an energetic *coopérative* is bringing about improvements. The environment and the soil give the white wines based on Sauvignon and Chenin Blanc a rather rustic bouquet, and Pinot Blanc has not yet proved itself in the area. At the moment seven varieties are grown for the production of reds and rosés and there needs to be a more critical approach if technical and commercial viability is to be achieved.

The evocative names of Cheverny, Vendôme, Valençay and Orléans immediately suggest the poetry of Ronsard and some of the most famous episodes in French history. These quintessentially French wines have appeared on the tables of kings and princes.

Cheverny also has a complicated list of grape varieties: a range of fourteen for white, red, rosé and sparkling wines seems somewhat excessive. However, on certain good sites individual growers are producing some sound wine from both classic and local varieties (Gamay, Pinot Noir, Côt, Romorantin and Sauvignon).

In the quiet green valley of the Loir the Coteaux du Vendômois keep up a

small-scale output of a pleasant Gamay. Jasnières and Coteaux du Loir are more familiar *appellations*. The former owes its reputation to a very delicate white wine based on Pineau Blanc de la Loire; this is quite out of the ordinary but has a tiny output of about 500 hl per year. Coteaux du Loir has a larger yield consisting of almost 1,000 hl of a light fruity red (Pineau d'Aunis, Cabernet, Gamay or Côt), 250 hl of dry white (Chenin or Pineau Blanc de la Loire), and some 200 hl of rosé.

The Valençay growers seem undecided whether they want to produce more than a simple *vin de table*. When they do aim at quality they achieve some very pleasing wines based on Gamay, Côt, Pineau d'Aunis and other varieties.

The wines of the Orléans region descend from some excellent wines produced in the Middle Ages which were sold in Paris and to the court, but they are now just emerging from a period of difficulty and obscurity. Various grape varieties are grown, with varying results, but the local Gris Meunier seems the most worthy representative of the region.

BOURGUEIL AND SAINT-NICOLAS-DE-BOURGUEIL

VINEYARDS in these villages were mentioned in the archives of the Benedictine abbey of Bourgueil as early as the eleventh century. They are planted mainly on old gravel terraces and the whole area was once part of Anjou. The river port of Chouzé once had a flourishing wine trade, of which the only remaining traces are a few rusty mooring rings on the long, empty quays.

Today the Bourgueil wine region has spread up beyond the original terraces, onto south-facing Turonian chalk slopes. This sector represents barely one third of the whole AOC Bourgueil region, whereas at Chinon the ratio of slopes to terraces is more or less reversed. South of the river Authion, there are good isolated sites on so-called *montilles* of sand and gravel situated higher up on the more recent Loire alluvial deposits: these are also included in the AOC Bourgueil *appellation*.

Saint-Nicolas-de-Bourgueil is unlike the others in having half its vineyards sited on old gravel terraces and the other half on chalk slopes, with no *montille*-grown vines. Because of its uniform quality the wine from this village only is entitled to use the Saint-Nicolas-de-Bourgueil AOC label. However, there is a single

growers' union which manages AOC wines of both Bourgueil and Saint-Nicolas-de-Bourgueil, and no distinction is made between Saint-Nicolas growers and those in the other seven villages of Benais, Bourgueil, La Chapelle-sur-Loire, Chouzé-sur-Loire, Ingrandes, Restigné and Saint-Patrice.

AROMATIC WINES

THE whole Bourgueil region conveys a mood of peaceful continuity and the wines have a subtle scent of flowers. Red Bourgueil grown on gravel terraces is especially aromatic, with refined and supple tannins. Probably the reason why these wines are so successful is that they have a very easy-drinking character, and can be enjoyed in the year they are produced for their distinctive aromas of fruit and flowers. The wine from the chalk slopes is much more robust, especially in a great year, and can achieve astonishing complexity and aromatic intensity. Some of these *coteaux* plots are becoming very well known – Evois at Restigné, Grand Mont at Benais, Chevrette and Beau

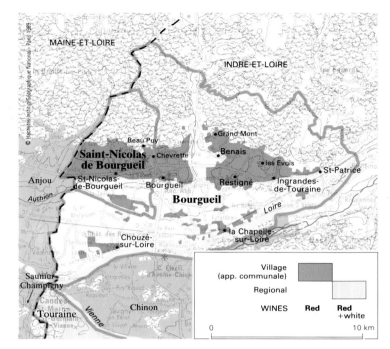

Puy at Bourgueil. The succession of vineyards running from the Loire up to the chalk plateau can be seen particularly well at Bourgueil, on the same sequence of soils as at Chinon. Silt lies over Senonian sands at the top of the slopes where the forest of Gâtine begins.

The AOC area amounted to more than 1,100 hectares after the Second

World War, and has now risen to 1,050 hectares for AOC Bourgueil and 700 for Saint-Nicolas-de-Bourgueil. The two *appellations*, with identical yields, together produce about 90,000 hl. The Restigné *coopérative* system is unusual in that the wine is first vinified and then sent back to the producers for maturing before it is bottled. Bourgueil peasant growers are shrewd, cautious characters but get on well with their more outgoing neighbours in Rabelais's territory of Chinon. At Bourgueil and Saint-Nicolas-de-Bourgueil the Commanderie de la Dive Bouteille wine fraternity sees that local traditions are kept up in a dignified manner. There used to be two important yearly celebrations in the Bourgueil calendar: the Foire aux vins nouveaux in February on the first Saturday after the feast of St Vincent, and the Salon des vins in Easter week. These have been replaced by events organized jointly with other Loire *appellations*.

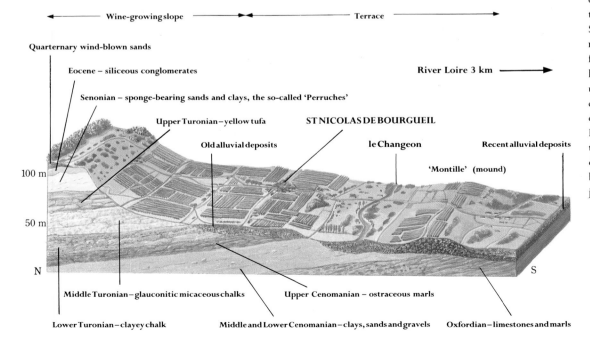

243

CHINON

CHINON lies at a crossroads between Anjou, Poitou and Touraine. Its wines have a quite different history from those of Bourgueil. On this side of the Loire the ratio of gravel to chalk slopes is reversed, which explains the different nuances of flavour in the two *appellations*.

Part of the castle of Chinon, seen from the Clos de l'Echo.

LINKS WITH RABELAIS

THE impressive fortress dominating the town was built by Henry II of England, the feudal lord of Normandy, Maine, Anjou, Poitou and Aquitaine. The Plantagenet king liked the weather and the wine in Chinon so the castle there was his favourite residence. Three centuries later it remained one of the last strongholds of the unfortunate *roi de Bourges,* the so-called 'King of Bourges', later to be Charles VII of France, when he was trying to defend his kingdom from Henry VI of England. It was to this miserable royal court that Joan of Arc came to declare her mission. At the end of these warlike times Chinon was to become famous for its links with the great Renaissance humanist, François Rabelais, born in 1494 at the nearby manor of La Devinière.

The wine-growing community, and their Confrérie des Etonneurs Rabelaisiens, seems to have retained the spirit of Rabelais's message to 'live as good Pantagruelians in peace, health and happiness, not forgetting copious dinners'. Wherever you are in Chinon, there is an atmosphere of friendly good humour, of tolerance and zest for life. In the direction of La Devinière, you can still see the castle of La Roche-Clermault described by Rabelais, and apparently intact in

spite of the way it is said to have been knocked about in the (imaginary) Pichrocholine Wars. The ruins of the Abbey of Seuilly are full of reminders of Brother Jean des Entommeures, the typical medieval monk immortalized in the words of Rabelais: 'It is a monkish precept, that no man of noble repute ever hated wine'.

THE PRINCIPAL CHINON VINEYARDS

THROUGHOUT the Chinon region there are sites similar to those of Bourgueil, but on the right bank of the river Vienne, between Crouzilles and Beaumont-en-Véron, vines are grown mainly on slopes of Turonian (glauconitic) chalk. In the Ligré and La Roche-Clermault village areas on the left bank, the only sites with a favourable aspect lie between the

Négron and the Veude, both tributaries of the Vienne, and it is here that the great Chinon wines are grown. They are matured in cellars hollowed out of the tufa and are long-lasting wines, based on Cabernet like Bordeaux and Médoc, and in no way inferior to them. Within the commune of Chinon these wines grow on sites mentioned by Rabelais: Saint-Louans, Clos de l'Echo and L'Olive. There are also the very well-known plots of La Roche-Honneur and Les Pigasses at Beaumont-en-Véron, and Les Roches-Saint-Paul at Ligré. Besides these Turonian slopes, there are sites higher up, on the plateau north of Chinon, where vines are beginning to take over from woodland on the thin sandy soils. The wines from here have a refined fruity bouquet, but nothing like the fullness of wines grown on slopes. Above the hillsides of Cravant and Avon-les-Roches, in

areas further east where wind-borne soils are unsuitable for vine-growing, the tops of the hills are given over to woodland. Lastly, there are the old alluvial terraces at the bottom of slopes beside the Vienne and in the Loire Valley, at Savigny-en-Véron, Avoine and Huismes. The more gravelly sites here give especially refined, fragrant wines, very much in the style of Saint-Nicolas-de-Bourgueil. At Chinon, however, the growers tend to blend wines from their different plots to give a distinctive character.

The Chinon wine region covers eighteen villages: Anché, Avoine, Avon-les-Roches, Beaumont-en-Véron, Chinon, Cravant, Crouzilles, Huismes, L'Ile-Bouchard, Ligré, Pauzoult, La Rivière, La Roche-Clermault, Saint-Benoît-la-Forêt, Savigny-en-Véron, Sazilly, Tavant and Theneuil. The recent revival has been considerable: around 1950 the area under vines had fallen to 500 hectares, whereas now there are 1,500 hectares with an annual yield of between 60,000 and 80,000 hl of red wine.

Chinon white wine made from Chenin should be mentioned, simply as a curiosity. It has a minute production (200 to 300 hl) but was once more extensive on the hillsides.

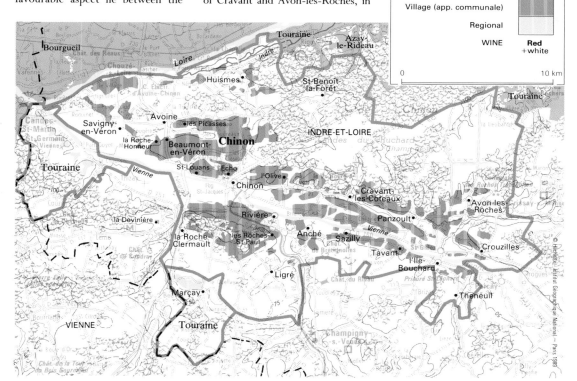

VOUVRAY AND MONTLOUIS

EVEN if Vouvray does not represent the whole of France, as some writers claim, at least one can say that it represents Touraine. Like the rest of the province, it has been shaped by the Loire and by all the little local tributaries such as the Cisse, and has characteristic geological formations (Turonian, Senonian, Eocene) which are widespread elsewhere in Touraine.

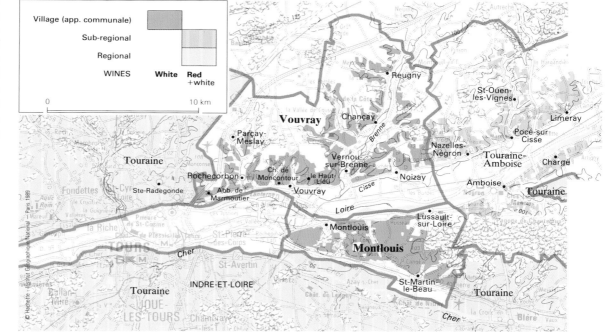

MAGNIFICENT VOUVRAY

ON the steep ledges of the right bank and in the sloping minor valleys are vine-growing soils typical of the region, like the famous *aubuis* and *perruches*. These give a very special

character to the Vouvray white wines, which are magnificent examples of Chenin Blanc, locally better known as Pineau de la Loire. It could scarcely be given the splendid south-facing situation, with so much sunlight and warmth that semi-Mediterranean plants like magnolia, cypress and the chamoerops dwarf palm all flourish there.

This special microclimate, at a junction of Atlantic and continental influences, probably results from a combination of the aspect, the chalky rock and the river environment, which all have a beneficial effect on both vines and wine. Vouvray has been highly prized from the earliest times; from the Roman occupation and the medieval monastic period, through the fourteenth century when the Dutch used to ship the wine through the port of Nantes.

The soil where the rows of Pineau Blanc grow is chalky but so rich in iron that the vines, often on *Riparia* root-stocks, do not suffer from chlorosis, and there are also areas of warm, well-drained flint pebbles. These extraordinary vines give lively, fruity wine, which is sometimes sweet or even lusciously *liquoreux* in a year favouring *pourriture noble*. This is how the wines from 1904, 1921, 1928, 1934, 1937, 1945, 1947, 1955 came to be so memorable, and still are for

those people lucky enough to possess some.

A fair proportion of the Vouvray crop is used for slightly sparkling and *mousseux* wines of well-defined character and high reputation. These wines seem to take on a sparkle very readily, and fermentation would often start up again spontaneously in the spring with the addition of a few grams of sugar. Nowadays, sparkling Vouvray is produced by the Champagne method.

Left, cellars at Vouvray.
Below, a cellar built into the cliff.

MONTLOUIS, A NOBLE WINE

ON the opposite bank of the ever-present Loire, between Amboise and Tours, lies the wine region of Montlouis. It was established in the fifth century and is famous for the château of Bourdaisière where Henri IV enjoyed the good local wine and the company of his mistress, Gabrielle d'Estrées. Conditions of production as well as type of wine are fairly similar on both sides of the river, although Montlouis acquired an independent *appellation* only in 1937.

Montlouis wine is well made and of dependable quality, but the area is now suffering from the creeping urban development at Tours. It has also been far more susceptible than Vouvray to the effects of spring frost. Nevertheless, some excellent wines are produced around Montlouis, Lussault and especially the village of Saint-Martin-le-Beau, which is now the core of the *appellation*. Certain vineyards (Mosny, Michet, Yvonnet, Grand Clos, Les Brunettes) still have a reliable reputation.

CENTRAL FRANCE

THIS central region, *'le coeur de la France'* or 'heart of France', lies between the Côtes du Forez and the Orléans region, on hillsides and plateaux formed over millennia by the Loire and its tributaries, the Allier and the Cher. As in Anjou and Touraine, it is the river that links all these wine regions, but the central area differs from its neighbours both in soil (Jurassic and Precambrian Massif Central types) and in climate, which is semi-continental with cold winters and hot summers, and fully continental in the Côtes Roannaises and Forez area.

The vineyards of Central France are all on well-exposed sites, and grow a limited range of grape varieties, mainly Gamay and Pinot Noir for reds and rosés, and Sauvignon, probably a native variety, for whites. The wines from these areas all have a similar fresh, light, fruity character which makes them very pleasant and easy to drink, as well as an ideal accompaniment to the local food.

THE LAND OF SAUVIGNON

BOURGES possesses a cathedral that is one of the highest achievements of Gothic architecture. It was the presence of this medieval city only a short distance away that was responsible for the development of vineyards at Menetou-Salon, where there are very suitable slopes, and the same soils and classic grape varieties, Sauvignon Blanc and Pinot Noir, as in the more famous neighbouring vineyards of Sancerre. All this helps to produce spicy, fresh-tasting white wines, some delicate, fruity rosés, and well-balanced, fragrant reds for drinking young.

Beside the river Cher, near Mehun-sur-Yèvre with its many reminders of the sixteenth century, the vineyards of Quincy and Brinay extend over about a hundred hectares on plateaux covered with layers of old sand and gravel. At Quincy only Sauvignon Blanc is grown and produces 3,500 hl of very light white wines whose fresh and fruity style has a certain elegance and refinement.

Once again, mainly Sauvignon Blanc is grown at Reuilly, on sunny hillsides along the pleasant river valleys of the Cher, the Arnon and the Théols. The *appellation* also extends over seven villages in the Indre and the Cher *départements*. Apart from its remarkably full-flavoured, dry and fruity whites, Reuilly also produces some unusually distinguished, rather delicate wine based on Pinot Gris, although this is now having to give way more and more to Pinot Noir and some full, fleshy reds.

Right, the fortified town of Sancerre.
Below left, vines at Menetou-Salon.
Below right, Gamay grapes.

Above, statue of the fifteenth-century
financier Jacques Coeur, Bourges.

Below, illustration for the month of October,
by Maurice Lenoir, 1904 (Bibliothèque des
Arts Décoratifs, Paris).

the reds and rosés gain a certain unity
of character from Gamay, and the
whites from Tressallier with some
added Chardonnay, Sauvignon or
other variety. These fine vineyards
cover 500 hectares of the fertile
Bourbonnais region and produce
23,000 hl of wine.

Both in the Puy country of
Limagne and in the Monts Dômes on
the eastern edge of the Massif Central, the Côtes d'Auvergne are based
on Gamay, sometimes combined with
Pinot Noir. These excellent wines
have a very long history and 21,000 hl
per year are now produced on about
500 hectares of land. There are some
amusing rosés, sometimes named as
whites, and some pleasant reds, particularly those from Chanturge, which
go well with the local *charcuterie*.

The Côtes Roannaises consist of
twenty-four villages covering 80 hectares on both banks of the Loire,
(here still a youthful river). Some very
good reds are produced, based solely
on Gamay, known here as Saint-
Romain, and, more rarely, some
fresh-tasting rosés. These wines have
just a hint of a southern quality which
intensifies as one moves down towards
the Côtes du Forez. Here the soils are
still volcanic or metamorphic in
origin, and the hillsides are often steep.
The moorland landscape of the south
seems not very far away and Gamay
wines from the Boën Cave Coopérative have faint Mediterranean
scents of rosemary and thyme.

GAMAY: THE COMMON DENOMINATOR

GAMAY does particularly well in
these central areas and produces red
VDQS wines with plenty of freshness
and fruit. On both banks of the Loire
are the Coteaux du Giennois, on
siliceous and limestone soils. This
region, with its own distinctive character, produces almost 4,000 hl of not
very tannic red VDQS wine based on
three traditional varieties: Gamay,
Pinot and Sauvignon.

At Châteaumeillant there is more
Gamay, growing on its favourite
gravels. The ancient soils here are
part of the Massif Central and, as the

local museum shows, there is a long
tradition of vine-growing in the area.
Châteaumeillant is famous for its *vin
gris*, a wine made from the immediate
pressing of black Gamay grapes. Its red
wines have a delicious lightness and
fragrance and should be drunk young
and fresh. Most of the growers sell
through the *coopérative*.

The river Sioule comes hastening
down from the hills of Auvergne and
was once famous for trout. Just before its confluence with the Allier, we
come to the vineyards of Saint-
Pourçain and the beginnings of jagged
volcanic and sedimentary terrain. The
wines are grown on differing soils but

SANCERRE

HILLS with a perfect aspect, plenty of wood for casks and posts, a broad river for transporting produce: a region with advantages such as these could hardly fail to attract wine-growers. On its hill above the majestically flowing Loire, Sancerre seems predestined for wine.

From the top of the Tour des Fiefs, you can look down across the quiet old rooftops and admire the comfortable prospect of vineyards in full sun with a steep stony hillside beneath to keep them dry. It is a site like this that makes one realize the full meaning of an *appellation*: homogeneous, fertile land, suitable grape varieties and vine-growers with the experience and energy to produce wine of distinction.

The Sancerre *appellation* extends over an area of 1,700 hectares which includes fourteen villages. Nowadays, there is a yield of almost 100,000 hl of white wine and 20,000 hl of red and rosé, from what are still mainly family businesses. The small local roads provide a kind of cross-section of the soil types which give Sancerre wine its character: they wind up through the vines, across chalky *caillottes* of varying hardness, over low hills and up into the marly *terres blanches*

('white lands'), or eastwards onto stretches of flinty pebbles. The different wine cellars offer a whole range of Sauvignons conveying all the subtle differences of soil: wines of refinement and breeding with notes of blackcurrant and boxwood from the *caillottes*; powerful, full-bodied wines scented with narcissus and tuberose from the *terres blanches*; hints of broom and acacia in those grown on flints or brown clay soils.

The different character of these soils is expressed in endless aromatic variations, but a particular locality invariably has its own dominant aroma. In its fresh, fruity style, Sancerre white wine is one of the best in France and is a model for all its neighbours. The quality of the Pinot Noir here depends on conditions of vinification as well as on the soil. It

Below, cooper's tools.

produces some opulent wine, with full flavours reminiscent of maraschino or morello cherries. Sancerre reds are very much in fashion at the moment, especially in Paris, and demand tends to outstrip supply. Some of them are made in Burgundy style and have almost reached the highest class.

Sancerre rosé has delicacy and breeding, with a bouquet of autumn fruit, and could also be considered as one of the most successful of the *vins gris* produced by direct pressing.

The environment of Sancerre is delightful, with a community of growers who have a strong sense of local pride. After all, it is not easy to produce fine wine from a late-ripening variety such as Sauvignon on some of the steepest vineyards in France, close to the northernmost limits of vine cultivation, and with fermentation taking place in the chancy late autumn period. White Sancerre is particularly delicious when drunk with dry goats' cheese like the famous *crottin* from the wine-making village of Chavignol, and also as an accompaniment to fish and main courses which are not too highly flavoured.

Below, vineyards at Verdigny.

POUILLY-SUR-LOIRE

HERE, too, vineyards are an integral part of the serene, light-filled river landscape. Pouilly faces south on a limestone promontory which makes the Loire swerve to the west at this point, and the vineyards here were planted centuries ago by Benedictine monks.

The soil is less chalky than at Sancerre and used to be devoted principally to Chasselas grape variety, which for a long time has been giving light, refreshing, typical 'bar' wines. With age, these have become slightly more respectable under the Pouilly-sur-Loire *appellation* (4,000 hl), and are quite pleasing when grown on flinty soil.

POUILLY FUMÉ

HOWEVER, the pride of the Nevers region is the Blanc Fumé de Pouilly, to which five-sixths of the area under vines is now given up. This wine is based on Sauvignon, which achieves its highest potential on limestone soils: freshness together with a certain firmness, a whole range of aromas characteristic of this grape variety, and refined by the environment in which it is grown and fermented.

Sauvignon is excellent at expressing the particular character of the *terroir*, and Pouilly Fumé, with its well defined fruit and firm structure, stands apart from wines produced nearby from the same grapes in more or less similar production conditions.

Seven villages, including Pouilly, Saint-Andelain and Tracy, maintain 600 hectares of vines producing 35,000 hl of white wine for the two local *appellations*. After a period of decline due mainly to natural disasters, particularly spring frosts, and to

The hamlet of Les Loges beside the Loire.

the overall economic situation, Pouilly is now making a new spurt of growth based on better quality, a more distinctive grape variety (Sauvignon Blanc Fumé) and a more highly motivated generation of growers.

The charm of the river landscapes of this region makes exploration essential. Just beyond the rows of vines, there are glorious views to be enjoyed from the wine village of Les Loges. If you climb up through Les Berthiers to the hill of Saint-Andelain and down again through Le Bouchot, there is a wonderful panorama with glimpses of vines and woodland, of the Loire of course, and in clear weather of the purple Morvan hills in the background. Above the foliage, you can just see the slate-roofed turrets of the château of Nozet, the largest estate in the region, hedged in by its 70 hectares of vines.

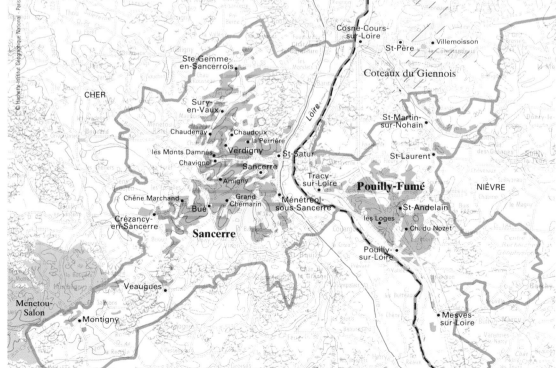

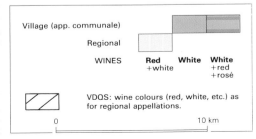

Village (app. communale)		
Regional		

| WINES | Red +white | White | White +red +rosé |

VDQS: wine colours (red, white, etc.) as for regional appellations.

0   10 km

GLOSSARY

AC See **AOC**.

Acidity Occurs naturally and is necessary for the balance of flavours in a wine, giving freshness and vivacity.

Ampelography The study of grapes.

AOC *Appellation d'origine contrôlée*: legal term guaranteeing place of origin and methods of production for any wine granted an AOC label.

Appellation See **AOC**.

Aspect For a vineyard this means the way the land faces, as in 'a southerly aspect'.

Assemblage Blending: in Champagne this is the process of mixing samples from different plots or vintages to produce a balanced wine before the final fermentation in the bottle.

Blanc de blancs White wine made from white grapes only. Applies principally to Champagne.

Botrytis *Botrytic cinerea*, a fungus which attacks grapes. In certain warm, humid conditions it becomes *pourriture noble* (noble rot), which shrivels the grapeskins and causes the juice to become intensely sweet and concentrated. It is this which produces the best Sauternes.

Brut Dry (usually applied to Champagne).

Carbonic maceration A process derived from the traditional Beaujolais method and now much used in warm climates to produce fresh, fruity wines. The method of fermenting uncrushed grapes in covered vats extracts all the fruit and colour but not the astringent tannins.

Cave Wine cellar.

Caveau Tasting cellar, open to public.

Cave coopérative Wine-making plant collectively owned and run. Nowadays the source of many excellent regional, 'non-estate' wines.

Cépage Grape variety.

Chai The building where wine is stored before it is bottled. In the Bordeaux area the *chai* is above ground as, owing to the high water table, traditional cellars cannot usually be constructed. The *maître de chai* is the man in charge or 'cellar master'.

Chambrer To bring a wine up to room temperature, supposedly from a cool cellar. Necessary for many red wines, although the concept of 'room' temperature comes from the days before central heating. Some red wines, such as Beaujolais, may even be served slightly chilled.

Champagne Method See **Méthode Champenoise**.

Chapeau The 'cap' of solid matter which forms on top of the fermenting grapes.

Chaptalization The process of adding sugar to increase alcoholic strength. This is both legal and often necessary to help fermentation in areas where there is not enough sun to produce a high level of natural sugar in the grapes.

Château Large country house or castle. In the Bordeaux region the term applies to any wine-producing estate, where the château may be an 18th-century mansion or a modest farmhouse.

Clairet A pale red wine from the Gironde area.

Claret A name derived from *clairette*, the medieval term to distinguish the light red wines of the Bordeaux region from the dark-coloured wines grown further inland. For historical reasons, the name 'claret' may legally be used for red Bordeaux in Great Britain, but not elsewhere.

Climat A term used in Burgundy for a small section within a larger vineyard, often with its own geological conditions, aspect and microclimate.

Clos A mainly Burgundian term for a vineyard enclosed by walls, often in monastic times. Many have now lost their walls but retain the name of *Clos*.

Collage See **Fining**.

Commune Roughly equivalent to the English 'parish', although without church connotations.

Confrérie Wine-growers' society.

Côte Slope: occurs in many French appellations, such as Côtes du Rhône.

Coteau Slope or hillside. See above.

Coulure Pollination failure – hence an inadequate grape crop.

Crémant Sparkling wine made by the Champagne method. It can be fully sparkling, as with *Crémant de Bourgogne*, or more gently bubbling like *Crémant de Loire*.

Cru Means 'growth', but is often used to refer to a single vineyard.

Cru classé 'Classed growth', term used for the top-ranking wines of certain regions. In Médoc, according to the 1855 classification system, it applies to the highest category of wines, ranked from First to Fifth Growths. The best châteaux immediately below this level are generally classed as *Cru Bourgeois*, subdivided into *Cru Grand Bourgeois Exceptionnel*, *Cru Grand Bourgeois* and *Cru Bourgeois*.

Cuve Wine vat. Related words include: *cuvée* for the contents of the vat or for a particular batch of wine; *cuvier* or *cuverie* for the building housing the vats; *cuvage* or *cuvaison* for the fermentation period. *Tête de cuvée* is an expression sometimes used to designate the best wine from a particular batch.

Cuve close This means 'closed vat' and is used to describe a method of making sparkling wine where the second fermentation occurs in sealed tanks rather than in the bottle.

Dégorgement The process of removing sediment from the wine bottles when making Champagne. Also known as *dégorgeage*.

Dégustation Wine tasting.

Demi-sec This literally means 'half-dry', but in practice designates a fairly sweet wine, usually sparkling.

Domaine Land belonging to one proprietor.

Dosage The practice of topping up Champagne bottles, after the sediment has been removed by *dégorgement*, with a wine and sugar mixture. Without this addition Champagne would always be completely dry.

Eau-de-vie Distilled alcohol spirit. *Eau-de-vie de marc* is distilled from the crushed skins, stalks and pips which remain after the fermented wine has been run off.

Elevage Literally 'bringing up', a term applied to all the stages between the original fermentation and bottling the wine. Applies to the period when wine is maturing in vats or barrels.

Feuillette Cask whose capacity varies between 114 and 140 litres.

Fining Clarifying the wine, usually by adding some form of coagulant which attracts all the impurities as it settles to the bottom.

Foudre Large cask in which wine is matured.

INAO Institut National des Appellations d'Origine: the organization controlling the AOC system.

Lees Coarse sediment deposited by wine in the cask. A wine labelled *sur lie* (off the lees), like some of the better Muscadets, has been bottled directly from the cask to retain flavour and liveliness.

Lie See **Lees**.

Lieu-dit Named plot of land, not necessarily a village or hamlet.

Maceration The softening or separating of grapes as a result of soaking.

Maceration, carbonic See **Carbonic maceration**.

Malolactic fermentation Secondary fermentation in which malic acid is converted to lactic acid and carbon dioxide. It has a softening effect on red wines but is often stopped in white wines in order to retain a fresh sharp flavour.

Marc The crushed skins, stalks and pips left over after the grapes have been pressed.

Méthode champenoise A 'Champagne method' of making sparkling wine by encouraging a second fermentation in the bottle. Carbon dioxide given off during this process is trapped in the wine as effervescence.

Mildew Downy mildew and oïdium, or powdery mildew Common fungus diseases of the wine.

Millésime Year when a wine was harvested.

Mis en bouteille Bottled: labels may say 'mis en bouteille au château' if the wine has been bottled on the estate.

Mousseux Sparkling.

Must Grape juice before fermentation.

Mutage Permitted addition of alcohol spirit to stop further fermentation in Vins Doux Naturels (sweet fortified wines); they retain some natural sugar and have a higher alcohol level than ordinary table wines.

Négociant Shipper or merchant (mainly in Burgundy), who buys wine in bulk from the grower and matures and bottles it for sale.

Noble rot See **Botrytis**.

Oenology Science of wine-making.

Oïdium Powdery mildew, a common fungus disease.

Oxidation Deterioration of flavour and colour when wine is exposed to air. Slight aeration can improve flavour, as when a bottle is opened to 'breathe' for a short time before being drunk.

Pasteurization Process of heat sterilization before bottling, named after Pasteur. Used to prevent deterioration in cheaper wines. Not used for fine wines as it would check further ageing in the bottle.

Pétillant Slightly sparkling. Used to describe wine less effervescent than either *mousseux* or *crémant*.

Perlant Describes wine with a very gentle effervescence.

Phylloxera *Phylloxera vastatrix*, aphid which devastated French vineyards in the late 19th century. Classic European grape varieties are now grafted onto phylloxera-resistant American rootstocks.

Pipe Large wine-cask.

Pourriture noble See **Botrytis**.

Primeur Applies to wine bottled for early drinking, especially Beaujolais.

Racking The process of clarifying wine by transferring it from one cask to another, leaving behind the lees.

Rancio Describes characteristics of certain *vins doux naturels* (from Languedoc-Roussillon) which are allowed to age in casks until they acquire a tawny, sherry-like character.

Remuage Champagne-making technique: the bottles are stored upside-down and are turned and tapped every day to dislodge sediment from the sides of the bottle and onto the cap. The necks of the bottles are then dipped in freezing brine, the cap removed and the frozen sediment ejected (*dégorgement*). Nowadays the whole process is usually mechanized.

Sélection de Grains nobles In Alsace this designation applies to wines made from late harvested grapes affected by 'noble rot'.

Soutirage See **Racking**.

Sur lie See **Lees**.

Tannin Astringent element in red wine, produced by the skins, stalks and pips. It softens with maturity and is an essential component in the complex structure of wines intended to age.

Tastevin Shallow, ladle-shaped cup usually made of silver and used in Burgundy for tasting. It has become a symbol for many local wine organizations (such as the *Chevaliers du Tastevin*).

Terroir Literally, 'earth' or 'soil', but also used to refer to the particular area in which a wine is made. Wine which has *'un goût de terroir'* tastes of its soil and has an authentic local flavour.

Tête de cuvée See **Cuve**.

Tirage See **Racking**.

Vendange Vintage, grape harvest. The *vendangeurs* are the grapepickers.

Vendange tardive 'Late harvest', equivalent to German *spätlese*. Applied to late harvested grapes in Alsace.

VDL See **Vin de liqueur**.

VDN See **Vin doux naturel**.

VDP See **Vin de pays**.

VDQS See **Vin délimite de qualité supérieure**.

Vigne Vine.

Vigneron Wine-grower.

Vignoble Vineyard; sometimes a wine region.

Vin de garde Wine intended for maturing.

Vin délimité de qualité supérieure (VDQS) Official second category of wine, after *appellation d'origine contrôlée* (qv).

Vin de liqueur (VDL) Fortified sweet wine made by adding brandy to wine (as with Pineau des Charentes), or by other techniques not covered by the rules for VDN.

Vin de pays (VDP) Regional wine. Third category (see above).

Vin de table Basic category of everyday table wine, not covered by the official regulations on origin and production methods.

Vin doux naturel (VDN) Fortified sweet wine, usually from the South.

INDEX

251

Touraine-Amboise 241–2
Touraine-Azay-le-Rideau 241
Touraine-Mesland 241
Tourbat 33
tourism, and wine 62–3
Tournon 182 192
Tournus 167 174
Tours 241 245
Tracy 249
training vines 31 35
Traminer 73 179
Tramontane wind 202 212 218
Travaillan 186
Tressallier 233 247
Tressot 131
Troesmes 134
Trogus, Pompeius 200
Trois Chardons 87
Trollinger 72
Trotanoy 24 117
Trottevieille 112
Trouillas 220
Trousseau 178
Troyes 122
truffles 224 225 226
Tuchan 216
'tuns' 14
Turckheim 70 75
Turin 205
Tursan 229
Tursan 229

Ugni-Blanc 30 199 203 204 206 207 208 212 226
Université du Vin, Suze-la-Rousse 63
Urban II, pope 128
USA
  phylloxera from 16
  vine-stocks 17 30 175

Vaccarèse 195
Vacqueyras 186
Vaissière 63
Val d'Or 166
Valençay 242
Valence 182 192
Vallet 234 235
Valmur 134
Valréas 186 187
Van Gogh, Vincent 208
Van der Weyden, Rogier 154
Var 18 202 203 204
Varades 234
vats 36 37 38 39
Vau de Vey 134
Vau Vigneau 134
Vauchrétien 238
Vauciennes 128
Vaucluse 186 199
Vaucoupins 134
Vaudésir 134
Vaupulent 134
Vaux-en-Beaujolais 173
Vaux Ragons 134
Vayres 106
VDQS 8 20 21
Vendaine river 155
vendanges tardives 76–7

PHOTOGRAPHIC CREDITS

From top to bottom and from left to right unless specified.

8: I.N.A.O. fiftieth anniversary poster, Arikha, 1985. 11: Book of Hours of the Duchess of Burgundy, September; around 1450 (Musée Condé, Chantilly; plate Lauros Giraudon). 12: J.-M. Labat (Explorer), R. Pratta (Explorer archives). 13: Devaux Collection (Explorer archives), P. Roy (Explorer), Hug (Explorer). 14: Bayeux Collection. 14–15: F. Jalain (Explorer). 15: J.-L. Charmet (Explorer). 16: J.-L. Charmet (Explorer, Pierre Mackiewicz (I.T.V.). 17: D. Clément (Explorer), Viollet Collection. 18: Viollet Collection. 19: P. Roy (Explorer). 20–21: F. Jalain (Explorer). 21: T. Bates. 22: F. Jalain (Explorer), P.-D. Forestier (Explorer). 23: H. Veiller (Explorer), Hug (Explorer). 24: F. Jalain (Explorer), P. Roy (Explorer). 25: P. Roy (Explorer), F. Danrigal (Explorer). 26: P. Roy (Explorer), F. Danrigal (Explorer), P. Roy (Explorer). 27: P. Roy (Explorer); above right G. Martin-Guillou (Explorer). 28: F. Danrigal (Explorer), R. Truchot (Explorer). 28–29: F. Danrigal (Explorer). 29: C. Errath (Explorer), F. Danrigal (Explorer). 30: F. Jalain (Explorer), P. Roy (Explorer). 30–31: P. Roy (Explorer). 31: Hug (Explorer), H. Berthoule (Explorer). 34: P. Roy (Explorer). 35: F. Danrigal (Explorer), Pujebet (Explorer), P. Roy (Explorer). 36: H. Veiller (Explorer), Martinez (Explorer), P. Tétrel (Explorer), P. Roy (Explorer). 37: P. Roy (Explorer), H. Veiller (Explorer); M. Mercier, S. Lafon-Lafourcade and B. Pucheu-Plante (Department of Electronic Microscopy, University of Bordeaux I. 38: F. Jalain (Explorer), P. Roy (Explorer), C. Portes (Explorer); N. Thibaut (Explorer). 39: N. Thibaut (Explorer), 4 middle photos, P. Roy (Explorer); M. Plassart (Explorer). 40: P. Roy (Explorer); bunch of grapes, P. Lanneluc. 41: N. Thibaut (Explorer), Hug (Explorer), F. Jalain (Explorer). 42: above and below, left, F. Jalain (Explorer); 3 right photos, P. Roy (Explorer). 43: P. Roy (Explorer), Samsons Cellar. 45: M. Plassart (Explorer). 46: P. Roy (Explorer). 47: P. Roy (Explorer). 48: P. Roy (Explorer). 49: P. Roy (Explorer). M. Plassart (Explorer). 50: 3 photos, above, P. Roy (Explorer); below, P. Roy-Villegier (Explorer). 51: Giraudon, Pataut (Maison de Marie-Claire). 52: Giraudon. 53: R.M.N. 54: Lauros-Giraudon, Giraudon. 54–55: M. de Lorenzo (Musée des Beaux-Arts, Nice). 55: Giraudon, Hug (Explorer). 56: 3 photos,

R.M.N.; painting by Chardin, Museum of Fine Arts (Springfield). 57: G. Dagli Orti, J.-L. Bohin (Explorer), Giraudon, Lauros-Giraudon, Alte Pinakothek (Artothek, Munich). 58: Giraudon, R.M.N. 59: Explorer archives. R.M.N., Lauros-Giraudon. 60: Jules (Galerie de Paris). 61: D.C.A., C. Cabrol (Kipa), Cinémathèque française. 62: Coordinating Committee for the Languedoc-Roussillon A.O.C. region. 63: C. Délu (Explorer), L. Salou (Explorer). 65: J.-P. Nacivet (Explorer). 68: F. Jalain (Explorer). 69: F. Jalain (Explorer). 70: F. Jalain (Explorer). 71: F. Jalain (Explorer). 72: I.N.R.A./I.N.A.O., I.T.V., I.N.R.A./I.N.A.O., P. Bouard (C.I.V.A., Colmar). 73: Rothan (Airdiasol), F. Jalain (Explorer), Desmarteau (Explorer), I.T.V., I.N.R.A./I.N.A.O. 74: F. Jalain (Explorer). 75: C. Cuny (Rapho); 2 photos, F. Jalain (Explorer). 76: S. Cordier (Explorer), F. Jalain (Explorer). 77: F. Jalain (Explorer), D. Clément (Explorer). 78: P. Roy (Explorer), Explorer archives. 80: Giraudon. 81: left, P. Mackiewicz (I.T.V.); 2 photos by J.-P. Nacivet (Explorer). 82: P. Roy (Explorer), J.-L. Charmet (Explorer archives). 84: P. Roy (Explorer), J.-P. Nacivet (Explorer). 86: P. Roy (Explorer). 87: P. Roy (Explorer), J.-P. Nacivet (Explorer). 88: P. Roy (Explorer). 90: J.-P. Nacivet (Explorer), P. Roy (Explorer), G. Boutin (Explorer). 91: P. Roy (Explorer). 92: Château Latour, F. Jalain (Explorer). 93: J.-P. Nacivet (Explorer). 94: J.-P. Nacivet (Explorer). 95: G. Boutin (Explorer), J.-P. Nacivet (Explorer). 96: J.-P. Nacivet (Explorer). 97: Musée des Beaux-Arts, Bordeaux. 98: P. Roy (Explorer). 100: P. Roy (Explorer). 102: P. Roy (Explorer); 2 photos below, F. Jalain (Explorer). 104: Domaine d'Yquem de F. Lyon (Rapho); F. Jalain (Explorer). 105: J.-P. Nacivet (Explorer). 106: F. Jalain (Explorer), Syndicat de l'Entre-Deux-Mers. 108: P. Roy (Explorer), G. Boutin (Explorer). 110: 2 photos above, F. Jalain (Explorer); P. Roy (Explorer). 112: F. Jalain (Explorer), P. Roy (Explorer). 113: P. Roy (Explorer). 114: Château Saint-Georges, Château de Francs. 115: P. Roy (Explorer). 116: P. Roy (Explorer). 117: P. Roy (Explorer). 118: C. Hervé, P. Roy (Explorer), Solaire Photo. 119: P. Roy (Explorer), F. Ducasse (Rapho). 120: H. Veiller (Explorer), Musée Saint-Rémi, Reims. 122: Moët et Chandon, Hug (Explorer). 122–123: Hug (Explorer). 123: N. Thibaut (Explorer), Moët et Chandon, Hug (Explorer). 124: Deutz, Laurent Perrier, Piper-Heisieck Collection.

125: Hug (Explorer), C. Huyghens (Pommery Cellars), Taittinger, Veuve Cliquot. 126: J.-L. Charmet (Explorer archives), J.-G. Auriol (Cahiers du cinéma Collection). 127: F. Danrigal (Explorer); painting, Bulloz. 128: Hug-F. Danrigal (Explorer); windmill, G. Boutin (Explorer). 129: P. Roy (Explorer). 130: F. Jalain (Explorer archives). 131: M. Plassart (Explorer), J.-P. Courau (Explorer). 132: F. Jalain (Explorer). 134: F. Jalain (Explorer). 135: G. Cros (Explorer). 136: H. Berthoule (Explorer). 137: M. Plassart (Explorer), B. Thomas (Explorer). 138: H. Plassart (Explorer), F. Jalain (Explorer). 139: M. Plassart (Explorer). 141: H. Berthoule (Explorer). 142: J. Mathiaut (Explorer), L. Salou (Explorer). 143: J. Dupont (Explorer), A. Berlin (Explorer). 144: M. Plassart (Explorer). 146: F. Jalain (Explorer). 148: M. Plassart (Explorer), L. Salou (Explorer). 150: F. Jalain (Explorer), Château de Corton-André. 152: J. Dupont (Explorer), M. Plassart (Explorer). 153: F. Jalain (Explorer), H. Veiller (Explorer). 154: L.-Y. Loirat (Explorer). 155: M. Plassart (Explorer). 157: F. Jalain (Explorer), H. Veiller (Explorer). 158: G. Marché (Photothèque S.D.P.), M. Plassart (Explorer). 160: F. Jalain (Explorer), R. Truchot (Explorer). 161: M. Plassart (Explorer). 162: J.-F. Bazin. H. Berthoule (Explorer). 164: H. Veiller (Explorer). 166: F. Jalain (Explorer), M. Plassart (Explorer). 167: H. Veiller (Explorer), M. Plassart (Explorer). 168: C. Cuny (Explorer), H. Veiller (Explorer). 169: M. Plassart (Explorer), A. Wolf (Explorer). 170: P. Lorne (Explorer). 172: M. Plassart (Explorer), Lauros-Giraudon, C. Errath (Explorer). 172–173: P. Cottin (Explorer). 173: L.-Y. Loirat (Explorer). 174: P. Cottin. 175: M. Plassart (Explorer), P. Lorne (Explorer). 176: Château de Pizay. H. Veiller (Explorer). 177: J.-L. Charmet (Explorer archives), H. Veiller (Explorer), M. Plassart (Explorer). 178: A. Le Toquin (Explorer). 179: F. Danrigal (Explorer), I.T.V., E. Sampers (Explorer). 180: G. Sommer (Explorer). 181: Fontana and Thomasset. 182: L.-Y. Loirat (Explorer). G. Dagli Orti. 183: P. Thomas (Explorer). 186: C. Errath (Explorer), P. Thomas (Explorer), P. Lorne (Explorer). 187: L.-Y. Loirat (Explorer), P. Mackiewicz (I.T.V.), F. Jalain (Explorer), P. Thomas (Explorer). 188: L.-Y. Loirat (Explorer). 189: P. Médard. 190: P. Thomas (Explorer). 191: J.-L. Charmet (Explorer archives). 192: P. Médard, F. Jalain (Explorer), P. Thomas (Explorer). 193: F.

Jalain (Explorer), P. Thomas (Explorer). 194: F. Jalain (Explorer), P. Thomas (Explorer), D. Rougemont (Cuisine et Vins de France). 195: P. Thomas (Explorer). 196: F. Jalain (Explorer), L.-Y. Loirat (Explorer). 197: P. Thomas (Explorer). 198: L.-Y. Loirat (Explorer); 2 photos below, P. Thomas (Explorer). 199: P. Thomas (Explorer). 200: F. Jalain (Explorer). 201: F. Jalain (Explorer). 202: painting, G. Dagli Orti, grape varieties, P. Mackiewicz (I.T.V.); capital and Sculpture, F. Jalain (Explorer). 203: E. Montalbetti, F. Jalain (Explorer); grape varieties, P. Mackiewicz (I.T.V.). 204: F. Jalain (Explorer). 204–205: D.P.A. (Explorer). 205: Château de Bellet, Dagli Orti. 206: F. Jalain (Explorer), right photo, L.-Y. Loirat (Explorer). 207: F. Lyon (Rapho), Fiore (Explorer). 208: Château de Fonscolombe, C. Délu (Explorer). 209: D. Délu (Explorer). 211: Pascale (Explorer). 212: G. Martin-Guillou (Explorer). 212–213: J.-P. Ferrero (Explorer). 213: R. Baillaud (Château de Flaugergues). 214: amphoras, Musée Archéologique, Ensérune; vinegrowers of the Gard region. 215: H. Veiller (Explorer). 216: G. Le Cossec (Explorer), F. Jalain (Explorer). 217: N. Thibaut (Explorer). 218: G. Martin-Guillou (Explorer), L.-Y. Loirat (Explorer), F. Jalain (Explorer). 220: G. Martin-Guillou (Explorer); painting, P. Willi (Top). 221: G. Martin-Guillou (Explorer). 222: J.-L. Nespoulous (Explorer). 223: C. Errath (Explorer), Mopy (Rapho). 224: J.-L. Nespoulous (Explorer), F. Jalain (Explorer). 225: Foucault, C. Portes. 227: F. Jalain (Explorer). 228: F. Gohier (Explorer), Ema-Photo. 229: I.T.V., N. Thibaut (Explorer). 230: P. Mackiewicz (I.T.V.). 231: P. Roy (Explorer), C.I.V.A.S. 232: Lauros-Giraudon. 233: P. Mackiewicz (I.T.V.), L. Salou (Explorer). 234: Frappier. 235: D. Clément (Explorer), Château du Coing de Saint-Fiacre. 236: C.I.V.A.S., N. Thibaut (Explorer), F. Jalain (Explorer). 238: C. Délu (Explorer), F. Jalain (Explorer). 239: F. Jalain (Explorer), C.I.V.A.S. 240: B. Hatala (Georges-Pompidou Centre), Roger-Viollet. 241: 2 photos, above, C.I.V.T.; below, Arsicaud (Explorer). 242: I.T.V., J.-L. Charmet (Explorer archives), H. Veiller (Explorer). 244: M. Plassart (Explorer). 245: P. Roy (Explorer), F. Jalain (Explorer). 246: F. Jalain (Explorer), Goudouneix (Explorer). 246–247: C. Délu (Explorer). 247: N. Thibaut (Explorer), J.-L. Charmet (Explorer archives). 248: Jean-Paul (Explorer), F. Jalain (Explorer). 249: F. Jalain (Explorer).

CONVERSION CHART

1 millimetre (mm)	= 0.04 inches	
1 metre (m)	= 39.5 inches (1.09 yards)	
1 kilometre (km)	= 0.62 miles	
1 gram (g)	= 0.04 ounces	
1 kilogram (kg)	= 2.2 pounds	

1 litre (l)	= 1.76 pints (US 2.1 pints)
1 hectolitre (hl)	= 100 litres = 22 gallons (US 26 gallons)
1 hectare (ha)	= 100 acres or 10,000 square metres = 2.47 acres

Temperature

Celsius to Fahrenheit

°C	−20	−15	−10	−5	0	5	10	15	20	25	30	35	40	45
°F	−4	5	14	23	32	41	50	59	68	77	86	95	104	113

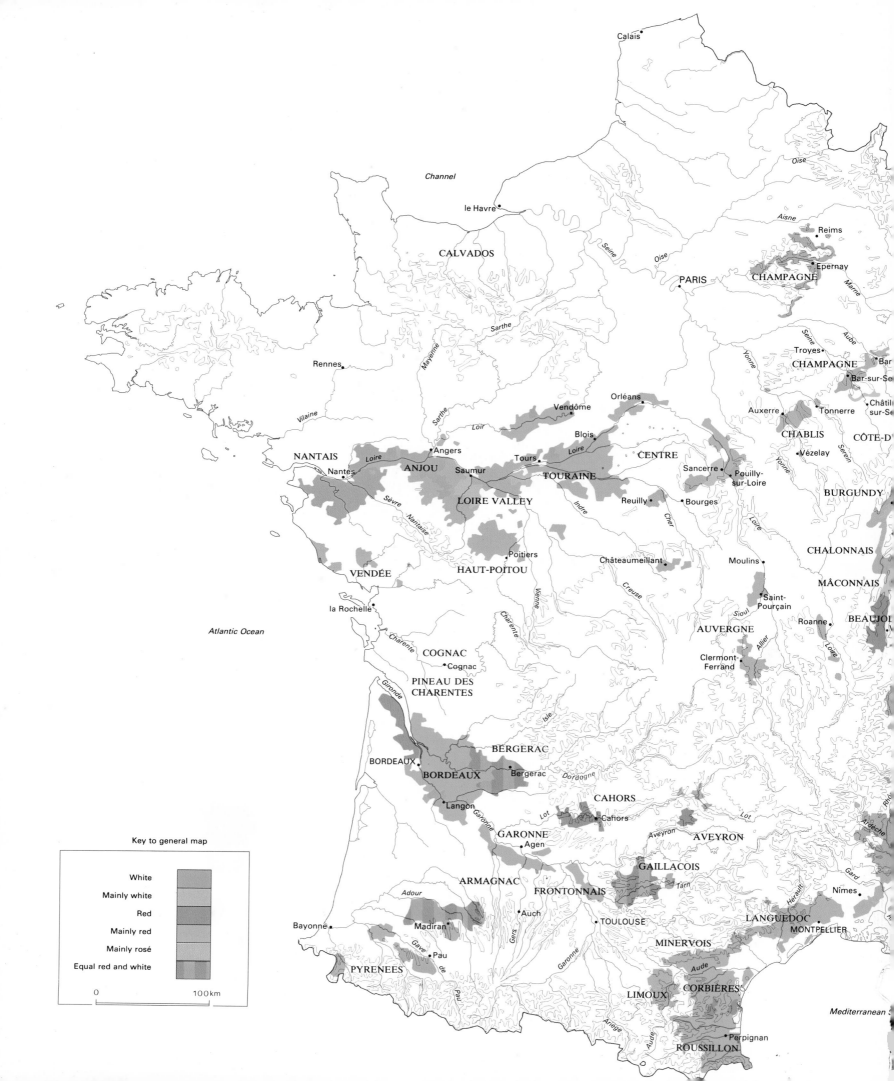

Channel

Calais

le Havre

CALVADOS

Aisne

Reims

Epernay

CHAMPAGNE

PARIS

Oise

Oise

Seine

Sarthe

Rennes

Mayenne

Sarthe

Loir

Vendôme

Orléans

Troyes

CHAMPAGNE

Bar-sur-Se

Auxerre

Tonnerre

Châti
sur-Se

CHABLIS

CÔTE-D

Yonne

Vilaine

Loire

Blois

Vézelay

NANTAIS

Angers

Tours

Loire

CENTRE

Sancerre

Pouilly-
sur-Loire

BURGUNDY

Nantes

ANJOU

Saumur

TOURAINE

Serein

Sèvre

LOIRE VALLEY

Indre

Reuilly

Bourges

Yonne

Loire

Nantaise

Cher

CHALONNAIS

Poitiers

Châteaumeillant

Moulins

MÂCONNAIS

VENDÉE

HAUT-POITOU

Creuse

Saint-
Pourçain

Vienne

Sioul

BEAUJOL

la Rochelle

AUVERGNE

Roanne

Charente

Charente

Allier

Loire

Atlantic Ocean

COGNAC

Cognac

Clermont-
Ferrand

PINEAU DES
CHARENTES

Gironde

Isle

Ardèche

BERGERAC

BORDEAUX

Bergerac

Dordogne

BORDEAUX

Lot

CAHORS

Lot

Langon

Garonne

Cahors

GARONNE

Aveyron

AVEYRON

Agen

ARMAGNAC

Adour

GAILLACOIS

Rho

Tarn

Gard

FRONTONNAIS

Nîmes

Auch

Hérault

Bayonne

Gers

TOULOUSE

LANGUEDOC

Madiran

Garonne

MONTPELLIER

Gave

Pau

MINERVOIS

PYRENEES

de

Aude

LIMOUX

CORBIÈRES

Pau

Ariège

Aude

Perpignan

ROUSSILLON

Mediterranean

Key to general map

White	
Mainly white	
Red	
Mainly red	
Mainly rosé	
Equal red and white	

0   100km